60-7154

10-19-62

HANCOCK THE SUPERB

Books by Glenn Tucker

POLTROONS AND PATRIOTS, 2 vols.
  (A History of the War of 1812)
TECUMSEH
  Vision of Glory
HIGH TIDE AT GETTYSBURG
  The Campaign in Pennsylvania
HANCOCK THE SUPERB

Major General Winfield Scott Hancock

★★★HANCOCK★★★
THE SUPERB

by

GLENN TUCKER

Maps by Dorothy Thomas Tucker

THE **BOBBS-MERRILL** COMPANY, INC.
A SUBSIDIARY OF HOWARD W. SAMS & CO., INC.
Publishers · INDIANAPOLIS · NEW YORK

COPYRIGHT © 1960 BY THE BOBBS-MERRILL COMPANY, INC.
Printed in the United States of America

First Edition

Library of Congress Catalog Card Number: 60-7154

A   441006

To my friend David Laurance Chambers, who gained knowledge of history under Woodrow Wilson and writing under Henry van Dyke. A story is often told that he won more academic honors than any student ever graduated by Princeton except Aaron Burr. Unfortunately it seems to be apocryphal on both counts, but it is so plausible on the first that a wonder at times expressed is how Burr surpassed him. In recognition of innumerable achievements during a distinguished career as publisher for fifty-seven years before his inconclusive retirement last year at the age of eighty, this volume is affectionately dedicated.

Contents

Illustrations

Maps

HANCOCK THE SUPERB

★ ★ ★ **I** ★ ★ ★

Summoned to the Army

Second in War, Second in Peace

If, as Ralph Waldo Emerson says, "there is properly no history, only biography," then the wartime career of Winfield Scott Hancock, perhaps more than that of any other man, is the story of the Army of the Potomac.

Hancock unloosed the advance on the Peninsula at Williamsburg, helped hold the center along the "Bloody Lane" at Antietam and rode in the whirlwind of death against the heights at Fredericksburg.

He conducted the rear while the confused Hooker, stripped of his bombast, was being extricated from the Chancellorsville thickets. He saved the army and the Union on each of the three days at Gettysburg.

At Spotsylvania, where he crashed through the Confederate trenches at the single moment of opportunity and captured Edward Johnson's fog-blinded division, he won the only spectacular success of Grant's victory-starved Northern army as it inched toward Richmond.

Grant picked Hancock's veteran Second Corps to lead in the Wilderness, deliver the main impact of the ghastly assault at Cold Harbor and head the march on Petersburg. For McClellan, Burnside, Hooker, Meade and Grant, Hancock was invariably dashing, resourceful, reliant and in most instances successful.

The comparison with Themistocles, employed so fittingly in another connection by the British historian Sir Edward Creasy, might be applied with equal pertinence to Hancock.

When after the battle of Salamis, as Plutarch recounts, the Greek archons voted to determine who was most worthy of the prizes for the victory over the Persians, each cast the first ballot for himself, but all gave second place to Themistocles.

So it was substantially with Hancock. From the remarks of his superiors it may be judged confidently that, had they balloted like the Greek archons, each in reflection would have awarded, for the period of his command, second place in merit to Hancock. That was especially the case as the war advanced and he had opportunity to display his qualities.

McClellan, his first commander, commented on his "chivalric courage," "superb presence" and "wonderfully quick and correct eye for ground and for handling troops."[1] Meade kept him within arm's reach and said "no commander ever had a better lieutenant." Grant, in the objectivity of his last days, called him "the most conspicuous figure of all the general officers who did not exercise separate command."[2]

In the heat of the last campaign Grant recommended Hancock, not his own young protégé Sheridan, to replace Meade as commander of the Army of the Potomac.

Sherman, always the student of war, digressed while marching north after the surrender of Joseph E. Johnston in North Carolina, to go by way of Spotsylvania, view the salient Hancock had stormed and voice his commendation. "Write all the good things you can think of, and I will sign it," he blurted expansively in a later appraisal.[3]

Many of the officers who began their military careers under Hancock's stimulating leadership went on to high places or distinction. The young lieutenant, Nelson A. Miles, newly from a Boston crockery store, became commander in chief of the United States Army and led it during the Spanish-American War. George A. Custer, fresh out of West Point and a green lieutenant at Williamsburg, saw Hancock's aplomb, became emboldened and strutted into a history that received him not unkindly for all his vainglory and rashness. Under Hancock the high-spirited Thomas Francis Meagher, lately associated with Daniel O'Connell in the cause of

Irish independence, won glories for his celebrated Irish Brigade; and Nugent, Kelly, Burke, Cavenaugh and others, along with their predecessor Corcoran, wrote into New York history the fame of the "Fighting 69th" Regiment.

Henry M. Stanley, the Welsh-born ex-Confederate and ex-Union soldier who afterward found Livingstone and explored the depths of darkest Africa, learned from the general's guarded self-confidence. Breaking in as a newspaper correspondent for the *Missouri Democrat,* Stanley won his job on the New York *Herald* while accompanying Hancock against the Indians on the Northwest plains.

The analogy with Themistocles might be carried further. After the Persians were back across the Hellespont and the Greek states again breathed secure in their freedom, the victorious Athenian attended the Olympic games. When he was seen entering the course, the excited spectators abandoned the athletes and devoted the day to watching their hero, pointing him out, hovering about him, clapping their hands in gratification.

Thus it was that the unsuspecting Hancock, forgotten at first amid the official Congressional credits for Gettysburg, won the popular applause no less when after the war he visited the capital and entered a Washington theater. Though Sheridan, whom Grant and the Radicals of Congress were touting for public favor, was prominently in the city, Sickles was in a nearby box and other notables were present, all were forgotten by the enraptured crowd intent on the magnetic Hancock.[4]

Pre-eminent as a general, Hancock was one of the relatively few Northern soldiers possessing broader than military talents. As his tactical skill had won him the quick admiration of adversaries who had come to know him as the "Thunderbolt of the Army of the Potomac," his restraint and farsighted compassion gained their lasting affection after the war was over.

When other commanders of the Southern departments were resorting to bayonet rule, Hancock was the first to restore civilian authority in conquered states. The electrifying words of his General Order No. 40 were hailed as forming one of the great documents of American civil liberty. The order set forth that, while in war force must be repelled by force, when peace is restored and the civil authorities are prepared to perform their duties, military power must cease to command. The heart of the order was: "The great principles of American liberty are still the inheritance of this people, and ever should be."[5]

Welcomed by much of a nation weary of blood and vengeance, Hancock's ringing appeal and patriotic conduct brought a stanch endorsement from President Andrew Johnson, who proclaimed that he acted in keeping with the precepts of Washington, always a custodian of civil rights and a warrior whose strongest claim was to be first in peace as well as in war.[6] And John B. Gordon, late lieutenant general in Lee's army, declared the order "must canonize this soldier . . . with the lovers of civil liberty in all lands and all ages."[7]

When he died, the Charleston, South Carolina, *News and Courier* recorded the wondrous reversal of sentiment that had occurred among his old enemies:

The South has changed but little in some respects since the day when the men who recoiled from Hancock's lines at Gettysburg began the retreat which ended in Appomattox. But the men who stood with him on the summit of the hill that day and who cheered him in triumph as he rode along the lines, scarcely mourn his loss . . . more sincerely than do those whom he opposed.[8]

The espousal of so forthright a doctrine as General Order No. 40 naturally provoked the open hostility of the Radical leadership of Congress, which was intent on bringing a full measure of humiliation to the defeated South. Grant, in covert purpose with the Radicals before his election to the Presidency and tolerant of their excesses after, parted company with his former subordinate over the famous order. Much as Themistocles had been ostracized for his virtues, Hancock was sent into frontier obscurity because of his wise and healing magnanimity. Sherman undertook a reconciliation, but the breach was never fully healed. Grant used belittling words about Hancock. The subordinate maintained a chill aloofness in social relationships and a strict punctiliousness, but nothing more, in the military amenities.

From the years he had devoted to the study of history and constitutional law, a course of reading encouraged in his youth by a high-minded father, Hancock recognized that vengeance, especially of the strong against the prostrate, is never attractive in the cold light of history. Had his reconstruction measures been given slight heed by an immoderate Congressional leadership, much of the bitterness against the North that still abides in many Southern homes, fanned and rekindled from generation to generation, likely would have been averted. For bitterness came, not from military defeat, but from the only harsh peace the United States ever imposed on a conquered enemy. Some of the vengeful Radicals, indifferent to Hancock's great services as well as his moderation, sought to strip him of his major general's rank. Their ill-tempered attack merely brought into bolder relief his forbearance and statesmanship.

These qualities gave him in time a Presidential nomination for which he did not lift his hand. He lost the election partly by a forthrightness that seemed political naïveté, and partly by a handful of what some of his followers termed craftily counted New York ballots. Close as was the result, he scorned the suggestion of a contest, but he went to his grave believing that he, like Samuel J. Tilden, had truly won.

Though a Pennsylvanian and a Federal general, he was the first Presidential candidate to carry the "Solid South."

In political history he was second best, an "also-ran." But, as one of his wartime aides said, "He needed no Presidency . . . to round out the fullness of his fame."[9]

He possessed to a high degree the qualities that distinguished Lee, Stonewall Jackson, George H. Thomas, Sherman and other noted commanders, a self-reliance and mystic reserve that imparted a feeling of calmness and sureness to his men and made them comfortable when he was close at hand. These qualities are as important as shell and cartridges on the firing line, and without them a military leader does not rise to greatness.

He was as systematic in his preparations as McClellan, but prudently vigorous and swift when it was time to strike. He was as talkative and gregarious as Sherman and evidently as candid, but never cynical or embittered. His temper carried him into controversies, and he could have given lessons in profanity to Sheridan's toughest trooper. His oaths were full-bodied, welling up from deep anger, but he had nothing of Meade's capricious petulance or Sherman's nervous impatience. The storm was violent but passed quickly. He was so handsome that he drew the eyes of all men,

the envy of many and the interest of most women. He bore with
seemliness the title of "the Superb," which could have rested gracefully on the shoulders of few other Americans.

Though always a subordinate, he undoubtedly ranks as one of
the great soldiers of American history.

Second in war, second in peace, Hancock is reached by scratch-
ing through the softer surface of the rarely skillful high command
of Mr. Lincoln's Eastern army and finding beneath it the solid
structure which made this army so dogged and unyielding even in
defeat.

Hancock's story as a soldier began with an extraordinary coin-
cidence early in 1840 in Philadelphia, and at his home in Norristown, Pennsylvania.

An Offer Comes in the Night

John Benton Sterigere, farmer, schoolteacher, lawyer and at
length Congressman, enjoyed a wide acquaintance across the rolling farm lands north and west of Philadelphia. From the time he
was admitted to the bar in Norristown in 1829 until his death there
in 1852, he was a dominant Jacksonian Democrat of the sprawling
countryside that embraced some of the country's most treasured
historic shrines: Germantown, where Washington's scattered forces
battled in the fog; Paoli, where "Cold Steel" Grey surprised Anthony Wayne in what the Continental Army knew as the "Paoli
Massacre"; and Valley Forge, where Washington suffered and
hoped through the most trying winter of the Revolutionary War.

Sterigere, born near Ambler in Montgomery County, at times
justice of the peace, state senator and editor of the Norristown
Register, owed his political fortunes to the contacts he maintained
by constant riding on horseback over his district, often on emergencies that seemed as urgent as those of a country doctor and lasted
as late into the night. His spirited horse must have been a good
vote getter, too, for Sterigere, having no wife, prized the animal
almost with a family affection. He was deeply grieved when by
early 1840 the mount became too old for the arduous campaign
journeys required in the ardent politics of the Jacksonian era, and
at a time when the Whigs were demonstrative in preparing their
Tippecanoe "Log Cabin" campaign.

Rather than sell the horse, Sterigere, then out of Congress but not out of politics, gave him to a Delaware County friend, explaining that the animal was no longer fit for long journeys but would serve well enough in family carriage work. The gift was made on the express understanding that the noble mount would be used for only light duty until his death.

Some time later the former congressman, passing the Montgomery Hotel in Philadelphia, saw his handsome horse hitched to a dray, "quivering with excitement under the heavy load, covered with foam."[10] The drayman was plying the whip callously. Sterigere stormed into the street, seized the whip and demanded to know how the cloddish driver got the horse. The drayman said he had bought him for $75, but had been cheated because the horse was too light and old for the heavy hauling of a drayman.

Furious, Sterigere offered $100 for the horse, which the subdued drayman eagerly accepted.

The incident had repercussions. While in Philadelphia Sterigere learned that the acquaintance who had shamelessly sold the horse had meantime moved temporarily to Montgomery County in an effort to qualify his son for an appointment to West Point, knowing a vacancy existed in that district while no appointment was procurable in his own. Sterigere's wrath grew. Exchanging districts, later recognized, he had never heard of. The man was not a bona fide resident of the district but was practicing subterfuge just as when in sheer villainy he had become the seller of an enfeebled horse.

Returning home on horseback that evening, ex-Congressman Sterigere formed his plans. He rode through Bridgetown, situated immediately across the Schuylkill River from Norristown, and stopped at the house of the incumbent congressman, a younger Montgomery County lawyer, Joseph Fornance, to whom he explained the circumstances. Then he rode across the Schuylkill bridge to the home of the schoolteacher-lawyer, Benjamin Franklin Hancock, at the head of DeKalb Street, in Norristown. He arrived late but guided his horse to the door and rapped loudly, without dismounting. A nightcapped head appeared.

"Mr. Hancock, would you like your son Winfield sent to West Point as a cadet?" he inquired of the figure who finally answered his summons.

The father was astonished. "Really, sir, I hardly know how to reply to such a question," he said. "It is a very sudden one to be proposed at this time of night."

The conversation, preserved, shows that the two chatted at some length, in the doorway, over Winfield's qualifications.[11] When the father pointed to Winfield's youth—he was a few days past sixteen—Sterigere explained that the other candidate for the appointment was no older. "Winfield is a smart boy," he went on with eager salesmanship, "a *very* smart boy; a great deal smarter than the other one. He has the talents for it, sir, just the talents, and if you will say the word, he shall go."

Benjamin Franklin Hancock, cautious in all things, even in answering the beckoning of opportunity, thanked his night caller and said he would reflect until morning. The Hancocks always rose with the sun and the weighty message that had come in the night was discussed before, at and after breakfast.

Obstacles to acceptance were apparent. Winfield was one of identical twins. West Point would mean parting company with his brother Hilary, with whom he had been inseparable. His father, an ardent Baptist, was deacon of the church and superintendent of the Sunday school, and, while he had himself been a soldier, he had become a devout man of peace. The attitude in the pacific Philadelphia neighborhood was not fully in sympathy with making a lifelong profession out of military service. It was necessary to reflect.

But ex-Congressman Sterigere had one important supporter, Winfield's mother, the strong-willed daughter of Edward Hoxworth, a frugal farmer of the neighboring community of Hatfield. Her great-great-grandfather, Jenkin Jenkin, was one of the band of adventurous Welsh pioneers who had come to Pennsylvania in the seventeenth century, settled in the wilderness, named Montgomery County after the shire in Wales, cleared and cultivated Gwynedd Township and, with accessions of immigrants who soon followed from Wales, set up the neighboring community of Bryn Mawr and others of the Philadelphia back country that still retain their old Welsh names. Her grandfather had served in both the French and Indian wars and as a captain under Washington in the Revolution. He had so enervated himself on the long campaigns that he died, mainly from exposure, in camp in 1777. Her father, Edward Hoxworth, likewise a soldier of the Revolution, had gone to sea as a lad, had been seized by the British and had languished in Dartmoor prison until he won his freedom to serve under Washington.[12] Naturally she had no scruples against essential military service.

Elizabeth Hoxworth Hancock had already observed the strong traits of leadership developing in young Winfield, whom she could distinguish quite readily from Hilary, though others in Norristown found such a strong likeness between the twins that they could never be sure which they were meeting.[13] She cast her not inconsequential vote immediately in favor of acceptance. The father was still uncertain. Early that morning he sought counsel at the home of his pastor, the Reverend Davis Bernard, a sensible man who promptly rendered an opinion that as long as the country needed protection, soldiers would have to provide it and they should be of the best material available in the citizenry. He added that a high-spirited lad like Winfield would do well under the West Point discipline.[14]

So Benjamin Franklin Hancock returned home with his mind resolved.

True to his promise to come early, Sterigere was at hand with the single question: "Shall Winfield go?"

"Yes, sir," the father replied firmly.[15]

The visitor did not wait for longer conversation. He wheeled his horse and made off across the Schuylkill to Congressman Fornance's house. That morning's work was important also for the congressman. When his biography came to be prepared for the *Directory of the American Congress,* in which the deeds and achievements of congressmen are summarized and recorded for history, the only incident found worth preserving about Fornance, aside from the mere dates of his education and service in political offices, was that he "appointed Winfield Scott Hancock to the United States Military Academy at West Point."[16]

Amateur Scientist and Drillmaster

Sterigere had observed what was apparent to others in Norristown, that Winfield, the more enterprising of the twins, possessed unusual talents. He had read the Declaration of Independence with sureness and emphasis at the town exercises when he was fifteen years old, and his clear strong voice gave promise of speaking ability.[17] His collection of minerals and geological specimens had attracted notice to him as an amateur geologist. He was an artist and cartoonist of promise, whose caricatures had enlivened the classes at the academy conducted by Eliphalet Roberts, William Hough, the Reverend Ashbel G. Harned, Jr., and Stapleton Bonsall.[18] He was musical and could write verse.

But none of these abilities disclosed his inquiring mind as fully as his experiments with chemistry and electricity. At the age of fifteen he became the motivating spirit in the Youth's Improvement Society of Norristown, a group that had to be discontinued when he left for West Point.[19] The society's neat little account book, still preserved by the Montgomery County Historical Society, shows an orderly mind and a peculiar devotion to paper work that came to be a characteristic of his army service. The entries include such items as "copper, 75 cents"; "W. S. Hancock for breaking glass receiver (his share) 37½ cents"; "Spirit of wine for lecture, 6¼ cents"; "Turning block for electric magnet, 25 cents." In one instance the meticulous order understandably collapsed. The entry was merely "Lot of sand, 3 cents."[20]

The stimulating teacher, William Hough, had generated keen interest among the Norristown youth of the late 1830s in scientific experimentation.[21] The subject was appropriate for the area. The great eighteenth-century mathematician and astronomer, David Rittenhouse, had lived a short distance out on the Germantown Road. Nearby on the Reading Pike was the home of the naturalist and ornithologist, John James Audubon, already engaged in preparing the pages of his treasured work, *The Birds of America*. These were the men being pointed to in the Norristown neighborhood, and the youth were inspired.

Winfield's first achievement was building an electric battery. After that he commandeered a portion of his father's house for laboratory purposes, and the experiments became graver. He began to examine the reactions of nitrous oxide, or laughing gas. Winfield took the role of what the others termed the "grand lecturer" of the course, which was attended by his twin brother and a group of companions, and Winfield ordinarily served both as program chairman and the guinea pig for the experiments. The occasion which caused the most hilarity was when they induced a reticent Norristown youth whose first name was Washington to

inhale the gas as Winfield administered it slowly, all the time inton-
ing in the lad's ear, "Sing, Wash! Sing! Sing!" Wash soon felt the
full effect of the exhilaration. He assumed a stiff operatic stance
and pealed forth the old gospel tune:

> On Jordan's stormy banks I stand,
> And cast a wishful eye
> To Canaan's fair and happy land,
> Where my possessions lie.

The young scientists found this convulsively funny. The direct
effect of laughing gas was mild by comparison. Winfield, elated
over breaking the boy down into expressiveness, shouted, "Well
done, Wash!"[22]

The era of Winfield's youth in Norristown was dominated by
memories of the Napoleonic Wars. Much as the lads of a later day
came to be thrilled by fanciful accounts of the pioneer West, so
the boys of the 1830s played at Austerlitz and Waterloo, stood
with the Old Guard, marched with Desaix and charged with Murat.
The gentle Quaker ascendancy over the Philadelphia area did not
dampen the ardor of Norristown youths in their military drill. Most
of the stories of Hancock's early teens deal with his sham battles.
They were told in later years to show his fighting soul and empha-
size that he came by his military fame through destiny—that he
was born to be a soldier. That should have been clear to all the
world after his conduct at Gettysburg and Spotsylvania, where his
tactical abilities were strong enough to stamp them as innate.

Winfield led his little company of junior militia on Saturday
afternoon parades through the Norristown streets. His hard-work-
ing but compassionate mother, who at periods was the family's main
earner, had helped make the uniforms, the mimic colors and much
of the equipment and had procured the small drum and flageolet.[23]
Once in the early history of the drill, when he was seven, he was
humiliated by being ordered home to wash the dishes. He sheathed
his wooden sword in obedience, but his privates followed and
through the window watched him fasten the apron, then wield the
dish cloth. Their insubordinate taunts so enraged him that he
rushed on them with a fury that drove the tormenters seven blocks
before he stopped.[24] The burst of anger gives a color of accuracy
to the tale. At the age of twelve, while still captain, his personal

appearance was considered "striking," and it was noticed that he "always commanded respect at the head of his little troop."[25]

Small but spirited and sharp-witted, he became a quick and active partisan in a controversy. Eliphalet Roberts told of carrying him bodily into the schoolhouse to end a stubborn battle.[26] One of his lifelong friendships resulted from his guardianship of a weaker lad, whose helplessness was an invitation to the pestering of a neighborhood gang. Johnny Everman had moved to Norristown when he was three years old, and soon the death of his father impoverished the family. Winfield became acquainted with him when he was nine, shared with him the few pennies he was able to earn, fought for him and protected him from older boys.[27] Johnny went to Philadelphia, gained wealth and position and reappears at moments in the Hancock story.

Debater and Stanch Democrat

Winfield and Hilary were born February 14, 1824, at Montgomery Square, eleven miles north of Norristown.[28] Since their father had been named after a distinguished man, he followed that course with one of the twins. He had served under Scott on the Canadian border in the War of 1812.[29] He honored his old commander by naming one boy Winfield Scott Hancock; the other he named Hilary Baker Hancock, though the reason for the selection does not seem to have been preserved. A later, third boy he named John.

The year of Winfield Scott Hancock's birth was epochal in the Philadelphia area. Tucked away in the news columns was an item that the first railroad in Pennsylvania would be built from Philadelphia to Columbia, which prompted a correspondent to the Philadelphia *Gazette* to inquire, "What is a railroad?" Construction of a Delaware-Chesapeake canal was begun at Newbold's Landing on the Delaware River opposite Pea Patch Fort. Water from the Schuylkill was introduced into nearly 4,000 Philadelphia homes. The Franklin Institute was being formed.[30]

James Monroe, a soldier of the Revolution, sat in the White House. Lafayette returned in his old age to the scenes of his early struggles at Brandywine, Germantown and Valley Forge. Hailed by the Walnut Street masses, he was received by the city fathers and the Society of the Cincinnati in Independence Hall, paraded in a barouche behind six matched cream horses, with the handsome

City Troop as an escort, and was feted and honored at dinners and reviews for his great part in the achievement of American independence.[31]

Great Britain and the United States signed that year a convention for the suppression of the African slave trade, which, coming four years after the Missouri Compromise, appeared to put the slavery issue to rest.

At Montgomery Square, Benjamin Franklin Hancock farmed and taught school while his wife learned to make ladies' hats. They had been reared on adjacent farms in Hatfield Township, and at times after they were married and were establishing a family, they continued to attend church in the old neighborhood. Winfield carried the memory of it through his life. Fifty years later on revisiting the church he noticed that the young men of the region still remained outside during services, as they had in his childhood. From their perches on the fence, looking, he said, "like so many crows," they ogled the fair worshipers. Winfield judged that they lacked "strong-minded mothers and fathers" who would take them inside.[32]

When the twins were four, the Hancocks moved from Montgomery Square to Norristown and settled in a two-story brick house on Airy Street, facing the end of DeKalb Street, commanding the half-mile sweep of DeKalb to the bridge across the Schuylkill.[33] The ample current ordinarily was dotted with boats, but the canal along the southwestern bank was the main artery of commerce from the rich agricultural lands into Philadelphia. In this house the father studied law while his wife, now an expert milliner, made hats for Norristown women. When Benjamin Franklin Hancock was admitted to the bar, he opened a law office next door to his wife's millinery shop.[34]

Elizabeth Hancock was a woman of striking beauty who retained her charm and grace into late life. One of her close friends described her as not only lovely in appearance, but earnest, mentally quick, and possessing strong leadership characteristics. The twins were indebted to her for their sharp, handsome features, noted already in their early teens, and their upright carriage.

A few incidents were preserved showing the devotion of the boys to their mother. Arriving home one evening, they found their father absent and their mother busy with shopwork that would keep her up until late into the night. They declined to go to bed and leave her laboring alone, but took turns at sentry duty until she finished her task.[35]

Winfield's lively young mind won him a place in the conversations around the stove in the grocery store across from his house. He was never rashly contentious but always positive, with the unshaded opinions of youth, when his views were sought. Known in school as a good debater, he could hold his own in adult political discussions as well. Like his father, he was a stanch Jacksonian, an admirer of Old Hickory and an adherent of what he accounted the party of the common people, a loyalty he retained through life.

When a high school was established in Norristown under Ashbel G. Harned, who had taught under Eliphalet Roberts, Winfield moved to it and studied under Harned, an excellent teacher. He was busy in his classes there, intending to follow his father in the practice of law.

Already he was toying with ideas and words. "My youth now excludes me from hope of preferment," he wrote ponderously, "but I mean to prepare for futurity."[36]

Then the horseman came to his father's house in the night. "Futurity" was upon him. His military career was less a choice than a summons.

His Father Slips in Blackstone

After the decision for West Point had been made, the Hancocks provided the congressman with information to support his recommendation to Secretary of War Joel R. Poinsett. Winfield wrote a formal application in his precise script, ornate with shadings and flourishes, to which his father appended an assent in slightly less artistic but still embellished penmanship. The father stated that Winfield was well grounded in mathematics and that "he has paid much attention to Natural Philosophy, Chemistry, Algebra, English grammar, geography, and has been for some time past and is now engaged in learning Latin."[37]

One bit of information his father supplied shows that Winfield had a late but very rapid physical growth. At the time he submitted the application in February 1840, he was five feet, five inches tall. When he entered the Army on graduation he stood six feet, two inches. This accounts for conflicting statements about his size at the Academy. Most of the cadets thought of him in later reflection as tall, but William B. Franklin remembered him as "a small boy, scarcely of regulation height."[38]

Francis A. Walker, who became his adjutant general, stressed that Hancock was but "half grown" when he entered the Academy, and explained that his "large frame and powerful physique, his unfailing flow of animal spirits, and his impulsive disposition required a longer period in the preparatory stage."[39]

As Winfield departed for the Military Academy, his attentive father put two volumes into his valise and added some advice that was to have a profound bearing on the son's career and be a factor that lifted him to the rank of statesman. The books were the *Constitution of the United States* and Blackstone's *Commentaries*.

The admonition was that Winfield should read each book at least once a year. The father emphasized his point: since the young man was about to become a soldier, he should know his government. He should understand the principles of civil law and respect them because, said the father, when republics have fallen, generally it has been by soldiers' swords.[40]

Blackstone whetted his interest in his father's profession. Throughout his life he was continually captivated by the logic of the law.

West Point and Mexico

The Academy Meets the Test

West Point was still an experiment at the time Hancock entered. None of its graduates had yet been distinguished in an important war. Congress watched, uncertain of its value.

Among the strictures aired in the House were that the Academy had become "a hotbed of aristocracy" conducted for the purpose of educating "the scions of our nascent nobility"[1] and sons of congressmen and officials; that the poor man's son had no more chance of getting a bunk overlooking the fair Hudson than a rich man had of procuring a berth inside the pearly gates of Heaven. Enormous sums were being appropriated, ran the complaint, to educate the "wasp-waisted vampyre" or the "small species of political leech applied to suck out some of the surplus revenue of the plethoric body politic."[2] Grant, bored with the curriculum, watched hopefully the beguiling legislation pending in Congress in 1839 that would abolish the Academy and release him from the annoyance of his far from onerous studentship there.[3]

The animadversions, emanating from a Midwestern farm society that still lived close to the sharp edge of necessity—reproofs which were to recur from time to time until after the Civil War—were launched in the 1830s mainly by the Kentucky farmer-congressman, Albert Gallatin Hawes. They were answered in detail for the public by an unidentified graduate who, in demonstrating that the rich and poor received like opportunities, cited one Southern boy

28

who was so destitute he had walked all the way to Washington to procure an appointment.[4] The defending graduate, "Justitia," might have added a short time later that T. J. Jackson, a bucolic, orphan cadet from Virginia, was as impoverished, and though he rode a horse from Clarksburg to catch the Washington coach, he carried everything he owned in his saddlebags. He was twenty-four days older than Hancock, but two years behind him in entering the Academy.

Even after a cadet was admitted, the weeding-out process was no respecter of persons. One of Henry Clay's sons had been ejected for not making his marks while another son, during a period when Clay's political prestige was in eclipse, had led his class and been graduated handsomely.[5] "Justitia" insisted that the cost of supporting the Academy did not equal that of maintaining one frigate, and deck swabbing and barnacle scraping did not come high in the days of iron men and wooden ships.

Admission requirements in Hancock's day were simple. Good physical condition was imperative. The candidate had to know how to write an ordinary descriptive letter, how to calculate and, as has been said respecting geography, "know the North Pole from the Equator." A leading objective of the severe course of study and training was to teach the young man to conduct himself as a gentleman. It was well established that none could remain "if he be transparently stupid or inherently bad."[6]

The courses conducted in the forbidding gray buildings were, for those who liked to learn, thought-provoking and stimulating. Traditionally the worst crime was to lie, and the most cutting insult was to be charged with that offense.

West Point, far from failing, was just coming into its full flowering at the time Hancock entered.[7]

A Handsome Lad Wins His Way

Red-haired Sherman—he had dropped the "Cump" and was becoming known as "Bill" Sherman[8]—remembered the "tall slender boy, with fair hair and blue eyes" and "cheeks with the down of the freshly-riped peach."[9] Hancock was a plebe the year Sherman was graduated. Twenty-five years would pass before Sherman saw

him again, for they served in different theaters and at different
posts, but they corresponded much and Sherman followed the
younger man's career with marked interest and fatherly esteem.
William B. Franklin, who was only one class ahead, noted that
Hancock entered a mere boy, was very handsome and "at once
became a pet." But none "ever outgrew the boyish condition sooner
than he did," and by the time Franklin was graduated, he judged
Hancock "as manly a fellow as the academy ever produced."[10]

Orlando B. Willcox, a year behind Hancock, remembered "his
tall, slender and handsome person, which he bore without haughti-
ness or condescension, even to plebes."[11]

William Farrar (Baldy) Smith, destined to be his commander for
a time, who was with him three years at the Academy, judged
him a "strikingly handsome boy," with genial outlook, but still
possessing an inflexible code to live by. His own conscience was
his guide and he would not be swayed by others. Don Carlos Buell,
his senior three years, thought he looked even younger than his
sixteen years when he arrived, but saw in him "a fair-haired, handsome boy, well-bred, good-tempered, and manly." According to
Buell he was one of the few plebes admitted at once into the fellow-
ship of the older classmen, and "he was a special favorite of my
most intimate friends."

Buell, who was warmly attracted to Hancock and became his
close friend and an influence in later garrison days, was a peculiar
admixture of temperament and resolution, which Hancock could
not fully understand. Though he was to be known as the top martinet among the general officers of the Civil War, he was for a time
at the very bottom of the conduct roll among the academy's 219
cadets.[12]

Fellow cadets agreed about Hancock's handsome appearance and
self-control. Egbert L. Viele, a plebe when Hancock was a senior
and later a New York congressman, found him pleasant, with a
ready smile and kindly word even for the newcomers. Hancock,
then twenty, was "tall, lithe, manly" and "as well known to one
class as to another."[13]

Hancock's own class, when mustered for entrance on the spacious parade grounds on July 1, 1840, consisted of fifty-four cadets,
but it was culled down to twenty-five by graduation time. This
lackluster class was set in the middle of a golden era of West Point
talent. Apart from Hancock, few members attained pre-eminence.

The tall Kentuckian, Simon B. Buckner, rose to be lieutenant general in the Confederate Army and governor of Kentucky, and earned from Lew Wallace, the Indiana general and author who served against him at Fort Donelson, the acclaim that he was "a soldier in all the higher meaning of the word."[14] He outlived all the others and died at the age of ninety. Alexander Hays was the son of an immigrant from County Donegal, Ireland, who had settled in Venango County, Pennsylvania, and had become a militia general and, while Alexander was at West Point, a congressman. The son stood fifth from the bottom in Hancock's class, but he made an excellent officer on Cemetery Ridge and died leading one of Hancock's brigades in the Wilderness.

Probably Hays was Hancock's closest friend at the Academy, though the relationship was a bit paternal, for Hays was a few days short of twenty-one when he entered, Hancock's senior by nearly five years.

Classmate Alfred Pleasanton, vain and bantam-weight, rose to the command of the Federal cavalry at Fleetwood and Gettysburg. Of the twenty-five who graduated with Hancock, five were killed in the Mexican War and five died before the War between the States began, while six others resigned before the war, leaving but nine in the military service in 1861.[15] Among the civilians was William G. Peck, who led the class and became the distinguished professor of mathematics at Columbia College in New York and author of numerous books on physics, mechanics and astronomy.

The Academy schedule was rigid indeed for youths who, like Hancock, had been attending small classes a few hours at a stretch and enjoying leisure for antics with laughing gas the rest of the day. The rising hour was 5:00 A.M. in summer and 6:00 A.M. in winter. The plebes performed the menial chores assigned by higher classmen, and were required to be obsequiously deferential. Hancock did the work cheerfully but stopped abruptly when he felt he was being imposed on unduly. They made their beds, scrubbed floors, cleaned their equipment and tidied their uniforms. Life at West Point was not so much the "wasp-waisted vampyre" idling that the back-country congressman envisioned as it was hard, purposeful work for the coveted commission.

In June the cadets left their barracks for the plain, where tenting savored more truly of campaign conditions. They posted pickets, mounted guard, laid out entrenchments, built fortifications, fired artillery, learned to launch pontoons, and drilled and maneuvered until driven back to the barracks by the arrival of autumn. Indoors, apart from the book studies, they learned fencing, practiced horsemanship in the riding hall, and drilled indoors or out, depending on the weather.[16]

One of Hancock's choice textbooks was *Elements of Descriptive Geometry* by Charles Davies, a professor of mathematics at the Academy. In it he wrote his name, with the date April 21, 1841, then exquisitely lettered his surname on the leather cover.[17] On the reverse side of the charts and diagrams, which were inserted in the volume like maps in a history book, he drew carefully his own variations of some of the propositions, which show his initiative, competence and neatness. The book must have been dear to him, for he kept it until his death.

Hays's Fists Win a Lasting Friendship

Orlando Willcox told a story, the details hazy and names missing, of an occasion when Hancock challenged another cadet (Willcox thought he was an adjutant) to a fist fight. They squared away and slugged it out, and Hancock must have behaved well for Willcox asserted that his "audacity and pluck on the occasion made him one of the few notables in a class not particularly distinguished by men of character."[18] The real suspense of the combat appeared to be "alarm lest the authorities should get wind of it,"[19] but apparently they never did.

This may have been a phase of the running antagonism between Hancock and William Logan Crittenden, a haughty, assertive cadet from Kentucky, who was to die before a firing squad and leave a vigorous, laconic remark that in other circumstances might have become one of the treasures of the American heritage. Pleasanton, thirty-odd years later, recalled the details of the feud and attributed Hancock's trouble to his puny stature—he was the smallest boy in the plebe class—while Crittenden was "a big bully" who "treated Hancock very meanly." Whatever the cause may have been, Hays, "a big, honest fellow," interceded and told Crittenden to stop pestering the younger lad. The result was open hostility between Hays and Crittenden.

They met behind the Kosciuszko Monument, in a secluded area, and the ensuing battle was a classic for punishment and perseverance. Hays, though badly used, was the unquestioned victor because he was able to stand. Crittenden was so badly battered that he had to lie in bed several days.[20]

Another version, heard from eyewitnesses by Captain David Shields who later served on Hays's staff, was not at much variance with Pleasanton's. The battle lasted hours and both fighters were on the ground at the finish. Hays was finally able to get to his feet and therefore was declared the winner. As a result Crittenden stopped harassing Hancock, and Hancock never forgot how Hays had befriended him. Long afterward he recalled the incident to Mrs. Hays, in a letter written after Hays's death.[21]

Unfortunately the thrashing did not curb Crittenden's general truculence. He appeared again in an abusive role when Cadet George Horatio Derby of Massachusetts, small but spirited and, like Hancock, an artist and caricaturist, resented the Kentuckian's language when he was merely looked upon.[22] The unarmed Derby received some sword gashes. Crittenden resigned from the army after a few years.

His story should be completed. He joined the filibustering expedition of Narciso Lopez against the Spanish government of Cuba. After Lopez had been garroted in 1851, Crittenden was captured, condemned and taken before a firing squad. When told to turn his back and kneel, he faced his foes proudly and declared: "An American never turns his back to his enemies and kneels only to his God." West Point had taught him something.

Hancock's friends in other classes included many whose army careers were outstanding in the War between the States. George E. Pickett, the debonair, carefree Virginian for whom Abraham Lincoln had procured an appointment from Illinois, clung unshakably, reeking with demerits, to the bottom rung in the class of 1845. He was one year behind Hancock, while the handsome, Dutch-stubborn James Longstreet lingered near the bottom of the class three years ahead.

The roster of the seven classes that were with Hancock in the Academy contained many of the great names of American military history, and the two classes that preceded and the three that followed his entrance were destined to be showered with stars.[23]

One of the strong factors producing this outpouring of brilliant soldiers was Richard Delafield, commandant of the Academy from 1838 to 1845 and again from 1856 to 1861. The scion of a noble French family that had fled the Revolution by way of London, he had been born in New York in 1798. His father, John Delafield, who had managed to carry off his wealth from Alsace, became a prosperous New York merchant remembered in the city's early history as "Father of Wall Street." Richard became a West Point cadet at sixteen and was graduated at the head of his class in 1818. Thereafter he gave forty-eight years of competent service to the army and, as soldier, engineer and educator, proved an inspiration to Hancock and a host of others. While Hancock was at the Academy, Superintendent Delafield's adjutants were two tall, handsome lieutenants, Joseph Hooker of Massachusetts, of the class of 1833, and Irvin McDowell of Ohio, of the class of 1834.[24]

Perhaps Hancock's closest companions after Hays were McClellan, Buell, Burnside, T. J. Jackson, Reno, Franklin, Longstreet, Grant and D. H. Hill. Jackson, with his scant schooling, was able to make up in effort what he lacked in solid preparation. Hancock worked as hard, but had more diversions.

Art a Satisfying Diversion

Hancock was a spotty student. Growing nine inches is a demanding matter. Undoubtedly he was dragged down in some of his courses by his devotion to art, at which he labored rapturously at every opportunity. He excelled in the courses involving drawing, was proficient in ethics and in infantry and artillery tactics,[25] but was weak on languages. Long afterward his close military associate, Francis Walker, conceded that while he was born to be a leader, he was not cut out to be a scholar.

Some of his drawings were good-natured, cartoonlike jibes at Academy life. They were not well remembered, probably because of the more deft work of Cadet Derby, the "Veritable Squibob," who under the pen name of John Phoenix became the celebrated humorist of the West Coast.

One of Hancock's caricatures that caused amusement was entitled "Jineing the Pint."[26] It depicted the practical joke, common among the cadets, of telling strangers who came to the gates that all they had to do to enroll and become future officers was offer

"JINEING THE PINT."

themselves to the authorities inside. Many a bucolic passer-by was
thus entrapped, to while the time away. Hancock's drawings of
fortifications, arsenals and military installations were executed with
fine exactness. His neatness and attention to details were comparable to Robert E. Lee's, whose precise drawings distinguished
his early courses in advanced mathematics. Lee was fifteen years
ahead of Hancock at West Point and finished second in his class
whereas Hancock was eighteenth, but there were common elements
in their studentship. Back in the Academy at Norristown his in-
structors had spoken of Hancock's neatness. They had never
found a knife mark on his white pine desk. Hancock himself
thought he entered the Academy too young. It may have affected
his standing but not his scrupulous care with his papers.

What time he was not working on class drawings, Hancock was
busy with handsome, well-executed pictures in color of the West
Point buildings or with nature sketches.[27] His work in art stamped

him as possessing strong creative talents and sensitivity. As has been well pointed out, the artistic temperament is not unrelated to military leadership.[28] Even so unimaginative and blunt a general as Grant was dabbling with painting at West Point, in such time as he could spare from idling and reading novels.[29]

Class standing was not wholly a matter of book learning. A cadet might be perfect in geometry, but if he never found time to shine his boots he was certain to be pulled down by demerits at inspection. If he accumulated 200 of these hated marks, out he would go, though conceivably he might be book perfect. Some of the tailenders quite obviously were more negligent than stupid.

At West Point Hancock met the distinguished soldier, the oracle, the big, garrulous gourmet, Winfield Scott, after whom he had been named. His father's old commander, a striking military figure not yet grown fat, gouty and puffy, took a friendly interest in Cadet Hancock, looked up his marks and satisfied himself that the youth was making a go of it at the Academy. Scott was chairman of the visiting committee which examined the graduating class of 1843, a year ahead of Hancock's.[30] The details of the meeting of the two Winfields have not been preserved, but they were sufficiently vivid to Scott that he remembered Hancock a few years later and made it a point to give him a place in the army going to Mexico.

A Restless Lieutenant Yearns for Action

Winfield Hancock was on recruiting duty in the Cincinnati area when war erupted with Mexico in the spring of 1846, and for a time it appeared he would be stranded while his West Point companions won glory beyond the Rio Grande.

He was a second lieutenant of the 6th Infantry Regiment,[31] but his detached service in gathering recruits and transporting them from point to point seemed even more essential in war than peace. One of the first of the adjutant general's actions was to freeze all officers engaged in recruiting work, which brought from Hancock a protest that he should be excluded from the terms of the order because he was not regularly a recruiter, but only temporarily so.[32] But a solid, reliable officer finds that his services can rarely be dispensed with wherever he happens to be.[33] By the time news of Zachary Taylor's encounters with the Mexicans reached Ohio, Hancock had become so restive that he bombarded the adjutant general's office with requests for orders to the front.

Hancock had spent the intervening period of nearly three years after West Point serving on the upper stretches of the Red River, assigned to the Regular Army guard maintained to protect the southwestern frontier from skittish Indians not yet familiar with the conditions of "Manifest Destiny." His detachment had headquarters at Fort Towsen and later at Fort Washita,[34] the far southwestern army posts of a country that then terminated with the western border of the Mississippi basin. There he had accomplished little more than to satisfy his sporting instincts, engaging avidly in hunting.[35] Game was abundant in the wild country his troops patrolled. He had ample time for reading his lawbooks, one of which appears to have been sent to him at this period by his brother Hilary, who, now that Winfield had elected to become a soldier, had fallen into line at his father's elbow and was reading law in the Norristown office.

Hancock had begun his campaign for transfer to the border even before reaching Cincinnati.[36]

"I am exceedingly anxious to go," he wrote the War Department, but when it came to advancing a reason, the only one he could offer was: "as I have not been there."[37] Another letter directed to Washington from Fort Washita, June 30, 1846, was followed by still another on August 14, adroitly suggesting that his earlier communication might not have been quite clear. Such letter writing was unusual for Hancock. Throughout his army career he was to address the adjutant general sparingly, while many others, on the squeaking-wheel theory, loaded the War Department with their observations, in search of axle grease.

Punctiliously he reported the details of his conduct of sixty recruits from Newport Barracks, Kentucky, to Fort Scott, Missouri, in March and early April 1847. Then as now, the oncoming of war brought psychological problems to the individual soldier. Hancock said he "lost one man by drowning who jumped overboard whilst laboring under a stroke of insanity." Did not the man just dread the unknown mysteries of war? One deserted in St. Louis and another at St. Charles, but Hancock brought in the remaining fifty-seven, nine of whom were sick on arrival.[38] Health was a much greater army problem in 1847 than enemy bullets.

In May he wrote to Hilary how he grieved that he could not get to Mexico. "I made an application today to join the army going to the front," he said. "Whether the Adjutant General will favor it or not I do not know; but think it doubtful."[39]

The adjutant general did favor it at last and in June directed him to go to New Orleans. Winfield Scott had been assembling an army on the Isle of Lobos and was looking for capable young officers. He had noticed Hancock's name among those unemployed on field duties and requested his services, as many others would do later. Good junior officers were needed on the firing line, and Hancock, whose first two names were so easily remembered by the commander in chief, had had the shine of promise when they met at West Point. Still, by the time cumbersome processes of the War Department ground out the orders, Zachary Taylor had penetrated deep into northern Mexico, and Scott had not only taken Vera Cruz but was headed into the mountains. Hancock's authorization was to proceed to his old command.

His regiment, the 6th, meantime had gone on with Scott, commanded by Colonel J. S. Clark. Hancock's battalion was under Captain William Hoffman, a West Point graduate of 1829, in a class that had given the army two other intrepid young officers, Joseph E. Johnston and Robert E. Lee. Hoffman had been with the 6th Infantry since 1836, while Hancock had been assigned to the regiment as a brevet second lieutenant on his graduation from the Academy in 1844.

Hancock Moves to Mexico at Last

The lieutenant fell in with a detachment of the 12th Infantry Regiment, commanded by Colonel Milledge Luke Bonham, which with other troops, including a sizable group of doctors, joined Brigadier General Franklin Pierce.[40] Pierce was bringing up a brigade to strengthen Scott's pitifully weak army. Scott meantime had battled past the mountain citadel of Cerro Gordo and was waiting at Puebla for the assembly of a force of sufficient strength to hazard a move on Mexico City.

Serving as adjutant for Bonham's column, Hancock traveled through Vera Cruz, safely held by the American garrison, past the miasmal swamps behind the city—breeders of yellow fever, the *vomito* of the Mexicans—and up over the "national highway," at

times little better than a mule route connecting the seaport with
the inland capital. After ascending 8,000 feet, past snow-capped
Orizaba that towered above them, the party finally reached Scott
at mountain-rimmed Puebla, on August 6, 1847. The arrival of
Pierce's fresh brigade of 2,500 men, after previous reinforcements
had come in under Generals George Cadwalader and Gideon J.
Pillow, the President's partner-at-law, was a signal for Scott's immediate advance, which he began on the day following Pierce's coming. The army moved August 7, with two divisions of regulars
and two of volunteers, the regulars commanded by Generals William J. Worth and David Twiggs; the volunteers by Pillow and
John A. Quitman. Hancock's regiment was under Worth. Colonel
Clark took command of one of Worth's brigades, which gave command of the 6th Regiment to Captain Hoffman. Hancock led a
platoon. Colonel William Selby Harney, the hussar who had conducted the brilliant flank movement at Cerro Gordo and with
whom Hancock would be closely associated in later army life,
headed a brigade of light dragoons.

Commenting on this march in his later memories, Hancock said
it was "as good as a picnic."[41] Though he conceded that the movement was "conducted with care," he could not but note that the
army placed no pickets except on the roads and relied for security
mainly on the guards which each regiment posted for its own comfort. He was to become a specialist on pickets, one who was never
surprised in a long military career.

Now the army labored past lofty Popocatepetl and at length
looked out from the heights on a scene of rare beauty, the vast
panorama of the valley of Mexico.

Hancock was elated with his adventure, as his letters home,
written after the pressure of the campaign, attested. He was
twenty-three years old when he joined Scott's army, the youngest
officer of the 6th Infantry. Thirty-year-old First Lieutenant Lewis
A. Armistead had joined the regiment in 1839, five years ahead of
Hancock, having been dismissed from West Point because of unruly conduct alleged to have consisted of no more than throwing
a plate at Jubal Early and breaking it across Early's head. Hancock's classmate, Simon B. Buckner, and John Sedgwick, a rugged
Connecticut mountain boy who had been graduated from the
Academy in 1837, were alongside him. Sedgwick was a first lieutenant in the 2nd Artillery but was attached to the 6th with his guns.

Swinging wide around Mexico City to the south and west, Scott's army skirted Lakes Chalco and Xochimilco, Worth's division in the lead. The route avoided the lakes and marshlands that protected the city on the east and southeast and approached from the south and west, a course which allowed operation on firm ground. But the lava and rock-strewn fields of the *pedregal* were commanded by a series of citadels and forts garrisoned by forces vastly superior to any Scott might bring against them.

Though Scott in his enthusiasm, never tempered by modesty, was to speak of the first battle at Contreras as the most brilliant and decisive in all the annals of war,[42] the main test came in the companion battle of Churubusco on the same day, August 20, 1847.

After Contreras the little American army swept past San Antonio, a strongly held village, and approached the hamlet of Churubusco, situated on a river of that name and dominated by the fortified convent of San Mateo.

The object at Churubusco was to rout the Mexicans from their main defensive line running along the stream and anchored on strong points, among them a church and a convent. The Churubusco River, employed as a canal, was approached by a causeway and spanned by a large stone bridge, the focal point of the battle

A Citation and a Brevet

Conspicuous in the sanguinary and decisive battle of Churubusco, fought from noon until 3:00 P.M. along the little river, were Hancock's 6th Infantry and its companion regiment, the 5th. Major Martin Scott commanded the 5th, while Captain Hoffman still had the 6th. Scott was a Green Mountain boy who had served in the War of 1812 and had later become a lieutenant in a rifle company, a crack shot, of whom the story was told that when he treed a coon the animal wailed for mercy: "Don't shoot. If you're Martin Scott, I'll come down."[43]

Hoffman of the 6th was not to be outdared by the Vermonter, and though it was a frank invitation to competent Mexican marksmen when they stood up in front of the firing line during the preliminary exchanges, before the rushes began, neither regimental commander would stoop for a minute. Nearby, Hancock, in his first battle, stood also.

Hoffman finally called down the line to Martin Scott, "Major, you had better lie down."

The old soldier's reply was contemptuous: "The ball was never molded to kill Martin Scott."[44]

The next one caught him in the heart and he fell instantly. He rested his head on his hat while Hoffman rushed over, in time to take his pocketbook and hear the words, "For my wife."

Hancock a moment later was hit by a musket ball on the leg below the knee, but the contusion was minor and he paid no heed to it. That day's fighting won him his first citation.

Advancing with their platoons abreast Hancock were Lieutenants Armistead, Buckner and Longstreet, while Sedgwick with his guns was close behind.[45] When his company commander was wounded, Hancock took command. The charge of the 5th and 6th Regiments, along with the 8th and 14th, was impetuous.

The Americans carried Churubusco, the third brilliant triumph in a single day. Victory began at Contreras, was carried along at San Antonio, and at midafternoon was still with the Americans as they pressed the defending army back to its last ramparts. They were now only four miles from Mexico City. But there had been hard fighting. Taking Mexico was no mere matter of marching.

Hancock was brevetted first lieutenant dating from August 20, 1847, the day of Churubusco, and was mentioned in dispatches. The Pennsylvania Legislature named him among those from that state distinguished in the fighting.

After Churubusco, the army moved on Molino del Rey, the King's Mill, which the 6th, with Hancock leading a company, helped storm on September 8. There fell two of his West Point classmates, Erastus B. Strong of Arkansas and William T. Burwell of Virginia.[46] Burwell was bayoneted just as he reached the works, while Hancock fought nearby. The assault on the Mexican batteries began at 3:00 A.M., and Hancock was in front of his men as they pushed through the blasts of grape, reached the main gate, broke into the fort and captured 800 prisoners.

Then came Chapultepec. The frequently recorded account which describes how Hancock charged against the citadel alongside James Longstreet, George E. Pickett and Lewis Armistead—men who would meet at a high moment of history on a later day—is in error. Hancock, stricken with chills and fever after Molino del Ray, was ill in his tent when the American army reached the great fortress

that commanded the Mexican capital. But he could not lie quietly
when the firing commenced, and though enfeebled by high fever,
he wrapped his blankets around him and crawled to the roof of the
nearest house.

"The balls whizzed around me," he wrote to Hilary, "but I kept
my post, doing what I could; and when I learned that the colors I
saw hoisted on the conquered walls were those of my own regiment,
my heart beat quick at the glorious sight."[47]

He recovered sufficiently to join in the final four days of fighting
by which Scott forced his army into the Mexican capital. At Chapultepec another of his classmates, Joseph P. Smith of New Hampshire, was killed, knocked into the ditch while mounting a ladder
on the wall.

Lingering in an Entrancing Realm

Scott's capture of Mexico City terminated the shooting war.
Then came the long occupation while the peace terms were drafted
and haggled over by commissions and governments. Though assigned for a short period to General Cadwalader's outpost at
Toluca, Hancock remained in Mexico City during most of the
occupation.

In his letters to Hilary and his parents he was moved to super-
lative outburst about a country that has never ceased to delight
newcomers with its bountiful yield of a varied produce, its gracious
people, salubrious climate and scenery as sublime as any the world
offers.

"The summits of lofty Popocatepetl," he wrote, "are capped with
more snow than is usual." . . . "The Almada, or Great Square of
the Capital, is far superior to anything of its kind in the United
States."[48] He told of the carriage roads that rimmed the city and
of the pleasant walks where the fashionable disported themselves.
He mentioned another snow-capped peak overlooking the city, the
Neviado, and said, "When the wind blows from that direction it
is bitter cold." Mexican houses did not have even fireplace heat.
Northern-born invaders found that tropical winter nights could be
most uncomfortable—at such an elevation. The liberal offerings of
nature impressed him: "The variety of fruits produced is astonish-
ing. On one of the market days recently, over fifty different kinds

were for sale. Think of opening a fine, fresh, ripe watermelon in the month of January!"

What had Hancock learned from the Mexican War? Mainly how to conduct small infantry units in attack, which was the basic phase of nineteenth-century warfare. Somehow he had instinctively come by the understanding that men respond to leadership; they quickly sense its quality and will advance eagerly when a confident officer is with them.

Perhaps it was observing the regimental commanders, Hoffman and Martin Scott, vying with each other for the post of danger at the front of the action, that gave Hancock his lifelong pattern of command. As courage inspired him, so it must inspire others. Was it only foolhardy? His future conduct showed he did not judge it so. Out of these actions came Hancock's decision that he was a front-line officer, a conclusion he never forgot during the stresses of a much greater war. Likely he enjoyed the excitement of combat. Men sometimes instinctively do.

But he had observed also one of the most audacious and successful enterprises by a small army, operating without a base, in the history of warfare. "Scott is lost," the great Wellington had declared when he read how the American had cut his communications and headed for the interior.[49] Scott handled his army superbly in each engagement. Always maintaining the offensive, he rarely relaxed his pressure and was willing to take long chances for grand results. It is not surprising that from this relatively small operation involving 15,000 men, there developed a host of highly capable officers who would conduct vast armies in the desperate and prolonged war just ahead, and that among them—the more careful and gifted observers, perhaps—would be some of the great names of military history.

Though he was a natural field officer, Hancock was continually called into the army's managerial work, which gave him few opportunities for the infantry drill he relished or for interesting side excursions. Loaded with staff duties, he labored in Mexico City until time came for the last brigade of Worth's division to withdraw. The treaty of Guadalupe Hidalgo had been signed and ratified by both nations. Hancock looked on while with flourishes and salutes the Stars and Stripes were lowered from the National Palace and the Mexican flag was raised in its old place. Worth had his trim division on parade in the Great Plaza. Then the bugles called, the drums beat and the rear guard of the American army that had surprised the world by penetrating to the heart of a populous nation moved out on the road to Vera Cruz.

On the return Hancock served as regimental quartermaster of the 6th Regiment. His reliability with the records was casting him inevitably into the staff and supply assignments.

The 6th tarried at New Orleans, then moved up the Mississippi to Jefferson Barracks, where in the autumn of 1848 the distribution of troops was effected for the winter. Hancock went as quartermaster to Fort Crawford at Prairie du Chien, Wisconsin, and in the spring of 1849 to Fort Snelling, Minnesota. On reaching St. Paul in May, he obtained leave for five months to visit home. He had been absent from Norristown for five years.

★ ★ ★ 3 ★ ★ ★

Formative Army Years

Buell Reappears to Some Purpose

After a short adjustment period St. Louis became Hancock's army station during his years of service as adjutant under Brigadier General Newman S. Clarke.

The old 6th Infantry officer, a Connecticut Yankee who had won his first brevet for bravery on the Niagara border in the War of 1812—and there was no overabundant supply of courage on the border during much of that peculiar war—had gained his brigadier's star for outstanding performance in the capture of Vera Cruz.

In St. Louis Hancock had a reunion with his close West Point friend Don Carlos Buell, brevet captain and department adjutant general. Buell found that in the nine years since they had parted at the Academy, Hancock had ripened into manhood but about him "there was that same generous and genial nature."[1] Hancock's position as regimental adjutant, though he was still a second lieutenant, was proof to Buell that "he had developed the qualities of an efficient officer."

Meeting this old friend was of the first significance to Hancock through the balance of his life, for Buell introduced him in St. Louis to Almira Russell, daughter of Samuel Russell, one of the two partners in the prosperous St. Louis retail commercial house, Russell and Bennett.[2]

Sherman knew the family from his early days in Lancaster, Ohio, for the business had had its beginning in neighboring Zanesville. Russell and Bennett had started work as Zanesville store clerks and each had married a beautiful Creole girl, daughter of French

45

immigrants who had come as part of the influx to the Ohio River
towns of Gallipolis, Marietta and Belpre during the French Revolution. They had taken their brides to St. Louis, set up their business and, as Sherman put it, by "labor, industry and thrift, rose to
great eminence as merchants."[3] He noticed that they lived in
splendid houses set in parklike grounds and were among the most
respected residents in this throbbing new city of the West.

The marriage of Almira Russell and Lieutenant Winfield Scott
Hancock, adjutant of the 6th Regiment, on January 24, 1850,
was a social event of grand proportions, made newsworthy not
only by the union of wealth and military prestige, but more so by
a curious rumor which swept the city and brought out a crowd of
onlookers even in a freak winter thunderstorm.

The era was one of unusual glass blowing, in which the Germans
newly arrived at St. Louis were adept, and word spread that the
merchant's beautiful daughter was to be married in a bridal gown
of spun glass. The crowd—Almira called it a "mob"—soon blocked
off access to the invited guests. Somebody summoned the police,
which irritated those who had come only to glimpse the extraordinary costume, and for a time unpleasant friction threatened. As
the bride viewed the event, it was a stormy beginning for a marriage
career, yet one which did not prove prophetic.[4]

Buell was a groomsman, as were Lieutenants Nelson D. Anderson, a Kentuckian of the West Point class of 1841, and Orlando B.
Willcox, the Michigan cadet of the class two years later, who had
been Hancock's warm friend at the Academy. Willcox, serving
with Lovell's battery at Jefferson Barracks, described the bride as
"one of the sweetest reigning belles of St. Louis." Recognizing
Hancock's striking appearance, "in the prime of his manhood with
his Mexican laurels on his brow," he found the couple "as handsome a pair as can be imagined."[5]

One of the notable social festivities for the wedding was the
reception given by Colonel and Mrs. William Selby Harney, who
were to become the new family's close sponsors and friends.

A Brush with the Bureaucratic Bragg

Shortly after the marriage the army for economy reasons directed
General Clarke, commander of the Department of Missouri, to
move his headquarters from St. Louis to Jefferson Barracks twelve

miles south of the city. Hancock made the transfer with him, greatly to the delight of the bride, who enjoyed the novelty of garrison life in the country.[6]

Here Hancock encountered almost at once the bureaucratic penuriousness of Lieutenant Colonel Braxton Bragg, temporarily the camp commander. The story was told that when on detached duty at an isolated post and the only officer present, Bragg wrote a requisition for badly needed supplies for the troops. Then, having gone to the other side of the desk and reviewed the requisition through the eyes of the acting post quartermaster, his parsimony overcame him and he rejected the request.

At Jefferson Barracks Hancock found the quarters assigned him untenantable; the doors were off their hinges and had to be nailed shut at night and too much else was in disrepair for a young lady accustomed to an elegant St. Louis residence. When he complained, Bragg held that the quarters had been sufficiently good for Major Gabriel J. Rains, whose rank greatly exceeded Hancock's, and that no relief could be granted. Although the matter was trivial, Hancock felt himself wronged and went into considerable correspondence with Bragg, who delighted in such letter writing. Eventually through General Clarke's intercession Hancock got his house repaired.[7] The incident grew to the point of causing bad blood between department and post commanders, each feeling he should exercise the active command at the barracks. Here as usual the general's rank prevailed.

Army legislation following the Mexican War provided for three new regiments, and the barracks buzzed with the expectancy of promotions. Under the custom then obtaining, officers might quite properly apply for higher rank when opportunities occurred. Hancock did so at the invitation of President Franklin Pierce, with whom he had marched over the mountains to join Scott at Puebla. He had been made a first lieutenant in 1853, but Secretary of War Jefferson Davis either did not appreciate Hancock's qualities, or else thought he fitted best where he was. He was passed over in 1854 when the new regiments were organized, though some of his juniors, even those who had entered the service three years later, won promotions.[8]

The pattern followed by Hancock in this instance governed him in future cases where promotion was at stake. He did not hesitate to submit his qualifications to the War Department. When the ap-

pointment was made and he lost, he never nursed a grievance
but seemed to erase the matter from his mind promptly. After the
1854 promotions he wrote congratulatory letters to all the fortunate
young officers of his acquaintance. Mrs. Hancock, who observed
him closely, noticed that he immediately turned to new activities,
such as planting trees and cultivating shrubbery—to the pleasure of
generations of army officers who followed him at the Western post.

Mrs. Hancock said he bore a "strange, jealous love" for everything he planted.[9]

William B. Franklin noticed that Hancock made no effort to
push himself unduly but had a tendency "to await events and be
prepared." When those who might be less qualified were jumped
ahead of him, he gave no hint of jealousy. Said Franklin: "He felt
sure that the day would come, as it did come, when his dearly-
bought experience would serve him and his merit would be acknowledged."[10]

Davis unbent in 1855 and appointed Hancock a captain of cavalry assigned to the Quartermaster Corps. The promotion was
made on the solicitation of John Cadwalader, Pennsylvania congressman, who undertook to request it because Hancock was "absent at a remote western post." Cadwalader had contact with
Hilary Hancock, who assumed the responsibility of saying that
Winfield would prefer a captaincy in the adjutant general's department or else in the pay department, because the latter would lead
to a majority at once. Cadwalader wrote his thanks to Secretary
Davis, March 9, 1855: "The promotion of Captain Hancock already announced will be a cause of great pleasure to my constitu-
ents of his native county where he is much beloved and highly
respected."[11] Hancock accepted, though he preferred line to quartermaster duties.

Roles of Reporter and Healer

While in the St. Louis area Hancock watched over his friend
Buell with zealous care. Buell, now a major, took passage from
St. Louis to Alton on the *Kate Kearney,* a river steamboat. Just
off the wharf a weak boiler exploded, scalding and burning many.
Buell, at first believed hurt fatally, was really the hero of the inci-
dent. With an unidentified helper, he saved a substantial number

from burning or drowning. Hancock called immediately at Buell's hotel and found the major mutilated almost beyond recognition.

To Hancock's annoyance, his friend's conduct received scarcely a line of mention in the newspapers. Hancock regarded it as a gross oversight and called personally on the editor of the leading St. Louis journal, the *Republican*. The editor promised a story but nothing more appeared. So the lieutenant became his own reporter. The newspaper, apparently indisposed only to the writing chore, published Hancock's amateurish account, an editorial panegyric rather than a news item:

As a matter of justice to a gallant gentleman, now on a bed of suffering, it should be known that after the explosion occurred on board of the *Kate Kearney,* nothing saved the boat from being entirely destroyed by fire, and with it other boats in the vicinity, but the personal exertions of Major Buell, United States Army, assisted by another gentleman whose name is unknown. They continued to throw water on the fire, which had broken forth in two places, until the arrival of the fire-engines, which were enabled to reduce the flames, so manfully kept at bay. It is certain that several persons who were wounded, if not others, who are now alive, would have perished but for such prompt and efficient action. In times of danger, presence of mind in a soldier is expected; but it is thought that under the circumstances Major Buell's conduct deserves especial notice, he having been previously so injured by the explosion that for some time afterwards his life was despaired of.[12]

When illness struck the army post, Hancock won the affection of the soldiers by his potions.

While the Hancocks were at Jefferson Barracks a cholera epidemic broke out in the St. Louis area and the losses to the army garrison became so heavy that bodies had to be carried away in wagons after darkness to prevent a panic among the troops. Lack of confidence in the doctor in charge added to the unpleasantness. The distressed physician also had to make daily visits to the St. Louis arsenal and recruiting depot twelve miles away, and neither they nor the barracks had sufficient medical attention.

Hancock, the boy chemist of the laughing-gas days, offered his own treatment, a "cholera specific," which he prepared in large quantities and handed out to the crowds of soldiers who came, distrusting the army physician and imploring Hancock not to send them to the hospital.[13] For one reason or another, the remedy appeared to work. At the height of the scourge Hancock was ordered to take a party of recruits to St. Paul. The specific seemed to lose its efficacy outside the barracks, for many soldiers had to be buried on the Mississippi River sand banks.

Command at Jefferson Barracks passed from General Clarke to General Twiggs, a courteous officer whom Hancock was pleased to serve as adjutant, and to Colonel Edwin V. Sumner, "Old Bull" to the troops. The 6th Regiment was given an alert for a prospective march to California, but trouble threatened with the Sioux and early in 1855 it was ordered to Fort Leavenworth instead.[14]

Heavy Duties on the Alligator Run

Hancock remained at his old post, moving between Jefferson Barracks and St. Louis, until February 1856. Then the restive Seminoles stirred again and Adjutant General Jesup ordered him to report at once in Florida. Their son Russell had been born in St. Louis and Mrs. Hancock and the boy made the trip with him.

The army was organizing a campaign against Billy Bowlegs, the Seminole who was not content to hide in the depths of the Everglades. Hancock, a captain in the Quartermaster's Department, took charge of the difficult supply job, first from Anastasia Island off St. Augustine, Florida, and then from Tampa and Fort Myers on the lower Gulf Coast.[15]

At St. Augustine, he occupied his spare time by making sketches of the old Spanish houses, forts and notable sites of the surrounding country, art work with which the walls of his father's Norristown house soon came to be decorated. On the military side, largely for practice in draftsmanship, he made drawings of the ground plans of Spanish fortifications.

At the time of Hancock's arrival Lieutenant Thomas M. Vincent, five years Hancock's junior at West Point, was adjutant general of the forces along the Big Cypress and the Everglades, commanded by the Scotch-born Colonel John Munroe. Something about Hancock's bearing seemed to impart confidence even then. Officers who recognized that getting up the supplies would be the main problem in the isolated country were reassured by the presence of their new chief quartermaster officer. "Concern disappeared when we knew Hancock was to have charge of the base," Vincent said.[16]

Mrs. Hancock was the only army wife on the remote expedition. A supply line was set up from the army base on Tampa Bay to the quartermaster depot at Fort Myers. Captain and Mrs. Hancock first found a small house in Tampa which Orlando Willcox described as "a perfect oasis in the desert for the rest of us." There the Hancocks dispensed a hospitality that "shed a glow of sunshine over our precious visits to Tampa."[17]

Almira Hancock found the country "prodigal only in the number and variety of venomous snakes and insects of every kind."[18]

Here in the Florida heat the precious daughter of the Hancocks, Ada, idolized from her birth by the soldier-father, was born. Mrs. Hancock recorded one of his statements at the time, which showed he recognized the potential conflict between family love and the soldier's duty to which he gave first obedience: "Things have gone well with us, and we have many inducements to make life worth living, and painful to give up."[19]

When the Hancocks moved their quarters from Tampa to Fort Myers—in a prolonged rainy season that made it almost impossible to light campfires for cooking—Mrs. Hancock kept open house for the officers "and the table was stretched to its full capacity."[20] The proximity of the Indians restricted their exercise mainly to walks on a wharf that extended into the Caloosahatchee River. At times they would row on the river, the captain at the oars, while Russell, then four, would lie in the bottom of the boat, covered with a rubber blanket—this when Seminoles would suddenly exhibit themselves along the shore. Mrs. Hancock was vexed sometimes to learn that what she mistook for Indians in red blankets were no more than flamingos feeding along the banks.

The tough old hussar, Colonel William Selby Harney, who had given the wedding reception in St. Louis, commanded the expedition and impressed Mrs. Hancock with his "energetic mode of expressing himself."[21] One of the rugged and dominating officers of the old army, Harney would likely have become a great name in American history had the War between the States come five to ten years earlier. Through a series of circumstances he was given scant employment in the actual conflict, but he had a sharp influence over Hancock and many others who were to play leading roles in it.

Harney had not gone to West Point but had come up through

the dragoons. A native of Haysboro, Tennessee, in the Nashville area, he was nevertheless intensely Unionist in sentiment and a highly competent officer in the Black Hawk, Seminole, Mexican, western Indian and Kansas wars; he was in command during the threatened British war in the far Northwest. In the many ways Harney impressed himself on Hancock, not the least arresting was the effective acquisition by the younger man of the proper inflections and emphasis for trooper oaths.

The purpose of the Florida expedition was to keep Billy Bowlegs and his followers south of the Caloosahatchee River and Lake Okeechobee, a substitute objective for the original long-term plan of removing them to the West over the "trail of tears" taken by other tribes. When Billy Bowlegs had been moderately contained, Harney, now appointed a brigadier general, was transferred to Fort Leavenworth, Kansas, because of threatened disturbances in that area. Hancock, still a captain in the Quartermaster Corps, followed at Harney's request. There they remained until March 31, 1858, when the expedition to Utah and California was organized.

In the practical adjustment of ideal textbook protocol to campworthy military standards, Hancock had as tutor canny old Brigadier General Andrew Jackson Smith, the post commander, who was to lead a division in the western Federal armies in the Civil War. There was an occasion when Hancock saw an orderly coolly refraining from saluting him. He called the man to account.

"I did not salute you, Captain Hancock," the soldier replied, "because when you passed me the last time you failed to return my salute."

"Because I was guilty of an oversight," replied Hancock, "you think you must be also—is that it?"

The orderly was beginning to argue warmly when General Smith, who had overheard, popped his head from the window with a command: "Orderly, you will pace the sentinel's beat in front of the door of this house for one hour and salute Captain Hancock every time you pass him. Captain Hancock, you will remain in your present position for the same period and return the orderly's salutes."

Hancock many times chuckled over this. For one with his strict sense of discipline and justice, it must have amused him as a straddle verdict, no verdict at all. But to the old general it apparently was Solomon-like, to hand each one half a baby and give both time to consider who was at fault.[22]

The March Across the Plains

Nothing in the peacetime history of the early American army was quite so spectacular as the march of the 6th Infantry across the plains and over the mountains to the West Coast, a journey on which the regiment was now about to be ordered.

For Hancock the past year at Fort Leavenworth had been pleasant. It had allowed fresh association with numerous companionable officers. Mrs. Hancock found that "the cream of our army in every branch of the service" had gathered there. She encountered annoyances, to be sure, on the disturbed border. Her husband would never permit her to travel alone into town for shopping; her main protection was an Irish coachman, Benden, of ready fists, who used them at times when she journeyed to Weston, Missouri, eight miles north of Leavenworth. Hostility between the sections smoldered in Kansas and was already erupting into bloody warfare.

Much as he enjoyed Fort Leavenworth, Hancock was delighted with the break from garrison duty into field operations. The unconventional Mormons had been elbowed successively out of New York, Ohio, Missouri and Illinois, and in the winter snow of 1846 had been pushed again on the long trek to Utah. In their new home, relations with the Federal government continually worsened until, in 1857, President Buchanan appointed a non-Mormon governor and late in the year sent Colonel Albert Sidney Johnston with 1,500 troops to enforce Federal authority. Bad weather impeded Johnston's advance over the mountains until early 1858, and in March General Harney was sent from Fort Leavenworth with reinforcements. Harney made Hancock his quartermaster, assigned not only to procure and conserve supplies for the long march, but to maintain transportation as well.

The "Mormon War" was an occupation instead of a conflict and there was no plausible use for the 6th Infantry. Units of the 6th continued to reach Fort Bridger until finally, after sixteen years of scattered duties, the entire regiment was concentrated there. Harney went on to other assignments. Officers and men expected to go back to Fort Leavenworth, but Colonel Johnston, who had the discretion of reassignment, directed the regiment to march to Benicia, California, between San Pablo and Suisun bays, near San Francisco.

Having covered the 1,000 miles from Fort Leavenworth to Fort Bridger, Hancock now made ready for the additional march of

1,119 miles across the wastelands and over the Sierra Nevada to Benicia.

Already the animals were in poor condition and the wagons in disrepair, but he labored long hours to make everything serviceable. Fresh supplies had to be gathered. The transportation he readied consisted of 128 wagons, five ambulances and one traveling forge, drawn or accompanied by 1,000 mules. He supervised and inspected the repair of harness and saddles, hired teamsters and herdsmen, packed the quartermaster stores and procured an ample herd of cattle. Though the season was well advanced and apprehension was expressed that the regiment would be caught in the Sierra Nevada snows, the march was begun on August 21, 1858.

The march of the 6th Infantry from Fort Leavenworth to Benicia, California, with only a brief halt at Fort Bridger, was regarded in its day as the longest ever made by infantry troops. The wild, rugged territory, infested by hostile Indians, was broken by mountain ranges deep with snow, reaching to elevations of 16,000 feet. One of the officers of the Utah expedition gave a hint of the difficulties: when the men wanted to turn back, the officer opened the Bible for guidance and read the passage, "Go on, and search the mountain, and the gates of the city shall not be shut against you." That kept him moving forward.

Hancock wrote both a journal of the march and letters to his wife about it. "We followed the valley of the Carson River . . . in eight-tenths of a mile are the gold diggings . . . I thought better of the Chinamen after seeing these specimens." "The march was resumed . . . in the midst of a snow-storm, which covered the mountains and the plain."[23]

One of his letters contained a humorous drawing showing him in midair, tossed by an unruly mule. Even this mule, later made contrite by a snake bite, seemed to know that Hancock dispensed potions. While a group of officers were seated in the quartermaster's tent the suffering animal put his head inside the flaps. Nothing could be done for him there so he sought aid elsewhere, and made a long swing down the line of officers' tents before he died.[24]

Hancock, the amateur geologist and scientist of the early Norristown years, made close observations of the geography and botany of the country traversed, reported on the varieties of trees, the types of grasses and the available water supplies. His report reflected great labor. It has been looked on as of general and scientific excellence, though it was prepared under the adverse conditions of continual movement by one whose duties were constantly present and exacting.[25]

Mrs. Hancock, who followed the journey as closely as she could on the maps, reflected on the easier services and recalled her husband's reply when she had asked him why he preferred the infantry arm: "Because I am only a soldier," he answered. "This resting fancifully upon my guns, or making guns for others to shoot with, or being a professor at West Point, as you desired, is all well enough, and there must be capable officers to perform such duty, but it does not belong to me."[26]

On the march Hancock had to watch almost constantly over his equipment and supplies. How efficiently he discharged his duties might be seen by the fact that when the 6th Infantry arrived at Benicia, after four months, he delivered his wagons and other equipment in what was alleged to be better condition than when they had left Fort Leavenworth, and without having suffered any accident of moment. The traveling forge had been kept continually at work. The distance covered each day varied—twenty-five, twenty-nine, and up to thirty-six miles, depending on terrain and weather.

Francis Walker, later his corps staff officer, was to say of Hancock that "he could conduct a long march over bad roads, with artillery and trains, better, in my humble judgment, than any other officer of the war, Federal or Confederate."[27] The experience of the journey to Benicia was always with him.

Some Benefits Gained from the Garrison Years

What had Winfield Hancock been studying and learning during this preparatory period? He left no bibliography of his reading, but his books suggest that he was acquiring a substantial background of military history.[28] One prized volume was Caesar's *Commentaries,* a leather-bound book that sold for $1.50 in 1844. The translation was by William Duncan, who prefixed a discourse on the Roman art of war, giving much attention to the principles of attack and defense of fortified places. Appended was a history of Cataline's conspiracy and the Jugurthine War, a translation of Sallust by William Rose. The book shows considerable usage and must have been one of the first Hancock purchased after leaving West Point.

W. F. P. Napier's four volumes, the *History of the War on the Peninsula and in the South of France,* also gives evidence of substantial wear and possible exposure to campaigning.

Some of Hancock's theoretical views of battle methods obviously were obtained from British Lieutenant Colonel J. Mitchell, author of a *Life of Wallenstein,* as well as his more useful *Thoughts on Tactics, and Military Organization.* This book is a less doctrinaire and perhaps a more common-level approach to military methods than the more widely acclaimed studies of Jomini[29] and Clausewitz. The German's works were scarcely a factor in pre-Civil War learning, not being available in English at the time.

Mitchell devoted close attention to the campaign methods of such innovators as Caesar, Frederick II, Gustavus, the Prince of Orange, Charles XII, Napoleon, and others. The author was not without a vein of humor of the sort that delighted Hancock, as when he spoke of the change brought about by introduction of the rifle, and of the skill with which Americans had employed it in the Revolution and the War of 1812. To it was commonly attributed, for example, the devastating nature of Pakenham's defeat at New Orleans.

He went on to observe:

But the tales of wonder related to that skill prove how ignorant men usually are to the real power of fire-arms; for no arms ever constructed by human hands could, if fixed and leveled with mathematical precision, come within fifty degrees of what is told of every Kentucky rifle.[30]

There was one section on which Hancock must have reflected in the years after Cemetery Ridge and Cold Harbor. The author's findings might also have proved advantageous if they had been fixed in the memory of Robert E. Lee before the encounter on the third day at Gettysburg. Colonel Mitchell, after discussing the use of solid formations by the French Republican generals ("Napoleon Bonaparte overran continental Europe with masses twenty-four deep"), observed the coming of a new order:

At a time when swarms of skirmishers already cover the front of every line or position; when artillery is so powerful, and when grape and canister sweep the ground at hundreds of yards, all idea of deep and solid formations must be given up; we must substitute for the weight of masses, extended lines, celerity of motion, and the skillful use of efficient arms.[31]

Here was a writer, ahead of most of the generals, who had learned the clear lesson of Badajoz and New Orleans. The section on "Military Custom" was passed over by Hancock, some of the pages not being cut.

Another book Hancock was studying at this period between the wars was Francis Hilliard's *Elements of Law,* which offered itself as a "Comprehensive Summary of American Jurisprudence." It was presented to Winfield by Hilary Hancock May 5, 1855. Another of his lawbooks was Simon Greenleaf's *Treatise on the Law of Evidence,* published by the Harvard professor in 1850.

While at St. Louis under General Clarke, Hancock received what might be termed a postgraduate course in army paper work. The requirements of the War Department were exacting and many officers found writing the reports so irksome as to deprive soldiering of its rightful pleasure. Hancock, accustomed to taking great pains in his drawings and caricatures, found such writing easy, even entertaining. This caused him to be looked on as beyond doubt a freak by less diligent associates. But there was a certain beauty in the order and balance of a completed account that satisfied the artist.

Clarke was thoroughly imbued with the routine of the familylike army which in the early 1850s sprawled over the West and South, mostly in garrison, occasionally fighting Indians. Under his tutelage—and there was no better paper man in the service—Hancock's control over this phase of military life became "skillful, accurate and concise."[32] Writing reports and handling correspondence gave him experience in setting forth his ideas on paper. Eventually his style grew terse and vigorous.

Francis Walker of his staff termed him "a perfect master of the regulations" and added that he "was perhaps the greatest hand at 'papers' the army ever knew." Then Walker went on to say that it is quite the army custom to express contempt for "regulations and red tape," but: "It is more likely that a mill or factory or railroad will be well managed whose accounts and correspondence are always in arrears, in confusion, in error, than that a brigade or division or corps will be well administered under the same conditions."[33]

How his discharge of office duties impressed another of his staff was told by Major E. W. Clark, one of the small group that handled his corps executive work:

> If I recall one trait of Hancock's character more than another, I would name his conscientious devotion to details and his thoroughness in the minutiae of affairs. Nothing seemed too trivial to claim his consideration, and yet he did not magnify the minor things to the exclusion of weightier matters. His mind seemed happily formed to take the lesser with the greater; his eye to be equipped with a wonderful sweep for the particulars of the business.[34]

The years between the Mexican and Civil wars, his adjutant, Henry W. Bingham, found to be characterized by "observation, thoughtful reflection and training."[35]

Walker, who looked on those fourteen years as "one long term of military education"[36] for Hancock, analyzed the qualities fused in his character: "He had courage—fiery, enthusiastic courage." Another quality was his "positive, unfaltering loyalty to country and comrade. . . ." "He had industry beyond measure" and "the ambition that stirs to do great deeds." Above all, he had "an unrest while anything remained to be done, a dissatisfaction with what was incomplete."[37]

Parting with Old Friends

Colonel Lee Offers Family Advice

Leave in Washington! Orders awaited Hancock at Benicia allow-ing him two months to return east, visit his family and, if he wished, transport his wife and children to California.

Delightful were those late winter and early spring weeks in the capital city, never to be forgotten by the Hancocks. Almira Han-cock was entranced with Harriet Lane, bachelor President Buchan-an's niece and the sweetheart of all Washington. No more radiant young lady ever presided over the White House.

Almira had opportunity to meet other outstanding ladies of Washington society. Mrs. Jefferson Davis, wife of the Mississippi Senator and recent Secretary of War, she found to possess "many remarkable qualities" that made her a "presiding genius" at her entertainments, where the most cultivated of Washington society assembled.[1]

Especially was she attracted to Mrs. Joseph E. Johnston, whose unusual intelligence and quick repartee distinguished her and made conversation with her sparkling. "Our happiness that winter was complete," Mrs. Hancock said in later reflections.[2] They could look out over the raw, straggly city, the Capitol not yet completed, where the lights burned at night during the almost continuous de-bate over slavery in the territories. Across the beautiful Potomac stood the stately edifice of Arlington, which had passed from George Washington Park Custis, adopted son of President George Washington, to Mrs. Robert E. Lee.

Perhaps the outstanding memory of that visit was the meeting with Colonel Lee, a thorough gentleman who seemed to take a fatherly interest in the Hancocks. Lee was not then the gray-haired and gray-bearded soldier of the war pictures; he wore a black mustache and retained a youthful trimness in his courtly middle age. On the evening before their departure for New York when he came to bid the Hancocks godspeed, he suddenly disrupted Mrs. Hancock's plans. If she ever repeated his admonitions, Lee must have benefited other army wives and husbands on later occasions. At an opportune moment the colonel turned to her and volunteered a suggestion:

I understand that you contemplate deserting your post, which is by your husband's side, and that you are not going to California with him. If you will pardon me, I should like to give you a little advice. You must not think of doing this. As one considerably older than Hancock, and having had greater experience, I consider it fatal to the future happiness of young married people, upon small provocation, to live apart, either for a short or long time. The result is invariably that they cease to be essential to each other. Now promise me that you will not permit him to sail without you.[3]

When the California steamer the *St. Louis* weighed anchor for the Isthmus of Panama on April 27, 1859, packed though it was with 1,150 passengers, Almira Hancock and her children were on board.

The crowd experienced great suffering in the tropical heat. When the Hancocks reached the Pacific side, after the transfer across Panama, they found a smaller steamer, the *Golden Gate,* loaded even more heavily, with 1,750 passengers, while the captain was muttering, "God knows what will become of us in the event of disaster."[4]

Among the difficulties of the trip up the Pacific—always a trial in the 1850s—was the vengeful spirit of the steerage passengers, who overran the ship and defied anyone to challenge them. According to a warning given Hancock by a friend, they plotted to throw him into the sea because he represented authority. He sent word indirectly that he was not afraid of the plotters, then proved it the next morning when he learned that six men armed with knives had seized his son, Russell, and were dragging the lad by his hair across the deck. Hancock charged onto them, put the entire crowd to flight—mainly by his wrath—and warned them that he would kill instantly the next man who laid a hand on the child. The docile ship's captain who looked on said he never saw "a fiercer assault and quicker rout."[5]

They reached San Francisco May 23, where they found orders sending Hancock to Los Angeles 500 miles down the coast. The quartermaster chore was with him again. A ship was available that afternoon and thirty-six hours later they were at anchor off Wilmington. Still later, after a ride of eighteen miles behind some frisky California ponies, they reached Los Angeles, the little town of adobe houses and 4,000 residents—only a dozen of whom were English-speaking North Americans—which for more than two years was to be their home. Ada and her mother were stricken almost immediately with what the Californians called Panama fever, an illness believed to be contracted in crossing the Isthmus, and probably a type of dysentery. From it the daughter, then three years old, almost died.

Setting a Guard on Guns and Powder

Even on so remote an assignment life had many pleasures for the Hancocks. They rode to the beaches eighteen miles away, helped organize the first Protestant Church in the community—at which Almira Hancock played the organ—and kept open house for officers who occasionally visited the Southern California area on army assignments. George Pickett and Dick Garnett came—Hancock had known both of them at the Academy, though Garnett had been graduated the year after Hancock entered. Lewis Armistead, now a major in the 6th Infantry and one of his closest army companions, came occasionally from San Francisco, where Brigadier General Albert Sidney Johnston had his headquarters as commander on the West Coast.

Hancock had developed into an easy conversationalist whose friendly manner inspired confidences. Captain James H. Merryman, of the U. S. Revenue Marine, met him in Los Angeles and remembered that he had a "pleasant voice, always soft and low."[6] Talk with the Virginians—Armistead, Pickett and Garnett—inevitably drifted to the impending war and dwelt on the course Southern officers should follow if their states left the Federal Union.

In politics Hancock remained a Democrat, as much as anyone could who was changing posts constantly and had never voted.[7] His attitude—reflected in some of the conversations and recorded in rather formal language by Mrs. Hancock—is of interest because it shows the normal reaction of a Northern Democrat. Part of the swelling Republican propaganda of the period, given some color by the attitude of President Buchanan, held that *most* Democrats were at heart appeasers.

He would not wrestle with the problems of others. The summary of his remarks to his close Southern friends was:

I can give you no advice. I shall not fight on the principle of State-rights, but for the union, whole and undivided. I do not and will not belong to a country formed of principalities. I cannot sympathize with you. You must be guided by your own convictions, and I hope you will make no mistakes.[8]

Mail arrived occasionally but perhaps merely added to the concern, for from all appearances there was as much excitement in California over the Lincoln campaign as there was in Springfield, Illinois. Hancock was disturbed and felt keenly the danger of secession should Lincoln triumph. Almost everyone in Los Angeles sympathized with the South or else favored an independent Western republic composed of the territory that had been wrested from Mexico. The "Bear" flag of an independent California was being raised in nearby towns. Old-time Spaniards had a formal maneuver to suggest their desire for hostilities: they would ride in line past a disliked headquarters or house and turn their faces menacingly in that direction. The Hancocks had seen one such a procession before they were apprised of its implications; on the second occasion Captain Hancock, sensing that his army supplies were endangered, was prepared.

Probably all that saved the faraway section of Southern California for the Union at this critical moment was Hancock's care in seeing that his precious guns, ammunition and supplies were adequately protected. He assembled twenty or so derringers for his own use in an emergency, then recruited every Union sympathizer in the neighborhood to be ready on a moment's notice. He armed Mrs. Hancock, who had learned to shoot in Florida. The commissary depot was an inadequate building that could be entered easily, and there were rumors that this was exactly what the hostile inhabitants intended. He hid the boxes of guns and ammunition underneath great heaps of grain, drew up his wagons to form a barricade and prepared to fight it out. No other officer was closer than a hundred miles, but Hancock faced attack with some confidence. Finally a squadron of cavalry arrived from Fort Tehone, a hundred miles away, and paraded, and the danger of the loss of Southern California was minimized. Many credited Hancock with holding it for the Union cause.[9]

Armistead Weeps at the Farewell Party

At length across the mountains came the distant rumble of the cannon at Fort Sumter. The moment of decision had arrived. Remembering how he had been neglected at the outbreak of the Mexican War, Hancock began at once to petition for active service. He wrote the adjutant general requesting orders east. When he heard nothing, he renewed the request in a letter to General Winfield Scott. Then he wrote to his friend Postmaster General Montgomery Blair, an appeal that went outside military channels to be sure, but he knew the dangers of being stranded, as in 1847, and he was desperate. Blair did him no good. At about this time the Postmaster General was asserting to the Cabinet that he could march to Richmond with 10,000 men "armed with staves."[10] Hancock would not be needed from the far West Coast in any such war as that!

When all of his requests went unanswered, Hancock realized that the war would be fought mainly by state volunteers. He wrote to Governor Andrew G. Curtin of Pennsylvania, asking for command of one of the volunteer organizations being mustered into Federal service. This request also lay unanswered.[11] So pressed were national and state officers with war preparations that they could give no attention to the man who was to contribute almost as much as any individual soldier toward winning it.

Meantime a minor crisis was precipitated on the West Coast by the arrival of "Old Bull" Sumner, who had come surreptitiously, his name not being on the passenger list regularly sent overland to reach San Francisco ahead of the Panama boat. Mrs. Hancock, in San Francisco at the time, met General Johnston on the morning the ship docked. She noticed that Johnston had tears in his eyes.[12]

"You are not aware," he said, "that General Sumner was among the passengers who arrived on the steamer this morning, and who came to me unannounced, expecting to catch me in treasonable intentions. I have not yet seen him, but I understand that he has been sent out to relieve me of my command."

Mrs. Hancock tried to reassure Johnston, saying he was hasty in his conclusions.

"But why was the General's name omitted from the passenger list that was sent by the overland mail?" he asked. "If my suspicions are correct, I shall at once resign."[13]

Undoubtedly Johnston, then looked on as the outstanding officer of the United States Army, would have resigned in any case, to go with his own section. His name was second, led only by that of Samuel Cooper, on the list of five officers President Davis submitted later to the Confederate Congress for confirmation as full generals. Born in Kentucky, he had been appointed to West Point from Louisiana and had identified himself early with the Republic of Texas, where he rose from a private in Sam Houston's army to be Secretary of War of the new republic. Mrs. Hancock and, in her opinion, many others were satisfied that he would have remained loyal to Federal interests as long as he stayed in the United States service. She had no sympathy with the treatment accorded him. She found both Northerners and Southerners denouncing the manner in which the matter was handled and said, "The unwarrantable suspicion shown by the Government was considered humiliating and discreditable."[14] Her view and her husband's could not have been far apart.

General Johnston took his family to Los Angeles, where his wife's brother was a physician. There other Southerners seeking means of reaching their home country began to assemble. Johnston's resignation had been the signal for everyone to choose sides. Lewis Armistead and Dick Garnett arrived. By June 15 the party was ready to leave on the overland trip to Texas.

That night the Hancocks gave a farewell dinner for their close friends of many years, mostly the old 6th Infantry crowd that was breaking apart forever. Mrs. Hancock called it a "never-to-be-forgotten evening," and it was heavy with the sadness of severing friendships.[15] General Johnston was in a sentimental mood. As midnight approached—the officers were to depart soon after the hour of twelve—he called to his wife, "Come, sing me one or two of the old songs you used to sing, 'Mary of Argyle,' and 'Kathleen Mavourneen.' "[16]

Mrs. Johnston was reluctant to perform. She, too, was deeply stirred. She remarked that she thought her music days were ended, but she played and sang and there was not a dry eye in the party, though Mrs. Hancock maintained that all were trying with smiles to conceal their true feelings. Armistead was the most deeply affected. He seemed to sense the bitter finality of parting with Hancock, alongside whom he had fought at Churubusco, served in the Everglades and made the long, toiling march across the plains and mountains from Fort Leavenworth to Benicia. His tears, streaming down his face, were contagious. He put his hands on Hancock's shoulders, looked him in the eye and said: "Hancock, good-by. You can never know what this has cost me, and I hope God will strike me dead if I am ever induced to leave my native soil, should worst come to worst."[17]

What this seemed to mean was that Armistead would fight a defensive war for his native North Carolina and home state of Virginia but would not go elsewhere to oppose Federal authority. Many others entered with that resolution. Then he handed a small satchel of mementos and personal items to Mrs. Hancock and asked her not to open it unless he should be killed. In that case, he said, he intended that the small prayer book in the satchel should go to her. When she examined it after his death at Gettysburg, she saw he had written on the flyleaf: "Lewis A. Armistead. Trust in God and fear nothing."[18]

That night he removed his military apparel and donned travel clothes—he would not need the blue major's uniform of the United States Army again. He handed it to Hancock with the words that it might come in handy some time.[19] It never did, because Hancock jumped the grade of major.

Mrs. Hancock did not give the full list of her dinner guests but she did say that three of the six who left that midnight were killed in front of Hancock's lines at Gettysburg.[20] Armistead and Garnett were two—the other may have been one of Pickett's colonels, most of whom went down in the sanguinary assault.

Armistead, a warmhearted officer much beloved by all who knew

him, was to become the object of unmerited calumny, for reasons
that have never been determined. One defamatory story was that
he fought on the Union side at the first battle of Manassas—misin-
formation which spread over the South and which the Northern
gèneral Abner Doubleday worked into his book, *Chancellorsville
and Gettysburg.*[21] The Johnston party after leaving the Hancocks
made its way across the southern mountains via Yuma to Mesilla,
New Mexico, on the Rio Grande above El Paso, where they arrived
well after the battle of Manassas had been fought. Other stories
derogatory of Armistead—one closely related to Hancock—arose at
Gettysburg.

Sounding the Call of No Retreat

The summer rolled on, the war went on and Hancock still awaited
his transfer orders.

Being the only army officer in Los Angeles, he was called on to
deliver the Fourth of July address of 1861 and in it he made an
earnest plea for the seceding states to return to the Union. He could
not know at that moment that blood had already been spilled, that
the hostile forces already were on the field, that a Federal army had
crossed the Potomac and invaded Virginia and that General Irving
McDowell had already submitted to Winfield Scott his plan for the
movement on Manassas. For Hancock and most of the West Coast,
bloody, relentless war between close friends was unthinkable. In
his peroration he spoke of the common heritage of Revolutionary
War battles, fought in both North and South. He urged the South
to consider. "Let them return to us—those who would secede. We
will welcome them as brothers who have been estranged, but have
come back."

The remark is of interest as showing that Hancock's partiality to
conciliation over vengeance, an attitude which caused him to break
with the Radical control of Congress after the war, was what he had
felt from the beginning, the idea of erring members returning to an
inseparable family. But his firmness showed through his conclud-
ing remark: "The government resulting from the union of these
states is a precious heritage, that we intend to preserve and defend
to the last extremity."[22]

Even more pointed was a later summation: "My politics are of a practical kind. The integrity of the country. The supremacy of the Federal government. An honorable peace, or none at all."[23]

Back in Washington Winfield Scott was reviewing 20,000 troops who marched down Pennsylvania Avenue in the Fourth of July parade, drums beating a quickstep, banners fluttering, dashing Zouaves disporting their gay uniforms, the sun glinting off the polished rifles of the three-months volunteers. Crowds assembled in the rotunda of the Capitol, beneath the unfinished dome, to sing "The Star Spangled Banner" with eager enthusiasm.[24] The newspapers called, "On to Richmond!" and the power to march seemed to be assembled. While the prudent Scott doubted, the Cabinet strategists demanded that the war be wrapped up in the shortest possible time. Here again it appeared that the main actions might be completed without Hancock, who would have to make the long journey by way of the Isthmus, even if the expected orders should be forthcoming.

At length Hancock's orders came but they were not for the line duty he craved. The cramping curse of the Quartermaster Corps was still with him. He was assigned to be chief supply officer for General Robert Anderson, "hero of Fort Sumter," now in the department of Kentucky.

The Hancocks' departure was marred by a distressing accident. One of the small boats built to carry Los Angeles passengers from ocean-going craft to the shore had been named the *Ada Hancock* in honor of their daughter, five and a half years old, and the little girl had presided at the christening ceremonies. But early in its service, while it was loaded with a large party including many women, the boilers blew up and most of the passengers were killed or injured, among the dead being General Albert Sidney Johnston's eldest son.

Amid this sadness the Hancocks left Los Angeles. As August ended they sailed from San Francisco for Panama and New York. Military careers already had been made. Bethel, Bull Run and the West Virginia battles had been fought. And by now the war had already taken on a new complexion. Richmond would not be captured with staves. Hancock would arrive in time for some serious campaigning. George B. McClellan had been called to Washington and was building the army which, however it came to be used or abused by others, would always bear the marks of his organizational

genius. News had moved slowly to the West Coast. On reaching
Panama Hancock, eager for information, induced some sailors to
row him ashore. There he obtained the latest Eastern newspapers,
only two weeks old. The principal account dealt with the battle of
Wilson's Creek, where General Nathaniel Lyon, Hancock's senior
by three years at the Academy, had been killed.

Lyon had relieved Hancock's old commander, Harney, in command at St. Louis, when Harney came to be looked on with some
question by the Washington authorities. Apparently the trouble was
not Harney's Tennessee birth so much as the fact that while en
route to Washington he had been seized by Confederates at Harper's Ferry and taken to Richmond, to be closeted with Lee and
Joseph E. Johnston as they urged him to join the Southern cause.
That he withstood the pressure proved insufficient vindication and
he was soon retired from the army rolls.

Hancock was compelled to read his newspaper aloud to the
group of passengers, who included future officers of both armies.
Among the strange features of this extraordinary war was the fact
that the same vessel was transporting old companions who still
fraternized on the best of terms, but who immediately upon their
arrival would become relentless enemies on bloody battlefields. As
the Atlantic-side steamer approached New York, the Southerners
managed to have themselves landed on the Jersey shore, where
they obtained railroad transportation connecting with the South.

Assigned by McClellan to a Combat Brigade

Hancock, disquieted by his Quartermaster-Corps assignment, did
not take time to stop either in New York or at his Norristown home,
which he had not visited for more than two years. He proceeded
by the first train to the capital, to apply for line duty. Scarcely had
he arrived when the attentive McClellan, who had a fair understanding from the Mexican War days of Hancock's combat abilities, sent his father-in-law and chief of staff, General Randolph B.
Marcy, to Hancock with instructions for him to wait at Willard's
Hotel until the commanding general had time to see him. Marcy
told him that McClellan intended to recommend him to President
Lincoln for appointment as brigadier general. He would not need
Armistead's uniform after all!

Hancock was elated. Mrs. Hancock thought it "incredible" until she commented in that vein to another officer who had just been given the same grade. "That's all right," said the officer, "but if a cannon should be fired down Pennsylvania Avenue it would hit a hundred or more newly created brigadiers."[25]

That night at ten o'clock McClellan summoned him and the men talked until well past midnight. McClellan could size men up. He had known Hancock since West Point days. The Quartermaster-Corps duties were forgotten. Hancock would command a brigade in Baldy Smith's division, in what was soon to become a part of Old Bull Sumner's corps.

Several of Hancock's staff officers or close associates have left their impressions of him as he seemed at this time. Francis Walker thought he had only one blemish in his impressive military character. That was his "extravagant indulgence" in "harsh and profane speech."[26] And even here Walker offered mitigating circumstances: the "traditions of the old regular army in this respect were very bad."[27]

Profanity had been a vexation since the days of George Washington, who had issued an order on August 3, 1776, against "that foolish and wicked practice of profane cursing." He admonished his officers to check it by their example and said, "We can have little hope of the blessing of Heaven on our arms, if we insult it by our impiety and folly."[28] The worst evil was employing profanity against troops. Corporal punishment had been abolished by the enlightened armies—in the British armies as recently as William Cobbett's outcry against it earlier in the nineteenth century—and the use of oaths had become a moderate substitute when calling men to account. Cursing enlisted men was no more tolerable in a democratic army than the profanity of enlisted men against officers, and that was by no means a novelty in either the Northern or Southern army.

Nowhere is there evidence that Hancock ever employed profanity in direct dealings with his men. He was, in fact, always a defender of the volunteer soldier. His orders on the battlefield were delivered with calmness and restraint, at times softly. With him, cursing was impersonal, a means of letting off steam. But as Walker pointed out, the tales told around the campfires of the peacetime army had dwelt on the "extravagant profanity of a few generals" and this had "set the fashion among the officers coming into promi-

nence at the outbreak of the Rebellion."[29] Hancock, he held, was
not more of an offender than others. Sheridan was perhaps worse.

Others of Hancock's conspicuous traits were his dash—a touch
of swank and elegance which did not descend to dandyism—and a
warm hospitality. Never a heavy drinker, he always seemed to
have whisky available for the amenities. He was thirty-eight years
old, "a perfect blond . . . powerfully formed yet easy and graceful
in his movements." He was strong "yet without a trace of ferocity
or even habitual severity."[30]

Conscious of his handsome presence, he was mindful of his dress
and bearing and did not allow his appearance to become slovenly.
Lee had the same attentiveness. Soldiers liked this trait: "Just as a
dash of puppyism is an excellent quality in a junior officer, so a
shade of physical self-consciousness in an officer of high rank is certain to give a tone . . . to the troops he may command." Hancock
was never forbidding "except in some tremendous explosion of
wrath." Always he was well mounted and well dressed.[31]

The year 1861, his aide Henry A. Bingham declared, "found
him a soldier of mature years, devoted to his career, absolute in
his faith and fidelity to his government, and knowing no other duty
than the upholding of the honor and integrity of his country's
flag."[32]

★★★ 5 ★★★

The Charge at Williamsburg

Hancock "Whispering to His Brigade"

Hancock's brigade was formed on September 28 on the south side of the Chain Bridge at what was known as Camp Advance. At 5:00 A.M. the next day the bugles called. It was so early the recruits thought an alarm was being sounded for an enemy attack but it was merely Hancock beginning drill.

That afternoon they held their first dress parade, then continued drill with proper rests until nightfall. The next day the brigade advanced two or three miles to a camp called "Vanderwerken," the day after to Camp Griffin at Lewinsville, its headquarters until the following spring. Drills in the school of the soldier, squad, company and battalion were held regularly at Camp Griffin.

Hancock's trumpetlike voice was such as to inspire awe among recruits, who would come from other commands to see the brigade's performance. The 5th Wisconsin, one of his regiments, was under Colonel Amasa Cobb, a distinguished lawyer and state legislator from Mineral Point, who had served as a private in Mexico. But he was rusty on army drill and Hancock often had to correct him, to the secret amusement of his soldiers, who knew he had been the distinguished speaker of the house, adjutant general and a celebrated figure in his home state.

Members of the 6th Wisconsin, camped nearby, would assemble to look through the willows along the riverbank as Hancock shouted commands. Cobb would sometimes march his men off on a tangent, and Hancock would bellow, "Colonel Cobb, where in the name of Heaven are you going with that battalion?"[1]

The men came to call the drill "Hancock whispering to his brigade."[2] When Cobb was in earshot and Hancock at a distance, they would mimic through the bushes, "Colonel Cobb, where in the name of Heaven are you going with that battalion?" But Cobb learned along with his men and made an intrepid officer who won citations and remained in the service until after Appomattox.

Hancock's other regiments were the 49th Pennsylvania, 43rd New York and 6th Maine. The last was probably the farthest down-east regiment of the army, having been built around the Brownville Rifles, with a Bangor lawyer, Abner Knowles, its first colonel.

Merely by chance a second lieutenant of Company F, 49th Pennsylvania, was John Hancock of Norristown, the general's younger brother, who was soon appointed assistant adjutant general at the brigade headquarters. The regiment had one other volunteer officer who would be closer to Hancock even than his brother almost to the end of his life. Lieutenant William G. Mitchell of Company H soon became his aide-de-camp, rose to the rank of brigadier general, served Hancock as chief of staff, and was one to whom he turned for any paper and on almost any problem until Mitchell's death. The regiment's arms of ancient .68-caliber flintlock muskets that fired three buckshot were as dangerous to their owners as to the enemy. Hancock eventually had them replaced with .54-caliber Austrian rifles firing Minié balls.

Occasionally there were exciting breaks in the drill routine. The brigade took part in the great review of November 20, 1861, held by McClellan at Munson's Hill. This grandest spectacle of the war to that date was participated in by 70,000 men of the divisions of Smith, McCall, McDowell, Heintzelman, Porter, Franklin and Blenker—ninety confident regiments with twenty batteries aggregating 100 guns.

Hancock's uncompromising discipline was revealed during the review. After Colonel William H. Irwin had taken the 49th Pennsylvania past the reviewing stand, his showmanship overcame him and he began to drill his snappy Pennsylvanians on the parade ground, blocking the units behind him and halting the entire parade. Hancock, angered, dashed to the front, liberated the column, rebuked the colonel and put him under arrest. Though Hancock had him tried by court-martial, he was retained in command.

Baldy Smith, who commanded the division, credited Hancock with "indefatigable labors" in drilling and disciplining his brigade during the winter months and said that for the balance of the war it retained the impress of his teaching.[3]

One of Hancock's practices was revealed at once. He made no distinction between volunteer and regular army officers. At an early stage of the war when there was still clannishness and some snobbery, he never gave a hint of regular army arrogance. Others noticed this respect for the volunteer soldier and observed, near the end of the war, that with a single exception—and this an officer Hancock had inherited from Sumner and Couch—Hancock always picked volunteers for his close military family and never gave a regular army officer an important staff assignment. Perhaps he felt the regulars were needed for line duties, or possibly it was mere chance, but at a time when he could have had any young officer in the army, he chose volunteers who had distinguished themselves.[4]

Baldy Smith termed his treatment of volunteer officers "a surprise and mystery to them." They were accustomed to aloofness and stern words. Smith found his reproofs "prompt and sharp," but when the officers were off duty the brigade commander's geniality and hospitality—what Smith called his "courteous and unrestrained" attitude—put the subordinates at ease.[5] Officers fresh from civilian life came to understand that there were two distinct phases of soldiering. On duty, performance had to be quick and unfailing; in quarters, officers were presumed to be friends and gentlemen.

The forging of the Army of the Potomac into a powerful fighting force could not be accomplished in the mid-nineteenth century without some brutalities. A few regular officers bullied and intimidated the volunteer regiments. Volunteer officers themselves often were unduly severe because they thought that by being tough they were following regular army practices. Hancock, though a strict disciplinarian, was incapable of "silly brutalities."[6]

His lack of cupidity and his desire to be free of obligations to others already were established in his character, as well as a sense of the fitness of things. At Lewinsville, during the winter training, some of his officers asked if he would accept as a mark of the brigade's esteem the gift of a silver service. He told them frankly he did not approve of such presentations. In any event, he pointed out, it would be best to wait until the war was over, because the officers might come to have altogether different feelings about him. Nothing more was heard of the suggestion.[7]

During the drill Hancock showed his sense of justice to a captain of the 2nd Division attached to his command. The captain, a reliable soldier, saw his name published in the list of those A.W.O.L. Angered, he stormed in on his colonel to resign, but the superior ordered him to see General Hancock. He was so indignant he would not comply for four days but finally went to Hancock's tent. "General Hancock," he said, "I have come to you against my will, but because of my personal respect for you."

"Sit down, Captain," said Hancock cheerfully, "sit down and tell me about it."

The captain poured out his story of how without cause he had been publicly disgraced.

Hancock listened, then asserted: "I want you to understand, Captain, that I consider the personal honor of my officers and soldiers as sacred as my own. . . . Now, Captain, go back to your tent and leave the whole matter to me. There has been some gross bungling somewhere, and I am going to find it out and have it remedied. I promise you that if I do not set this whole thing right in a week, both to your satisfaction and my own, I will give you an honorable discharge."

He set an investigation into motion and learned that not only this captain, but also twelve other officers, had been abused by the War Department due to an irresponsible inspection by an aide-de-camp who had gone through the camp and listed as A.W.O.L. every officer he did not chance to see on duty. The hastily prepared list had been published in the newspapers. The War Department was quick to make a correction after Hancock's vigorous protest.[8]

Mary Todd Lincoln Remembers a Kindness

Mrs. Hancock rented a Washington house to be near if her husband happened to be wounded. She found Washington society frivolous even under the shadow of war. Mrs. Lincoln insisted on maintaining formal receptions and early in the season gave an "exclusive" ball that brought her much criticism. But with it came some praise also because of the "spirit of independence" with which she inaugurated the social season.[9]

Though invitations went only to Cabinet members, the diplomatic corps, senators and the major generals of the army, Mr. and Mrs. Hancock, to their puzzlement, were included. Later Mrs. Lincoln explained that the invitation was in return for the courtesies members of her family had received from Mrs. Hancock's mother when they were on St. Louis visits. Mary Lincoln had overruled the President, who had demurred over an invitation to a single brigadier general.[10]

Once she was at the White House, Mrs. Hancock became disturbed by the President's careworn face. She remarked that she would show greater consideration if she did not require him to shake hands. She quoted his response in more resounding phrases than were customary for Lincoln:

Ah, if this were all that I was called upon to do, how willingly would it be done for all time; but to say No to the poor unfortunates who come to me, in the belief that I am all powerful to pronounce that little word of only three letters, and who do not and will not understand that I cannot always act as I wish, but have others to consult—this keeps me always unhappy.[11]

Secretary of War Stanton a little later felt free in talking to her to dwell on a Presidential weakness. "Mr. Lincoln," he said, "has the biggest heart of any man in the world, and for that reason we have to watch him, or the Southern women, with their winning ways, would get his permission to carry with them enough contraband goods to supply the Southern army."[12]

Stanton sometimes would have a Lincoln pass recovered at Alexandria when the holder was trying to go through the lines, and impudently torn up without explanation. He did precisely that with an unoffending acquaintance of Mrs. Hancock. With difficulty she prevailed on him to relent.

Stanton, who could be the most implacable of enemies but was useful as a friend, warmed to General Hancock. One incident particularly impressed the new Secretary of War. Agitated by a minor setback in West Virginia, Stanton asked Hancock, a new acquaintance, how long it would take him to make ready a special train for the front.

"As long as it will take me to reach the station," Hancock replied. At Stanton's word he set out. The Secretary of War was holding a reception on the next evening.

Hancock had insisted that his wife attend in his absence. She was in the next room when she heard Stanton inquiring, "Where is Mrs. Hancock? I want to see the wife of that soldier who is ready for an order in ten minutes."

When he greeted her, thoughts of McClellan's slowness, contrasted with Hancock's alacrity, must have been in his mind. "If we had more such soldiers," he said, "if our generals were all so ready, so unquestioning in obeying an order, what materials we would have for our army!"[13]

How Is All This Unhappiness to End?

Hancock's brigade moved with McClellan in early March to Centerville, (then Centreville) Virginia, in the odd "practice" campaign, to find Joseph E. Johnston's trenches empty, as expected. Then the army returned to Alexandria to board the transports for the Peninsula and the grand march on Richmond. Johnston had already transferred the advance elements of his gray-clad force to that area.

When the Federal divisions debarked at Fortress Monroe, they were organized into corps. Smith's division, containing Hancock's brigade, was assigned to the corps commanded by Old Bull Sumner. Later it was transferred to the Sixth Corps.

Edwin Vose Sumner, under whom Hancock was to serve in the sanguinary early battles of the war, had been a trouble shooter during the period of secession. A native of Boston, educated privately instead of at West Point, he had risen through the Black Hawk and frontier fighting to be a captain of dragoons and commander of the cavalry school at Carlisle, Pennsylvania. Distinguished in the charge that broke the Mexicans at Cerro Gordo and in the equally intense cavalry action at Molino del Rey, he won wounds, brevets and such honors in Mexico that the army sent him to Europe for military studies. A series of garrison assignments thereafter marked him as one of the outstanding officers of the old service.

When the states began to secede and Lincoln appeared endangered on his journey to Washington to be inaugurated, Sumner commanded the President-elect's escort from Springfield to the capital, a trip on which he gained Lincoln's confidence. After appointment as a brigadier general, he was sent to relieve Albert Sidney Johnston and secure the West Coast for the Federals. He was sixty-three years old when the Confederates fired on Fort Sumter. He could see the prospect of a back place on the retirement shelf with other sixty-year-olds; still, he was rugged and dominating, and Lincoln liked him, and during the first two years of the war he was frequently mentioned as a possible commander in chief.

Age had brought caution and tended to make a bit of a steer out of the Old Bull. Probably the main trouble was that the size of the armies appalled him after a lifetime of small-unit soldiering. Hancock, as a second lieutenant, had tiffed with him mildly over a careless remark made during the assignment of quarters at Jefferson Barracks, but the misunderstanding had passed with the years. Some of his qualities Hancock liked: "He was never known to doubt. . . . He never failed to obey an order. . . . He was never too late."[14]

When the elements of Sumner's corps embarked at Alexandria March 23, 1862, Hancock wrote to his wife:

I am off at last, and it is a matter of great pain to me that I am unable to see you again before we part—God alone knows for how long. I rode all last night, and while I rode, did not cease to think of how and where all this unhappiness is to end.[15]

McClellan marched through the slough of the lower Peninsula amid the rains of early April, opposed as much in the rear by the Washington authorities as in the front by John Bankhead Magruder's and Joseph E. Johnston's Southern armies.

Stanton schemed and waited almost as eagerly as Johnston for the opportune moment to bring his fist down on the little Napoleon; Attorney General Edward Bates inveighed against him to Lincoln.[16] The President was irresolute himself, fearful that the whole Peninsular plan of invasion, to which he had consented with reluctance, was fully as faulty as he had at first believed, and that Washington was being unblocked to the vast Confederate hordes about whom McClellan always seemed to be writing. Nor were McClellan's four corps commanders, McDowell, Sumner, Heintzelman and Keyes, sympathetic to his leadership, however loyal they were in obedience to his orders.[17]

Looking on from Washington, John Hay, the President's secretary and never McClellan's friend, made it clear that the general was in danger: "Not in front, but in rear."[18] Behind the lines buzzed the black gossip that he was in covert league with the enemy, an iniquitous charge to which Stanton lent a ready ear and eager tongue.[19] He did have an enthusiastic army and ardently loyal subordinate officers, and Hancock was among the most confident.

McClellan might have overcome his obstacles with speed and resolution, neither of which were qualities in his generalship. Arrived at Yorktown—a ripened fruit ready for his taking—he came up against the Confederate Magruder with 15,000 men holding a line along the Warwick River, which cuts almost across the Peninsula at right angles to the York and James rivers and empties into the James.

Baldy Smith's division, with the Vermont brigade in the active role and Hancock in support, made a reconnaissance which developed the enemy's line and on April 16 assailed it at Lee's Mills. Here, still in support, Hancock had his first minor brush with the enemy, though for the Vermont brigade, which was lured into an attack across the river, the affair became spirited and costly. The Green Mountain unit here gave notice that in the War between the States it would be no less intrepid than it had been in the Revolution. It lost heavily in regaining the Federal side of the river when the enemy threw in support.

Hancock continued skirmishes almost daily along the creek until early on the morning of May 4, when two Negroes came into his camp with the surprising intelligence that the Confederate army was no longer in his front.[20] This was the first news of the Confederate withdrawal, which had been conducted stealthily during the night. Hancock sent four or five volunteers across the Warwick River to verify the report.[21] Heintzelman soon had confirming information, which he obtained by ascending in a balloon and looking over the deserted Confederate lines.

Thus after McClellan had devoted a month to shelling Yorktown and the Warwick line and had settled down for a siege which under his method of warfare would likely prove protracted, he was spared further effort. Lincoln was relieved and elated. He would learn to be patient later through more prolonged sieges at Vicksburg and Petersburg, but fretted each day while McClellan—methodical to the point of irritation, yet parsimonious in the matter of casualties—stood in front of Yorktown.

Hancock's brigade was on the left as the Federals followed the retreating Confederates thirteen miles up the Peninsula to Williamsburg. This point the Confederates could not hope to hold permanently because McClellan controlled the York River on their flank. He could bypass Williamsburg, send his gunboats and transports to West Point and establish a beachhead in their rear at any favorable moment.

But Magruder wanted to fight at Williamsburg, and the reason might have been found even in so remote a quarter as the Cologne, Germany, *Gazette,* to which a Prussian officer with the Confederates sent an item. It was difficult, he said, to persuade Magruder to give up his Williamsburg works, "for he loved the position as a father loves his child, and to tell the truth, all the fortifications had been constructed with much talent under his personal direction."[22]

Hancock Seizes the Empty Trenches

So the first major battle of the new Army of the Potomac and Hancock's first opportunity in action came near the historic old Virginia capital and college town, with neither army having its commander actively in charge and neither having more than a plan-of-the-minute to govern its operations.

McClellan was back at Yorktown, supervising the embarkation of Franklin's division for transport up the York to West Point in the Confederate rear. Johnston was present but went about the battlefield humming "Camptown Races"—"I'll bet my money on a bobtailed nag"[23]—and left the resistance mainly to Longstreet on the right, D. H. Hill on the left and Magruder's division in the center. Much shifting of Confederate units occurred in the mud. When, on the morning of May 5, the Federals began to show in their front, the Confederates had a line drawn across the Peninsula, two miles in front of Williamsburg, the strong point being earthen Fort Magruder in the center, from which radiated Magruder's series of redoubts comprising three main defensive lines.

Fort Magruder was at the junction of roads leading to Williamsburg from Hampton on the James River and Yorktown on the York
River. As the Federals approached, Smith's division of Sumner's
corps, now commanded by Keyes, which had been on the extreme
left at Lee's Mills, passed to the extreme right, and Hancock's brigade became the right element of McClellan's army.

Hooker's division opened the battle for the Federals by assailing
Longstreet on the opposite end of the line, with Kearny later moving
to his support. Desultory and at times bitter fighting developed all
along the line.

Hancock had brought his brigade to the woods in front of Fort
Magruder when at 11:00 A.M. General Smith summoned him to
army headquarters in the Whittaker House. There he found Sumner, commanding the army in the absence of McClellan. Sumner
told Hancock to take four or five regiments and a battery, move by
road to the right for a mile and a half, cross Cub Dam Creek, a
branch of Queen's Creek, which empties into the York River, and
seize, if possible, the Confederate works commanding the dam.
Sumner had information that these works had been evacuated.
Smith added orders allowing Hancock to advance farther if it
seemed advantageous and to send for reinforcements if they were
required.[24]

Hancock took three of his own regiments—the 5th Wisconsin,
49th Pennsylvania and 6th Maine, plus two regiments from David-
son's brigade, the 7th Maine and 33rd New York, then acting under
his orders, and Lieutenant Andrew Cowan's 1st New York Battery
of six guns. He had an unusual opportunity to conduct an operation apart from the immediate supervision of his superiors. Success would depend on his own efforts.

The regiments moved circuitously, cutting their way at times
through the woods to cross the dam and approach Fort Magruder
from the north while the balance of the Federal army assailed it
in front. Emerging into the open country, Hancock could see the
York River a mile to his right, but before approaching it he turned
to the left and soon reached the dam, about seventy-five yards long.
The tributary was a series of ponds that could be crossed only at
the dam. Hancock found the works unoccupied. He learned from
Negroes in the neighborhood that they had been held by the Confederates in force on the previous evening, but had been evacuated—

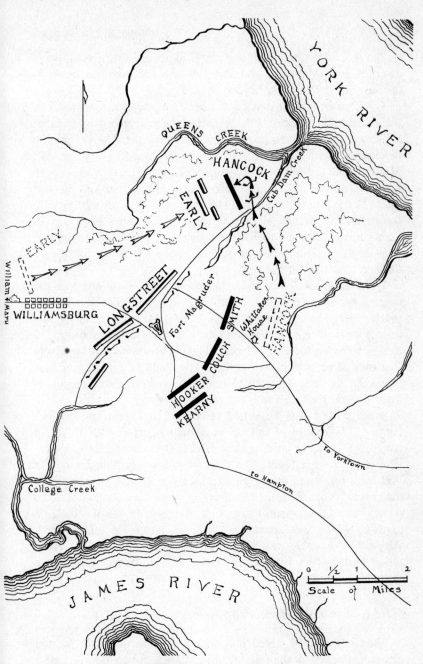

BATTLE OF WILLIAMSBURG, May 5, 1862. Hancock's flank march and attack on the Confederate left.

on the theory, it developed, that the Confederate army would soon abandon Fort Magruder and Williamsburg and continue its withdrawal up the Peninsula beyond West Point.

That had been Johnston's aim until Longstreet, in command of the retirement, had begun to reinforce the rear guard in front of Williamsburg and had gained such advantages over Hooker that he determined—with Johnston's assent—to prolong the engagement. Mindful that the left of Fort Magruder, where only a few South Carolina companies held the redoubts, was almost naked, he had asked D. H. Hill for help, and Hill had ordered Early's brigade to countermarch. It had already progressed two miles beyond Williamsburg on the road to Richmond when it was halted. The brigade returned and lolled on the campus of William and Mary College, awaiting further orders.

When Hancock issued from the woods he found himself on the edge of a clearing roughly two miles long and a mile deep, with a patch of trees in his immediate front. Fort Magruder with its bastions was on the southern edge of the clearing, two miles away. No troops were visible in his front. Hancock observed instinctively that by a sharp attack the Southern line could be turned and Fort Magruder carried. In order to undertake such a promising movement he sent back to Smith for reinforcements.

Smith replied that he would send four regiments and another battery. On receipt of this information but before the arrival of the troops Hancock pushed forward 1,200 yards and took possession of the next redoubt. But this did not satisfy him, for he felt that if his flank and rear were adequately protected, he could oust the enemy troops from the trenches remaining between him and the fort, demonstrate against the fort and greatly assist Hooker's division, which was attacking it without much success in front. Already he was able with his artillery to dominate the plain reaching toward the fort, from which he was now little more than a mile distant.[25]

"Old Bull" Orders Hancock to Retire

Wheeler's battery joined him with four guns and with his ten pieces he opened on the fort. An incident which occurred just after he occupied the second line of trenches showed the Confederates' uncertainty about the disposition of their army. Southern troops in the trenches between him and the fort were puzzled about the identity of the fresh force that had suddenly appeared and signaled to one of Hancock's staff officers asking who the newcomers were.[26]

Hancock answered by ordering the national colors placed on his front parapet. When the flag was unfurled the enemy deployed skirmishers and began an annoying fire along the Federal line, which Hancock's skirmishers answered. Soon Confederate artillery let loose a reply to Cowan's and Wheeler's batteries. Hancock, seeing the precision of the Federal fire and recognizing that the line in his front was not strongly held, again grew impatient to advance and watched anxiously for the arrival of reinforcements. Directly astride the left of the Confederate position, he sensed that increased pressure would force Longstreet to evacuate Fort Magruder and retire into or beyond Williamsburg.

But, instead of reinforcements, Hancock received a message from General Sumner ordering him to fall back to the first works he had taken after crossing the dam. The order disturbed Hancock not only because he saw a great opportunity cast away, but also because he knew that his division commander, Smith, had intended to support him.[27] It was now 2:30 P.M. Hancock decided to hold for a time and sent Lieutenant C. K. Crane, Smith's ordnance officer, to both Sumner and Smith with a discreet protest against the withdrawal order. Crane quoted Sumner as saying, "I have just ordered General Hancock to fall back to his first point, sir, and cannot send him reinforcements."[28]

Smith returned this message:

Go at once to General Hancock and tell him that I have wanted and have tried to reinforce him, but that General Sumner has positively forbidden to allow any reinforcements to be sent to him until more troops come up from the rear.

When Lieutenant Crane delivered these two messages Hancock recognized that he was in a most trying situation. Here at the very outset of McClellan's Peninsular campaign he had to make a decision calling into play his full capacity and courage. The easy course would be to comply with Sumner's orders and retire three quarters of a mile over the ground he had captured. He knew that his troops, whose spirits were now thoroughly aroused, would suffer

a sharp loss of morale. They too could recognize the importance
of their situation on the enemy flank and could understand that a
great many casualties might be required to recover the ground once
it was abandoned.

Hancock's ability to make quick and bold decisions now asserted
itself. Instead of withdrawing, he determined to protest again. It
was 3:30 P.M. He sent Second Lieutenant Francis V. Farquhar,
an engineer officer, to describe the terrain and his position to Sumner. His object, as he explained it, was to show the "disadvantage
of falling back . . . and giving up the advantages we had already
secured, for which we might have to fight again the next day . . .
besides the bad impression it would make on my troops, and the
inspiring effect it would have on the enemy, who were then engaged
in a furious contest . . . in front of Fort Magruder."[29] Farquhar
was to tell Sumner that Hancock would wait a reasonable time for
a reply and, receiving none, would obey the order to fall back.

Farquhar found Smith at Sumner's headquarters. Smith told
him to locate Sumner and tell him that two brigades of Smith's
division might be sent to Hancock. Sumner at first consented; then,
before the brigades could move, he countermanded the order and
diverted them to reinforce his center battling in front of the fort.[30]

These transactions required time. When Farquhar did not return promptly, Hancock at 4:20 P.M. sent a written message to
General Smith that he would wait "a reasonable time" for word
from Sumner. Fifty more minutes passed. The skies unloosed a
heavy downpour which drenched the troops.[31] It was 5:10 P.M.
Hancock's position was desperate, not with the enemy but in his
relations with his own chief. In final capitulation to Sumner's orders, he prepared to withdraw.

A Bold Lieutenant Looks on with Rapture

Perhaps the best account of his stubborn refusal to budge from
his favorable line on the enemy's flank and his anguish at the turn
of events was provided by Second Lieutenant George A. Custer of
the 5th Cavalry, a close observer.

Custer had been graduated from West Point the previous summer without much promise. He had been present at the fiasco
along Bull Run. When the Peninsular campaign opened he became

attracted to Hancock and worked himself into a status which Hancock described as a "volunteer aid." As such he had led, as a lone horseman, the brigade's march through the woods and across the dam to the enemy's flank. During the fighting later he watched enraptured at Hancock's elbow, ready for odd jobs as they developed, and with a quick military perception that had not been so apparent at West Point he evaluated and recorded everything that happened. His account of the battle was found among his papers after his death on the Little Big Horn.[32]

Hancock's supreme achievement, in Custer's opinion, was in maintaining his forward position resolutely in the face of orders to retreat. That was the sort of independent judgment which delighted one of Custer's temperament. Hancock saw the importance not merely of holding, but of advancing, and as early as eleven o'clock, by Custer's timing, sent a member of his staff to Smith for more men. Again and again Hancock risked the impatience—even the drastic action—of his superiors by renewing his request. Custer pictured him as angered: "Those who have seen Hancock . . . can imagine the manner in which he received the order to retire. Never at a loss for expletives, [he] was not at all loath to express his condemnation of the policy, which . . . in the end, must prove disastrous."

Hancock took out his watch and turned to Custer. "It is now two o'clock. I shall wait till four. If no reply reaches me from headquarters I shall then withdraw."

Four o'clock finally was at hand. Custer noticed that Hancock's impatience increased minute by minute and almost with every musket discharge. "A fourth staff officer was dispatched at a gallop to hasten, if possible, the expected and long-hoped-for message from 'Old Bull.'" At four o'clock Hancock decided to wait half an hour more. "If no orders reach me during that time," he again told Custer, "I must retire." His entire staff was now in the rear, urgently requesting a reversal of the retreat orders and the dispatch of fresh troops.

The Enemy Launches a Sudden Assault

At 5:10 P.M., as he was about to begin his withdrawal, Hancock noticed that the enemy was being reinforced.

The trenches in his immediate front were filling rapidly. A detachment of Confederate horse moved out of the woods to survey his lines from a distance. He immediately sent a messenger to General Smith informing him that the enemy was concentrating on the Federal right.

Seeing a fresh Southern regiment enter the woods on his left as if for a flanking movement, Hancock brought back his two left regiments to the crest of an incline that formed a better defensive line, halted them and faced them again to the front. The other regiments he brought back a short distance to conform to this new position.

This rectification of his line, which the enemy understood to be a retirement, was the signal for a sudden and desperate assault by Early's brigade, which had been brought over from the William and Mary campus.[33] Major General D. H. Hill, seeing that Hancock was unsupported and isolated on the Federal right, had judged that he could be dislodged by a vigorous assault. Johnston had assented, though Longstreet was not in sympathy with the attempt.[34] Hill accompanied Early's brigade. Longstreet pointed out the objective of the old Confederate works to the left of Fort Magruder. Hill had brought up the brigade of Gabriel J. Rains to give Early support. When all was in readiness, he ordered the charge.

The Confederates came on impetuously, shouting, "Bull Run" and "Ball's Bluff," until they were within thirty paces of Hancock's line.[35] The assault suffered from too many generals. Early accompanied his old regiment, the 24th Virginia, which had given him distinction at Manassas, and which now advanced on the brigade's left. Early commanded the left regiments, Hill the right. The 5th North Carolina was on the far right, while the center was held by the 23rd North Carolina and 38th Virginia. The two flank regiments moved with vigor, those in the center so deliberately that they never got out of the woods but remained content with long-range firing. Early's brigade consequently attacked with the two flank regiments, or about half of its 2,300 men.[36]

The 5th North Carolina executed an unusual movement in its advance. Seeing the 24th Virginia unsupported on its far left, and the center regiments of the brigade lagging, it moved entirely across its own brigade front until it formed a line of assault with the Virginians.[37] These two regiments threw themselves impulsively against the Federal line.

Hancock watched them admiringly. That night he told one of his prisoners that "immortality ought to be inscribed on the banners of the 24th Virginia and 5th North Carolina for their great bravery" in the charge.[38]

That, too, was the conclusion of the historian of the North Carolina regiment: "The charge of the 5th North Carolina on this occasion has rarely been surpassed in the history of war for its heroism and gallantry."[39]

Custer observed Hancock as the enemy advanced. He rode along the line saying, "Aim low, men. Aim low. Do not be in a hurry to fire until they come nearer."[40] The Confederates marched a thousand yards across the cleared ground. There was no longer a question of retiring. Hancock had no alternative now but to fight and win a battle. He found himself suddenly involved in what promised to be a most heated engagement. He had acted contrary to repeated orders, and he understood that the only thing that could save him was victory. Custer heard him tell one group, "You must hold this ground or I am ruined."[41] When the action was joined he galloped along the line, his hat off, indifferent to the hail of bullets.

The assailants never were able to come to close grips with Hancock's solid defense. Early was hit in the shoulder at a critical moment and lost so much blood he had to leave the field.

According to Custer, when the Confederates were within twenty paces and while the Federal line was firing at will, the attack languished. The ground over which the gray soldiers advanced was soft and lumpy, which would have made the going heavy even had there been no opposition. The confident yelling of the assailants began to trail off. At this instant Hancock sensed his opportunity and ordered the counterattack. His manner had just the poise and finesse that would appeal to young Custer, who in his journal described it thus:

With that excessive politeness of manner which characterizes him when everything is being conducted according to his liking, Hancock, as if conducting guests to a banquet rather than fellow-beings to a life-and-death struggle, cried out in tones well befitting a Stentor: "Gentlemen, charge with the bayonet."[42]

Hancock had timed the movement nicely. Custer saw the men— "no, the gentlemen," he said, correcting his narrative—bring down their bayonets and spring ahead in a cheering, charging line. The

Confederates, already wavering, were astonished and swept back. The retreat soon degenerated into a rout. The fresher Federal soldiers overtook many of the retiring enemy, capturing about 500 prisoners and bringing in the first enemy battle flag captured by the Army of the Potomac. On the advance, Hancock, hat off, went along with his men.[43]

The Duc d'Orleans, one of the French princes on McClellan's staff, attracted by the heavy battle on the right, reached Hancock's line just as the colors were brought in and at Hancock's request bore the trophy to army headquarters. Custer had captured it.

McClellan Gives Lavish Approval

After the repulse of Early the fortifications behind Hancock began to fill up with masses of Federal troops. Darkness was coming on but shouts in the rear soon explained the extraordinary activity. McClellan had ridden up from Yorktown, arriving on the field as news reached headquarters of Hancock's repulse of the Confederates and his brilliant counterattack.

Even while he was being cheered by his admiring troops, McClellan was listening to the account and grasping its implications. He saw the decisive nature of Hancock's battle and recognized what Sumner had not seemed to fathom, that the Confederate left had been turned and that reinforcements to Hancock, who sat astride the enemy flank, would force them out of Fort Magruder and Williamsburg.

McClellan gave his own picture of conditions: ". . . grasping at once the fact that he [Hancock] held the key of the field of battle, I ordered Smith, who was chafing like a caged lion, to move as rapidly as possible to Hancock's support with his two remaining brigades and Naglee's. Within five minutes of the time I reached the field Smith was off as rapidly as his men could move."[44] Naglee followed immediately with a brigade of Casey's division.

After ordering a forward movement of his center, McClellan rode at once to see Hancock's line personally. Before reaching the dam he encountered the column of prisoners Hancock was sending back. He numbered them at between 500 and 600 and placed Hancock's loss at only 31 men.

"This was one of the most brilliant engagements of the war," he wrote later, "and General Hancock merited the highest praise." He commended Hancock inferentially for not heeding Sumner, by referring to "his perfect appreciation of the vital importance of his position."[45]

No such charge as Hancock's had been made to that moment in the war, and though darkness and a heavy storm prevented further action in that quarter, McClellan meant to take full advantage of it. By sending in more troops he was preparing to develop a full-scale action on his right in the morning. He was spared that necessity. That night the Confederate army, its left flank turned, retired.

McClellan, on the night of the battle, sent a telegram to Washington: "Hancock was superb today."[46] The words were so appropriate that they never left Hancock. Until his death he was "Hancock the Superb."

Though McClellan had complimented the troops on his arrival at the close of the fighting, two days later he paid the brigade the further tribute of calling personally, parading each regiment and thanking it for its part in the brilliant action on the army's right at Williamsburg.[47] After such glory the brigade naturally became attached to its commander. Greenleaf A. Goodale, an enlisted man of the 6th Maine, voiced this sentiment: "Certainly after Williamsburg, if not before, the brigade believed that whatever General Hancock ordered was exactly right."[48]

Smith, who all along had had a better perception of Hancock's movement than Sumner, was effusive in his report:

The brilliancy of the plan of battle, the coolness of its execution, the seizing of the proper instant for changing from the defensive to the offensive, the steadiness of the troops engaged, and the completeness of the victory, are subjects to which I earnestly call the attention of the commander-in-chief for his just praise.[49]

★★★6★★★

Our Country, and No One Man

Enduring Admiration Formed for McClellan

Brigadier Generals Hancock and William T. H. Brooks and Colonel Alexander Hays were on the steamer *Montreal,* August 24, 1862, going from Fortress Monroe up Chesapeake Bay and the Potomac to Alexandria, following their troops on the transports.

McClellan's Peninsular campaign had passed into history. Talk among the officers was incessant—how the battles had been fought, the opportunities and failures, the requirements that the army be reorganized and, as Hays put it, the material and driftwood that would have to be cut loose. About one matter there was full agreement: "We are still for Little McClellan, and the people must not throw him overboard without cause."[1]

This ardent admiration of McClellan, which Hancock shared as fully as any private in the ranks, was a peculiar by-product of an abortive military campaign. But Hancock and the men were not without discernment. McClellan possessed, in addition to his organizing talents, perhaps to a greater degree than any other Northern military figure of this war, the capacity for inspiring his troops and winning the lasting admiration of their officers, which is no small part of competent generalship. Hancock's solid friendship for him was to endure until their deaths within a few months of each other. The affection was to be one of the deepest of Hancock's life, surpassed only by his devotion to his family and the cause of the Union.

Through the battles of the Peninsula his brigade had fought stanchly in Baldy Smith's division of Franklin's Sixth Corps, at Garnett's Hill, Golding's Farm, Savage Station and White Oak Swamp, and in numerous minor affairs and skirmishes. After the army had changed its base and was finally retiring from Harrison's Landing, Hancock marched the brigade overland in good order to Fortress Monroe.[2]

For him the Peninsular campaign had involved no failures, but rather a series of brilliant engagements all the way from Williamsburg to the sad withdrawal. For his consistently gallant service McClellan recommended him to be a major general of volunteers and to receive three brevets in the regular army.

One or two of his engagements had been notable. While standing as the rear guard of Smith's division and McClellan's army, he had beaten off a savage attack, launched just before darkness, at Garnett's Hill. The action had continued the next morning at Golding's Farm and again the assault had been repulsed.

That morning Hancock's men brought in a prisoner who was destined to become one of the country's great men and to wield a powerful influence in cementing the South with the Union in the years after the war. He was Lieutenant Colonel Lucius Quintus Cincinnatus Lamar, head of a Georgia battalion. Later he served as a Mississippi senator, a member of President Cleveland's Cabinet and an associate justice of the United States Supreme Court.[3] His brother, Mirabeau B. Lamar, had been president of the Republic of Texas and his father-in-law was the distinguished Georgia educator and writer, Augustus B. Longstreet. Here he first met Hancock, to whom he gave his friendship and political assistance in later years.

The turn of McClellan's fortunes for the worse on the Peninsula might have been read in the attitude of Hancock's Negro groom, Charles. The general, always mounted on a splendid horse, had a fine sorrel and a handsome bay. As Hancock was about to go into action Charles asked which horse he would ride.

"I think I will ride the bay today, Charles," he responded.

Charles reflected deeply, then demurred. "I think you better ride de sor'l today, Gineral," said the groom. "He's de swiftest."[4]

When the brigade landed at Alexandria, too late to be sent to Pope before he met Lee, Hancock moved with the rest of the Sixth

Corps to Centerville, where he occupied part of the works while
Pope brought his shattered Federal army back to Washington after
the second battle of Manassas.

Victorious on the Peninsula and in Northern Virginia, Robert E.
Lee, who had succeeded Johnston in the Confederate command,
crossed the Potomac. Lincoln, who had stripped McClellan of his
troops in order to augment Pope's army, was compelled to turn
again to the Little Napoleon. After McClellan had been fortuitously
apprised of Lee's campaign plans by finding a copy of his marching
orders, he closed on the Confederate army, then hastily concentrating behind Antietam Creek at Sharpsburg, Maryland.

Holding the Center at Antietam

While Antietam was a battle of great fury and significance, for
Hancock it was mainly a parting with the brigade he had drilled
and loved, and a progression to the higher responsibility of division
command. It meant the renewal of his association with the Second
Corps of the Army of the Potomac, with which his name would be
linked until the closing days of the conflict.

On McClellan's movement from Frederick to Sharpsburg, Hancock's brigade, being in reserve, merely exchanged artillery fire
with the Confederates at Crampton's Gap, which Franklin and the
rest of his Sixth Corps forced on September 14, while Hooker and
Burnside were carrying Turner's Gap five miles farther north.

On the Antietam battlefield Hancock became engaged when
Franklin sent Baldy Smith's division to the support of Sedgwick
after that general's spectacular but costly attack on the West Woods,
from which he was ousted. Howard, who took command of the
division after Sedgwick was wounded, said of Smith's assistance,
that "like all other supports in this ill-managed battle, it was a little
too late."[5] Taking no chance that his artillery might be captured
by a Confederate counterattack, Smith assigned Hancock to protect the guns, which Hancock did by scattering regiments between
the batteries all along the line.

At high noon Major General Israel B. Richardson was mortally
wounded. He had come to the assistance of French's division and
attacked the Confederates under D. H. Hill along a sunken road

known thereafter as the "Bloody Lane." McClellan sent hastily for
Hancock and personally directed him to take command of Richardson's division.

No appointment could have won wider acclaim in the army,
where the admiration of Hancock had become almost universal.
Walker pointed out that he had so thoroughly prepared himself for
the larger responsibilities of division command that, within an hour
after assuming his new duties, "none could have told—he himself
hardly knew—he had not commanded a division for years."[6]

An enlisted man in the 64th New York told in a letter home
how Hancock had appeared before the division at 2:00 P.M., "riding along without aide or orderly."[7] Another said his actions were
so decisive he mistook him at first for the commander in chief of
the entire army.[8]

The only disappointment was in the Sixth Corps which he was
leaving. The corps commander, Franklin, was to pay him a splendid tribute. Franklin said the longer he knew Hancock the more
he admired him, and: "I never met a man who, as a general officer,
while under my observation, combined so well as he did the pru-
dence which cherished the lives of his command, with the dash
which was his distinguishing characteristic." He went on to say that
a man like Hancock was "worth hundreds of ordinary commanders," and "to be under his command, to know him . . . was to have
a complete military education."[9]

Hancock's new command, the First Division of the Second Corps,
already had been distinguished even at this early stage of the war.
Sumner had drilled it in the winter of 1861-1862 and the brigades
of Caldwell and Meagher had engaged in some of the hardest fighting on the Peninsula. Both were important elements in the repulse
of Lee's army at Malvern Hill. At Antietam the division had been
involved that morning in the most sanguinary phase of the battle
along the sunken road.

Hancock now commanded the center of McClellan's army. The
division occupied a single line in close proximity to the enemy; consequently, part of French's division was sent to fill in Hancock's
gaps, though Hancock's request for artillery could not at once be
satisfied. Referring to the great length of Hancock's line, McClellan
found the subordinate general confident he could hold his position,

yet lacking in strength to undertake an offensive.[10] Finally he obtained some batteries which aided greatly in repulsing enemy thrusts.

The centers of the two armies, with Hancock opposed to D. H. Hill, faced each other at close range during the afternoon of September 17. The fighting scarcely slackened, though the charges abated, but the main action rolled off toward the Federal left, where Burnside with great deliberation was crossing Antietam Creek, only to find that Lee's weak right had been made secure by the arrival of A. P. Hill before he finally came to grips with it. Hancock continued to hold the center as the two armies sullenly faced each other throughout the next day and the night of September 18, when Lee silently recrossed the Potomac.

The Antietam campaign had brought promotion but not great battle distinction to Hancock, nor to scarcely any other high officer. It had disclosed McClellan's faith in him. With the first opportunity for advancement, the commanding general had confidently assigned him to new troops and a different corps, and had entrusted him with one of the foremost responsibilities of the battlefield, guarding the center against the assaults of the high-spirited, hard-fighting D. H. Hill, on the hottest section of the field.

One incident in the battle Hancock's staff remembered with amusement. On the night of September 16, as the facing armies waited for the desperate encounter they knew would follow in the morning, and brisk firing occurred along the lines, Hancock met one of the many new regiments having their first experience under fire. The men were hugging the brow of a hill, shells bursting around them, musket balls cutting the ground. The colonel lay prostrate with the men, so that when Hancock rode up in the moonlight he could not see that the regiment had a leader.

"Who commands this regiment?" he inquired.

The colonel bobbed his head out of a hole, then dodged back as a bullet whizzed by, but he managed to get out the reply, without saluting, "I do, sir."

Hancock sat on his fine horse in front of the regiment, his staff about him, indifferent to the enemy firing. "How many men have you got on duty, Colonel?" he asked.

"About eight hundred, I guess," said the colonel, again dodging back and forth from his cover.

Hancock was entertained and amused himself by drawing out the colonel. "Are you about ready to advance?"

"I rather guess we shall be when we're ordered," the colonel said none too convincingly.

One of Hancock's aides then stepped forward. "Perhaps General Hancock shall order you to," he said, pointing his sword to designate the general.

"General Hancock!" exclaimed the colonel, who now jumped to his feet and saluted. "I beg your pardon, General. I feel ashamed to be caught in this position. It is my first fight, sir. I await your orders. I will follow you anywhere."

The general and colonel laughed together. The newcomer, a distinguished lawyer who proved in later fighting a brave and capable officer, saw the drollery of the situation, with the general on horseback out in front while he and the regiment timidly hugged the ground. He shouted his orders: "Regiment! Up, men! Face front. Present arms!"[11]

They made a good showing in the moonlight as Hancock passed along the line. Thereafter the colonel, inspired by Hancock's presence under fire, distinguished himself, was wounded and was cited.

"I Do Not See Any Great Blunders"

The Second Corps with Hancock's division was near McClellan's headquarters at Rectortown, north of Warrenton, on November 7 when in a driving snowstorm the messenger from Washington brought to McClellan orders relieving him from command of the Army of the Potomac and appointing Major General Ambrose E. Burnside in his place.

Along with the rest of the army, Hancock was deeply shocked, yet as a soldier his immediate instinct was to accept the order without question and make the best of it.[12]

While the army seethed with mutiny,[13] there were grumblings in Hancock's own division over a more earthy matter than loyalty to a fallen chief. On taking over the new division he had issued strict orders against pillaging. Now that the division was camped on a cold, open plain between Salem, where Burnside had his headquarters, and Rectortown, and little wood was available, Hancock's prohibition was so adamant that the officers refused to allow the men to burn a rail fence conveniently in front of their camp. As they brought in scant supplies of fuel from long distances through the snow, they grumbled over Hancock's injunction. Even Mc-Clellan, they recalled, countenanced the use of the top rails for firewood.[14]

Hancock's discipline had provoked an amusing incident a few days before. Atop Snicker's Gap his division could look out on the fertile Shenandoah Valley and the rolling country devoted largely to sheep raising. He saw a group of his men huddled over a sheep. Spurring up to them, he denounced them scathingly for violating orders and butchering an animal before his very eyes. When some of the men tried to reply, he cut them off sharply with a fresh outburst. Just as his anger was at its height, the prostrate sheep suddenly jumped to its feet, issued a bleat and made off with healthy speed. The delighted soldiers, to perpetuate the memory of the incident, named their Snicker's Gap bivouac "Camp Mutton."[15]

Probably the Federal cause was never in more desperate condition than at the moment the army learned of McClellan's dismissal. One or two firebrand generals might easily have set off a revolt. Veteran regiments seemed ready to throw down their arms. John Gibbon heard of instances where they actually did so. One of the generals told McClellan: "Lead us to Washington, General. We will follow you there."[16]

Gibbon, though West Point-trained and a veteran of the old army, came up with an extraordinary suggestion himself. To another general he proposed that the leading officers of the army should write to President Lincoln requesting suspension of the order removing McClellan, so as to allow breathing time and enable McClellan to finish whatever operations he had under way. He found no supporters for such a move and abandoned the suggestion. He pointed out that McClellan personally stopped all talk of resisting Lincoln's order.[17]

Hancock's course was consistent. Whenever he heard open complaints of officers or mutinous sentiments, he checked them with the admonition, "We are serving our country, and not any man."[18] He would neither stoop to the gross offense of ingratitude to the chief who had given his confidence and promotion, nor lose sight of the main objective of preserving the Union, which could not be accomplished by rebellion against its established authorities. His words were almost identical with those of McClellan, "Gentlemen, please remember that we are here to serve the interests of no one man. We are here to serve our country."

The same words occurred in the letter Hancock wrote to his wife:

The Army are not satisfied with the change, and consider the treatment of McClellan most ungracious and inopportune. Yet I do not sympathize with the movement going on to resist the order. "It is useless," I tell the gentlemen around me. "We are serving no one man; we are serving our country."[19]

So ended the military career of George B. McClellan, Hancock's close personal friend, from the days of West Point to Antietam. Had the junior officer been called on to summarize his opinion about his chief's conduct of the army, he probably would have chosen words not greatly different from those of McClellan himself: "I do not see any great blunders." For Mrs. Hancock, McClellan was "that great soldier so often misrepresented and misjudged."[20]

Now the army looked for orders and presumably swift action from Burnside, whose slowness, as all the world knew, had been McClellan's major obstacle to a more resounding triumph at Antietam.

Storming Marye's Heights

A Testy General Will Not Be Countered

Burnside moved down the north bank of the Rappahannock, intending to establish a base at Falmouth, cross and seize the heights south and west of Fredericksburg, then operate against Lee's army and Richmond.

Sumner, who came up first to Falmouth, might easily have passed the river with Hancock's division and taken Fredericksburg, but Burnside would not consent until his lines of communication were established and his pontoons were brought over from Harpers Ferry, all of which meant a delay of about a month. During that time Lee concentrated his army behind Fredericksburg to dispute a Federal crossing. Winter began to settle over the Virginia countryside, and it was not until December 11 that the laying of the pontoons across the Rappahannock was begun.

One of the riddles of the war is why Lincoln picked Burnside to succeed McClellan. The great humanitarian's early ineptness in selecting leaders was fully illustrated when he handed the army to Burnside, who was among the first to concede, both before and after the event, that he lacked the talents to direct so large a force.

Burnside seemed to be groping for comfort by sharing, as far as he could, the responsibilities of the high command. He divided the army into three large units, which he called Grand Divisions. To the command of them he appointed Sumner, Hooker and Franklin.

Sumner's Right Grand Division was composed of the Second Corps under Major General Darius Nash Couch, and the Ninth Corps, formerly Burnside's, under Brigadier General Orlando B. Willcox. Hancock commanded the First Division of Couch's Second Corps, while Couch's other two divisions were commanded by Brigadier Generals Oliver O. Howard and William H. French. On Couch's corps fell the heavy brunt of the desperate assault on Marye's Heights, the most sanguinary phase of the battle of Fredericksburg.

Couch was a native of Putnam County, New York, and a graduate of West Point two years behind Hancock, in the class with McClellan, Burnside and Stonewall Jackson. He had distinguished himself at Buena Vista but had resigned from the army after the Mexican War and gone into business in New York City. When war broke out between the states he raised the 7th Massachusetts Regiment, became colonel, hurried it to Washington and rose rapidly from regimental to corps command under his close friend McClellan.

He was of slight build and was modest and retiring, but in battle he "became sublime" and "the high-mounting sense of duty took complete possession of every power and faculty, every thought and feeling. . . ."[1]

The season was anything but happy for campaigning and only Lincoln's extreme impatience over McClellan's slowness could have justified Burnside in making a winter attack which, even though it might dislodge the enemy, could not likely be followed up over the miserable Virginia roads in such unfavorable weather.

Snow fell all day December 5 and reached a depth of several inches while the army awaited the pontoons. The litterateur De Trobriand told how the pine trees beneath which his regiment camped curved and bent and "formed arcades above the tents."[2] He compared the sentinels on their posts to plaster statues. As he grew poetic in describing the scene, which Hancock probably would have painted if he had had more leisure, he said one would think that "Death, not satisfied with the bloody part reserved for him, wished to bury us all under the same winding sheet."

Bitter cold weather continued on the seventh and the snow formed a sparkling, icy crust. Drill was suspended, and the men, believing there would be no more campaigning, began to put up log houses for winter quarters, but on the night of December 10 orders were passed through the commands that the army would move in the morning. De Trobriand described the preparations:

The night was full of suppressed agitation, and of those distant rumors which denote preparations for battle. . . . In the different sections was heard the rolling of wagons to the rear, and cannon going to the front. Confused noises indicated the march of regiments changing position. Their bayonets flashed . . . lighted up by the bivouac fires.[3]

Burnside had no battle plan except to go over the river and storm the enemy's entrenched position. While the army waited, Sumner had called a council of his general officers, which filled the Lacy house, for it included everyone down to brigade commanders. The comments were candid and, despite Sumner's efforts at moderation and full support of Burnside, there was pointed objection, mainly from Couch and Hancock, to the proposal that the army should cross and rashly attack the waiting Confederates.

The meeting was held on the night of December 9, and the next morning Burnside was informed what everyone had said. He was particularly indignant at Hancock.[4] This surprised Couch, who had thought his own opposition to the assault less moderately expressed than Hancock's. But Burnside took the position that he had decided on the attack and needed not objections but the loyalty of his army to carry it out, which caused Hancock to disclaim any lack of personal respect, though he retained his opinion that it would be most difficult to carry Lee's fortified line.[5] He remembered Badajoz and New Orleans.

Burnside's stubborn adherence to error during these preliminary councils was clearly evident when Couch passed to him information gained from deserters, Negroes and citizens of the area about a canal between Fredericksburg and the Confederate lines on Marye's Heights. Francis Walker, who conveyed Couch's message, said Burnside answered "with asperity" and cut him off with "Say to General Couch that he is mistaken."[6]

Burnside declared he had occupied Fredericksburg with his corps the preceding August, had ridden out from the town, covered the plain and hills, and was certain there was no obstacle between town and Marye's Heights. Other information on Burnside's attitude came from General Zook, who attended a council at which Colonel

Benjamin C. Christ of the Ninth Corps told Burnside of this canal. It merely infuriated the commanding general, who denounced Colonel Christ and claimed it was not the first time the colonel had tried to thwart his plans.[7] Mr. Lincoln's substitute for McClellan was already proving peevish to a point where he seemed emotionally unstable.

While Hancock's division was making ready, one of the brigade commanders, Zook, inspected a newly arrived regiment at Falmouth and saw that the Belgian rifles known as "contract weapons" were not only unfinished but of poor material, some of them having springs so weak they would not fire a percussion cap. The soft iron bayonets were little better than toy tin swords. When Zook thrust one at the ground it bent almost double. He tested a percussion cap half a dozen times and it failed to explode. He stood off and declared there was only one thing satisfactory about such firearms, which was: "I'm satisfied they're not worth a damn."

He reported the miserable condition of the arms to Hancock, who had no surplus weapons available and could only suggest: "Tell the men to look around them as soon as they get into a fight. They'll find plenty of guns on the field."[8]

The attack on Marye's Heights came two days later; the regiment had scant opportunity to hunt for discarded guns, and according to an account which Hancock appeared to have approved, this regiment lost half its numbers without much likelihood that it killed a single enemy soldier.[9]

Hancock's Men Help Sack a City

On the night of December 10 Hancock was ordered to send two regiments to the Lacy House, Sumner's headquarters opposite Fredericksburg, to serve as protection for engineers who would lay the pontoon bridges across the Rappahannock, beginning at daybreak. He detailed the 57th and 69th New York regiments, which went to the water front and soon were losing heavily to Barksdale's Mississippi sharpshooters stationed in houses and rifle pits in Fredericksburg.

Barksdale's fire proved so effective that the work had to be suspended until Hancock could put some of his men into boats and gain a foothold on the other bank. He asked for volunteers and got a goodly number who crossed the river, scaled the bank, worked their way into the town and by steady pressure drove the Mississippians out of the houses and rifle pits. As Hancock's boats pushed off, a Michigan drummer boy rushed into the water, held to one of the craft and swam and reached the other side safely, to win the name of the "Drummer Boy of the Rappahannock."[10]

Hancock marched his full division close to the pontoons, but as the bridges were not completed on the eleventh, he halted in a protected valley and had the troops stack arms and go into bivouac. That night the division of 5,006 men slept in the open, on the frozen ground, without fires, the general lying with his soldiers.[11]

At 8:00 A.M. on the morning of December 12 the division made the passage of the river.[12] French's division crossed on a pontoon farther upstream. When Howard also was across, the three divisions of the Second Corps made a line of battle and moved through the streets, sweeping out the remaining remnants of Barksdale's Confederate brigade. The Ninth Corps, which with the Second Corps made up Sumner's Right Grand Division, then crossed.

Here the lack of planning began to show itself, for orders were issued that Sumner's men should cross Hazel Run on their left, move down the Rappahannock and fall in behind Franklin's Left Grand Division, which had made the passage farther down the river. To carry out this maneuver, three bridges were built across Hazel Run, a creek that enters the Rappahannock below Fredericksburg. Late on December 12 orders came from Burnside to defer the march downstream until the next morning. By that time he had changed his mind again and gone back to his original intention of assailing Marye's Heights, where Lee had his main defenses about a mile back from the river.

On his left, Lee held the line with Longstreet's corps, while down the river Stonewall Jackson's corps confronted Franklin's Left Grand Division. Hooker's Center Grand Division was the Federal reserve. The Federal lines extended about seven miles along the river. Lee's lines were longer, for they ran along the semicircle of hills commanding the level plain, or river bottom, about a mile in depth at the center.

Marye's Heights, the focal point of the main action, was the seat of a family established in Virginia by James Marye (pronounced Mareé), a Huguenot minister who had founded St. George's Church in Fredericksburg, and whose academy George Washington had attended. A great grandson, John L. Marye, was an able Virginia attorney before the war.[13] The Marye house, called Brompton, a modest mansion with a great oak tree in its front, stood on the high ground south of the Plank Road and west of the Telegraph Road.

In the face of the desperate assault which the men could foresee, and in retaliation for the stubborn resistance Barksdale's gray-clad sharpshooters had offered in the town, the troops of Hancock's division, with others of Couch's corps, began a systematic looting of the Fredericksburg houses, which were soon stripped of all property of value. Even so unbending a disciplinarian as Hancock could not check the stealthy plundering, but Couch had a provost guard stationed at the pontoons so that none of the property could be carried to the Federal side of the river. "An enormous pile of booty was collected there by evening," Couch said.

Most of it apparently was carried off later, not by the original looters or the owners, but by soldiers who found it at the bridge-heads after the army became too much occupied with the enemy to guard it any longer.

Francis Walker undertook to minimize the plundering by saying Hancock's and French's soldiers did it in a spirit of levity rather than hatred.[14] He saw a "gigantic" private of the Irish Brigade decked out with a white satin bonnet that had been part of a bride's trousseau. Another was wearing what he termed an antique "scoop" bonnet, and still another toted a feather bed about the town so that he might sleep on it that night. A soldier carried around a ten-gallon coffeepot used for church socials, while one clowned about with a woman's chemise over his uniform.[15]

The looting, according to Walker, occurred at night or early the next morning before there had been time to place guards. Some of it was clearly wanton:

There were many things done which had not even the poor excuse of frolic. Pianos were thrown into the street, elegant furniture chopped up, family portraits split with bayonets, choice libraries scattered and mutilated, frescoed walls done over with charcoal sketches of military amateurs.[16]

As Hancock's and French's men appeared to be the principal offenders, clearly Hancock's warnings about fence rails and mutton had influenced his new division only lightly.

Hancock's Attack "Launched like a Catapult"

The battle of Fredericksburg, one of the most disastrous defeats of American military history, was fought on December 13, mainly by Sumner's Right Grand Division, though Hooker brought some of his men into action late in the day and Franklin engaged in a spirited attack against Jackson, with Meade's division threatening for a time to maintain a lodgment in the Confederate works.

The main impact of Sumner's attack was delivered by the divisions of French and Hancock, with Howard later coming to their support.

After the heavy snow, which had been followed by days of biting cold, December 13 was "radiant as a fete day,"[17] the air soft, the sky cloudless. The heavy river fog lifted by midmorning. As the sun thawed the frozen ground it became slippery and sticky with red Virginia mud.

De Trobriand looked out through his field glasses at the area embraced by the great curve of the heights beyond the Rappahannock, with the river cutting through the wide bottomland like a chord, and as the orders came for his own command to go down into the arena, he thought of gladiators entering an amphitheater. The words that came to his emotional mind were "Ave, Caesar! Morituri te salutant."[18]

Hancock received his attack orders at 8:00 A.M. on the thirteenth. They notified him that French would occupy the first line and that he should move in support. The formation would be a brigade front, with intervals of 200 paces between the brigades. In his division Zook was in the lead, followed by Meagher and Caldwell.

Samuel K. Zook was, like Hancock, a native of the Philadelphia area, having been born in Chester County, and, also like Hancock, had been attracted in his teens to scientific experimentation. But Zook continued his work in electricity and made some developments and inventions that attracted notice and took him to New York. There before the outbreak of war he joined a militia company. Soon he was colonel of the regiment and then brigade leader.

On moving out from the town, French and Hancock found that Burnside had been wholly wrong about the lack of obstacles be-

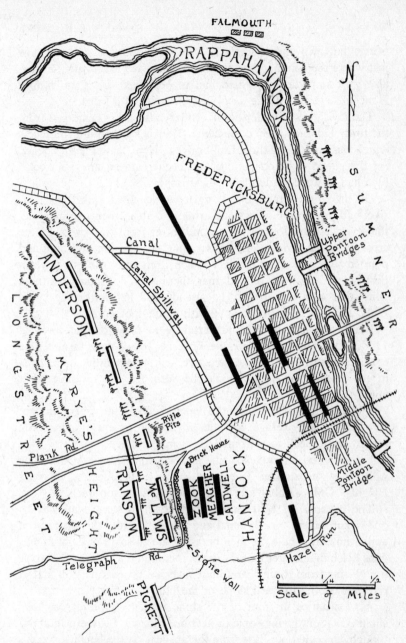

BATTLE OF FREDERICKSBURG, December 13, 1862. Attack by Hancock's Division on Longstreet at the stone wall in front of Marye's Heights, marking the farthest advance of the Right Grand Division of the Federal Army.

tween the town and Marye's Heights. A canal, or spillway, was
just where the commanding general had insisted it was not. Fences
also were impediments which had to be pulled down under fire;
Hancock said each fence destroyed the unity of a brigade.

The division was under heavy artillery attack as it emerged from
the town and encountered the canal—Hancock called it a millrace—
which was crossed by three frail bridges. Here came the first delay,
for the planking on one bridge had been removed and Hancock's
men had to walk single file on the stringers.

On the Confederate side, Longstreet, delighted with the defensive, had prepared his lines and artillery emplacements so carefully
that every square foot of the ground in his front was swept by the
crossfire of his cannon. Lee rode along the line that morning and
pointed to a section of artillery which Longstreet did not have in
position. Longstreet replied that there was no room for these
guns—that with the artillery he already had in position he could
"rake the ground in front as if with a fine-tooth comb."[19]

Longstreet had ordered his artillery to open on the town at
11:00 A.M., an hour before the Federals began their assault. He
considered the fire "very destructive." It "frequently made gaps
in the enemy ranks that could be seen for the distance of a
mile."[20]

The Federal artillery, on the heights across the river, did not
give adequate coverage for the advancing infantry and served
mainly as a check to a Confederate counterattack.

French's division attacked first and was hurled back at the stone
wall along the sunken Telegraph Road, at the base of Marye's
Heights. Only Kimball's brigade made a close approach.

The distance of 1,700 yards from town to stone wall was an
open plain except for the canal and fences. Across this distance of
approximately a mile the men breasted the crossfire of Longstreet's
guns belching canister and shrapnel, then met the sheets of infantry
fire blazing from troops carefully concealed behind the wall and in
rifle pits on the forward slope of the hill.

At a distance in front of the stone wall the ground rose to a
slight elevation, giving some protection from the Southern infantry,
though concealed but little from the artillery on the heights. Zook's
assault, "launched like a catapult,"[21] swept past this incline, charged
rapidly through the ranks of French's broken division, and approached the stone wall, where those who had not gone down in

the inferno of bursting shell and shrieking bullets were stopped
short and forced to fall back.

The men retired to the slight incline, where they formed a line
and began returning the Confederate fire. They piled up all the
wood they could find as a barricade and here maintained a position
for the rest of the afternoon. A brick house and outbuildings between the canal and the stone wall gave them some protection.

Zook claimed that no other infantry advanced farther than his
men that day, though he conceded that part of Kimball's advance
of French's division reached the same line.[22] Howard, who from
the rear watched Hancock's attack, observed that Zook advanced
with "great speed" and gained ground by his impetus.[23]

Hancock went forward with his men. A bullet cut through his
overcoat, grazing his abdomen; when he wrote home about it he
said half an inch nearer would have meant a fatal wound. Back
and forth he rode across the open plain with his staff, giving directions, urging on the men. Of his five staff members, four had
horses shot from under them and three were wounded.

The Irish Brigade Outdoes Fontenoy

Close behind Zook came Meagher's Irish Brigade. Hancock had
reviewed it a few days before the battle and had complimented it
on three points—its health, cleanliness and soldierly bearing.[24]
Woefully reduced in numbers at Antietam, it had had an opportunity to refill its ranks only partially since that costly battle.
Though lame from an ulcerated knee joint and a wound taken at
Antietam, and unable either to ride or walk any distance, Meagher
accompanied his men. When he was hit in the leg again, he left
direction of the assault to the regimental commanders.[25]

The green flag carried in this action—the Irish Brigade always
had one—was that of the 28th Massachusetts, commanded by Colonel Richard Byrnes. Every soldier of the brigade sported a sprig
of green in his cap.[26] Meagher's own "green and gold trappings
gleamed at the head . . . like a battle flag."[27]

Colonel Patrick J. Condon of the 63rd New York, Irish Brigade,
wrote:

I see Gen. Hancock riding along on the left-hand sidewalk
opposite me, hunting up stragglers who were sheltering themselves
by a house on the left. We cross the canal, some dashing through,

up to their hips in water, the three temporary planks thrown across it not affording sufficient accommodation under such a heavy fire. . . ."[28]

The brigade threw away its rations as it advanced. Everything was too heavy except ammunition.

They formed into line of battle at the double-quick, moved fifty yards up the slope, lay down for a minute behind French's line, then re-formed and pushed on. Here they passed Meagher, who flashed his sword and encouraged them.

George E. Pickett, who a little later would lead an assault himself, was on the heights where the Confederate lines ran. The next night he wrote to his fiancée, LaSalle Corbell:

Your soldier's heart almost stood still as he watched those sons of Erin fearlessly rush to their death. The brilliant assault on Marye's Heights of their Irish Brigade was beyond description. Why, my darling, we forgot they were fighting us, and cheer after cheer at their fearlessness went up all along our lines.[29]

A correspondent of the London *Times* at Lee's headquarters overlooking the battlefield watched this second wave of Hancock's division "burst" out of the town and deploy under the fire of the Confederate batteries:

Never at Fontenoy, Albuera, nor at Waterloo was more undoubted courage displayed by the sons of Erin than during those six frantic dashes which they directed against the almost impregnable position of their foe.

When he surveyed the field after they had been forced back, the correspondent grew more eloquent:

That any mortal men could have carried the position before which they were wantonly sacrificed, defended as it was, it seems idle for a moment to believe. But the bodies which lie in dense masses within forty yards of Col. Walton's guns are the best evidence what manner of men they were who pressed on to death with the dauntlessness of a race which has gained glory on a thousand battlefields, and never more richly deserved it than at the foot of Marye's Heights on the 13th day of December, 1862.[30]

The bands had played. The New York *Herald* printed two days after the battle a line jotted down by a soldier in the advance: "There is music behind us, death in front."

By chance Meagher's regiments assailed a section of the Confederate line held by the Irish-born Confederate Colonel Robert McMillan of the 24th Georgia, who took command of Cobb's brigade, behind the stone wall, along the sunken road, after Brigadier General Thomas R. R. Cobb was mortally wounded early in the fighting. The private letter of a Georgia soldier told of Hancock's attack.

They watched the forming of Hancock's brigades, a column stronger and heavier than that of French's first assault. They held their small-arms fire until the Federals came into short range. Hancock's men poured a leaden hail through the clouds of smoke that billowed up in their front as they advanced.

Colonel McMillan walked along the line. At his order the brigade suddenly stood up and let loose a ruinous volley into the Irish now close at hand. "Again and again was the assault renewed, and again and again was it repulsed with tremendous slaughter," the Confederate soldier wrote.

The men seemed to catch McMillan's spirit, he said, and as he passed along at the height of the fight they gave him three lusty cheers. The Irish brigade was finally beaten back to the line still held by Zook.

The Richmond *Whig,* which printed the letter to show "that Meagher met his match at Fredericksburg in the gallant son of the Emerald Isle," offered the grisly suggestion that it would "like to see McMillan at the head of the lamented Cobb's Brigade pitted against Meagher or Corcoran in an open field."[31]

Nelson Miles Thinks He Can Carry the Hill

Caldwell's brigade, the largest of the division, was the last taken into action by Hancock. It pressed ahead through the fragments of French's division and Hancock's two other brigades—those of Zook and Meagher—until it met the sheet of flame issuing from the Confederate wall.

The brigade was stopped on the same line where Zook and Meagher had been arrested, though Colonel Edward E. Cross contended that his regiment, the 5th New Hampshire, "advanced farther than any regiment of the division, and held its place as long as there was any organization left."[32]

The brigade leader, John Curtis Caldwell, born in Lowell, Ver-

mont, had settled in East Machias, Maine, after graduation from
Amherst College. He was twenty-eight years old when the war
broke. Though without previous military service, he became colonel of the 11th Maine, proved a combat leader of great courage
and aggressiveness, and early in the Peninsular campaign was
appointed a brigadier general of volunteers.

Colonel Nelson A. Miles, commanding the 61st and 64th New
York regiments of Caldwell's brigade, marched them at Hancock's
personal order, moving against the Confederates with guns at the
right shoulder shift.

"The two regiments were as quiet and kept as good a line as
though they were on parade," he said.[33]

Miles held to the right. When within forty yards of the stone
wall he thought "it only needed a spirited charge with the bayonet
to close in . . . and carry the works."[34] He asked Caldwell's permission to try to storm the hill with his two regiments, using Zook's
remnants to support him, but when Caldwell and Zook discouraged
him he desisted.[35] Later he said, "I only regret that I did not make
the attempt."[36] The remark was based more on youthful zest than
sound judgment. Zook had nothing with which to support him.

Miles's 64th New York Regiment was armed with Austrian
rifles and the men were able to pick off some of the Confederate
canoneers.[37] While this firing was in progress Miles was hit in the
throat by a rifle ball and compelled to leave the field. Aside from
the late hours at Antietam, it was his first fight under Hancock,
with whom he would have extensive later associations.

Caldwell was hit by a musket ball in the left shoulder but did
not leave the field. Then he was hit again, more critically, in the
same shoulder and was carried off.

At this point on the line some Confederates made a sortie.
Among those they shot down was a Federal soldier about seventeen
years old. They rushed out to get his canteen and clothing. The
first man to reach the body turned it over and looked down on the
face of his brother.[38]

Caldwell said all his regiments "behaved gallantly and fought with
steadiness" except the 145th Pennsylvania, which broke and fell
back when its colonel, Hiram L. Brown, was severely wounded.[39]
But the regiment must have behaved stanchly, because when the
returns were in, it was found to have lost more men at Fredericks-

burg than any other regiment in the entire army, and a heavier percentage of its force as well.[40]

Caldwell's regiments pushed ahead to the brick house that stood in front of the Confederate line. "The fire here was terrific," he said, "the hottest I have ever seen. The men fell by hundreds."[41]

Hancock's bolt was now spent and Howard's division advanced to take up the attack. As Miles was being carried back on a stretcher, he held together the lips of his deep neck wound and sat up, so he could describe to Howard, on whose staff he had served, where the fresh troops might be put in to advantage.[42] Howard said he had observed from a knoll "the havoc among the two divisions preceding mine,"[43] but his men did not reach Hancock's farthest advance. Manifestly the Southern defense was not weakening.

Members of the Philadelphia brigade, Howard's division, defined glory as "being shot at and having your name spelled wrong in the papers."[44] They came up behind Hancock, encountering little opposition at first except occasional artillery bursts. The band of one of the fresh battalions was playing "Bully for You" when a shell exploded in its midst. The survivors did not tarry. Ahead they could see Hancock's men almost at the wall, where for ten minutes they stood before the murderous fire, then were sent reeling back."[45]

Colonel Joshua T. Owen, commanding the Philadelphia brigade, reported back to Howard: "I was sent out here to support General Hancock's division but there is not much left of it to support."[46]

When, after the battle, the Confederates went along the lines in front of the stone wall they found bodies of Federal soldiers within forty yards of the wall and a few as close as twenty-five yards.[47] From the regimental markings they were able to identify those closest as soldiers of Colonel Robert Nugent's 69th New York, Colonel Edward E. Cross's 5th New Hampshire and Colonel John R. Brooke's 53rd Pennsylvania.[48] Thus all three of Hancock's brigades were represented in the farthest Federal advance toward Marye's Heights. Two brothers of the 88th New York, Irish Brigade, were found dead, locked in each other's arms.[49] Hancock had advised against the foolhardy assault but when ordered to make it had given it his most energetic efforts. He had gone the farthest.

Hooker Loses the Required Number

The repulse of Sumner and Franklin did not satisfy Burnside; it goaded him to fresh sacrifices. Pacing back and forth across his headquarters portico, he demanded that Franklin align his troops and renew the assault on the left. Since Franklin occupied a two-mile front, his men could not be massed that late in the day for another futile, close-order effort. Piling division on division was not likely to break a line that had gained firmness by successful resistance.

Hooker, who had sent supports to Franklin, saw the disaster about him and, determining that his own Grand Division should not have a further share in it, sent a message to Burnside recommending that the attack be abandoned. The messenger could not have reached Burnside at a more inopportune moment. The commander in chief had his blood up. His reply was an order to continue the action with everything Hooker could assemble.

Meantime Couch had told Hooker frankly that Marye's Heights could not be carried by a frontal assault—precisely what he and Hancock had been telling Burnside two and three days before. Couch thought it might be turned by a night attack on the Confederate left.

"I will go and see Hancock about it," Hooker replied as he rode away. The reply caused Couch to observe that "very often did a Union general in doubt of what to do, 'go to see Hancock about it.' "[50]

Hooker did talk to Hancock, then returned to Couch and said, "Well, Couch, things are in such a state I must go over and tell Burnside it is no use trying to carry this line here."

About that time the aide returned with Burnside's adamant decision to continue the attack. Hooker, angered, rode his white horse across the river and unloaded on the commander in chief such a torrent of vituperation that Pleasanton, who was at headquarters, went to another part of the house to avoid the criminations. But he was still close enough to overhear part of the exchange and said Hooker "made the air blue with adjectives" about how the battle was being managed.

Burnside still would not yield to vituperation or entreaty. He was singularly obstinate for a man who had no trust in his own competence. After an absence of two hours, or at 4:00 P.M.,

Hooker returned to his command bearing Burnside's order to continue the action. By that time Humphreys' division had attacked, supported by Sykes, both marching at the command of the corps commander, Butterfield.

Humphreys moved with high ardor and vigor but did not get so close as Hancock. Hooker on his return to the front did not push the rest of his Grand Division with any zest. After Humphreys and Sykes were hurled back, he commented that he had "lost about as many men as he was ordered to sacrifice,"[51] and therewith he cut off the battle. This was the final futile attack of the Federal army.

Deep sarcasm came from the Richmond *Examiner,* which predicted "decapitation" for Burnside:

To judge of his ability as a commander it is only necessary to state that from the balcony of the Phillips House, in Stafford County, he sent his troops to the fight in columns of attack "doubled on the center," thus furnishing ready food for every musket ball, slug, shrapnel, canister and fragment of shell discharged by the Confederate army.[52]

The Cincinnati *Commercial* correspondent in his dispatch said it could scarcely be possible "for men to show more valor, or generals to manifest less judgment." A similar remark was that "lions were led by asses into the very jaws of death."[53] The castigation of the generals was largely misplaced; the blame might more properly have been assessed against *a* general.

Hancock reported his killed and wounded: in Zook's brigade, 38 officers and 491 enlisted men out of 92 officers and 1,440 men engaged; Meagher's brigade, 53 officers and 488 men out of 92 officers and 1,323 men engaged; Caldwell's brigade, 62 officers and 932 men out of 116 officers and 1,871 men engaged. Of the 5,006 officers and men Hancock took into action, 2,064 were killed or wounded.[54] The Second Corps lost more than any other and more than half of the Second Corps loss was from Hancock's division.

Casualties for the entire army were placed at 1,180 killed, 9,028 wounded and 2,145 missing, an aggregate of 12,353.[55] Lee reported taking "more than 900 prisoners" which suggests many of the missing were killed or wounded.

The army's medical inspector, who reported casualties of 15,000, remarked that even this return may have been too small. Many soldiers thought the figures were kept low purposely to conceal from the army and the home public the staggering cost of the ill-conceived battle.[56] Most of the dead and wounded fell in an area less than a quarter of a mile deep, in front of the stone wall.

That night Burnside, in an emotional outburst, wanted to lead personally a charge of the army against the heights, headed by his old Ninth Corps. But his subordinates who had been unable to dissuade him from sending in the troops managed to prevail on him not to head a new assault personally, so the three Grand Divisions were withdrawn to the north side of the river.

The full depth of the tragedy only gradually came to be realized in the North. Christmas that year was bleak in Northern homes.

★ ★ ★ 8 ★ ★ ★

Pray, Could We Expect a Victory?

"Fighting Joe" Is Marked by the Printer

Returning from the Fredericksburg battlefield, Hancock's division rattled around in its old quarters, three men having the space formerly occupied by five. Already the soldiers had built winter huts of logs and mud, with shelter tents for roofs, and here they remained for four months. Meantime the ludicrous "Mud March," on which the army bogged down in the Virginia mire, had laughed Burnside out of the command when the serious business of maltreating the army in front of Marye's Heights had not.

Hancock's division did not make the Mud March. Its role was to cross and take Fredericksburg if Lee could be drawn away by the flanking movement to his left, but that did not eventuate. Hancock devoted four months to rebuilding the division, drilling it and outfitting it with new clothing and equipment, and restoring its morale after the costly defeat.

As Lincoln had appointed Burnside after his slowness had thwarted McClellan at Antietam, so he now picked for the high command the least co-operative of Burnside's generals, Hooker.

One of the depressing aspects of this period of the war was that generals such as Hancock—well read in military history and practices and thoroughly in harmony with the responsibilities of leadership—or Sedgwick, Couch, Reynolds, Meade and others, were called on to serve under Pope, Burnside and then Hooker, who does not appear to have refurbished his military education, apart from his Mexican War service, since leaving West Point.

115

The nature of the high command under which the Army of the Potomac operated had a sharp bearing on Hancock's military standing and development and on the fortunes of the army to which he was giving his most devoted service, and is an important phase of the Hancock story.

Someone has said that Hooker's florid complexion was not a result of the Virginia winter sunshine, and others have applied to him the term of "genial toper." Charles Francis Adams considered him "little better than a drunken West Point military adventurer." He thought the Army of the Potomac was at its low point at this time:

During the winter when Hooker was in command, I can say from personal knowledge and experience that the Headquarters of the Army was a place no self-respecting man liked to go and no woman could go. It was a combination of barroom and brothel.

War Clerk Jones in Richmond noted in his diary that an acquaintance in the old army said Hooker had sunk so low before the war that many refused to associate with him. Jones added on his own account—in order to get in his customary disparagement of the Northern character—that when Hooker resigned from the army in California he "worked a potato patch, Yankee-like, on speculation —and failed."[1]

Ten years before secession the word was that he was living hard, drinking hard, disporting himself with a mulatto mistress and otherwise acting contrary to the standards of an officer and gentleman.[2]

Lincoln had, indeed, reached low in the barrel when he brought up Hooker. But repeated disappointments had put Lincoln in the position of President Madison in the War of 1812, to whom Jefferson wrote consolingly from Monticello: "The Creator had not thought proper to mark those on the forehead who are of the stuff to make good generals. We are first, therefore, to seek them, blindfolded, and then let them learn the trade at the expense of great losses."[3]

If Hooker were in any way marked, it had been by a typographical error. The typesetter of the New York *Courier and Inquirer,* intending the slug line "Fighting—Joe Hooker," left out the dash and allowed the word "fighting" to become an adjective, so that the phrase read "Fighting Joe Hooker."[4] Soon it became a nickname, which Hooker himself disliked. "It sounds as if I were a private," he said.[5]

Gibbon considered him at heart an intriguer and thought that he would sacrifice principle to gain a political end.[6] Still, the instance he cited of the promotion of the Quaker colonel, Solomon Meredith, to brigadier general, which Gibbon opposed, was not impressive. Meredith rated it. His brigade later performed heroically at Gettysburg.

The red-faced, fast-talking, superficially shrewd Hooker ordinarily did not shun action in an army where a surfeit of caution was displayed. He had taken a wound in the heel at Sharpsburg, then had been feted about Washington by the Chase coterie as the most dashing and talented general of the war, just the man to outwit Lee and march into the Confederate capital. It was incidental that he might be used as a convenient tool in Secretary Chase's intrigues to unseat Lincoln for a second term.

Hooker reorganized the army, called in the deserters under a general amnesty, sent the camp followers back to Washington, instituted a system of regular furloughs and appeared, at the beginning, to impart new vigor to troops dejected by a long series of fruitless combats.

On the Peninsula General Phil Kearny had required his men to wear a red diamond patch to distinguish his division. Hooker now extended this practice to the entire army, giving each corps identifying insignia, designed by his chief of staff Butterfield. The Second Corps received the trefoil, or clover leaf, called by the Irish the "Shamrock" and by some of the others the "Ace of Clubs."[7] Each division in the corps had a color, the first, red; the second, white; and the third, blue. Hancock's division wore a red trefoil. The men liked the badges. They were beginning to be pleased with Hooker.

Hooker Challenges God to Deliver Lee

The story of Chancellorsville is that of an overpowering army with an erratic general who was defeated almost at the firing of the first shot.

The campaign opened propitiously. In skillful maneuvers Hooker distracted Lee by a feint march of troops under Sedgwick down the river. The bulk of the army went upstream to cross at different fords and concentrate at a road center and clearing called Chancellorsville, named after the big brick Chancellor plantation house that stood with its outbuildings on the northwest corner of the crossroads.

Hooker had abolished the awkward Grand Divisions and the army would now fight by corps. Couch, the second-ranking officer, commanded the Second Corps and in this corps Hancock commanded the First Division. Howard, who had led the Second Division at Fredericksburg, had been elevated to the command of Sigel's corps, the Eleventh, composed largely of Germans, and John Gibbon had replaced him as a division commander in the Second Corps. French still commanded the Third Division of the Second Corps. At Chancellorsville the three divisions served separately. Hancock's division held the left of the Federal army, reaching toward the Rappahannock at Bank's Ford, between Chancellorsville and Fredericksburg. Howard's Eleventh Corps was on the army's extreme right.

Hooker went into the battle with approximately 130,000 men, while Lee—who had sent Longstreet with two divisions, those of Hood and Pickett, to the south side of the James River—had his force cut to about 60,000.[8] Never had prospects seemed so auspicious for the Army of the Potomac as on May 1, 1863. Hooker had concentrated 80,000 men at Chancellorsville and had left 22,000 under Sedgwick to cross and occupy Fredericksburg, once Lee had abandoned his defenses and turned to confront the main Federal army on his flank and rear. He had sent Stoneman with the Federal cavalry on an abortive ride toward Richmond.

Hooker had been so sanguine that he told Lincoln he would either win a victory or be in hell, whereupon the President cautioned him to "carry plenty of water along."[9]

He emitted considerable bombast at this stage, maintaining in words variously quoted that Lee could not escape him. As the old soldiers had it, all versions simmered down to the assertion, proclaimed as he slammed his fist on the table, that "God Almighty cannot deliver him from my hands."

Lee, if not through the intercession of the Almighty, then through his own and Stonewall Jackson's quick perception, set about promptly to recover the initiative which, through Hooker's swift movements, had passed from Southern arms.

The two main elements in the battle of Chancellorsville were, first, Hooker's sudden and strange timidity on May 2, the day after his bold assertion, which caused him to withdraw Hancock and Sykes from the favorable ground they occupied on the army's left; and, second, the bold strategy of Lee and Jackson, by which Lee divided his army and sent Jackson on the memorable flank march that shattered Howard's Eleventh Corps and rolled up the right flank of the Federal army.

Much of the Eleventh Corps broke up into bands. Some were halted by Sickles at a stone wall in the woods, as they were trying to reach Chancellorsville. Other bands rushed through the fields and woods toward the Rappahannock, intent only on gaining the security of the north bank. Many plunged into the water and swam across.

Francis Walker noticed that some of the distracted soldiers were running in the other direction—they were so beside themselves with fright that they fled past the Chancellor house, plunged through Hancock's lines and fell into the arms of the Confederates.[10] One "ingenious German" approached Hancock and asked to be directed to the pontoons. "The answer he received has been handed down in tradition, but it is best not to put it into cold and unsympathetic type," said Walker.[11]

Prior to the rout of Howard, Second Corps commander Couch had gone out with Hancock to reinforce Sykes, of Meade's corps, on the army's left. Hancock had just put his division into line when Couch received Hooker's amazing order to withdraw to Chancellorsville.[12] The offensive, so hopefully assumed, was about to be surrendered. Brigadier General Gouverneur K. Warren, the army's chief engineer, who was with Hancock and Sykes when Couch received the order, counseled disobedience to it.[13] But Couch complied, though he left favorable high ground open in his front for the Confederate artillery, which was soon in position there, shelling the Chancellorsville area in which Hooker was huddling up his army like refugees. Paralysis appeared to have stricken the high-spirited force which a day before was expecting a quick victory and rapid descent on Richmond.

The Confederate bombardment from the high ground severely

wounded Colonel Francis A. Walker, adjutant general and later the historian of the Second Corps, and the early military biographer of General Hancock.[14]

On retiring, Hancock stationed parts of three regiments—the 57th, 64th and 66th New York—under Colonel Nelson A. Miles in a bushy ravine three quarters of a mile east of Chancellorsville. The employment of this force as a protective shield for the left flank of the army later came to be regarded as a classic example of the use of skirmishers in defensive warfare.[15] By having Miles extend his regiments across the entire division front, Hancock was able to maintain a skirmish line of a man for every three paces. Miles dug rifle pits and felled abatis in his front, and held off the Confederate pressure during a series of heavy attacks. Nowhere was an aggressive enemy able to reach Hancock's main line of battle. Late in the day, after making one of the most stubborn defenses at Chancellorsville, Miles was carried off on a stretcher, again, as at Fredericksburg, severely wounded.

Hooker had cast away the offensive and entrenched under the impression that Lee would be compelled to attack him. When Jackson delivered the bolt where it was least expected, the Federal commander ceased to be much of a factor in the battle.

Jackson was mortally wounded that night, but his wing of the Confederate army, grievously exposed in its isolated position, was allowed to reunite with Lee's main body when the Third Corps of the Federal army under Daniel E. Sickles was called and pushed back from the key elevation of Hazel Grove, southwest of Chancellorsville. No one had paid attention to replenishing ammunition, and supplies were running low enough to cripple the Third and Twelfth Corps and jeopardize the army.

History has softened the story of what occurred at Hooker's headquarters on the morning of May 3, when there were still ample time and sufficient unengaged troops for a great victory. Usually his incapacitation has been attributed to the concussion of a shell bursting nearby, or to the falling of a brick or a porch pillar torn loose by the explosion. Couch, the senior major general, opposed any further aggressive movement of the army because of his complete lack of confidence in Hooker. This does not sound like the effect of a temporary injury.

As Francis Walker summarized it:

That army had, in truth, no longer a head. Hooker had suc-
cumbed to the strange lethargy which had afflicted him ever since
the morning of the 1st of May. The rout of Howard's corps had
finished him. . . .[16]

The army was pulled back across the Rappahannock, despite
the opposition of Reynolds and Meade, who had been virtually unengaged, and of others.

The question of whether Hooker was drunk, injured or suffering
from amnesia or emotionally induced illness, while in command at
the battle, probably never will be answered. Nobody ever established positively whether it was a bursting shell or a popping cork.
Couch seemed to think it was not liquor but suddenly being deprived of liquor that contributed to Hooker's mental strain and
amounted to almost complete incapacitation.[17] But the army was
needlessly recalled by Couch at the insistence of the commander in
chief, who then abandoned it and went to the north bank of the
Rappahannock a thoroughly beaten man.[18]

The stupefied Federal commander, singularly unnerved at the
fateful moment of his career, when the full measure of his alertness
and judgment was imperatively needed, was pusillanimously returning to the security of his Falmouth entrenchments. Said the
historian of the 1st Minnesota:

His officers ridiculed his generalship; his rank and file swore at
him, and tens of thousands of them could not understand how they
had been defeated in a battle in which they had not fired a shot.[19]

"I Became a Hero by That Man's Influence"

The extrication of the army was left to Couch, and, since he delegated the rear-guard duty, to Hancock.

As the different corps were withdrawn to the river the thin line
at the Chancellor house was finally held by Hancock's division and,
on its right, by John W. Geary's division of the Twelfth Corps.
Geary's right flank was being turned and though Couch thought he
made a gallant fight of it, Hancock's men had a different view.

Hancock's "wagon guard," which had seen no wagons in a

week, was the last Federal detachment left between the burning Chancellorsville farmhouse and the oncoming Confederates. It was commanded by Colonel Cross of the 5th New Hampshire and consisted of that regiment, the 81st Pennsylvania and part of the 88th New York. For about thirty hours these men had been under a "hellish crossfire" which they considered "almost worse than Fredericksburg," before Hancock brought them personally back to the new rear-guard line in front of Chancellorsville.

Just then Brigadier General Geary, a high-tempered giant, came rushing up in agitation—in "considerable disorder," one of the men termed it—and yelled at Hancock's soldiers, who were stationed to cover his own retreat: "Charge, you cowards, charge!"[20]

Geary was leading the remnants of his division, and all of them, according to the account from one of Hancock's men, were making haste to the rear.

Hancock's soldiers were "disgusted" with Geary. Two of them were irked into turning both their bayonets and their oaths against him as he charged through their breastwork with his insulting language. One was Private John Sparks, who had been helping that day to drag off Leppien's Battery abandoned near the Chancellor house after most of its men and all but one of the horses had been killed.[21] The other was an Irish private named Burke of the 88th New York. An adjutant deflected their bayonets to save Geary.

In his excitement Geary almost ran into Hancock's horse, then appeared amazed as Hancock admonished him severely, "General Geary, I command here." The men had no time to chuckle at the discomfited general, who disappeared rapidly.

The wagon guard broke the Confederate rush with a volley, and Hancock then moved it back, closer to blazing Chancellorsville. There in the open the guard made its last stand. The Confederates were pressing forward in heavy masses. In the laconic language of the chronicler of the wagon guard, "the guns were saved and a few of the men."[22]

One of Hancock's privates named Paxton, a lad of eighteen, gave a picture of Hancock in this encounter. The army seemed to be going to pieces around him, Howard's corps had been shattered, the Chancellor mansion was in flames, shells were bursting, men

were groaning, and "I was scared to death and would have run."
Just then Hancock appeared:

Suddenly in the midst of our collapse a man on a horse rode
down the line. It was awful, but that man rode down the line, tall,
magnificent. . . . He rode on a horse, not a muscle quivering, and
looking us in the face said, "Gentlemen"—he called his soldiers
gentlemen—"we are left to keep them in check until the second
line is formed." . . . I became a hero by that man's influence. No
Plutarch could have done that for me.[23]

Hancock's horse was shot from under him. A shell almost severed the horse's leg, which dangled by a bit of skin, but the animal
went to work busily cropping the grass as though nothing had happened.[24] The general jumped from his saddle and threw his arms
around the noble mount's neck, then told an aide to dispatch him.
The substitute horse Hancock procured was so small that his feet
almost raked the ground.[25]

At one halt in the rear-guard assignment Hancock stationed a
brigade and said to its commander, an anxious and not always a
stubborn fighter, whom the accounts do not identify, "General,
whatever happens, I want you to hold this ground."

The brigade commander looked about him and as Hancock was
departing called: "General, where are my reserves?"

Hancock turned sharply, rode back to the subordinate and said
severely: "General, it is none of your business where your reinforcements are. That is my business. I have placed you here to
hold this ground, and that is all you are required to do, and I want
it done, sir."[26]

Hancock wrote his wife at the first opportunity, 6:00 A.M. on
the morning of May 4:

We have had tremendous fighting at Chancellorsville. The losses
on both sides are very heavy, more so than any battle of the
war. . . . I am unhurt, though I was struck several times with
small fragments of shells. . . . My horse was shot twice. My
division did well. . . .[27]

He had been genuinely shocked by the commander in chief's
impiety. In another letter, he expressed the thought that Providence
had perhaps favored the other side:

The day before the fight, Hooker said to a general officer, "God Almighty could not prevent me from winning a victory tomorrow." Pray, could we expect a victory after that? . . . Success cannot come to us through such profanity.[28]

Couch complimented him on covering the army's retirement, saying he had a close shave to get his division back safely. He did lose 500 prisoners on his left, at Mott's Run, because a lieutenant who had the responsibility there did not exercise vigilance. "Under the circumstances," said Couch, "the division was retired in better shape than one could have anticipated."[29]

Lee had piled his men in at the end to try to turn the Federal retirement into a rout. But both Hancock and Sedgwick, who had marched on Lee's rear and for a time was in great danger because Hooker gave him no co-operation, finally gained the north bank of the Rappahannock, bringing the Chancellorsville campaign to a close.

Hancock confided to his wife that "Hooker's day is over," and:

I have been approached again in connection with the command of the Army of the Potomac. Give yourself no uneasiness—under no circumstances would I accept the command. I do not belong to that class of generals whom the Republicans care to bolster up. I should be sacrificed.

Manifestly he was thinking of such Democrats as McClellan and his good friend Don Carlos Buell, who had saved the day at Shiloh and repulsed Bragg's invasion at Perryville, only to be investigated by Congress and a military commission and removed from the Western command.

He felt that Chancellorsville "should have been a brilliant victory." The fault was in not putting in the two large corps of Meade and Reynolds, when the enemy apparently had "used up all their troops."

Couch, contemptuous of Hooker's leadership, asked for a leave of absence and when this was refused, requested to be relieved of command of the Second Corps. He persisted in the request even though Hooker asked him to reconsider. President Lincoln finally acceded and on June 9, 1863, appointed Hancock to command the Second Corps.[30]

$$\star \star \star 9 \star \star \star$$

Picking a Battlefield

Hays Adds a Rejuvenated Brigade

Lee had already grasped the offensive and had been on the move six days when Hancock, who was to have the outstanding role in the new campaign, took command of the Second Corps.

In the early summer of 1863, as the wheat ripened and the Confederacy seemed in the full flush of victory on the battlefield, Lee brought the war to a dramatic climax by invading Pennsylvania. On June 3 he began a stealthy movement around the right flank of the Federal army along the Rappahannock, easing north and west until his progress was eventually detected by Hooker. After some correspondence with Washington the Federal general began a pursuit, moving his army between the enemy and the capital until he had followed Lee across the Potomac. Hancock, last to leave Falmouth, brought up the rear of the Federal army as Hooker marched leisurely northward.

Trudging through Dumfries to Wolf Run Shoals, the begrimed Second Corps got a chance to bathe in the clear water of the Occaquan River, then pushed ahead to Centerville.

Brigadier General Alexander Hays, Hancock's classmate and protector at the military academy, commanded a brigade at Centerville when Hancock's corps burst into the town. Mrs. Hays was with her husband and was appalled at the high antics of soldiers on the march. She wrote to her father, James B. McFadden, in Pittsburgh:

The Second corps, commanded by General Hancock, arrived last evening, and such a sight I never saw. The men were completely demoralized, no order or discipline. . . . They were committing some depredations when Alexander would stand it no longer. He called for "Dan," buckled on his sword and pistols, and dashed in amidst them, ordered them to move on.[1]

Then he went to Hancock, his superior, told him that he, Hays, commanded the post at Centerville and Hancock would have to find another place for his artillery. He doubled his own brigade guards and ordered them to shoot the first man who interfered with them. The old spirit he had shown at West Point had not abated a whit. Hancock seems to have been well aware that Hays was in the right, for he accepted the subordinate's admonitions docilely; there were few officers in the army for whom he had so much respect as for Hays.

Still, Mrs. Hays's description was severe, for the corps was blamed for the misdeeds of a few unruly soldiers such as could be found in any command.

Hancock moved on for a brush with Jeb Stuart at Haymarket, which deflected Stuart and sent him skirting farther south and east to get around the rear of the Federal army—a journey of tragedies that was to take him out of effective participation in the Gettysburg campaign.[2]

At Gum Springs, while the skies let down a soaking rain, an event occurred of major significance to the future of the Second Corps. Hays's brigade was incorporated into the corps. Hays, by virtue of his seniority, became commander of the Third Division, while Colonel Willard took command of the brigade. Other brigades in this division were those of Colonel "Sprigg" Carroll and Colonel Thomas A. Smyth. All were destined to play heavy roles at Gettysburg.

Along with Hays, Hancock added to the Second Corps one of the army's most picturesque and peculiar regiments, the 39th New York, the "Garibaldi Guards." They were a temperamental, untamed, capriciously officered, courageous body of men, the first three-year regiment recruited in New York, whose career had become more checkered as the war progressed. They were a goodly representation of most of the armies of Europe, three companies being Hungarian, three German, one Italian, one Swiss, one French, one Spanish and one Portuguese. They were at both battles of Bull Run, with Frémont at Cross Keys, and with Blenker; and it was not a surprise to hear either that one of the companies had mutinied or that they had stood heroically in some action.

When at Centerville their Hungarian count-colonel, Frederick G. d'Utassy, lived in the most splendid house and had his meals sumptuously cooked in Washington, thirty miles away, then gently transported by ambulance, packed so artfully that they could be placed before him warm and palatable.[3]

The "Guards" became involved with Colonel Dixon S. Miles in the Harpers Ferry garrison during Lee's Maryland campaign. When Miles ignominiously lifted the white flag and they became prisoners and parolees, their *esprit de corps* plunged downward. The soldiers of fortune among their officers slackened the reins. The men were anything but responsive soldiers when they passed under the command of Alexander Hays.

They claimed for one thing that they had not been exchanged properly, and consequently were still on parole and not subject to duty. D'Utassy encouraged them in this belief, which Hays, who knew it was groundless, "knocked out of their heads."[4] Then he reorganized the regiment. Among the first to go was D'Utassy with his caterers. He mustered out a goodly number of lackadaisical noncommissioned and some commissioned officers, and put an efficient Prussian, Major Hugo Hildebrandt, in command. Thus this regiment of many tongues was made into a sturdy fighting unit in time for service under Hancock at Gettysburg.

Colonel George L. Willard, a man of "princely presence," who had commanded the 125th New York, succeeded Hays in command of the brigade that included some Harpers Ferry units. He was a native of New York City and had been a sergeant at Chapultepec. When cited and made a second lieutenant he had remained in the regular army and had risen to captain in 1861. At Troy, New York, he recruited two regiments and accompanied one as colonel.

"It seems a little strange," wrote Mrs. Hays to her father a little later, "that Mr. Hays should command part of a corps that two weeks ago he had pointed two of his guns at to make them obey. The corps was a fighting one, but was demoralized."[5]

There was another major change. Brigadier General J. T.

"Paddy" Owen, who had commanded the Philadelphia brigade, had fallen into arrest, an easy misfortune to encounter on the tense march to Pennsylvania. The brigade was assigned to General Alexander Webb, an artillery specialist. By the swift developments of a few days Webb was brought from staff duty and given the brigade which happened to be stationed at a little clump of trees at the center of the line where the blow fell on July 3 at Gettysburg.[6]

Meade Sends a Proxy to the Front

Hancock crossed the Potomac at Edwards Ferry and brought his corps through Maryland to Uniontown.

Nobody could anticipate the notable role to which he would assign the 1st Minnesota and it received no special consideration on the march up, except that its spirited colonel, William Colvill, was placed under whimsical arrest by Colonel Charles H. Morgan, Hancock's inspector general and chief of staff, and a hard man with the troops.

The trouble arose from the crossing of Linganore Creek, a tributary of the Monocacy River, where the water at the ford was knee-deep. The men were ordered to "bulge" the stream, which meant marching straight through, indifferent to wet feet, though there were two large foot logs at the ford, hewn flat on top and laid with planks, on which it was easy to cross dryshod.

Morgan was at the ford when the 1st Minnesota came up. To show his authority he ordered Colonel Colvill to march through the water and not let the men straggle. But a goodly number capered blithely over the logs and fell into ranks on the opposite shore. Inspector General Morgan was wroth.

Immediately behind the 1st Minnesota came the 15th Massachusetts. Morgan again ordered the men to wade through the water. A little farther along, when the regiments were resting, Morgan trotted his horse between the lines lying along the roadside and the Massachusetts soldiers gave him some hearty groans. The two regiments were so mixed that in his white anger he thought the Minnesotans were the sole culprits. He placed Colvill under arrest and stripped him of his command. Then he rushed to Brigadier General Harrow to tell his story and have Harrow, who temporarily commanded the division, confirm the arrest. So the veteran regi-

Hancock and three of his division commanders during the Wilderness campaign. Standing *(left to right)* are Brigadier General Francis C. Barlow, Major General David D. Birney and Brigadier General John Gibbon.

Died

RECENTLY, OF

Chronic Profanity on the Brain, and Protracted Decay of the Patriotic Cardaic Tissues,

Gen. W. S. Hancock, U. S. A.

(TARQUINIUS SUPERBUS.)

Funeral will be held on Tuesday, Nov. 2, 1880.

Preliminary arrangements for the funeral will be made at the Ocean Street Wigwam (15th Ward) on this Friday night, August 27, at which time pall bearers and torch holders will be selected.

Requiescat in pace—if he can.

Hancock's oaths were Titanic enough to make a campaign issue. An example of the free-swinging attacks in the Presidential canvass of 1880.

Library of Congress

Hancock and his principal officers in the Wilderness. Barlow (in checkered shirt) leans against the tree; Birney and Gibbon stand to the right of Hancock.

From Brady Collection, National Archives

Almira Russell Hancock,
wife of the general.

From Reminiscences of
Winfield Scott Hancock
by His Wife, *New York, 1887*

The profile sketch by Kelly
in 1879 is a good likeness
of Hancock just prior to
the Presidential campaign
of 1880.

*From Dr. Ryder's Collection,
photographed by the
Signal Corps, U. S. Army,
National Archives*

The Governor's Island years. Hancock in the 1870's was reaching toward the 250 pounds he weighed as a Presidential candidate.

Hancock's earnestness, shown clearly in this studio portrait, impressed many as his outstanding characteristic.

ment, the first accepted when Lincoln called for volunteers after
Fort Sumter, went on without its colonel leading.[7]

Lincoln had finally decided that he could not risk Hooker in another battle and on the early morning of June 28 transferred the
command to the most scholarly appearing and least exciting of his
corps commanders, George Gordon Meade.

Meade had formed a sincere admiration of Hancock from observing him on the Peninsula and at Fredericksburg and Chancellorsville. George Meade, the general's son and aide, had been with
his father, then a division commander, just after Fredericksburg,
when a handsome officer rode up, said some words of greeting and
left at a full gallop. The younger Meade said "his bearing was so
striking" that anyone would have asked who it was. When he
inquired, his father answered with surprise. "Don't you know who
that is? Why, that's Hancock."[8]

Hancock gave his men a good rest, all of June 30, at Uniontown,
where the enthusiastic citizens brought out varieties of food. On
the early morning of July 1 he had just written a general order for
the corps when a messenger arrived directing him to march at once
to Taneytown, where Meade had his headquarters. The general
order was never issued. Adjutant General Walker retained the
draft, and the conclusion suggested the tenor: "To the patriotic
brave I have said enough. Upon those who desert their posts in
the hour of trial let instant death be inflicted by their comrades."[9]

Marching up from Uniontown on July 1, Hancock's corps
reached Taneytown at 11:00 A.M. and were given a rest for coffee
while the general went to headquarters.

He looked around the village of Taneytown with interest. He
told Major St. Clair A. Mulholland that his grandfather as a soldier
in the Revolutionary War had gone to this same village to pick up
prisoners after Burgoyne's surrender and conduct them to General
Washington at Valley Forge.[10]

At headquarters, Meade informed Hancock of his plan to fight
behind Pipe Creek, which, according to his examination, was the
strongest position he could find.[11] Engineers were then scrutinizing
and mapping it, and Meade had prepared the order for the army to
occupy this line.

Hancock went back to his corps, but Meade, just after his departure, received a message that Reynolds, with the First Corps and

Buford's cavalry, was fighting west of Gettysburg. Another messenger brought word at 1:00 P.M. that Reynolds was dead.[12]

Not waiting to summon Hancock, Meade went directly to Second Corps headquarters, gave Hancock the information about Reynolds, and told him to transfer the corps to General Gibbon, and proceed himself to the front at once and take general command there.

Hancock was disturbed about rank. He told Meade that Caldwell ranked Gibbon in the corps, but this did not seem to bother Meade. He explained also that both Howard and Sickles, the two major generals already at the front, were his seniors. While he and the other two had been commissioned major generals on the same day, both had been brigadier generals ahead of him and that determined their present rank.[13]

To ease Hancock's mind, Meade showed him a letter from Secretary Stanton authorizing him to make any changes he wished among the army officers and saying he would be sustained by the President and Secretary of War in what he did.

Meade has been criticized for not going personally to Gettysburg. Quite obviously the reason for his not doing so was that at this stage he felt the main battle of the campaign would be fought along Pipe Creek. But since he did not choose to go himself, Hancock was the most prudent selection as a substitute. No other corps commander could have carried such confidence and influence, along with such a clear understanding of topography and logistics.

One of the not infrequent commentaries about the army at Gettysburg was that most of the corps were not strongly led. No doubt Sedgwick would have been capable of the role, as would Slocum, but neither so surely as Hancock. Sedgwick was thirty-five miles away from Gettysburg at Manchester. Meade could not have entrusted so heavy a responsibility to Howard, Sickles or Sykes. After the death of Reynolds, clearly he would have to put his first reliance in Hancock.

Meade's order giving Hancock, the newest of the corps commanders, the authority of a commander in chief at the point of action, was novel in the army to that date. It disclosed not only Meade's justifiable lack of confidence in Howard after the Eleventh Corps fiasco at Chancellorsville, but also his independence and freedom from conventional restraints. Censure would be heavy if Hancock made a false move.

But he relied on Hancock in the same measure that he doubted Howard and the power he delegated was absolute. He told Hancock to proceed to the front and "by virtue of this order, in case of the truth of General Reynolds's death, you assume command of the corps there assembled—viz., the Eleventh, First and Third, at Emmitsburg. If you think the ground and position there a better one on which to fight a battle under existing circumstances, you will so advise the general, and he will order all the troops up."[14]

Hancock began the journey of thirteen miles from Taneytown to Gettysburg in an ambulance. He had what Francis Walker termed a "poor little map" of the Gettysburg area and he studied it as he rode. If he took a nap in the ambulance it was brief, for he soon called for the horses, mounted his sorrel—the horse his groom preferred as the swiftest—and galloped ahead.

Four miles southeast of Gettysburg they met the ambulance carrying the body of General Reynolds. After that the party rode along in silence.

Hancock Likes the Gettysburg Position

Meantime conditions at Gettysburg were growing desperate for the Federal cause.

Major General John Buford, commanding a division of Meade's cavalry had begun the battle west of Gettysburg early on July 1 and had held his thin cavalry line until Reynolds arrived with the First Corps. After Reynolds fell, Doubleday took over and continued the fighting. Howard, arriving about 10:30 A.M., aligned the Eleventh Corps north of the town at right angles to Doubleday, with his right flank exposed to the advance of Early's Confederate division by roads leading to his rear.

When Early attacked, Howard's line collapsed. Doubleday at almost the same moment was dislodged by Pender's Confederate division and survivors of the two Federal corps rushed back into Gettysburg, and then to Cemetery Hill. There the broken remnants of the Eleventh Corps and the better conducted elements of the First Corps were met by Hancock.

Buford, a man of both military acumen and candor, had been telling Meade what was needed. In one message, sent via Pleasanton, he closed with the remark, "In my opinion there seems to be no directing person." In another, summarized later by his signal officer, he wrote Meade directly: "For God's sake, send up Hancock. Everything is going at odds, and we need a controlling spirit."[15]

Hancock said that "owing to the peculiar formation of the country, or the direction of the wind at the time" he did not hear the roar of the battle until within a few miles of the town.[16] On his arrival he saw the troops "retreating in disorder and confusion," pressed closely by the Confederates. Howard on Cemetery Hill was trying to rally them but they were going over the hill and running down the Baltimore Pike. Part of Steinwehr's division that had taken no part in the battle remained in position on the hill.[17]

The hour of Hancock's arrival is one of the many uncertainties of the battle of Gettysburg, but Francis Walker insisted that since Hancock placed it at 3:30,[18] this must be correct, for no officer in the army had so many aides who jotted down important matters in notebooks. This was a phase of his thoroughness. Nevertheless, the picture he gave of conditions suggests that he reached Cemetery Hill about 4 o'clock or even later.

Carl Schurz claimed there was no element of dissolution in the army at the time,[19] but Hancock's party found panic among the crowds pouring down the Baltimore Pike—"stricken men mixed up with led horses, artillery, ammunition wagons, and ambulances loaded with wounded." It was a field of "wreck and disorder."

How grievously the Eleventh Corps had been shattered might be seen from the fact that the provost guard of the Twelfth Corps picked up 1,200 fugitives on the Baltimore Pike.[20] Considering the large number of prisoners the Confederates had captured, and the killed and wounded, this was clearly more than a third of the part of the corps surviving the action.

Hancock had sent his aide-de-camp William G. Mitchell ahead to advise Howard of his coming and the scope of his orders. Then he explained them more fully when he met Howard at the cemetery gate. He offered to show the orders but Howard said he did not want to see them.

Howard was anything but cordial. "Why, Hancock, you cannot give orders here!" he exclaimed. "I am in command and I rank you."

Doubleday gave the conversation, and said "quite a scene occurred."[21]

Major E. P. Halstead, adjutant general of the First Corps, offered substantially the same version of the exchange—but reported an important addition. Hancock cast a glance over the terrain from Culp's Hill to the Round Tops. Referring to the line proposed for the battle behind Pipe Creek, Hancock turned to Howard and said: "But I think this the strongest position by nature on which to fight a battle that I ever saw, and if it meets your approbation I will select this as the battlefield."

When Howard replied that he, too, thought it was a very strong position Hancock concluded: "Very well, sir, I select this as the battlefield."[22]

In view of this conversation there is little doubt about who in the final instance determined that the army should fight on the Culp's Hill-Cemetery Ridge-Round Top line. Undoubtedly Buford and Reynolds had seen the advantage of the hills behind Gettysburg and had drawn their line in front of the town in order to save the heights for the rest of the army as it arrived. Still, Hancock had no information about their earlier intentions, when he determined that there the Union army should make its stand.

Howard's resentment at the turn of events was expressed in a letter to Meade that night, saying "General Hancock's order to assume command . . . has mortified and will disgrace me."[23] He took the position that Hancock was "assisting" him in carrying out his own orders. He did not seem to recognize that the mortification should be in the manner he had conducted the battle of July 1. Hancock thought it "only natural that a soldier should feel chagrined at being thus relieved, by a junior, on the field," but he did no gloating over it.

Carl Schurz, who commanded one of Howard's divisions, could understand that the appearance of Hancock was a blow to Howard's pride. But, unlike Howard, Schurz was quick to recognize Hancock's value to the broken Federal army. He described Hancock's arrival as "most fortunate."

It gave the troops a new inspiration. They all knew him by fame, and his stalwart figure, his proud mien, and his superb soldierly bearing seemed to verify all the things that fame had told about him. His mere presence was a reinforcement, and everybody on the field felt stronger for his being there.[24]

Howard was a darling of the Radicals and it was not difficult to persuade Congress a little later that he was the hero of Gettysburg, the one who selected the position that was all-important to victory. When that august body came to pass its resolution of thanks it mentioned Meade, the commanding general, and Howard, but forgot Hancock. Reynolds and Buford, who began the battle, likewise were neglected. Reynolds and Buford were dead—out of sight, out of mind. Hancock was a Democrat.

Howard in a magazine article thirteen years after the battle[25] was still trying to keep his anguish alive by explaining that Hancock's function was that of "a temporary chief of staff for Meade." He added:

I noticed that he sent Wadsworth's Division, without consulting me, to the right of the Eleventh Corps, to Culp's Hill; but as it was just the thing to do I made no objection. . . .

Howard's article contained more than a bit of fictionalizing, which Hancock was able to refute easily in a little pamphlet he issued entitled "Gettysburg." It gave a concise account of his actions on the first day of the battle.[26] He said Howard's inaccuracies were "glaring"[27] and should be pointed out in the interests of historical truth.

His "Very Atmosphere . . . Invigorating"

In his own story of his arrival, Hancock said he "lost no time in conversation" but began making dispositions that would prevent the enemy from seizing the vital point of the battlefield. From that moment, he said, he exercised "positive and vigorous command over all the troops present. . . ."[28]

Few incidents of the War between the States were as gripping in their sheer excitement as Hancock's arrival on Cemetery Hill and the manner in which he turned a disheartened, fleeing army into a formidable force that might hope to resist the oncoming Confederates stimulated by their initial triumph.

So striking was the change in the army's condition that nearly everyone took note of it and not a few wrote memoranda about it that night or later.

Lieutenant Edward N. Whittier, commanding a Maine battery, found when he went to get orders that Hancock's "very atmosphere was strong and invigorating."

. . . and I remember (how refreshing to note!) even his linen clean and white, his collar wide and free, and his broad wrist bands showing large and rolling back from his firm, finely molded hands.[29]

Whittier's battery was near the cemetery gate, resting after a day of fighting west of the town. Hancock at once put it into action again. He pointed to Culp's Hill and told Whittier to find a position where he could prevent the enemy from coming up the valley between Culp's and Cemetery Hills. In an instant Whittier had the battery rolling.

The Philadelphia *Times* gave the story of Hancock's impact on the army. It said confusion and retreat already had begun. Troops were flowing through the town almost in a rout and within a few minutes Cemetery Hill would be in enemy hands.

But what a change came over the scene in the next half hour. The presence of Hancock was magnetic. Order came out of chaos. The flying troops halt and again face the enemy. The battalions of Howard's Corps that were retreating down the Baltimore pike are called back, and, with a cheer, go into position on the crest of Cemetery Hill.[30]

Certainly Hancock carried an inspirational power to the battle line. Sherman, who understood leadership, put the quality into words:

There is a soul to an army as well as to the individual man, and no general can accomplish the full work of his army unless he commands the soul of his men as well as their body and legs.[31]

Hancock possessed this mystic appeal as did few others and in no instance was it more apparent than on the late afternoon of the first day at Gettysburg.

Colonel J. W. Hofmann of the 56th Pennsylvania, whose troops had fired the opening infantry round of the battle, had his first sight of Hancock at what he thought was the sublimest moment of that general's life, just after he reached the field to take command. He sat on his horse on the crest of Cemetery Ridge to look over the scene, the surging mass of troops, and brought order to it, establishing the lines along which on the following days the enemy met a sanguinary repulse.[32]

Doubleday thought the great service rendered by Hancock on the first day was in creating the impression that the Federal line had been strongly reinforced, and thereby causing the enemy to delay their attack until the day following.[33]

The first order Hancock gave was to push the Eleventh Corps troops forward to the stone walls, which Howard had neglected to do, so as to create the impression of strength and deter the enemy's advance. Then he spoke in an inspirational vein to part of Howard's command to encourage it to hold while he was forming the lines elsewhere. His actions refuted Howard's later contention that he organized the troops on one side of the road and Hancock the other, for the truth was that Howard had become no more than an additional annoying problem to Hancock and, a little later, to Meade, both trying to save a battle Howard had all but lost by exposing his flank to Early's oncoming division. He had not learned the lesson of his exposed flank at Chancellorsville.

Hancock next placed remnants of the First Corps on the left of the Eleventh. On his arrival he had found only a small part of Cemetery Hill covered by Steinwehr. Soon he had a line running the full length of the hill, after which he was able to turn his attention to Culp's Hill, the companion eminence on the right. He had it garrisoned with Wadsworth's First Corps division. He put Buford's cavalry on the flat ground below and to the left of Cemetery Hill, giving protection to his left while he was forming his line on the crest. Colonel J. P. S. Gobin quoted him as saying on his arrival, "If we can hold these hills, here is the place to fight a battle." Then he prepared to sweep the approach up the Baltimore Pike from Gettysburg.

To the captain of a battery he said: "Place three guns on this pike and the other one at right angles and remain in this position until I relieve you in person."

Not being satisfied with these direct orders, he called an aide
to listen to the order as he repeated it:

I am of the opinion that the enemy will mass in town and make
an effort to take this position, but I want you to remain until you
are relieved by me or by my written order and take orders from
no one.[34]

Geary Sent to Occupy Round Top

Schurz, whose division had largely dissolved in the face of Early's
and Rodes's attack, tended to agree with Halstead's version of the
meeting of Hancock and Howard. Schurz was riding up Cemetery
Hill with Howard when they met Hancock, who saluted "with great
animation, as if there were no time for ceremony."[35]

The anxieties of that moment made a deep impression on Schurz.
Hancock, as soon as he had formed his defensive line, seated himself on a stone wall where he could get a good view of the Confederate position. Schurz joined him and through their field glasses
they watched the Confederate columns and batteries on the opposite ridge. They studied the movements but could not discern the
purpose of the enemy as infantry and artillery moved here and
there.

Schurz frankly confessed that he felt nervous. He thought the
Federal line was grievously thin after the day's losses, however
strong its position might now be. He was relieved when he found
his attitude was not personal timidity; Hancock freely admitted that
he was not entirely sanguine either, though he thought they could
hold until the Twelfth Corps came.

They saw finally that the enemy was not forming for an immediate attack, and Schurz grew more tranquil. At sundown the
Twelfth Corps was up and the Third was arriving, and the position
began to seem secure. By that time Hancock's own corps was
approaching.[36]

Hancock's first message to Meade was carried at 4:00 P.M.,
Hancock's time, by Major William G. Mitchell, his aide-de-camp,
who advised the commanding general that Hancock said he could
hold the position until nightfall and that he thought it was the place

to fight the battle, "although somewhat exposed to be turned by the left."

That was the conclusion of Longstreet when he first viewed the position from the Confederate lines at about the same time. Thus these two generals, perhaps the outstanding subordinate officers of the war after the passing of Jackson, reached almost instantly the same opinion about the possibilities of the terrain.

Mitchell reached Taneytown about 6:00 P.M. and delivered Hancock's message to Meade in person. Meade's reply was "I shall order up the troops."[37] Now he threw aside his Pipe Creek plans and decided to fight at Gettysburg.

Before Hancock made his report to Meade that the Cemetery Hill position was favorable for the battle, he took the precaution of going over the terrain with Warren, the army's chief engineer, who confirmed his judgment. Warren reached the field after Hancock. He left Taneytown earlier but lost the way and went by Emmitsburg.

Brigadier General John W. Geary, commanding a Twelfth Corps division, rode ahead of his troops and came to Hancock on Cemetery Ridge at a time given by his aide as 4:00 P.M. Neither referred to their recent meeting at Chancellorsville.

Geary dismounted and saluted Hancock, who said: "Geary, where are your troops?"

"Two brigades are on the road advancing," Geary replied. He had left his third brigade in the rear at Two Taverns.

"Do you see this knoll on the left?" Hancock designated Little Round Top. "That knoll is a commanding position, and we must take possession of it, and then a line can be formed here and a battle fought. If we fail to fight here we will be compelled to fall back about seven miles. In the absence of Slocum [commanding the Twelfth Corps] I order you to place your troops on that knoll."

Hancock's orders from Meade had put him in command of the First, Third and Eleventh Corps, though not the Twelfth, but he felt that in the emergency he could give directions since Slocum had not yet arrived.[38]

Geary turned to his adjutant and said, "Veale, ride back and order General Greene to double-quick his troops diagonally across the fields and take possession of the knoll."

Adjutant Veale found Greene, who commanded one of Geary's brigades, and Greene occupied Little Round Top on the early evening of July 1. After the battle Veale commented that Hancock had at a glance visualized the lines on which the battle would be fought. Unless they held Little Round Top, a key point, the Federals would have to retire behind Pipe Creek.

Geary was in position on the army's left by 5:00 P.M. He covered the summit of "the range of hills," the Round Tops, with two regiments, regarding them "of the utmost importance," since from them the enemy might enfilade the entire Federal line.[39]

★ ★ ★ IO ★ ★ ★

Two July Days

The Minnesotans Save the Army's Center

Hancock's battle line, which he had laid out so carefully on the late afternoon of July 1, was badly disorganized on the afternoon of July 2 when Sickles suddenly moved his Third Corps a half to three quarters of a mile forward to take advantage of high ground at the Peach Orchard. In so doing he left the Round Tops—the importance of which Hancock had pointed out so earnestly to Geary, and Geary had emphasized to a representative of Sickles before moving to the army's right—stripped of troops at the very moment when Longstreet was launching his formidable assault on Meade's strung-out, angular left.

Unquestionably the main factor in saving the left of the Federal army was Hancock. Longstreet's blows dented and shattered Birney, who commanded the left division of Sickles' Third Corps, reaching from the Peach Orchard to Devil's Den in front of Little Round Top. Sickles, his leg shot away, was carried out of the action. His line seemed likely to break at any instant. Meade turned to his main reliance, Hancock, and placed him in command of the Third Corps as well as his own.

Hancock had foreseen how the battle would develop when Sickles advanced his corps to the Peach Orchard salient. He had been holding Caldwell's division in readiness for the oncoming emergency. The Irish Brigade had been given absolution by its chaplain, Father William Corby. This was Hancock's old division.

140

It had stood with him at Antietam, followed him at Federicksburg and held the last lines at Chancellorsville. He looked on with pride as it marched past, Zook in the lead, followed by Cross, Brooke and Kelly. Kelly, formerly colonel of the 88th New York, had replaced Meagher as the Irish Brigade commander.

Knowing how well Cross had fought on every field—he was one of the best brigade leaders in the army—Hancock sought to give him encouragement. "Cross, this is the last time you'll fight without a star," he shouted as the brigade passed.

The colonel did not tarry. "Too late, General," he shouted back. "This is my last battle."[1]

The premonition was accurate. He fell ten minutes later.

Hancock accompanied the division as it went to Birney's relief. Meantime the Confederate brigades of Barksdale and Wofford were cutting in behind Birney as he battled the brigades of Kershaw, Semmes, Anderson and Benning in front.

Hancock met Birney near the Trostle house behind the Wheat Field. "General Birney, you are nearly surrounded by the enemy," he said.

"I know it, General Hancock," Birney replied. "I am doing my best against a superior force."

"I have brought you these reinforcements." Hancock pointed toward Caldwell's splendid division rapidly advancing across the fields. "You will place them at your discretion, General Birney, and I will hold you responsible for their lives. . . ."[2]

Caldwell's arrival allowed Birney to extricate most of his men, though the loss to both his and Caldwell's division was staggering. Here both Zook and Cross met death and Brooke was wounded. The New Hampshire troops never recovered from the loss of Colonel Cross and always looked on his successors as substitutes.[3] Hancock grieved over the passing of so noble a subordinate.

Gibbon's division of Hancock's corps, which held the line along Cemetery Ridge in the center of the Federal army, watched the assaults on Birney with growing apprehension and saw him give ground first slowly, then in disorder as he was beaten back from the Wheat Field and the Trostle farm. But Meade was rushing troops from all parts of the field and eventually he had a new line behind Plum Run where the advancing Confederates were arrested. The crisis of the battle was moving from the left to the center. Anderson's division of A. P. Hill's corps now advanced to support Longstreet.

The other division of Sickles' Third Corps, commanded by Major General A. A. Humphreys, had been stationed by Sickles in a difficult position along the Emmitsburg Road, far out in front of the Federal line. Now it was assaulted in force and pressed back in what seemed likely to degenerate into a rout. The brigades of Wilcox and Lang, of Anderson's division, menaced the gap Sickles had left between his corps and Hancock's, at the moment when Hancock had been unable to fill the equally wide space left by the withdrawal of Caldwell to support Birney.

Hancock was, as usual, at the point of danger. He directed Willard's brigade of Hays's division—the soldiers who had been surrendered by Dixon Miles at Harpers Ferry—to charge the oncoming Confederates. Willard made the attack but was shot dead almost by his side. Colonel Eliakim Sherrill of the 126th New York took the brigade. Exposed to Wilcox's fire and with its right uncovered, it desperately needed help. Hancock told Colonel Sherrill to stand fast until he could find succor, and Sherrill held firmly until he, too, was killed.

Into this gap Wilcox's Alabamians were advancing rapidly, supported by Lang's Florida brigade on their left. Hancock saw a body of men coming out of some woods and underbrush and, judging them to be a fragment of the Third Corps in flight, he spurred his horse to rally them. But he was speedily brought to a recognition of the supreme emergency when the newcomers sent a volley in his direction. Luckily he escaped, but his aide, Captain Miller, was wounded and wounded again. The general directed the aide to find safety at the rear while he himself rode into a swale that protected him from the Confederate fire.

Here, suddenly, in front of him appeared a fresh body of men, unmistakably Federal, moving down the hill into the swale. They were eight companies of the 1st Minnesota, the advance element of Harrow's brigade, of Hancock's corps, coming into action. Earlier that morning Brigadier General William Harrow, who was in fact too ill for fighting, had resumed command of his brigade, declaring that he would not "play sick" during a battle.[4] Colonel William Colvill, chafing under the arrest that had resulted from the groans of the Massachusetts regiment, had proposed to Harrow that, with

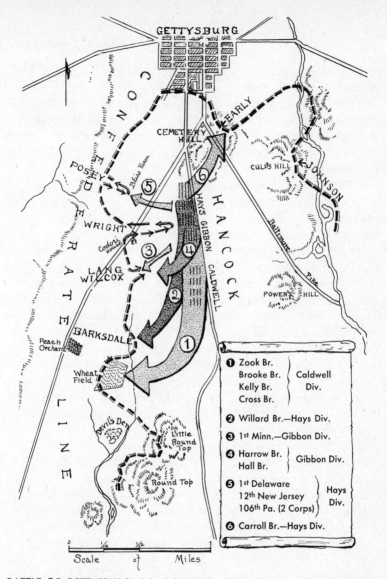

BATTLE OF GETTYSBURG, July 1-3, 1863. Hancock's corps was dispersed to meet successive attacks delivered against the Federal left, center and right, July 2. (1) Caldwell's division going to rescue Birney in Wheat Field. (2) Willard's brigade moving from Hancock's far right to check the triumphant Barksdale on Plum Run. (3) Charge of the 1st Minnesota against Wilcox advancing on Cemetery Hill. (4) Brigades of Harrow and Hall meeting onslaught of bulk of Anderson's division against Federal center. (5) Elements of Smyth's brigade checking Posey at Bliss farm. (6) Carroll's brigade saving East Cemetery Hill after break-through of Confederate brigades of Hays and Avery of Early's division.

a battle in prospect, a court-martial could wait; he had been temporarily restored to duty.

Three companies of the 1st Minnesota had been detached for skirmish duty, leaving 262 men in the ranks. When Hancock saw the regiment on the hillside, marching in column of fours toward the front, he dashed to it at a gallop. "What regiment is this?" he demanded.

"First Minnesota," Colvill answered briefly.[5]

"Colonel, do you see those colors?" Hancock asked, pointing to Wilcox's Confederates. When Colvill replied, Hancock spoke sharply, "Then take them."[6]

The regiment recognized at once that it was being sacrificed to gain time. Happily for the Union cause, Colvill was with his men. At his prompt order they deployed in a "perfect line" and moved down the slope, heading directly at the center of the Confederate brigade. As they came close Colvill gave the order to charge, and the Minnesotans plunged ahead with lowered bayonets. They caught the Confederates at the moment when the front line was slightly disordered as it crossed the bed of the dry stream and drove it back on the second line. The impetuous charge was just what Hancock had hoped for. The regiment then took a position along the shallow stream bed and with a volley arrested the advance of Wilcox's entire brigade.

But the odds were too great for a prolonged stand. The Confederates poured in a deadly fire from their flank regiments that had been halted but not pushed back. Within fifteen minutes, Colonel Colvill, all of his field officers and 215 of the 262 men who made the charge, were lying dead or wounded in front of the Confederate line. Only three company officers were unscathed. A captain took the 47 survivors back.[7] Meantime Hancock had brought in the balance of Harrow's brigade and the attack of Wilcox and Lang faltered.

Hancock later, in a conversation with Senator Morton Smith Wilkinson of Minnesota, told of his desperate need at the moment he encountered the Minnesota regiment:

I had no alternative but to order the regiment in. We had no force on hand to meet the sudden emergency. Troops had been ordered up and were coming on the run, but I saw that in some way five minutes must be gained or we were lost. It was fortunate that I found there so grand a body of men as the First Minnesota. I knew they must lose heavily and it caused me pain to give the order for them to advance, but I would have done it if I had known every man would be killed. It was a sacrifice that must be made. The superb gallantry of those men saved our line from being broken. No soldiers, on any field, in this or any other country, ever displayed grander heroism.[8]

Similarly, when a Federal battery had been seized a bit later by the enemy and was about to be turned to ply the Federal lines, Hancock appealed to the 13th Vermont of the First Corps, which happened to be nearest. When he asked Colonel Francis B. Randall if the Vermonters could recover the guns, the colonel's reply was simple: "We can! Forward, boys!"

They dashed into the fighting, regained the guns, then pushed on over what Randall judged to be half a mile to the Emmitsburg Road, where they wrested two brass cannon from the Confederates, the only pieces of Lee's artillery captured during the three-day battle.[9]

As the attack moved farther to Hancock's right, the thrust of Wright's Georgia brigade into the heart of the Federal center was finally beaten off by Webb's brigade. The Confederate attack on the Federal center languished. Hill had sent in his brigades in such slow succession that Hancock had been able to repulse them in detail without having to meet any concentrated assault along his front.

Again on July 2 Meade had revealed the same supreme confidence in Hancock that had impelled him to send the newest of his corps commanders to the field of disorder and defeat on the afternoon of July 1. By entrusting Hancock with the command of the Third Corps as well as his own, Meade had given him virtually complete authority over the left and center of the Federal army during the period when it and the Union cause were in great peril from Longstreet's relentless hammering.

A "Happy Inspiration" Holds Cemetery Hill

Now, after saving the army on the left and in the center, Hancock was about to direct his attention to a fresh menace on the right.

As the day of blood and tragedy began to pass, Longstreet's attack was subsiding on Meade's left and Hill was being repulsed in the center. Now Ewell's corps belatedly came into action against Cemetery and Culp's Hills, and with desperate courage and dogged enterprise threatened to carry those eminences and shatter Meade's lightly held right.

Early's division, with the brigades of Hays and Avery in front and Gordon in reserve, stepped off at sundown from the region of the Culp farm and moved toward the northeast face of Cemetery Hill. They had to breast artillery fire in their front and from the Culp's Hill batteries on their left, and face a heavy infantry fire as they advanced. Re-forming at the base of the hill, where they scattered the Federal skirmishers, they made an impetuous dash up east Cemetery Hill, broke through Howard's defending Eleventh Corps line and drove into the Federal batteries on the summit.

Close as Meade had been to disaster in other quarters, his army was never more imperiled than when these two Confederate brigades gained a lodgment in the very heart of the Federal position. From here they might, if supported, pierce Meade's army and sever the two wings.

Absorbed as he had been with the battle against Longstreet on the left and Hill's successive attacks on his immediate front, Hancock was not inattentive to developments elsewhere. He was deeply concerned over the increasingly heavy firing on his right. Howard was not adequately prepared, nor had he taken the precaution to call for reinforcements. Hancock did not have full confidence in the Eleventh Corps's sturdiness, enfeebled as it had been by the first day's battle. His decision to support Howard, even though that general had not requested it, was what the Federal chief of artillery, Henry J. Hunt, called a "happy inspiration," and it probably saved the battle.[10] Hancock was standing with Gibbon, who commanded the Second Corps while Hancock commanded the left wing, when the heavy firing on the rear slope of Cemetery Hill indicated the full gravity of the attack.

"We ought to send some help over there," he said to Gibbon. Then, in quick decision, he added: "Send a brigade. Send Carroll."[11]

Though darkness had fallen, Carroll was quickly in motion. He picked his way across the crest of Cemetery Hill from Ziegler's Grove to the critical point of the attack on the Cemetery Hill summit, guided mainly by the flashes from the Confederate muskets. Howard said the brigade advanced "with marvelous rapidity, sweeping everything before it." It struck the two Southern brigades along the line of the stone wall that at the outset had marked the Federal position. Weakened and scattered by their assault and unsupported by Early, the Confederates were hurled back to their old position at the Culp farm.

East Cemetery Hill was not again endangered.

That night a brigade officer put out a picket line close to the Emmitsburg Road. He made sure that his line joined other pickets on the right and left, then rode back to be met by Hancock, whose first question was what troops his pickets connected with. The officer sought to reassure the general: "I am sure the connection is perfect but did not ascertain the regiments."

Hancock sent him right back to the picket line to find out. At that stage of a desperate battle he was leaving nothing to chance.[12]

In Meade's council of war held at eleven o'clock that night, Hancock seemed a little bored by the entire proceeding. He voted to stay on the field and stay on the defensive. That was the clear course and no council was needed to confirm it. All the other corps commanders were of the same or similar judgment. The council broke up about midnight, and Hancock slept with Generals Newton and Gibbon in an ambulance parked near Meade's headquarters.

The Bombardment Shakes the Countryside

Lee's successes on the first two days at Gettysburg impelled him to continue the battle on the third. As he had assailed both of Meade's wings and judged that most of the Federal troops were massed there, he determined to make a frontal assault on the Federal center.

For the attack he selected Pickett's fresh division that had been guarding the Southern army's rear at Chambersburg, Heth's division, commanded by J. Johnston Pettigrew after Heth had been wounded, and two brigades of Pender's division commanded by

Isaac R. Trimble. The attacking force aggregated about 15,000 men. Under Lee's orders they were to converge on the little clump of trees held by the brigade of Alexander Webb on the left of Hancock's Second Corps line. The assault was under the general direction of Longstreet.

The hot morning wore on, quietly on the Federal left and center, but an inferno of shell and flame on the far right, which curved back almost to the rear of Hancock's position. There Edward Johnson's division, reinforced by Ewell with brigades from his other divisions, battled with Slocum's Twelfth Federal Corps for the possession of Culp's Hill.

On Culp's Hill, from 3:45 until 11:00 A.M., was fought one of the bloodiest battles of the war, with both sides trying to maintain an offensive, charging back and forth over the wooded slopes with a fury and determination unsurpassed in any other quarter of the field. Brigadier General Thomas L. Kane, commanding a Pennsylvania brigade assailed by Steuart's Confederate brigade, told of a dog that rushed forward at the head of the 1st Maryland Infantry and was killed by Federal fire. Says Kane:

He licked someone's hand, they said, after he was perfectly riddled. Regarding him the only Christian-minded being on either side, I ordered him to be honorably buried.[13]

With the battle raging behind him but with the action lulling along his own front, Hancock strengthened his position and made ready for the massed attack he was certain would be forthcoming as soon as Lee formed his columns.

While waiting for the Confederate move, Hancock passed along the rear of his line. He met a girl about six years old who was clutching a heavy musket in her arms and staggering under the load. She came up to the general, held the rifle a bit higher and, when he dismounted, fell into his arms weeping. Between sobs she said: "My papa's dead, but here's my papa's gun."

Hancock's eyes were no drier than hers when he related the incident. "I never recall that brave chit of a child's offering to our cause," he said, "without feelings of the deepest reverence."[14]

Finally the battle for Culp's Hill ended on the right. The troops of both armies were spent. In the center, behind the crest of Cemctery Ridge, a group of Federal officers had luncheon on a cracker-box table and blankets spread on the ground. Meade, Hancock, Newton, Gibbon and Pleasanton were there with their staffs, and the talk dwelt not only on the July 2 battle, but on where the expected fresh attack would fall. Meade believed his left would again be assailed, and Hancock the center. The generals had finished eating, had lighted cigars and were departing when the signal gun sounded from the Confederate woods a mile away and the air was suddenly alive with shrieking shells.

Thus the greatest cannonade of the battle opened. As a prelude Lee had massed his pieces on Seminary Ridge and directed a thorough artillery preparation. The opening gun was fired shortly after one o'clock, and for an hour and forty minutes the Pennsylvania countryside shivered under the bombardment. Hancock said: "It was the most terrific cannonade I ever witnessed, and the most prolonged." General Hunt, commanding the Federal artillery, replied from Cemetery Ridge and Little Round Top.

Pleasanton had ridden about fifty yards from the picnic scene when the shells began to drop. He looked back and saw, flying in the air, as he described it, "an indiscriminate mass of sandwiches, cheese, crackers, and stragglers all mixed up together."[15] One of the first shells had fallen directly on the improvised table from which Meade, Hancock and the others had been eating only moments before.

A Gallant General Rides the Lines

Just before the cannonading Hancock had ridden with Meade to a point behind the Second Corps lines near Meade's headquarters. He mounted at once and, followed by staff and orderlies, rode to his left and stood with Colonel John R. Brooke, commanding a brigade of Caldwell's division, watching the effect of the Confederate fire. Then, according to his own modest recital, he "rode along my line to the right of the Second Corps to the woods held by General Hays."[16] Hays's line extended into Ziegler's Grove. Finally he turned back and rode again to Meade's headquarters behind his center.

Hancock's ride along the shell-swept crest of Cemetery Ridge at the height of the Confederate bombardment was one of the spectacular events of the battle of Gettysburg, long talked about, without any exact agreement about the details, even on the color of the horse he rode,[17] by the Second Corps soldiers. His object, according to one of his staff, was to show every man that "his general was behind him in the storm."

Just as he started a regimental band struck up the "Star Spangled Banner."[18] Though it was not then the national anthem, something about the swelling music caused Hancock to take off his hat—he was wearing a black felt, stiff enough to keep its shape, with a general officer's cord[19]—and as he rode along he waved it and smiled at the men huddled behind the fences, never showing a trace of concern about the shells and solid shot dropping about him.

But his men were scarcely as hopeful about his safety. "Every soldier's heart stopped beating," said A. J. Bothwell, "for this seemed certain death to the general."[20]

Hancock had a habit of wearing his coat buttoned only at the top and open at the waist. Causes no doubt were the heat and the fact that he was already beginning to grow heavy, but probably the most important was that he invariably wore his sword belt under his coat. Meade rarely buttoned his jacket at all. Hancock's sword was a light rapier. At Gettysburg he had on what he called an "undress uniform," apparently of ordinary issue stock.[21] He wore no sash, such as general officers sometimes affected, mostly in the early stages of the war.

Some of his staff members began the ride with him, but he gave them assignments, until only the bearer of the Second Corps emblem, Private James Wells whom Hancock described as a "short, stout Irishman," continued to the end.

At one point their progress was interrupted by the intensity of the fire. Hancock was not bothered but his favorite sorrel, which he had always found remarkably steady under fire, became so terrified as to be unmanageable, refusing to move despite the fact that the general, in his own words, spurred the mount "severely."[22] From Captain Edward Brownson he borrowed a tall, light bay with a white mark on its face (a horse from which Brownson was later shot in the Wilderness) and rode it during the rest of the time he was on the battlefield.

Twenty-odd years later, after Hancock was dead, General Abner Doubleday would recall the dramatic picture:

I can almost fancy I can see Hancock again as he rode past the front of his command, just previous to the assault, followed by a single orderly displaying his corps flag, while the missiles from a hundred pieces of artillery tore up the ground around him.[23]

When a subordinate told Hancock a corps commander ought not to risk his life that way, he replied, "There are times when a corps commander's life does not count."

Finding Meade's headquarters vacated—the bombardment had caused Meade to move to Slocum's headquarters on Power's Hill—he went to a point on the line of battle behind Webb's brigade and awaited the attack.

Colonel Wheelock G. Veazey gave a picture of Hancock as he appeared just before the assault. Veazey, commanding the 16th Vermont of Stannard's brigade, had been in charge of the picket line in front of Cemetery Ridge on the night of July 2. As the morning of July 3 wore on, his men, skirmishing in the fields over which the oncoming attack would pass, were not relieved. About noon, as they were becoming exhausted, he hunted up Hancock, who was as much distressed about their condition as the colonel. Hancock thought the exchange of details so far out in front could be accomplished only with considerable loss and had been awaiting an opportune time. Now that things seemed quiet along the lines he would order up a relief. Always hospitable, he invited Veazey, who had been with him when he turned the flank at Williamsburg, to visit with him until the relief arrived. After the battle the colonel made a memorandum of the incident.

He had watched Hancock, he said, in various battles "and had often been thrilled by his proud and fearless bearing in action." Now, at Gettysburg, he was supreme.

I had never seen him when he looked every inch the magnificent, ideal soldier so truly as on this occasion. . . . As he repeatedly examined his line with field glasses, I could see the expression of satisfaction, confidence and impatience. But he had not long to wait, for just as the first detail he had ordered was approaching, the signal gun from the opposite crest was fired, followed in a minute by one hundred and forty others.[24]

Armistead Falls Inside the Lines

When the concentration of the Confederate fire showed clearly that the Second Corps position was Lee's objective, Hancock sent hurriedly to Brigadier General Henry J. Hunt, chief of Meade's artillery, for two batteries. Hancock's and Hunt's views on the use of artillery were not in accord that afternoon, and this request led to the first divergence. Hunt responded by sending two batteries of 2½-inch rifled guns that came at a gallop.

Hancock was displeased. "Why do you bring those guns?" he stormed vehemently to the officer in charge. "I don't want those pop guns! Tell General Hunt to send me some Napoleon guns." Before the officer could depart he added: "Stop! I will see General Hunt myself."[25]

He prevailed on Hunt quickly and the Napoleons—brass 12-pounders that could throw shrapnel, round shot, canister or grape—were soon in position. Hancock first threw round shot and shrapnel. Canister would be the main defense against heavy, massed lines of infantry, and that was what Hancock had the batteries fire when the attack commenced, beginning at a range of about 800 yards.

Hunt later criticized Hancock for not following his advice to hold his artillery fire during the Confederate bombardment. Hunt's point was that the Second Corps guns exhausted their long-range projectiles before Longstreet's men stepped off, and had to wait until the assailants came into canister range. Had the shells been conserved, he said, Pickett would not have reached the Federal line. He complained that one third of the fire of the Federal guns was thereby lost, and it was the important crossfire that would have doubled the effectiveness of the artillery.[26]

Francis Walker talked over this criticism at different times with Hancock and after the general's death wrote an answer embodying Hancock's views. The Confederate bombardment had to be answered, he maintained, to preserve the morale of the men waiting under the storm of shells behind the stone walls and in the ditches along Cemetery Ridge. "Every soldier," he said, "knows how trying and often how demoralizing it is to endure artillery fire without reply."[27] Walker himself thought it was a question of judgment and that Hancock's was about the best in the army concerning the temper of the troops and an infantry defense.

Hancock made one other surprising move before the attack. He and Colonel John R. Brooke, who had been wounded on July 2, rode, at about 2:30 P.M., to a farmhouse about two hundred yards in front of the Federal lines in an effort to see what effect their own artillery was having on the Confederates preparing to attack. They could not see much in the woods but Hancock observed enough to know what was being prepared for him. Before the party went back, he rode out in front of the officers and addressed them:

Gentlemen, after this artillery fire is over it will be followed by an infantry attack upon our lines. This battle is the turning point of the war; if we win this fight the war is practically over. . . . We cannot tell where any of us may be before this day is over; before leaving you I wish to say I speak harshly sometimes. If I have at any time ever said anything to offend or hurt the feelings of any one of you I wish now to offer an apology.

Adjutant Charles P. Hatch explained that neither he nor the others understood Hancock to mean it would be the last battle, but that the loss of Gettysburg would be vital and disastrous to Lee's army.

Meade, anxious to draw on the assault, for which he was fully prepared, at length ordered his own guns silenced, and Longstreet's artillery chief, E. P. Alexander, whose ammunition was running low, sent word to Pickett that he must come at once. When he noticed the slackening of the Federal fire he followed his first message with another, urging him to come quickly.

Out from their concealment in the depression in the woods, into the expanse of open fields guarded by Federal guns loaded and waiting, moved Pickett's three brigades, full of the zest and confidence that for two years had attended each forward movement of the Southern infantry. Garnett was on the left, Armistead recessed behind the center and Kemper on the right. With them rode Pickett, his long dark curls reaching to his shoulders, his fine horse prancing. Viewed from Hancock's lines as the artillery smoke lifted, it was perhaps the grandest spectacle of the war—long lines of men marching lightly in fine order, their gray merging into the white smoke, their gait unhurried.

Abreast Pickett on his left moved Pettigrew's brigades and close behind them Trimble. Closing ranks as the batteries from Little Round Top took them in enfilade, the gray-clad soldiers continued their steady forward march even when Hancock's infantry opened. They realigned their ranks in a declivity at the Emmitsburg Road and stormed up the slope toward the stone walls from where the Federal artillery shook the battlefield as it emitted its double charges of canister.

Thomas L. Livermore told of riding behind Hancock's line just before the attack and seeing a body of skirmishers who had been driven in by Pickett and Pettigrew come crashing through the Federal lines. These were apparently some of the exhausted men who had been on tense duty in the fields all night and much of the day, and no doubt were trying to find a place to sleep. But their withdrawal was impetuous and Hancock was angered, fearful that running might be contagious. He shouted to his staff to go after them and bring them back.[28]

His surgeon, Dr. A. N. Dougherty, medical director of the Second Corps, a fat, jovial, phlegmatic man whose mount was almost as rotund as he was, was the first to respond, with coattails flapping. Livermore was just behind him. They had a ludicrous but short chase, and in the security behind the lines the skirmishers were stopped before anyone at the front paid much attention to them.

Pickett's and Pettigrew's assault against the impregnable Federal position behind the stone walls was foredoomed to failure. Garnett was killed as he led his men up the slope and Kemper went down critically wounded, but Hancock's old companion of the Sixth Infantry days, Lewis Armistead, took part of his brigade over the wall and into the Federal guns. He put his hat on his sword so the brigade could see him clambering over the stones and called on those who followed to "give them the cold steel, boys." As he rested his hand possessively on one of the Federal guns he was shot down, mortally wounded.

One of the Federal soldiers battling where he fell said he whispered some words and gave a distress signal, the fraternal implication of which the private did not grasp, but which others nearby understood. Armistead's appearance caused the group of Federal soldiers, members of the 71st Pennsylvania, to think he was General Longstreet. Half a dozen of them made a litter and started with him to the rear. One took his sword and carried it until the end of the war.

Hill's soldiers supported Pickett courageously but made no better impression on the Union lines. Meade again rushed in a surplus of assistance. Taken in front and flank, the commands of Pickett, Pettigrew and Trimble withered. Those not killed or captured fell back, many retreating slowly, reluctantly, before an overwhelming fire, shooting as they went.

Hancock's account of his actions at this high point was contained in a letter he wrote in 1869 to ensure accuracy to the artist Rothermel, who was painting a picture of Longstreet's assault:

During the fight (the close contest) I passed behind the troops close to the line. I was cheered by some of the troops (one or two regiments) and spoke to one or two colonels . . . and encouraged the troops by a few words as I rode close behind the ranks. I do not know what regiments cheered me; they were on the left of the clump after I had passed it.[29]

From their position they were probably regiments of Harrow's brigade. Hancock surmised that those who had thought General Meade was so near the line at that stage of the battle had heard this cheering and "fancied it to have been for him."[30]

Hancock Felled by Nail and Bullet

Passing Harrow's and Hall's brigade and moving toward the left, Hancock came to the part of the line held by Doubleday's division of the First Corps, remnants of the first day's battle. Doubleday had been strengthened by the arrival of Stannard's fresh Vermont brigade, a mingling of veterans with green recruits.

Hancock rode over the crest to the forward side of the hill, where the infantry had no stone wall protection. The position was described as "a place where no mounted man had for hours been seen" and where "no mounted man could for five minutes hope to live."[31]

Hancock had gone to this part of the line thinking Stannard's troops belonged to the Second Corps; nevertheless, he had general command of the entire line, including the First Corps units, and he gave orders to Stannard's soldiers as freely as if they had been his own. He rode down its entire brigade front and told the officer in charge of a small force of "fifteen or twenty files" which had been thrown out in front that he was too weak to accomplish much and should fall back to the main line.

Then, just as Hancock met Stannard, he was hit in the front of the right thigh by a Minié ball that had passed through the pommel of his saddle. As the bullet entered his groin it carried with it some bits of wood and a bent iron nail, apparently from the saddle. He was able to pull the nail out unaided but mistook the source of it. "They must be hard up for ammunition when they throw such shot as that," he remarked to the group that gathered around him.[32]

Some uncertainty about the nail lingered. Some expert opinion has maintained that a Civil War saddle should not have had any nails and if any was there it must have come from some crude repair work, such as was not likely on one of Hancock's saddles.[33]

The only one of what Hancock termed "my own people"—his regular staff and orderlies—present when he was hit was Private Wells, the dragoon who carried the Second Corps flag.[34] As he fell he was caught by Lieutenants Hooker and Benedict of Stannard's staff, who laid him on the ground, where he bled so freely that his wound was at first judged mortal. Stannard, who also was mounted "where no mounted man could hope to live five minutes," and who was wounded a little later, jumped from his horse, fashioned a tourniquet from his pistol barrel and handkerchief and, by his quick action, undoubtedly saved the corps commander's life. The bleeding was checked but Hancock would not allow anyone to move him so long as the enemy was still attacking.

Colonel Veazey of the 16th Vermont was one of the first to reach his side. "Shall we not carry you to the rear, General?" he asked.

"No, I thank you, Colonel," said Hancock calmly, though he was obviously in great pain. "Attend to your commands, gentlemen. I will take care of myself."[35]

Mitchell of his staff arrived in five to ten minutes and a little later Parker and then Bingham, who had received a slight head wound. Hancock was able to relate the time he lay wounded with the progress of the battle by the fact that Bingham brought him a message from General Armistead, whom he had encountered as the Confederate was being carried off mortally wounded. This was of importance to Hancock not only because Armistead was an old friend, but also because it showed that he remained on the field until after Armistead's men had been repulsed and the victory won. It was one of the incidents that allowed him to reconstruct the sequence of events as he went over them in later reflections.

When Hancock was satisfied that his lines had beaten off the Confederate attack conclusively, his first thought was to get the information to the commanding general. Immediately on Mitchell's arrival he sent his aide to Meade with an oral message, the wording, as written down that night by Mitchell, being:

Tell General Meade that the troops under my command have repulsed the enemy's assault and that we have gained a great victory. The enemy is now flying in all directions in my front.[36]

Mitchell found Meade east of the Taneytown Road, riding toward the crest of Cemetery Hill, and carried back a reply:

Say to General Hancock that I regret exceedingly that he is wounded and that I thank him for the country and for myself for the service he has rendered today.[37]

After repeating this to Hancock, Mitchell rode to a woods some distance down the Taneytown Road and in fifteen to twenty minutes returned with an ambulance.

Dr. Dougherty, the Second Corps medical officer, was cleaning out his hospitals behind the lines when he received an urgent message to go to Hancock, whom, he said, he found under a little tree on the slope of the hill that faced the enemy. Hancock later corrected the doctor's account by saying he lay near a clump of small trees but not under a tree. Dougherty, like Mitchell, had brought an ambulance. Hancock was placed in Mitchell's and asked the doctor to lie alongside him as they started toward the rear.

When they reached a place regarded as less exposed to the enemy's fire, Hancock requested that the ambulance be stopped until he could dictate a message.[38] The doctor took it down with a lead pencil and dispatched it to General Meade as directed. Though he retained no copy he remembered it, repeated it often and said he had it nearly verbatim when he jotted it down later: "We have won a victory and nothing is wanting to make it decisive but that you should carry out your intention. I have been severely, but I trust not seriously wounded." He added that he did not leave the field so long as any of the enemy remained "upright" in his front.

Dougherty thought the wording might have been "nothing is wanting to convert it into a rout but that you should carry out the plan determined on." He understood the reference to the plan to

be a proposed vigorous attack by Major General John Sedgwick
with his Sixth Corps against Lee's flank.[39]

The message was carried by the general's brother, Colonel John
Hancock, assistant adjutant general of Caldwell's division, who had
heard that Winfield was wounded and ridden at once to see him.

Thomas L. Livermore came up to the ambulance and judged that
the resting place had not been well selected. A Confederate battery near Gettysburg was throwing shells down the Taneytown
Road every three or four minutes, some of them reaching as far
as Little Round Top. Finding that the ambulance was in easy
range, he told Hancock how the enemy was enfilading the Federal
line.

"We've enfiladed them, God damn them," was Hancock's only
answer.[40] He seemed to be thinking of the effective work done to
Pickett's advance by Stannard's Vermonters.

The Vermonters Assail Pickett's Flank

Hancock, while he was on his back, had directed General Stannard to throw out a regiment in front of the Federal lines and
attack Pickett's flank as the Confederate column advanced toward
the stone wall. The opportunity for such a maneuver had been
created suddenly by the lagging of the supports Lee had ordered
to move on Pickett's right. The brigades of Wilcox and Lang
wandered away in the smoke, leaving Kemper's brigade on the right
of Pickett's division exposed. Hancock, called "eagle-eyed" and
"easily the best tactician of the Potomac army," and "always on
the front line of battle"[41] saw the opportunity and seized it quickly.

When Captain Bingham of his staff arrived Hancock directed
him to order out a second of Stannard's regiments to intensify the
attack on Kemper's flank.

Some misunderstanding resulted in later years about whether the
flank movement of Stannard's brigade, so important to the repulse
of Pickett's attack, was the inspiration of Stannard or of the corps
commander. Stannard maintained that he threw out the two regiments—the 13th and 16th Vermont—of his own accord and that
Hancock cautioned him against it, saying he was "making a great
mistake" because it would leave a gap in the Federal line of battle.
But on Stannard's promise that he could get his men back before

any element supporting Pickett could reach the Federal line, the corps commander, though still opposed, did not further counter the order.

Hancock in his report took credit for directing the maneuver and later persisted in that version. "I had seen the importance myself and probably General Stannard had also, and may have given similar directions," he said.

Likely the confusion sprang from Hancock's order to the small detail of "15 or 20 files" to fall back because they were not in sufficient force. Sending out this detail may have been the flank movement claimed by Stannard. Hancock was positive when he said that with the exception of this small detachment, which was firing when he came up, "no flank attack was made unless directed by me."

His aide Captain Bingham verified that he carried Hancock's order to Stannard and that he rode with the troops while they were taking a position for the flank attack on Kemper.[42]

By the time Meade reached the lines Hancock had been carried from the field. He was emphatic in disputing claims that officers other than his own aide Mitchell had first announced the victory to Meade, among them Frank A. Haskell of Gibbon's staff. Possibly they did so later, he said, but he added testimony to show that the first word was conveyed by Mitchell. Captain James Meade of Brigadier General S. W. Crawford's staff was near General Meade when Mitchell arrived and later reported to Hancock what occurred.

The Rothermel painting, when completed, represented Haskell as taking the message to Meade. Mitchell wrote a mild protest saying he was at a loss to understand the error and again giving the details.

Undoubtedly Hancock's best personal version of the third day at Gettysburg was contained in the letters he wrote to Rothermel. His neat, small script, with its shaded down strokes and flourishes, was clearly the work of another artist, though it is at times difficult to read because of its sheer ornateness. No detail about the battle was too unimportant to command Hancock's attention or be recorded accurately.

He had heard it contended that Meade was at the front before the Confederates were repulsed and thus the artist intended to depict it. He conceded that it was doubtless within the prerogatives of an artist to bring the commanding general onto the field even though he was not at the place shown in the painting. But he asserted that Meade had not visited the Second Corps by the time he sent Mitchell with his message.

"If General Meade claims to the contrary," he concluded, "I will contest it."[43]

Hancock did not forget his own personal group in his commendations:

I had a most valuable staff of young officers, and although they became separated from me in the fight, you will find that they hunted up the place where they could be most useful.[44]

He gave especial attention to Mitchell of his own staff and Haskell of Gibbon's:

It is possible their behavior had as much to do with the success of the Second corps in repulsing the enemy as the acts of any other persons.[45]

As to his own part in the repulse Hancock was clear:

I commanded the whole line from Cemetery Hill to Round Top. I was the senior on that line, and the senior in the fight. I was also in fact the commander of the Second Corps which bore the brunt of the fight.[46]

Some place along the line he had noticed that a junior officer had made some movement contrary to established practices, which had averted a disaster of sorts. "If I knew the fool who ordered that movement," he said, "I would have him brevetted."[47]

Armistead's Alleged Recantation Challenged

Bingham gave Hancock an account of his conversation with Armistead that came to involve one of the grievous controversies about the battle, since it quoted Armistead as apparently recanting and expressing regret that he took service in the Confederate cause. Later he wrote the details as he recalled them and sent them in a letter to Hancock, January 5, 1869.

He said he was alongside Webb's brigade and first saw Armistead at the high point of the attack, when Webb's line was driven back. As he was helping to rally the troops he met several privates carrying a wounded Confederate to the rear. He ordered them back into the line, but they explained that they had an important prisoner, none other than General Longstreet.

Bingham saw from his insignia that he was an officer of rank and, as he explained it, was "impressed with the importance of carefully attending to the security of a commander holding the rank of Longstreet." The prisoner was suffering intensely. Bingham dismounted, asked his name, and was told that he was General Armistead.

"General," he said, "I am Captain Bingham of General Hancock's staff, and if you have anything valuable in your possession which you desire taken care of, I will care for it, for you."

Armistead asked if the general he referred to was Winfield Scott Hancock. Told that it was, he said he was "an old and valued friend" of Hancock's and asked to have this message delivered:

"Tell General Hancock for me that I have done him and done you all an injury which I shall *regret* or repent (I forget the exact word) the longest day I live."[48]

That was all of the enigmatical message. Bingham at his request took his spurs, watch, chain, seal and pocketbook, told the privates to take him on to one of the rear hospitals, then mounted and sought Hancock, whom he found lying wounded. He gave Hancock Armistead's message orally.

What is meant has never been clearly determined. The words came to be quoted with variations that did not seem greatly at conflict but which may have had a different implication from those given by Bingham. As often written, they were: "Tell Hancock I wronged him and wronged my country." Another version was: "Tell Hancock I have done him and my country a great injustice which I shall never cease to regret." The word "injustice" does not appear in Bingham's version, which is the only one that could be taken as correct.

The story that he lamented his action in supporting the Confederacy has been treated by Southern sources as "absurd."[49] The matter came up nineteen years after the battle, and apparently was first heard of in the South at that time, when Abner Doubleday published his book, *Chancellorsville and Gettysburg.* The quotation as Doubleday used it was: "Tell Hancock I have wronged him and have wronged my country," but Doubleday added his own comment that, in dying, Armistead "saw with a clearer vision that he had been engaged in an unholy cause."

Heated rejoinders were made by Southern writers and Armistead's friends. It was pointed out in the discussion that Armistead had made his choice calmly after a "perilous" journey to reach Richmond, that he had served "faithfully and gallantly" and that none of his associates ever had heard the faintest whisper that he doubted the righteousness of the Southern cause.

The Reverend J. William Jones, secretary of the Southern Historical Society, wrote to Hancock, July 10, 1882, stated that Armistead's relatives and friends were indignant, and said it was his understanding that Hancock had seen Armistead personally just after he was wounded.[50] Hancock replied that he had sent the message to Bingham, then a Congressman from Philadelphia. He expressed no opinion of his own on words attributed to his friend and spoken when he was not present, but said of Bingham: "He is the officer to whom the message was delivered and is the best witness in the case."[51]

Bingham replied to Hancock, who forwarded his letter to the Reverend Mr. Jones. Bingham could not then recall all the details of Armistead's condition and words, but he stood by the report he made to Hancock and what he had written in 1869. The words as he recalled them in 1882 were: "Say to General Hancock for me, that I have done him, and you all, a grievous (or serious) injury, which I shall always regret."

Bingham went on to describe him: "His condition at the time, was that of a man seriously wounded, completely exhausted, and seemingly broken spirited." He said the physician who attended his wounds could give better testimony as to his mental condition.[52]

The Reverend Mr. Jones analyzed Bingham's letter and found the situation different from the way he had understood it from Doubleday's book. Armistead, he recalled, had risen from a sick bed against his doctor's orders to go into the assault and had seen his men hurled back by overwhelming odds. Then he had "received an unexpected kindness from his old comrade and intimate friend, from whom he had been estranged by the events of the war, was deeply touched by it, and naturally sent the message." The implication Jones put on it was that "I have wronged you by cherishing bitter, vindictive feelings toward old friends, who, in this hour of extreme need, meet me with this great kindness."

An explanation that occurs to this writer is that he may have heard, by the time he spoke to Bingham, that Hancock had been wounded. He must have remembered the tenderness of their parting and felt deep regret that his old friend had suffered perhaps mortal wounds from his own assault. Naturally there was much confusion about the order of events after the attack was over, and word that Hancock was wounded probably had spread through the Second Corps before Armistead was carried back.

John B. Bachelder, who was to become the official governmental historian and map maker of Gettysburg, gave a clear picture of the variations in accounts and uncertainty of timing among Second Corps participants. While trying to establish the positions the various commands had occupied on the field of Gettysburg, he fell in with the corps at Brandy Station, after the return to Virginia.

At mess one night he said: "Well, I have been in the Second Corps today, and I believe I have discovered how Joshua made the sun stand still." He said he had gone to one regiment and had the officers mark on the map the hour of their brigade's position at a certain point. Then he had gone to another regiment in the same brigade, but the officers there declared with finality that the time was an hour or two earlier, or later.

So it went on, no two regiments or brigades agreeing, and if I hinted that some of them must certainly be mistaken, they would set me down by saying, with severe dignity, "We were there, Batchelder, and we ought to know, I guess."

He concluded that it would "take a day of at least twenty hours instead of thirteen at Gettysburg" to fit their accounts into the time:

So when Joshua's captains got around him after the fight and they began to talk it over, the only way under the heavens that he could ever harmonize their statements was to make the sun stand still and give them all a chance.[53]

In view of Bachelder's experience, no one can ever be sure of the precise times of events on Cemetery Hill on the afternoon of July 3.

Possibly the most plausible explanation is that Armistead did hear of Hancock's critical condition before he reached the rear. As he had wept when he parted from Hancock in California, his anguish over the wounding of his old 6th Infantry companion by his own brigade would be understandable.

Hancock did not offer his own interpretation. Not possessing firsthand facts, he could neither repudiate Bingham nor speak disparagingly of Armistead, so he treated it all with silence.

Recovery and High Honors

An Ingenious Doctor Draws the Bullet

On the night of July 3, while the two armies lay facing each other and Gettysburg and the surrounding country were being drenched with rain, Hancock was carried in an ambulance to Westminster and then by train to Baltimore, which he reached on the morning of July 4. He went on at once to Philadelphia, arriving at noon.

He had already sent a telegram to Mrs. Hancock in St. Louis advising her that he was severely but not mortally wounded and asking her to join him in Philadelphia. She started immediately.

The heat that July in Philadelphia was intense and unbroken. While both the general and Mrs. Hancock wanted to go on to Norristown, the physicians declined to allow further movement for a month. It was not until early August that Hancock was transported to his father's house on Swede Street in the home town on the Schuylkill.

The wound meantime had not yielded to treatment. The Minié ball had passed around from the front and imbedded itself in the back of the thigh bone. Several surgeons of high eminence probed persistently but could not extract the ball, and Hancock at length declared that he would prefer death to the torture of more probing. Although a partial scab had formed, the abscess was still draining.

Hancock's first theory was that he had been struck by a shell fragment; the bits of wood found in the wound, he thought, came from a fence rail which the shell had struck first. The surgeons therefore

165

did not expect to find any imbedded bullet and did not probe deeply for it.[1]

While Hancock was still lying in the Philadelphia hotel, the city, apparently indifferent to his great services at Gettysburg, was lavish in extolling Meade but gave Hancock scant attention. Details about how the battle was won had not been received, and praise went to the Philadelphian who had commanded the army. Crowds passed the Meade house and serenaders sang and cheered in front of it at night. Mrs. Hancock thought it evidence of her husband's "charitable, generous heart" that he considered it only natural for the public to express its gratitude to the army leader, and leave him out of the picture.

But Hancock's major role in the victory gradually came to be recognized in his home territory, where eyewitness accounts of the battle were being offered by the hosts of wounded soldiers of both armies. When at length the physicians allowed him to be taken to Norristown, the Philadelphia firemen, in full regalia, carefully transported him from the La Pierre Hotel to his special car, where the stretcher was placed over the backs of seats. In Norristown the Invalid Guards, veterans of many battles, carried him on their shoulders from the station to his father's house.

Soon after his arrival he had a telegram from Secretary Stanton asking him to suggest a successor as Second Corps commander. He recommended Warren, who received the assignment. Stanton followed with a letter expressing an apparently genuine warmth of sentiment: "Of the many gallant officers wounded on the great field of Gettysburg, no one has more sincerely my sympathy, confidence and respect than yourself."[2]

While he was still suffering, Dr. Louis W. Read, home to Baltimore on a brief leave from the army, called on him at Norristown. Dr. Read was able to extract the ball readily, even though it was imbedded eight inches deep. He had Hancock sit on a chair in the identical position he had occupied in the saddle, then followed with his forceps the course of the bullet and brought it to the surface without causing prolonged agony. A fragment of bone clung to the ball.[3]

Hancock was impressed with the surgeon's skill and recommended him in similar instances. Here was a man who applied common sense to surgery.

Later in the war Hancock met a gunner of Cowan's battery, W. E. Webster, of Auburn, New York, who had been hit in the upper left thigh at Cedar Creek. Frequent probing for the bullet had resulted in an abscess causing great suffering and threatening the man's life. The general said he knew a doctor who could extract the ball. Webster said he was "fed up with doctors," but when Hancock persisted the gunner departed at once for Baltimore and entered the McKim hospital at midnight. The diligent physician at once drew out the bullet with a fragment of bone attached to it, exactly as had been the case with Hancock.

The general called at the hospital next morning and when he learned of Doctor Read's success, exclaimed: "Why, that man could take a body out of the grave and make him live."[4]

Mentioned for Top Command

After the successful surgery but while the wound was still open and annoying, Hancock took his family on a visit to their home, Longwood, near St. Louis, which had come to them through Mrs. Hancock's family. Writing to his mother and father from Longwood on October 12, he was pleased with his progress: "I threw aside my crutches a few days after my arrival and now walk with a cane. I am improving but do not yet walk without a little 'roll.' "[5]

Though the wound remained unhealed, he nevertheless hoped to join his corps in two weeks, a desire he fell far short of realizing. He could not yet ride and found difficulty even in sitting on a chair. He occupied himself with his favorite hobby, tending the trees on the eleven-acre Longwood estate. The sap was not yet down but he went busily into the pruning. "I know it is not the time," he wrote, "but still it will do."[6]

As he regained the use of his leg, Hancock returned east, visited West Point, for which he retained the highest affections, and stopped at the Fifth Avenue Hotel in New York, the object of receptions and greetings wherever he appeared.[7]

Punctilious about army requirements, he had his physicians send regular reports to the Adjutant General of the Army from Norristown, St. Louis and other cities, certifying his inability to return to active duty.[8] It was a part of his thoroughness that no army regulation should be overlooked.

Although his wound still had not healed completely, he responded eagerly when on December 15, 1863, he was ordered back to Washington, where the high command of the Army of the Potomac was again the main topic of both official and sidewalk discussions. Hancock's name was mentioned frequently in both quarters. But the attention of Washington during the late fall and early winter had been directed toward the crises around Chattanooga and Knoxville. When the eastern army finally went into winter quarters, Hancock was sent to Harrisburg to stimulate re-enlistments among the veterans whose terms had expired. He spoke at public meetings, emphasizing that the restoration of peace depended on destroying the forces of the Confederacy in the field. The War Department looked on his brief tour of recruiting duty, after a lapse since the beginning of the Mexican War, as sufficiently successful to request him to return to it at a later date.

He was back in Philadelphia in February 1864 for the testimonials presented by the city as a result of resolutions introduced in the Select and Common Councils by the distinguished John W. Everman, the orphan he had shielded from the hostile gang when they were lads together in Norristown. The resolutions thanked him for his "brilliant services in the cause of the Union."[9]

The reception at Independence Hall, a distinction rarely granted, tendered by Mayor Alexander Henry and the presidents of the councils on behalf of the city, was regarded by the local press as one of the most imposing ever held in the "sacred Temple of American Liberty."[10] The event was reminiscent of the celebrations honoring Lafayette in the year of Hancock's birth. The day selected was Washington's birthday. The crowds were loud in their applause when Hancock appeared with his staff to review the volunteers and home guards of the Philadelphia area, who marched by with the aplomb of veterans. At the reception indoors he and the mayor exchanged felicitous remarks.[11]

After the festivities, as he was passing the La Pierre House on foot, Hancock noticed in the crowd an elderly, gray-haired man, and recognized him as his old school principal, Eliphalet Roberts of the Norristown Academy. The general halted, eagerly grasped the old teacher's hand, introduced his staff and others accompanying him and invited Roberts to call at his rooms.

"When I am a little stronger . . . I will return the call," he promised.

Roberts came the next day and found Hancock on his couch, resting from the exertions of the reception and review. But the general sprang to his feet at once, against the teacher's protest.

"No, Mr. Roberts," answered Hancock, "I shall always feel that I am under obligations to you."

They talked of old times at the academy. Roberts said it was an honor to have had Hancock as a scholar, and, beyond that, admired him because he always reverenced gray hairs.[12]

When the arrangements could be made, the citizens of Norristown presented him with a service of gold and silver consisting of nine pieces, which, according to Mrs. Hancock, he "always referred to with unmistakable pride."[13] Each piece was handsomely marked with the Second Corps trefoil.

The Union League of Philadelphia struck and presented a silver medal, but apparently kept a lingering hand on its recognition, watchful of his future conduct, mindful that he was well known as a Pennsylvania Democrat.

Other tributes came. At an informal gathering at the home of Edwin Forrest on Eighteenth Street near Race, in Philadelphia, the great tragedian, who was "never more delightful" and "kept the table in a roar," interspersed his recitations of "The Idiot Boy" and stray and heterogeneous bits from the classics with laudations of Hancock. Archbishop Wood of the Catholic Church and other guests were there, along with John W. Forney, clerk of the United States Senate and recorder of the event.

Forrest was no doubt the only American actor who ever had a riot in his honor, though it was altogether unsolicited by the noted Philadelphian. Forrest and his followers felt he had been impeded on the British and European stage by W. C. Macready, the most brilliant of the British actors, so when Macready in turn visited America in 1848 and concluded with *Macbeth* in New York, the Astor Place opera house riots ensued and culminated in a "tragedy of blood and death that shook New York to its center."[14] The play had to be suspended after the second act and Macready was spirited away in a closed carriage.

The mob scenes which followed an effort at another performance were a peculiar testimony of the fondness of the crowd for Forrest. The rioters maintained that no foreign rival, no "English hog," no "Devonshire bull," would be tolerated in New York, and for a second time howled the Briton down. Troops of cavalry and volunteer companies were called out. Twenty-two were left dead and large numbers were wounded.[15]

Intense, vibrant, willful, of handsome and powerful physique, unsurpassed as Spartacus or Hamlet, Forrest was in 1863 undoubtedly a greater idol of the Philadelphians than General Meade with all his fresh battle laurels. Now he became the champion of Hancock. Forney found him "in high glee" over Hancock's success at Gettysburg and eager to talk about it at every opportunity. As Forney explained it, Forrest, while an ardent patriot, was also an ardent Democrat and was "proud because so much glory and honor had been achieved by his friend, General Hancock." Like many other war Democrats, he had obviously been deeply incensed by the smugness of the Radicals in assuming that on them alone rested the responsibility of preserving the Union.

Congress Gives Its Thanks to Others

When Congress early in 1864 passed its resolution thanking Meade, Hooker and Howard for their services in the Gettysburg campaign but ignoring Hancock, considerable amazement was expressed in army circles. The *Army and Navy Journal* printed an article by "Truth," setting forth the great injustice perpetrated by the legislative branch. Hooker was largely passed over in the article—nobody could take commendation of him seriously. It was pointed out that he and Meade commanded the army in the campaign.

"But by what strange process of reasoning or distortion of facts is the name of Major General Howard placed in the resolution?" the article inquired. "On what ground is he alone of all the corps commanders selected for this high honor?" After dealing with the fiasco of Howard's corps at Chancellorsville, and referring to the broad powers granted Hancock by Meade on the first day at Gettysburg, the article continued:

No man who witnessed the advent of General Hancock on the field will forget the almost magic change his arrival created. Visiting every part of the field, his practiced eye caught at a glance the necessary dispositions to be made. His energy communicated itself to subordinate commanders. His manly bearing inspired the troops to new courage.

"Truth" went on to assert that the army gave the credit to Hancock which Congress had awarded to Howard, then with gusto censured the legislators:

The passage of the resolution may be the means by exciting discussion, finally of correcting a current but erroneous opinion; but the injustice done to General Hancock can hardly be remedied. Happily his reputation is fixed on too substantial a basis to be dependent on any action of Congress. The injustice lies in the fact that Congress has perpetuated what has always been a perversion of an impartial history of Gettysburg; the statement that Major General Howard was in any sense entitled to honors not shared by other corps commanders.[16]

The resolution in fact did not help Howard; it merely paraded the prejudice and fallibility of the Thirty-eighth Congress before the army.

Congress may have been either purposeful or confused when it awarded the credits for the Gettysburg victory, but Lincoln had a clearer picture. He interviewed Sickles on October 20, 1863, at the White House. Secretary of the Navy Welles entered just as the President asked if Hancock did not in fact select the battlefield.

Sickles said no, and went on to suggest that Howard and he were entitled to the credit more than others. But as he elucidated, the wary Welles noticed that in presenting the particulars he dwelt on his own role and relegated Howard to obscurity. The story Sickles told was a blatant and intensely personalized distortion of the facts and Lincoln must have been as alert to it as Welles. Hancock's name was not even mentioned again.

Howard, according to Sickles, had taken possession of the cemetery on July 1. He, Sickles, had arrived between five and six, followed shortly by Meade, who did not like the position and favored abandoning it. Having called a council, Meade was in earnest about falling back, so Sickles left the meeting and wrote an emphatic opinion in favor of maintaining the position. This, he said, "was finally agreed to against Meade's judgment." Sickles did not specify who made the decision overruling the commanding general! That night Welles's recordings reflected his own doubts about Sickles' objectivity and Meade's capacity: "Allowances must always be made for Sickles when he is interested, but his representations confirm my impressions of Meade, who means well. . . ." Meade, Welles thought, belonged in a secondary position.[17]

As time passed it became clearer everywhere that Hancock was indeed the individual who more than any other gave the Union the victory at Gettysburg. "I think he was distinctly the hero of that battle," said his old commander Franklin.[18] Sherman, when he went to Gettysburg after the war, pointed to where Hancock stood on the crest of Cemetery Ridge, when Pickett, Pettigrew and Trimble were advancing. "If there ever should be a monument erected on earth to man, there is the spot for Hancock's monument," he exclaimed.[19]

The approximate place was used for Meade's monument. It shows the army commander near the line, though he was well removed from it at the high point of the battle. Hancock's monument is farther north. There are many other sites that would be as suitable for Hancock, who so largely influenced the action on many parts of the field.

New Respect for the Trefoil

Hancock's absence from the army was felt severely in the fall of 1863 and was no doubt an important factor in the abortiveness of Meade's Mine Run campaign. Meade had written to Halleck about the want of energetic subordinates after Gettysburg and mentioned as most serious the losses of Hancock and Reynolds, whose places could not be filled.[20]

Meade expected to be relieved of the command. Others, viewing the record of the army, regarded it likely that Meade would go and speculated about the successor. Hancock in Washington heard the undercurrent of gossip, knew his own name was being mentioned and wrote Meade a letter of reassurance, saying he retained full confidence in the commander and hoped he would not be relieved.

Meade replied December 11, 1863, with a vein of cynicism:

As this army is at present organized, and as its commander is now regarded and treated at Washington, its command is not to be desired by any reasonable man, nor can it be exercised with any justice or satisfaction to yourself. While, therefore, I should be glad to see you promoted to a high command, as a friend and well-wisher, with my experience I cannot say I could congratulate you if you succeed me.[21]

Hancock's reply, written December 21, was a frank statement of his admiration of Meade. He must have harkened back to the days of Hooker's plotting, for in it he said:

I am no aspirant, and I never could be a conspirator, had I other feelings toward you than I possess. I would sooner command a corps under you than have the supreme command. I have faith in you. I would not like to serve under a bad commander. I would rather be out of command. I have always served faithfully, and so I intend to do. I would always prefer a good man to command that army than to command it myself. If I ever command it, it will be given to me as it was to you. I shall never express or imply a desire to command, for I do not feel it.[22]

A view of the high-command situation at about this time was contained in a letter written December 10, 1863, by Colonel Theodore Lyman of Meade's staff, who noted that the press continued to speculate about Meade's successor. Lyman ran over the possibilities and thought Hancock the most likely.[23] Meade himself, he said, thought he would be replaced, but the aide expressed doubts of the dearth of other talent:

General Sedgwick would, I think, refuse; General Warren is very young, and is, besides, under a cloud about his movement on our left. General Sickles, people would say, is too much of a Bowery boy. Generals French, Newton and Sykes are out of the question. General Humphreys has no influence strong enough to put him up. Any subordinate general would have to be of great note to be lifted thus high; there is no such one. I think they would not try a western general, after Pope's experience. The only one I can think of is Hancock, for a long time laid up by his Gettysburg wound, and not yet in the field. He belongs in this army, is popular, and has an excellent name. The New York *Herald* insists on Pleasonton, which *is* an original idea.[24]

The prestige and glory of the Second Corps had been firmly established at Gettysburg. That could be seen from the respect accorded Hancock's men by the enemy. Allen C. Redwood told of a small painting made by one of his fellow soldiers of the

Army of Northern Virginia. It showed a Confederate in his home-spun, carefully examining a flannel badge that decorated a hat he had picked up nearby. He was trying to answer the frequent question of "Who's in our front?" His gravity, according to Redwood, showed that the answer was not reassuring, because the badge was the clover leaf of Hancock's famous Second Corps.

"These little scraps of red, or blue, or white, were significant of much, as we learned to read them aright," said Redwood. He went on to tell how he and others of Jackson's men had encountered the Eleventh Corps crescent and Third Corps lozenge at Chancellorsville, but became acquainted with the trefoil on "the memorable afternoon of July 3 at Gettysburg. . . . The world knows the story of that encounter. . . ."[25]

Francis Walker, speaking in Massachusetts after the war, quoted Major General Charles Devans as saying no army was ever so well fed and clothed as the Army of the Potomac. Then he went on to add that of all the corps, not one was so well fed and clothed as the Second. He held this to be a factor in the corps's success, maintaining that "regular rations, well shaped shoes, and warm blankets bear a very positive relation to good marching and hard fighting."[26] Hancock, the commissary of the march to the Pacific, was still a good provider.

The Corps Was Never Surprised

Some comments of associates, while general, are appropriate as applied to Hancock's actions at Gettysburg. Slocum declared that "on the field of battle he had no superior in either army,"[27] while Artillery Major Harry C. Cushing compared him to Marshal Masséna, as having "the rare faculty of growing more clear-sighted the hotter the battle raged."[28]

Brigadier General James Grant Wilson, the Illinois cavalry officer, was equally laudatory:

He was certainly, in his uniform, among the grandest figures that I ever gazed upon, and always associated in my mind with Gen. Winfield Scott, whose name he bore, and that majestic Missourian, Col. Doniphan, who, early in the Mexican War, made one of the most marvelous marches on record.[29]

Colonel Samuel B. Lawrence found he was "lavishly equipped by nature with a handsome figure and noble presence."[30] The major

general of cavalry, David McM. Gregg, said he knew no other infantry commander with whom he felt it equally satisfactory to
serve in the field.[31]

Lieutenant Colonel Charles H. Banes, of the Philadelphia brigade, gave this impression:

There are some officers whose appearance on the battlefield, or
at the head of a column, imparts hope and secures the admiration
of those serving under them. Hancock not only possessed this
influence, but had the prestige that came from past success and
that inspired anticipation of brilliant achievements in the future.
During the period the corps had been under his immediate command, it had never met a surprise from an enemy or lost a gun in
action. For a considerable share of his success General Hancock
was indebted to careful attention to detail, and his habit of demanding prompt obedience to minor orders, as well as those of a more
important character. Until these traits were understood and known
to be the principles of his military action the general bore the
character among volunteer officers of a martinet.[32]

The general had come in for many bumps, but the permanent
ones were now subjected to diagnosis for those who might believe
in their significance.

A curious but strikingly accurate analysis of Hancock, which
time would sustain in several particulars, was published at about
this period by the *American Phrenological Journal,* in an article
and chart by Dr. Sam S. Fowler, of New York, known as an able
phrenologist in an era when the system had won considerable acceptance. The writer found Hancock in good health and of fine
physique, tough and enduring, with a good stomach and digestion,
and concluded that "there is no mud in brain or body." The near
prescience of the author was suggested by the remark:

There is nothing stimulated in body or brain, and if he will he
may achieve any position within the reasonable limits of ambition.
Throw a man with such an organization upon his own resources,
and he will make his way onward and upward.

Nothing but perversion, or wrong use of good faculties, could
prevent him from becoming a leader, for he has a spirit energetic,
persevering, and executive, with a clear, practical common-sense
intellect. . . .

Such a man bides his time and ultimately takes his place at the
head, where he belongs. . . . There is no vacillation or indecision
in his disposition.[33]

Hancock's hospitality, frequently referred to by his associates, was illustrated by a staff member. Entertainment was "an instinct with him." Once some Confederate prisoners were passing and Hancock in a burst of compassion, courteously asked a young Southern officer to step out of the column. "Lieutenant," said Hancock, "I am sorry to see you in trouble. Pray take a glass of whisky and water with me."

Later his adjutant Walker was taken prisoner. Confederate Lieutenant General A. P. Hill had a staff officer advise Walker that Hill had given orders that he should be treated with every kindness, in return for the kindness with which Hancock had treated Hill's men when they were his prisoners.[34]

Hancock was especially concerned that credits for good service should be recognized and that the receipt of intelligence should be recorded properly:

I have known him to keep a staff officer riding a day among the camps of the army, to find out the name of a lieutenant who, in the heat of some action, had brought him a message from another commander, that due acknowledgment might be made of it in his official report.[35]

The winter passed and Hancock, though still having difficulties with his wound, was anxious to rejoin his corps for the fresh campaign under the new commander in chief of the armies, Lieutenant General Ulysses S. Grant.

In the Wilderness

The Frigid Meade Warms in His Greeting

"Hancock arrived today at army headquarters. Grant is expected daily," wrote Alexander Hays from near Stevensburg, Virginia, to his wife, on March 23, 1864.[1]

The ground was covered with a foot of snow, the army was still being reorganized and numerous delays occurred before the hero of the West sounded the signal to break winter quarters and advance across the Rapidan.

Hancock's corps had been strengthened substantially by merger of the old Third Corps—which Sickles had commanded at Gettysburg—with his own Second, giving him four divisions, instead of the three he had led at Gettysburg. The three old Second Corps divisions had been compressed into the two divisions now commanded by Brigadier Generals Francis C. Barlow and John Gibbon. The old Third Corps divisions were those of Major General David B. Birney and Brigadier General Gershom Mott.

The consolidation deprived Brigadier General Alexander Hays of the division he had commanded at Gettysburg; he was assigned to command a brigade under Birney.

Glorious as was the record of Hancock's Second Corps, the old Third Corps soldiers wanted no part of it. They acquiesced resentfully in the consolidation. It was noticed that when Birney reviewed his division the men still wore the treasured "Kearny patch," the old Third Corps emblem, on their caps, and pinned the new Second Corps trefoil on their seats.[2]

Hays's division of the Second Corps was no better pleased over being merged and snuffed out. "The enemies of our country have, in times past, assailed it in vain," said Hays, "and now it dissolves by action of our own friends."[3]

The men of the division sensed misfortune in the air when they saw Hays go to corps headquarters upon the return of Hancock to the command. Crowds assembled to await him.

"When I announced the dissolution of 'our old pet,' " said Hays, "silence, and each lowered head spoke louder than words. . . ."[4]

The obstreperous Garibaldi Guards heard a rumor that Hays would return to his old brigade which he had left when he took the division. One of the soldiers was overheard to say, "Hell, old Hays is coming back and there won't be a man of us alive."[5] But a composite containing part of Kearny's old brigade petitioned for Hays and he went to it.

Lieutenant Morris Schaff, newly from West Point, chanced to be at Meade's headquarters when the Second Corps commander returned to the army for active duty.

"There's Hancock," someone said, as they saw him dismounting.[6]

Meade rushed hatless from his tent, his face, usually dour, lighted with pleasure, and in the deep rich voice that compensated amply for any number of other qualities lacking in his personality, welcomed his favorite subordinate, whom he had not seen since the cracker-box luncheon just before the great bombardment at Gettysburg.

"I'm glad to see you again, Hancock," he said, taking the general's extended hand in both of his own. It was about as near to a display of affection as Meade ever got and onlookers marveled at it.

Schaff, as had others, compared Hancock in appearance with Hooker, as "a very handsome, striking-looking man," who "moved grandly." He found Hancock "symmetrically large, with chestnut hair and rather low forehead, but authority was in his open face. . . ."[7]

Before the step-off into the Wilderness Colonel Theodore Lyman, Meade's staff officer, attended a review of the 5,000 men of Ward's and Hays's brigades of Birney's division and there for the first time saw the reviewing officer, Hancock. "He is a tall, soldierly man," wrote Lyman in a letter, "with light brown hair and a military heavy jaw; and has the massive features and the heavy folds round the eye that often mark a man of ability."[8]

After the review, the officers were invited to have a touch of whisky out of a bottle, and Lyman here met Sheridan, with whom Hancock would come into association during the approaching campaign. Lyman described the new chief of cavalry as "a small, broad-shouldered, squat man, with black hair and a square head. He is of Irish parents but looks like a Piedmontese. . . ."[9]

Grant had behind him for the 1864 campaign the most imposing army that had ever appeared on the continent and one of the most formidable to that time in the annals of war. Hancock's corps was the largest, aggregating on the day of the advance about 27,000 officers and men. Grant's entire army numbered 4,409 officers and 114,360 enlisted men, a total of 118,769,[10] an army which, in battle line two ranks deep and with one third in reserve, would extend twenty-one miles. His wagon train reached sixty-five miles. Meade retained command of the Army of the Potomac and issued orders, but Grant directed the operations through Meade—a clumsy arrangement unpleasant for Meade.

There was another peculiar feature of the organization, or lack of it. Burnside's Ninth Corps, an integral part of Grant's army, was still not a part of the Army of the Potomac, and was subject to Grant's, but not Meade's orders. Grant later had this corrected.

Lee's force in opposition, as calculated by the careful Federal General A. A. Humphreys, aggregated 61,953.[11] Disposed in two ranks with one third in reserve, it would form a battle line of twelve miles, nine miles short of Grant's line. Though an army on the offensive might move with stealth through the woods, such an advantage was partly offset by the ease with which the defenders could form barricades and ambuscades or concentrate in sudden limited attacks that would impede and frustrate the invader at every step.

Sleeping with the Chancellorsville Ghosts

Hancock's corps went first. The big Second Corps on Lone Tree Hill—a corps much larger than either army in the opening phases of this war or at any time in earlier American wars—awoke at midnight. At 2:00 A.M. on the morning of May 4, 1863, it marched through the woods, leaving the roadway open for War-

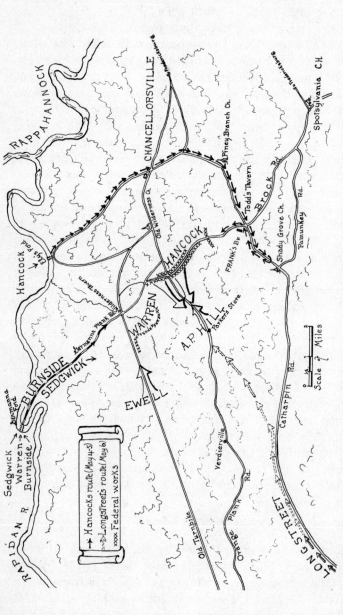

BATTLE OF THE WILDERNESS, May 5-6, 1864. Hancock's entrenched position along Brock Road just prior to his two-day battle with the corps of A. P. Hill and Longstreet. Longstreet, arriving on May 6, forced Hancock back to these trenches, from which he had launched his assault on Hill on May 5.

ren's Fifth Corps that moved abreast it. As dawn was breaking, Hancock's men reached the high northern bank of the Rapidan River at Ely's Ford. A pontoon bridge was laid quickly and the head of Grant's army began to enter the Wilderness.

"Hour after hour," said the observer Lieutenant Schaff, "this bridge pulsed with the tread of Hancock's twenty-seven thousand men, veterans of many fields." Then, as he reflected in later years on the scene: "Oh, gallant Second Corps, led on by Webb, Birney and Smyth; Hays, Brooke and Carroll; Miles, Barlow and Gibbon, my heart beats as I recall your deeds of valor!"[12]

After the crossing they marched down the country road, through "thickly sombre pines and surly oaks and by ragged forlorn openings"[13] to the old Chancellorsville battlefield. There the corps had stood as a rear guard in Hooker's retreat precisely one year before, to the day.

Hancock arrived with his staff at 9:30 A.M., and the last division of the corps was up at 3:00 P.M., having covered about twenty-three miles. The men carried rations for three days and fifty rounds, but did not expend a bullet. Lee offered no opposition to the crossing and the march through the woods proceeded in silence. Gregg, who screened the movement, took his cavalry south to the old Furnace Road, along which Jackson had passed on his march to Hooker's flank a year before. The Second Corps went into bivouac around Chancellorsville, with its pickets reaching out and maintaining contact with Warren's Fifth Corps on its right. While they slept the ghosts of countless old friends were about them.

At 5:00 A.M. the next morning, May 5, Hancock marched the Second Corps toward its assigned position at Shady Grove Church, moving southwest on the Catharpin Road. He was two miles past Todd's Tavern when at 9:00 A.M. orders came from Meade to halt at the tavern. The advance of Lee's army had been detected on the Turnpike.

The separate engagements on May 5 and 6, known as the battle of the Wilderness, were fought with the Federal army facing mainly west and the Confederates facing east. Grant, heading south, was assailed by Lee on his right flank and was forced to turn to his right and fight in the forests and underbrush. Artillery played small part. In few places were the clearings of sufficient size to allow it to be posted or given range.

The conflict, perhaps the most confused and disorganized of any in the war, though among the most stubborn and sanguinary of American history, was fought mainly along three roads, roughly parallel with one another and the Rapidan River to the north. Leading from west to east, these roads were the avenues employed by Lee in marching his army eastward and throwing it in separate attacks against Grant's flank. The road farthest north and nearest the Rapidan was the Orange-Fredericksburg Turnpike, or Old Turnpike. It ran substantially straight through the forest, passing Locust Grove, Old Wilderness Church and Chancellorsville. In accounts of the battle it is usually known as the Turnpike.

The first parallel road south meandered and at times was two and a half miles distant from the Turnpike. Known as the Plank Road, it ran from Orange, past Verdiersville and Parker's store, converged with the Turnpike at Wilderness Church, then left it at Chancellorsville and again ran parallel toward Fredericksburg. The third road, much farther south, was the Pamunkey Road. It merged into the Catharpin Road at Shady Grove Church, southwest of Chancellorsville, Hancock's objective when he resumed his march on May 5.

One road important to the battle cut across the west-east roads at right angles. This was the Brock Road, little better than a trail, which ran north and south. Near the Turnpike, with a jog, it merged into the Germanna Ford Road that led north to the Rapidan. During the battle the Germanna Ford Road marked roughly the line of the Federal Fifth and Sixth Corps under Warren and Sedgwick. Hancock's Second Corps, assisted by units from Burnside's Ninth Corps, occupied roughly the line of the Brock Road, extending south to the Catharpin Road.

Grant had hoped to get through the underbrush and fight in the open country to the south. But Lee had no intention of surrendering the defensive advantages of the Wilderness. When Lee's presence was discovered, Ewell's corps was marching east on the Turnpike and A. P. Hill—ill again and ineffectual as on the first day at Gettysburg—was moving abreast him on the Plank Road. Longstreet, far removed, had not yet reached the third of the parallel roads, the Catharpin Road to the south, where he would have encountered Hancock. As at Gettysburg, Lee had issued orders to Ewell and Hill not to bring on a general engagement before Longstreet arrived.

But Jones's brigade of Edward Johnson's division, Ewell's corps, advancing up the Turnpike, crashed into Griffin's division of Warren's Fifth Corps of Grant's army, and the battle could not be avoided. Meade and Grant were both confused at the outset, believing that Lee had merely left a division to fight a holding engagement while he prepared a defensive line behind the North Anna River farther south. But when Jones was driven back, Meade and Grant met solid resistance and recognized that they faced Lee's main army. Ewell not only pressed back Griffin, but Wadsworth's division of the Fifth Corps as well.

Hays Is Carried Out of the Woods

When it was clear to Grant that a battle had to be fought in the thickets, he ordered Hancock's corps to return to the junction of the Brock and Plank roads. Prior to Hancock's arrival, Getty's division of the Sixth Corps was in position on the Brock Road, where it had already sensed the approach of Hill's Confederates.

Thus the battle of the Wilderness began with Ewell fighting up the Turnpike against Sedgwick and Warren, and A. P. Hill, joined later by Longstreet, fighting up the Plank Road against Hancock. In most respects, two distinct battles were fought, almost as separate as though on different fields.

Hancock put his leading division, Birney's, into position on Getty's left, in two lines of battle. When Mott's and Gibbon's divisions arrived he extended them on the Brock Road on Birney's left and set all three divisions to work entrenching. Hancock's remaining division, Barlow's, was stationed on elevated ground on the far left, the only point in the line where artillery could be employed. Frank's brigade of Barlow's division was detached to cover the junction of the Brock and Catharpin roads. Soon Hancock had two formidable lines of log and earth breastworks running the entire length of his corps front along the Brock Road.[14]

At 2:30 P.M. he received word from Humphreys, Meade's chief of staff, that A. P. Hill's corps had driven in the Federal cavalry and was advancing up the Plank Road. Getty had been ordered to drive Hill back, and Humphreys said Hancock might have to send him assistance. Between 3:00 and 4:00 P.M. other orders followed for Hancock to attack with Getty down the Plank

Road toward Parker's store. Getty had already begun the attack, and Birney, commanding his own and Mott's division, went at once to his support.

The battle quickly became spirited. Hancock noted that "the lines . . . were exceedingly close, the musketry continuous and deadly along the entire line."[15] Carroll's brigade of Gibbon's division came to support Getty's right along the Plank Road, followed by "Paddy" Owen's Philadelphia brigade of the same division, and the fighting continued with great determination and heavy casualties in both armies.

Colonel Lyman gave an account of affairs around Grant's headquarters during the early fighting when Getty was attacking toward Parker's store. Grant sat on the grass and smoked a briarwood pipe, "looking sleepy and stern and indifferent." His smile was pleasing when he employed it and "that he believes in his star and takes a bright view of things is evident."[16]

Lieutenant Morris Schaff gave a description of Grant as he appeared at army headquarters. He was medium-sized, quiet, mild, unobtrusive, inconspicuously dressed. He possessed a "low, gently vibrant voice and steady, thoughtful, light blue eyes." Schaff could not detect in him any suggestion of impatience, restlessness or even self-consciousness, but, rather, the "pervasive quiet" about him seemed to communicate itself even to the orderlies.

Late in the afternoon Meade sent Colonel Lyman to Hancock on the army's left. Lyman took orderlies to carry reports to Meade on the progress of the fighting. He found Hancock at an intersection on the Plank Road, seated "on his fine horse—the *preux chevalier* of this campaign—a glorious soldier, indeed! The musketry was crashing in the woods, and stray balls—too many to be pleasant—were coming about." Lyman concluded that "it's all very well in novels, but *I* don't like such places. . . ."[17]

Most severely felt among the casualties in this early fighting was the loss of Brigadier General Alexander Hays, who commanded a brigade of Birney's division. He was carried back, covered with blood, only a few minutes after leading his men into the center of the fighting. Hays had called for reinforcements, but the army was still coming up and none was available.

Hancock replied, "I will send him a brigade in twenty minutes. Tell him to hold his ground. He can do it. I know him to be a powerful man."[18]

Lyman, who was apparently close by, described him as "a strong-built, rough sort of man, with red hair, and a tawny, full beard." The only wonder, he said, was that Hays had not been killed before, because "he always rode at the very head of his men, shouting to them and waving his sword."[19]

However rough he may have seemed to Lyman, Hays was a soldier of tender sentiments, as any officer must have been who remained one of Hancock's closest army friends, just as he had been closest when they were classmates at West Point. His warm, gentle nature was evident in the letter he wrote before going into the lines, mentioning the beauty of the morning, his last. He quoted:

> Lightly and brightly shone the sun,
> As if the morn was a jocund one.

Then he said:

Although we were anticipating a march at eight o'clock, it might have been an appropriate harbinger of the day of the regeneration of mankind; but it only brought to remembrance, through the throats of many bugles, that duty enjoined upon each one, perhaps, before the setting sun, to lay down a life for his country.[20]

Later, when Hancock could find time from his command duties, he wrote to Mrs. Hays in Pittsburgh. At his friend's passing the thing he recalled was the battle Hays had waged for him behind the Kosciuszko monument in the old days at West Point:

When I was a boy I once had a difficulty, and Alexander Hays was the first volunteer to assist me and in extricating me from my trouble became involved in the aforesaid difficulty himself. I never forgot his generous action on that occasion, and hoped some day to serve him. I never had the opportunity as to the time of his death he owed his prominence to his own good qualities.

He told her also that the army never had a more fearless soldier and said that to him "and to his reckless exposure of himself in times of greatest danger, I was often indebted to much of my success. . . ."[21]

Grant later visited Hays's grave in Pittsburgh. According to a press account, he "wept like a child."[22] He, too, had been a friend of Hays at West Point.

Darkness ended the battle of May 5 at about 8:00 P.M., with neither side having an advantage.

That night the Federal army lay along a line facing west, with Sedgwick's Sixth Corps on the right, and, down the line to the left, Warren's Fifth Corps, Burnside's Ninth and Hancock's Second.

For gallant service during the first day in the Wilderness, Hancock made especial mention of the Irish Brigade, commanded by Colonel Thomas A. Smyth, and Colonel John R. Brooke's brigade, both of Barlow's division, which attacked Hill's right flank and drove it back. Hancock was particularly proud of the performance of the Irish because four fifths of the brigade were recruits.[23]

Banes of the Philadelphia brigade, who found the Wilderness a gloomy "labyrinth of forests" filled often with tangled underbrush, told how the Second Corps lay exhausted that night "in the region of the shadow of death," after the fruitless struggle that had raged until darkness:

That night in the Wilderness will never fade from the memory of the survivors. When the noise of battle had entirely ceased, the contending forces, only separated by a few paces, were awaiting, like tigers in their lairs, the coming of day to spring upon each other; while all about the line were the dead and dying of both armies.[24]

Gibbon Falters When Victory Is Promised

As the morning of May 6 broke, the partridges were ahead of the bugles with their pert signaling of a new day of this glorious springtime. Dogwood bloomed and the cowslip hid in the deepest thickets. The day would be beautiful, cloudless. Soon the wild flowers would be trampled under the feet of the hostile armies, fighting a desperate war that few had wanted and few truly understood. Before 5:00 A.M. Hancock had his lines of attack formed, and promptly on the hour that Grant had ordered, Birney and Mott began their advance from the Brock Road into the thickets where the Confederates lurked.

Similar attack orders went to the other corps. Grant was a general of the offensive. Where Meade might have waited behind the entrenchments which shielded the entire Northern army, Grant would not yield the initiative to Lee.

Along with his orders, Hancock received an important warning. Longstreet's corps had been advancing up the Catharpin Road, which would bring it in on Hancock's left flank.[25] Hancock placed Barlow's division to guard the flank, stationed artillery to command the roadway, threw out a strong skirmish line and put General Gibbon in charge of the entire left of the corps, commanding both his own and Barlow's division. The corps was thus divided into two wings, with Birney commanding the right and Gibbon the left. They confronted Hill and awaited the arrival of Longstreet.

In compliance with Grant's orders, Hancock, at 5:00 A.M., had Birney begin the attack with his own and Mott's division, moving west on the Plank Road in concert with Wheaton, who had replaced the wounded Getty. Wheaton was supported by the brigades of Carroll and Owen. The fight was desperate but the Confederates soon began to yield ground.

Colonel Lyman of Meade's staff found Hancock on the Plank Road at 5:15 A.M., just as the Second Corps began its battle, and described him as "radiant."

"Tell General Meade," said Hancock, "we are driving them beautifully."[26]

The occasion was apparently what Meade had in mind when he remarked: "Bully Hancock is the only one of my corps commanders who always will go right in when I order him."[27]

Finally Hill's line broke in confusion, and Hancock's right wing advanced triumphantly through the woods for a mile and a half. Here it was necessary to re-form the line, made ragged by moving through the thickets. Here also Wheaton's fagged-out soldiers, who had been fighting for two days, were relieved by Alexander Webb's fresh brigade.[28]

It was 7:00 A.M. and a critical moment for the Federal army on the left. Hancock saw it as the great opportunity of the battle of the Wilderness. On the Confederate side the divisions of Heth and Wilcox, of Hill's corps, after wild and reckless fighting—some of the fiercest of the war, according to the Southern artillery man E. Porter Alexander—were thoroughly defeated. The fate of the Southern army depended on the arrival of Longstreet. Ewell was fighting obstinately farther north and was fully occupied by Warren and Sedgwick.

Hancock perceived that a splendid victory was within his grasp before the coming of Longstreet. By throwing a heavy force on Hill's right flank at a time when his front was shaky, he could roll up the corps on Ewell. At 7:00 A.M. Hancock sent a staff officer to Gibbon, followed by others, advising him of the victory already gained by the Second Corps and directing him to hurl Barlow's division against the enemy's right and press the attack toward the Plank Road.[29] Gibbon's failure to comply was never excused or forgotten by Hancock. He believed an invitation to rout Lee was wasted, a chance such as did not present itself frequently on the battlefields of this war.

Gibbon did send Frank's brigade, which felt the enemy's right and connected with Mott's left, but though it fought with much courage and enterprise, it was not in sufficient force to dislodge the Confederate line. Hancock thought Gibbon's fear of Longstreet's approach caused the inaction.[30] Whatever the reason, Barlow's fine division, the largest in the army, was, through no fault of the intrepid Barlow, left largely unemployed at the critical moment of the battle.

"Had my left advanced as directed by me in several orders," Hancock said, "I believe the overthrow of the enemy would have been assured." Again, in referring to the opportunity, he reiterated:

Had Frank's brigade been supported that morning by the remainder of Barlow's division the result must have been very disastrous to the enemy in his then scattered condition.[31]

Even without Gibbon's response, the battle of the Federal left had been going well for Hancock. He had struck Hill's advance, doubled it up and driven it for more than a mile, and for a time Lee's army was in great peril. Continual requests to Lee for help could be met only with the response that Longstreet was coming.

Longstreet was indeed on the last lap, on the run from Gordonsville, where Lee had left him, twenty-three miles from Wilderness Tavern, to guard against a crossing of the Rapidan by Grant farther upstream.

Hill's corps was so broken by Hancock's attack that Longstreet had to be diverted from Hancock's left, at which he was directing his march up the Catharpin Road, to retrieve the fortunes of the field along Hill's distressed front.

The failure of the battle from a Federal standpoint was that the attack on Hill could not be made conclusive.

Hancock had suffered from the lack of help expected from still another quarter. He had been told that Burnside would attack Hill's other flank with the Ninth Corps from Parker's store and sweep him from Hancock's front. Nothing was seen of any such attack by Burnside.[32]

"Old Peter" Staggers Mott's Division

Meantime Longstreet was now close at hand. He had only two of his veteran divisions, Kershaw's, which had been McLaws' at Gettysburg, and Field's, which had formerly been Hood's. They passed through Hill's disorganized ranks, free with their jibes at the soldiers who had retreated,[33] and struck the right flank of Mott's division, which Hancock felt would have been amply protected against such an assault had Gibbon not held the bulk of Barlow's division out of the action.[34]

Longstreet had come up the road and through the woods with what has been described as "a precision that was wonderfully beautiful," his men carrying their guns at "right shoulder shift."[35]

He made his way deftly to his point of attack in the woods. It might be said he had the law on his side, for he was guided by the sheriff of the county, who was familiar with every road and footpath.[36]

Longstreet's attack fell first on Frank's brigade, which alone had come from Barlow's division to assail Hill's right in compliance with Hancock's orders. The brigade had been waging a frenzied battle and was weakened and exhausted when struck by Longstreet's fresh troops, who, as Hancock explained it, "attacked with great vehemence."[37] They rolled over Frank's brigade and crushed it, then struck the left of Mott's division and threw it into confusion. Mott gave way in a twinkling and Longstreet next struck Birney, whose line was likewise broken.[38]

Apparently the first news at corps headquarters that Longstreet actually had arrived came from a Confederate prisoner. Those previously captured had been from Hill's corps. Then Lyman, suspicious, asked a prisoner if he was Longstreet's corps and the man answered, "Ya-as sir."[39] The hurried departure of Mott's men from the front told the story much more forcibly.

Banes of the Philadelphia brigade nearby thought Mott's rout "one of the strangest scenes of army experience." As he described it: the troops on his left, without any apparent cause that could be seen from the position of the Philadelphia brigade, began to give way and fall back toward the Brock Road.

Those pressing past the flank of the Second Division [Gibbon's] did not seem to be demoralized in manner, nor did they present the appearance of soldiers moving under orders, but rather of a throng of armed men returning dissatisfied from a muster.[40]

Some soldier might occasionally rush past terror-stricken, he said, "as if his life depended on speed." Mostly the retirement was deliberate. The officers were powerless to check the men. An officer hit a man across the back with the flat of his sword, but the frightened soldier merely thought it was another bullet.

Hancock and all his division and brigade commanders were unable to stem the rout. Said Banes:

No explanation can be given to this extraordinary affair, unless it might be that the rank and file were desirous of trying to take a new position on the Brock Road on their own responsibility, instead of "hammering continually" in the dense woods.[41]

Apparently it was the first show of dissatisfaction with Grant's costly attack methods, tactics with which the army had not been familiar since Burnside's attempt on the heights at Fredericksburg.

Everyone was willing to concede that Mott was among the bravest of officers. He had been wounded severely at both Second Manassas and Chancellorsville, and would be wounded even more critically before the end of the war. But banking rather than soldiering had been his profession and though he had been a junior officer in Mexico and a lieutenant colonel of New Jersey volunteers when Lincoln issued his first call, his wounds had kept him much away from the army and he obviously lacked experience in high command.

His grandfather, Captain John Mott, was the young officer who in the Revolutionary War guided Washington at the crossing of the Delaware and the march on Trenton. Gershom Mott had been collector of the port at Lamberton, New Jersey, and a banker in Bordentown before he answered Lincoln's call. His personal courage and conduct of his regiment at Second Manassas won him promotion to be a brigadier general of volunteers.

Grant was not impressed with Mott's generalship, but army opinion tended to the view that the division broke because it had been pushed around in the reorganization.[42] Colonel Lyman found the change in the division's morale curious:

It is Hooker's old fighting division, but has since been under two commanders of little merit or force of character; then there was some discontent about re-enlistments and about the breaking up of the old Third Corps, to which it had belonged; and the result has been that most of this crack division has conducted itself most discreditably.[43]

Thus the division that had been outstanding at Antietam was the main failure in the Wilderness.

Longstreet quoted Hancock as saying to him after the war: "You rolled me up like a wet blanket and it was some hours before I could reorganize for battle."[44]

The confusion was caused not only by the retreat, but by reinforcements crowding in from the rear, by wagon trains and horses, the mixing of commands, all a tangle that Hancock could unravel only with great difficulty.

Hancock hoped that he could recess his left and hold a line along the Plank Road, thereby preserving a part of the ground he had gained from Hill, but he found the troops too disorganized and close to exhaustion for anything but retirement. On the advice of Birney he pulled back the steady elements still making a stand in front of Longstreet and re-established his line along the entrenchments he had left when he began his advance against Hill. Longstreet's men pressed forward to within a few hundred paces of the breastworks, then halted and made no move toward an assault. Hancock next notified Meade of the effect of Longstreet's attack and advised that he had reoccupied his line along the Brock Road.

What slowed the Confederate attack at an unhappy moment for Lee was the critical wounding of Longstreet, shot by his own men, as Jackson had been a year earlier on almost the same ground. Hancock was given a respite of several hours to re-form his lines and strengthen his log and earth defenses.

During this period, while the Confederates were lethargic in his

front, he executed a surprising movement with a single brigade led
by Colonel Daniel Leasure, lent from the Ninth Corps, which
showed the paralysis that had come over the Confederate army due
to the wounding of Longstreet. Leasure moved from Gibbon's position on Hancock's left, entirely across the fronts of Mott's and
Birney's divisions, driving off a Confederate brigade in disorder.
He reached the Plank Road, then fell back again to his place
in the line.[45]

The Flames Are Allies of the Enemy

But Hancock's difficulties were not ended. Lee sent Anderson's
fresh division against his line.[46] The Confederates advanced again
at 4:15 P.M., halted at the edge of the abatis a hundred paces in
front of Hancock's first works, and poured in a heavy musketry
fire which they sustained for half an hour, causing some of the
Federals to waver.

Next part of Mott's division and Ward's brigade of Birney's division gave way and fled in disorder toward Chancellorsville. Hancock and his staff exerted their best efforts to rally the routed
soldiers and did bring some of them back into line, but others
could not be recovered until the end of the battle.

An officer came to Hancock with the news: "General Mott's
division has broken, sir, and is coming back."

"Tell him to stop them, sir!" Hancock shouted. Even then
Mott's troops—old Third Corps men not yet adjusted to being a
part of the Second—were streaming out of the woods.

Hancock was everywhere. "Halt here! Halt here!" he commanded, pointing to a new line. "Form behind this rifle pit. Major
Mitchell, go to Gibbon and tell him to come up on the double
quick."[47]

Soon the watchers saw Carroll's brigade coming at the head of
Gibbon's division, Sprigg Carroll riding in front "as calm as a May
morning."

When Mott's division gave way, Carroll was angered and disgusted, as was Hancock. He too rode among the fleeing men
shouting, "For God's sake stand your ground. Don't leave my men
to fight the whole rebel army."[48] It accomplished nothing.

Mott's second break was unusual in that it occurred from fire

superiority alone, delivered by the Confederates from among the
abatis against the Federals behind earthworks. When the Federals
were seen leaving their line the Southern troops pushed forward
into the breach, entered Hancock's lines and planted some of their
flags on the breastworks.[49] But their numbers were limited. Carroll's brigade, coming forward at a run, re-established the line,
killed a few Confederates who remained inside the breastworks and
forced back those who were firing from the abatis in front of the
line. Hancock noted that the enemy abandoned the attack "in
great disorder, with heavy loss. . . ."[50] If any one brigade could
be credited with having saved the Federal position on more than
one occasion in the Wilderness, it was Carroll's, whose night attack
at Gettysburg also had ousted the North Carolinians and Louisiana
Tigers from their lodgment amid the Federal cannon on Cemetery
Hill.

Samuel Sprigg Carroll, one of Hancock's best subordinates, was
a native of the District of Columbia, son of the clerk of the Supreme
Court, William Thomas Carroll, and a great-grandnephew of
Charles Carroll of Carrollton. He was graduated at West Point in
1856, a friend and classmate of Fitzhugh Lee, but after some
service in the 10th Infantry he was pocketed in the early stages of
the war with the assignment of quartermaster at West Point. He
got field duty at last, in time to perform as well as one could in
Shields's division against Stonewall Jackson. Next he rose to the
command of a brigade in the Third and later the Second Corps.
His red hair had led his West Point friends to call him "Brick."

Hancock attributed the disorganization in Mott's and Birney's
command to the spectacular fire that broke out in the woods in
their front. It developed into one of the most disconcerting elements of the battle, because of the intense heat.[51] "Flames spread
so rapidly," said Banes, "that the breastworks were soon enveloped."[52] The two armies fought back and forth through and
around the flames, but darkness finally ended the combat for Hancock's men.

The emotional De Trobriand saw the full drama of the battle
against both forest fire and enemy bullets. The Confederates happened to have what the sailors would term the weather gauge on
the fire, as the wind carried smoke and flames to Hancock's lines.
"The enemy took advantage of the accident," said the Frenchman,

"to charge home at that point. They literally fought in the midst of the fire, the flames licking the legs of the combatants."[53] Carroll's arrival had been the deciding factor. After the enemy was pushed back the fire ran its course.

The battle ended that night. Through the woodland in front of the entrenchments the ground was covered with the bodies of blue-clad soldiers wearing the trefoil badge. The Confederate Allen Redwood said, "In the dense woods bordering the Orange Plank-road the clover leaves lay thick."[54] As on the night before, neither side had gained an advantage.

Throughout the next day each army awaited the other's move.

Lee Expects Grant at Spotsylvania

The unanswered question about the battle was whether Hancock, had Gibbon complied with his orders, could have rolled up Hill's corps on Ewell and driven Lee's army from the field before the arrival of Longstreet. Some who have written about the battle have believed that he could. That was his own judgment.

His relations with Gibbon showed here the first evidences of the strain that later caused him to request Gibbon to find another assignment. When Hancock wrote his report, in February 1865, he made a frank statement of Gibbon's failure, as he understood it, but credited him with partial compliance with the orders by sending Frank's brigade. The dispatch of this brigade was a hard point for Gibbon to explain when in later years he took sharp exception to Hancock's report and implied that he had received no attack orders at all.[55] Why, then, had he sent Frank? Unquestionably he offered his sincere convictions, as did those who supported Hancock.

In the long controversy that followed and that trailed off into an exchange mainly between Gibbon and a member of Hancock's staff, Gibbon's contentions became a bit strained. He had been stirred, it seemed, because books that were appearing, by General Humphreys and by the war correspondent William Swinton, tended to accept Hancock's view. The facts seem clear. The staff members attested that they delivered Hancock's orders, and it was obvious to all that Barlow's division was not thrown into the battle as directed. Eighteen years passed before Gibbon challenged

Hancock's report and claimed the charges contained in it had been made clandestinely.[56]

Anyone would have to agree that whatever Hancock may have said in an official report could scarcely be regarded as clandestine.

Grant's able generalship shown on other fields was not apparent in the Wilderness, else he might have detected and taken advantage of the great gap between Ewell and the corps of A. P. Hill, a gap Lee had to risk because he was trying to contain the Federal army with only half Grant's numbers. Lieutenant Colonel Charles S. Venable of Lee's staff rode across the gap—he called it an interval of half a mile or more—and the only activity he discovered in it was two Federal soldiers "who had found it easier to desert to the front than to the rear."[57]

Lee's gamble of sending Longstreet to attack Hancock, by which he hoped to take the Federals in flank and drive them back across the Rapidan, was more of a risk than the Union leaders comprehended. A more conservative general would have used Longstreet to plug the hole. But Lee, and many others, always felt they would have achieved a great victory had not Longstreet fallen at the critical moment. Nobody but "Old Peter" could get the full effectiveness out of his corps.

The Confederates missed a similar opportunity to drive into a gap in the Federal line when Sedgwick's Sixth Federal Corps was found isolated on the Federal army's right. Gordon's Confederates were delayed by Ewell's timidity, then were unable to exploit the opportunity in the little daylight remaining after Lee learned of the possibility and issued an attack order over the head of the reluctant Ewell.[58]

At the end of the fighting it could be seen that Grant's campaign had not opened auspiciously. Said General Alexander S. Webb:

From personal contact with the regiments who did the hardest fighting, I declare that the individual men had no longer that confidence in their commanders which had been their best and strongest trait during the past year.[59]

Many of the Confederates thought the Federal army had been so severely handled that Grant, unable to advance, would be compelled to retreat. Lee at once countered this suggestion. "General

Grant is not going to retreat," he said. "He will move his army to Spotsylvania."

Gordon asked him if he had intelligence about Grant's intentions.

"Not at all. Not at all," Lee repeated, "but that is the next point at which the armies will meet. Spotsylvania is now General Grant's best strategic point. I am so sure of his next move that I have already made arrangements to march by the shortest practicable route, that we may meet him there."[60]

* * * 13 * * *

Spotsylvania Break-through

A Toilsome March Through the Night

Hancock was awake all of the night of May 11, 1864, marching and posting his men. Rain fell incessantly, making bogs of the Virginia trails crossing the rolling country south of the Wilderness. He had to work in deep, palpable blackness, and quietly, because the movement of the large body of troops had to be shielded from alert enemy sentries posted outside the Southern fortifications.

Grant had not issued his orders for the Second Corps to attack the Spotsylvania salient until 3:00 P.M. and Meade had not forwarded them until 4:00 P.M. Yet late as they were delivered, they were specific about the hour for the assault—4:00 A.M., with no cushion of time that would allow the corps commander discretion.

Why had Grant designated the Second Corps, three divisions of which lay on the army's right flank, for an attack that was to be made in the center? The corps would have to march across the rear of Sedgwick's and Warren's corps and come into line on the right of Burnside. Certainly it would appear more reasonable to entrust the attack to Burnside, since he was already in position alongside one face of the salient.

The answer could be found in Hancock's performance on the recent days in the Wilderness, where he had demonstrated again his pre-eminent ability to conduct large-scale movements. For an instant it seemed he had a great victory in his grasp, if he had been able to get a prompt and full response out of his division commander Gibbon. Still, even with no victory to offer Grant, in most respects the Second Corps had preserved in the thickets the reputation it had won on the open hillsides and among the boulders at Gettysburg. Here, in front of Spotsylvania, the Hancock of Williamsburg, Fredericksburg and Gettysburg was the leader Meade and now Grant recognized as one who could get the most from the men, however tough the assignment. He, not Burnside, would have to supply the shock in this assault to crush Lee's center.

Hancock's four divisions were reunited for the attack. Mott already was near the salient, where he had been feeling the Confederate lines gingerly, to find them unyielding. The night march was made by the divisions of Barlow, Birney and Gibbon. Gibbon would be in reserve and Mott in a second line. The impact would be delivered by the divisions of Barlow and Birney.

Barlow had been a newspaper reporter on the New York *Tribune* and then a New York lawyer before he was a soldier. He had gradually established himself as one of the army's most spirited division commanders, which may have accounted for the fact that his division was the largest. He had appeared to be breathing his last when Confederate General John B. Gordon found him on the Gettysburg battlefield. Fortune had accompanied him not only in his recovery, but also in the reassignment to go with Hancock in place of his old commander Howard. He had fought in the ranks as a private at First Manassas, and now the day's work on which he was about to engage at Spotsylvania would make him a major general.

Slight, youthful, close-shaven, he compensated for an apparent immaturity—the men called him the "boy general"—with a feverish enthusiasm that imparted ardor and zeal to those about him. Colonel Theodore Lyman of Meade's staff noted his enterprise, said he looked like a mounted newsboy. While Hancock was nearly always immaculate in a fresh white shirt—other officers often wondered how he could provide himself with a constant supply of clean ones— Barlow in the 1864 campaign wore a big-checked flannel that was not very fastidious for an officer of high rank and a Harvard honor student.

His trousers were "threadbare" and his blue cap battered. For side arms he carried a big, incongruous cavalry saber instead of the more conventional rapier. The expression on his young face usually was a smile, curled at times with a boyish cynicism. But "it would be hard to find a general officer to equal him or Joe Hayes, both my classmates," Lyman, another Harvardian, concluded.[1] With that opinion Hancock concurred. Hancock naturally would trust Barlow's men. This was his old division which he had commanded at Antietam, Fredericksburg and Chancellorsville.

Barlow would form the division in what was termed two lines of masses, which piled up much weight and meant in practical effect that the ranks would close during the advance and the men would attack in one solid, impetuous body.[2] The brigades of Colonels Nelson A. Miles and John R. Brooke would form Barlow's front, while the Irish Brigade under Colonel Thomas A. Smyth and the brigade of Colonel Henry W. Brown (formerly Frank's) would make the second line.

The niggardly Lincoln-Stanton promotion policy still existed as the war entered its fourth year; it had left brigade commanders colonels, though they had proved their capacity in some of the hardest battles of history. Capable division commanders remained brigadier generals. Corps commanders were major generals or in instances even lower in rank. Colonels commanded all of Barlow's brigades, though few would deny that such men as Brooke, Miles and Smyth rated higher commissions in recognition of their services at Chancellorsville, Gettysburg or in other desperate encounters.

While Congress retained control over the number of general officers, President Lincoln does not appear to have made any spirited fight, or transmitted any formal written recommendation whatever, to ease the situation and have the promotion policy overhauled and liberalized. It remained in sharp contrast with the more realistic policies followed by the Confederate government and by the United States under Presidents Woodrow Wilson, Franklin Roosevelt and Truman in the two World Wars, of awarding rank commensurate with performance and responsibility.

On Barlow's right, Birney's division would be deployed in two lines of battle, and Mott would be deployed in one line behind Birney. With Gibbon left in general reserve, the formation gave the main role in the crash-through to Barlow and his two front brigades.

Nobody doubted young Miles, whose career had been spectacular. He had studied the military arts at the school of the French colonel, Salignac, in Boston, while working as clerk in a pottery store, and when the war came he had raised a company that had been incorporated in the 22nd Massachusetts Volunteers. He became a lieutenant, being regarded too young for a captaincy. Even before he could overcome the handicap he proved the error of the judgment. Severely wounded on the Peninsula, at Fredericksburg, and in the gallant fight he made with his skirmishers on the army's left at Chancellorsville, he was now, at the age of twenty-four, confronted with his most difficult assignment.

Brooke, who would attack abreast Miles, was from Hancock's home county, Montgomery; he had entered as a captain of the 4th Pennsylvania Volunteers and by the time of the Peninsular campaign was a colonel of the 53rd Pennsylvania. As we have seen, he made the farthest advance with his regiment against the stone wall in front of Marye's Heights at Fredericksburg. Thereafter he commanded a brigade. Leading it he had managed to survive on the second day at Gettysburg, when his fellow brigade commanders of Caldwell's division, Zook and Cross, were being shot down during Hancock's rescue of Sickles' corps. He had been wounded at the fag end of Longstreet's assault. Another, much more serious wound would come to him at Cold Harbor.

Grant had sent his staff engineer, Lieutenant Colonel Cyrus B. Comstock, along with some junior officers, to make a reconnaissance of the ground in front of the salient and to guide Hancock in the placement of his troops. But Comstock got lost and reached the Brown House in front of the Confederate lines just as night was falling, too late for much examination of the terrain.[3] Then it was found that the Confederate skirmishers were far out in front and Grant's engineer and his helpers could not get close enough to survey the works. They could see the red clay of the freshly thrown up parapets here and there through the woods. Comstock was compelled to designate the positions for the columns of attack without positive information about the extent or depth of the fortifications or the meandering line they followed along the crest of the ridge.

In spite of all the difficulties, Barlow and Birney after a march of two hours reached the Brown House by 1:00 A.M.[4] Barlow called it a "laborous and tiresome march" through the dark over the heavy and muddy roads.[5] Though staff engineers were supposed to guide, Miles and Brooke rode ahead of their brigades and

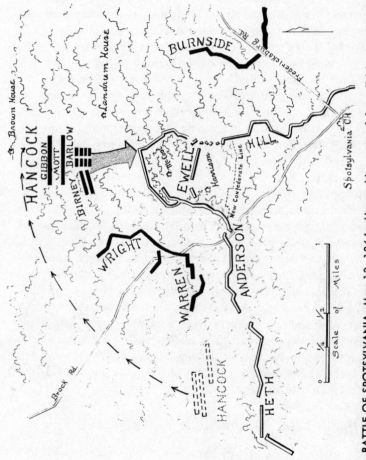

BATTLE OF SPOTSYLVANIA, May 12, 1864. Hancock's corps of four divisions poised
for dawn assault on "mule shoe" salient of Lee's fortifications.

were outspoken in criticism of the madness of such night enterprises. The young Barlow, for reasons he did not explain, said it
all seemed so ludicrous he could hardly sit on his horse for laughter.

Then Hancock's chief of staff, Colonel Morgan, rated almost as
deft with oaths as Hancock, arrived, and Barlow took up the criticism. "For Heaven's sake," he told the staff officer, "at least face
us in the right direction, so we shall not march away from the
enemy and have to go round the world and come up in their rear."[6]

A young West Point officer, Major George Henry Mendell of the
Topographical Engineers, took on the piloting assignment and conducted the divisions skillfully through the night. When they came
to what was described to Barlow as the base for the attack—the
Brown House—the men were allowed to sleep three hours, time
which the officers utilized in preparing for the step-off. Lieutenant
Colonel Waldo Merriam, who would live until sunup, had been on
the ground with Mott's division and helped Comstock align the
assault columns.

Between the Brown House, where Hancock formed, and the
enemy works was high ground on which stood the white Landrum
House, a barrier because it was held by Southern skirmishers, and
therefore an obstacle of much disadvantage to a surprise attack.

Daylight was beginning to show faintly when Hancock's preparations were completed.[7] The rain had stopped but the country was
covered with heavy fog. In the wooded areas the water dripped
heavily from the trees. At 4:00 A.M. Hancock was ready, but in
the dense fog and semidarkness the forward movement likely would
become hopelessly confused. The soldiers could not discern objects
in their front.[8] So he took the responsibility of holding the columns
until he had more daylight. Finally, at 4:35 A.M. he ordered Barlow and Birney to advance.

Lee Has the Guns Withdrawn

The night of May 11 had been one of high activity and deep
misfortune in Lee's army. In the part of the army removed from
his immediate supervision, the day had brought one of the heavy
losses of the war. Jeb Stuart with the cavalry had fought at Yellow
Tavern. That night Stuart lay in agony in Richmond, unwilling to
touch whisky even though told it would relieve his suffering.

Lee would not know of Stuart's death until the twelfth,[9] but he was concerned on the evening of the eleventh over indications that the Federal army was shifting its position in his front.

When Lee laid out his Spotsylvania lines after the hurried race with Grant from the Wilderness, he was confronted with the problem—not uncommon on battlefields of this war—of the existence of high ground in his front. A moderate elevation north of the town would prove advantageous to the Northern artillery, and the Confederate general decided to embrace it within his lines, though it created a salient roughly half a mile wide at its base and 400 yards at its front, and three quarters of a mile deep.

The men labored diligently on the trenches and soon had built well-engineered works. The large clearing of the Landrum farm lay immediately in front of the apex of the salient, with woods opposite the two faces, in which the enemy might find concealment.

Because of its shape the men dubbed the salient the "Acorn," the "Horse Shoe" or the "Mule Shoe," which, after the battle, was changed to "Hell's Hole," "Death Angle" or more often to the "Bloody Angle," the most famous of all the bloody angles of the war.[10] The line of Lee's trenches followed the crest of a spur jutting north from the ridge on which Spotsylvania was located. Though any salient is inherently weak, well-posted artillery gave the Mule Shoe great strength.

The village of Spotsylvania, settled because the Germanna iron works of colonial days were not far removed, had been named for the governor of Virginia who owned the surrounding grant: the Scotch soldier, Alexander Spotswood, who had fought in celebrated battles on the staff of the Duke of Marlborough, then, turning to the arts of peace, had emigrated to America and sought to bless Virginia by introducing the skylark.[11] While few if any of the skylarks that made up the shipload survived, some Virginians who lived in the Civil War era fancied they could still hear at times the joyous notes of this marvelous bird. But Spotswood's name would survive to be identified not with ornithology, but with one of the greatest carnivals of blood and death in the record of this sanguinary war—all because Lee elected to hold the Mule Shoe and because Grant, smarting under the reverses in the Wilderness and recognizing the superiority of his numbers, wanted to hit the hostile army a blow in its center that would destroy the illusion of Lee's invincibility.

From reports that Lee received as he went over his lines on

May 11, he concluded that he would not have to sustain another offensive in his Spotsylvania position. The several attacks already made had been beaten off. Young Emory Upton, a brigade commander in Grant's Sixth Corps, had been able to effect a lodgment in the works for a time on May 10, but had been compelled to withdraw when Mott's division failed to support him. The next morning, May 11, Grant, before ordering Hancock to attack at dawn on May 12, sent to the War Department his celebrated dispatch that he proposed "to fight it out on this line if it takes all summer."

Lee had formed a different conclusion and judged that after Upton had been ousted and assaults elsewhere had failed, Grant was moving toward Fredericksburg, an impression he gained from both his infantry on his right and his cavalry patrols reaching to Grant's rear. Lee's main aim was to preserve celerity of movement so that he might strike Grant on the move and defeat him in battle, for Lee distrusted his ability to stand a long siege. Recognizing that the army might have to move quickly to the right to counter Grant in that direction, Lee ordered that the guns defending the salient—posted mainly in the woods from which a quick withdrawal would be difficult—should be drawn back into the town and made ready for the march anticipated on the morrow. He had the men continue strengthening the trenches and as a precaution constructed a second line in rear of the Mule Shoe, which he did not expect to employ.

What followed was the old story of being once off guard. The artillery, twenty-two guns that could sweep the approaches to the salient across the Landrum House clearing, was pulled back into Spotsylvania early that evening, leaving the small arms of Major General Edward Johnson's infantry division the only custodians of the salient.

Johnson, like George E. Pickett and Ulysses S. Grant, had been in the bottom files at West Point and, like Pickett and Grant, had shown in the Mexican War an aptitude for fighting. He had been cited twice for gallant conduct, then had remained in the regular army until the states seceded. A native of Kentucky, he had elected to side with the South.

A wound taken in Mexico had affected a nerve and deprived him of full control of the eyelid, and he would wink spasmodically under stress. Another wound received while fighting under Jackson in the Shenandoah Valley left him with a stiff leg which caused him to limp and carry a round-headed cane heavy enough to earn the title of "Clubby" Johnson. Though he could not be sympathetic with Grant as the enemy commander in his immediate front, he had followed with delight his old friend's rise in the Western armies and commented on it frequently, claiming responsibility for the rescue when Grant was on the liquor skids.[12]

Steuart's Staff Officers Hear Strange Sounds

Johnson was one of Lee's readiest fighters, as he had proved by his unabating, bloody attacks on Culp's Hill at Gettysburg, but his division had been wasted to about half strength.

Mule Shoe as a term was not an accurate description of the salient. It would imply a curved front, whereas the front actually ran in almost a straight line and faced north, then bent back at a right angle and faced east. Three of Edward Johnson's brigades were stationed along the straight front of the salient. Walker's Stonewall Brigade was on the far left, joining with Rode's division on its left; then came Stafford's Louisiana brigade and Jones's Virginia brigade. The last reached to the point of the right angle. On the right of Jones, where the lines turned back sharply and faced east, was the brigade commanded by the pious Marylander, George H. Steuart, a mixed Virginia and North Carolina brigade. What was to all effects a gap existed on Steuart's right. Only pickets covered a space about a mile in length to where A. P. Hill's corps was stationed under command of Jubal Early.

Both Jones and Stafford had been killed in the Wilderness and the brigades were not accustomed to new leadership. In Jones's brigade in particular, the men were reported to be dispirited by the loss of their warmly admired leader and by the heavy casualties suffered when the brigade was broken in the Wilderness. The four brigades averaged about 1,000 men in the trenches, giving Edward Johnson an over-all strength of about 4,000.

While opinions about Lee's divisions vary greatly, Johnson's has been termed by competent authority the best of the Southern army.[13] More than any other element it carried on the tradition of splendid achievements and the aura given it by old Stonewall.

The ground in Steuart's front was heavily wooded with pine and oak and was crossed by small ravines, while at the angle a cleared strip sloped gently toward and beyond the Landrum House that stood less than a quarter of a mile in front of the works. Steuart's skirmishers were out all of May 11 without encountering evidences of the Federals excepts pickets on the left side of the angle.

When in the early evening the men in the salient saw the artillery limber up and move off, the matter was discussed with uneasiness, mainly because a salient, while allowing infantry fire from the two sides, does not permit the two lines to cover the ground immediately in front of the angle. The angle, here, being on high ground and having a clearing in its front, provided a good position for artillery, as did other points in the salient, but made a poor defensive station for infantry.

General Steuart went to sleep early on the night of May 11, but Major McHenry Howard and another officer of his staff walked out in front of the lines and then stood on the breastworks listening to low undercurrents of noise coming, despite Hancock's efforts at stealth, from the Federals. Howard said the sounds were "plainly audible on the still, heavy night air, like distant falling water."

Convinced that the salient would be attacked in force at dawn, the staff officers went to Steuart's tent, aroused him and had him send a message to Edward Johnson. This message said there was every probability that the Federals were massing along Johnson's front and requested that the artillery be returned immediately. Steuart then prepared a circular to the regimental commanders of his brigade. He sent it around that night and secured endorsements from each regiment. It stated that the brigade probably would be attacked and directed the colonels to have their men ready in the trenches half an hour before daylight.

But getting the guns back was found a more difficult operation than getting them out. By the time the requests and orders had cleared—from Steuart to Johnson to Ewell and then to the chief of corps artillery, Colonel Armistead Long, and on to the battalion commander Major Richard C. M. Page—most of the night had passed. It was 4:00 A.M. before the guns were rolling toward the Mule Shoe. It seemed likely that by daylight they would be in position to sweep the approaches.

Hancock's Men Crash Through the Lines

When Hancock at 4:35 A.M. gave the signal to advance, Barlow's and Birney's divisions moved abreast, though Birney's men had to make supreme efforts to push over the rough ground and through the wet pines while Barlow marched mainly down the clearing. Barlow's order was not to fire a shot during the advance, yet when they approached near enough to see the Confederate works before them in the fog, they let out a shout and rushed forward. Without any orders for the double-quick, the mass of men came on the run. Silence was no longer of any purpose, but still not a gun was fired. Some went through the abatis; others tore it away with their hands.[14] The section of trenches Hancock hit was only 400 yards wide.

The brigades of Miles and Brooke crowded over the parapet, bayoneting and clubbing as they went. The defenders, in spite of all the warnings through the night, were paralyzed by the great masses of blue soldiers suddenly falling on them. Birney was in the works at about the same moment.

Barlow said the attack began quietly, then the men broke into a run and began to cheer. They reached the enemy works in five minutes, but there was much uncertainty in later recollections as to just what happened in those five minutes. Miles thought the loss was heavy before they hit the Confederate lines; Barlow believed it was negligible. He saw only three or four fall.

As his men plunged ahead in the fog, Hancock, his battle spirits roused, sensed the tang of victory in the damp air and burst out: "I know they will not come back! They will not come back!"

Barlow and Birney struck the Virginia regiments of Jones's brigade, plunged through their line and forward until they had enveloped both Steuart's brigade on their left and Jones's, Stafford's and Walker's on their right. Steuart had his men face to the rear in an effort to beat off the masses of the enemy who had broken through. The Federals, "crazed with excitement," "could not be restrained"[15] and quickly overran a mile of the Confederate trenches, capturing the greater part of Edward Johnson's splendid division. The returning Confederate artillery which the gunners were trying to get into position was captured intact.

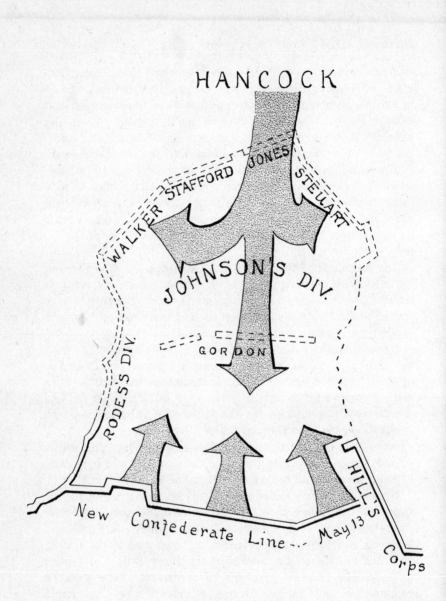

BATTLE OF SPOTSYLVANIA, May 12, 1864, showing Hancock's break-through at point of salient held by Jones's brigade and his envelopment and capture of Edward Johnson's division of Ewell's corps.

One Confederate gun was about to fire when someone close in the rear commanded, "Don't fire that piece."[16] The gunners looked around into the face of a Federal officer backed by hundreds of blue-coated soldiers with fixed bayonets. This gun, with the rest of the artillery, was scooped up and hauled back, though a North Carolina officer kept firing at the horses hoping to immobilize the artillery.

Colonel Hamilton A. Brown of the 1st North Carolina, Steuart's brigade, the regiment that had captured the Culp's Hill trenches at Gettysburg, was on the immediate right of Jones's Virginians when Hancock's main impact hit that brigade. Later he said:

The terrific onslaught of this vast multitude was irresistible, there being a rectangular mass of twenty thousand Federal troops, not in line of battle, but in column of regiments . . . supported by a division on each flank. . . . The clash of arms and the murderous fire around the bloody angle are indescribable.[17]

The blow struck not only Jones but the 1st North Carolina, Steuart's left regiment. Thirty of this regiment managed to extricate themselves; the others were captured. The colonel was captured and recaptured three times in the melee, the last time by his own men. After that the 1st North Carolina was no more than a company.

Immediately to the right of the 1st North Carolina, the 3rd North Carolina Regiment was captured almost in its entirety.[18] What remained was consolidated into the company with the 1st North Carolina, and sent into Cox's brigade, which fired the last shots at Appomattox.

Sergeant John H. Worsham, of the 21st Virginia, Jones's brigade, thought the capture of Johnson's division was a body blow to Lee's army:

This was Jackson's old division, and those were the men who had done so much fighting, and who had made those wonderful marches for him. . . . Jackson's old division was annihilated, and ceased to be a division from that date.[19]

Steuart's men maintained their brigade was not surprised, but it might as well have been. The Confederates here heard the shout of Barlow's division, then picket firing, and soon blue soldiers appeared in front of the trenches. A volley drove off this party; perhaps they had merely missed the angle and were coming down the outside instead of inside the works. Meantime the vivacity of the firing increased in the direction of Jones. Suddenly masses of blue infantry came down on Steuart from inside the angle and the line of trenches. Steuart's men saw the enemy overrun completely all the ground inside the salient. An officer backed by a line of bayonets demanded their surrender and, surrounded and vastly outnumbered, they threw down their arms. Major Howard noticed as he was being marched to the rear that a dense crowd of Federals was pressing up to the lines and into the salient. "I never saw an occasion when artillery would have done such execution," he said.

The fault, he felt, was not that the Confederates were surprised; it was in the shape of the entrenchments, the thinness of the defending line, the absence of supports on the immediate right of Johnson's division and the fatal absence of the artillery. Hancock had indeed attacked at the fortunate moment when the guns were gone, but it is not uncommon in warfare that, when a movement has been well prepared, luck also comes to its aid.

Banes of the Philadelphia brigade said some of the Confederates cried, "Yanks, you have got us this time," then surrendered.[20] One man wounded close in front of a Federal officer protested, "I am sorry that you shot me. I was coming to take the oath of allegiance." The officer said he had no copies with him but could offer a little whisky as a substitute.

"That will do as well," the wounded man agreed.[21]

Banes saw a Northern Irishman trying to fire a cannon with its muzzle elevated at 45 degrees. Someone told him to depress it, but he was elated with the multiplicity of targets. "Nivar fare, it's bound to come down on somebody's head," he declared.[22]

When the attack of Barlow and Birney was at its height, the excitement infected Carroll's brigade and the Philadelphia brigade under Owen, both of Gibbon's division. Though they were in reserve, they charged ahead and entered the works immediately behind Miles and Brooke. They were followed by McAllister's brigade which likewise, wildly excited, broke away from Mott and plunged forward.[23]

General Lee Shouted to the Rear

Brigadier General John B. Gordon, who commanded the Confederate supporting line deep in the salient, had stationed vedettes at various points to listen through the night for unusual noises. Between 4:30 and 5:00 A.M. one returned hurriedly and reported: "General, I think there's something wrong down in the woods near where General Edward Johnson's men are."

Gordon asked why he thought so, saying there had been no unusual firing.

"No, sir," said the scout, "there's been very little firing. But I tell you, sir, there are mighty strange sounds down there—something like officers giving commands, and a jumble of voices."[24]

Even before Gordon could saddle his horse a succession of couriers followed, bearing tidings of the disaster to Edward Johnson. Gordon found it difficult to believe the reports because there had been so little battle turmoil. But when he investigated he found that, as he stated it, "the surprise was complete and the assault practically unresisted."

"In all its details—its planning, its execution, and its fearful import to Lee's army—this charge of Hancock was one of that great soldier's most brilliant achievements," he said.[25]

Gordon ordered his troops into position and rode toward the captured salient, accompanied by Brigadier General Robert Johnston, whose North Carolina brigade followed. Along with Gordon's, it held the incompleted second line and had been in bivouac at the Harrison House, half a mile behind the works. Hancock had advanced so rapidly and silently that before these Confederate reserves were halfway to the front line they crashed into the solid advance of Barlow and Birney.

"The sudden and unexpected blaze from Hancock's rifles made the dark woodland strangely lurid," Gordon said.[26] His own brigade was on the left, so the first resistance to Hancock's oncoming tide was offered by Johnston's Carolinians.

Johnston at Gordon's side was severely wounded but his brigade, though confused, did not break. Twice as the brigade continued forward Federal line officers stepped to within ten paces of it and demanded its surrender. But it replied with volleys and charged

into the center of the attacking force. After a brief, bloody contest
the single brigade was pushed back; still, it had slowed the advance
and given other units a little time to come up. It was largely
Iverson's old brigade, which by its gallant fight at Spotsylvania
cleaned the record of its bitter defeat on the first day at Gettysburg, when it was poorly led.

Gordon's own brigade was in the rear and the brief check by the
North Carolinians allowed him to align it for a countercharge upon
which he believed the fate of the Confederacy rested. That, too,
was Lee's opinion, for, as Gordon stated, "His army had been
cut in twain by Hancock's brilliant *coup de main*." Gordon continued:

Through that wide breach in the Confederate lines, which was
becoming wider at every step, the Union forces were rushing like a
swollen torrent through a broken mill-dam. General Lee knew . . .
that the bulk of the Confederate army was in such imminent peril
that nothing could rescue it except a counter movement, quick, impetuous, and decisive. Lee resolved to save it, and, if need be, to
save it at the sacrifice of his own life.[27]

Here occurred one of the instances—perhaps the best known of
two or three similar occasions—when Lee, mounted on Old Travel-
ler, prepared to lead the Confederate attack personally, and found
the men unwilling to go forward until he went to a place of greater
safety. This famous "General Lee to the rear" incident showed the
army's devotion to its chief. Lee rode to the center of Gordon's
line of battle but was shouted back by the men on the line. With
Rodes's division coming in to help, followed by Mahone and Wilcox, and with some fresh Confederate batteries finally in position,
Gordon drove into Hancock's front mass, which had become disorganized by its own impetuous advance.

By the time Hancock's attacking column had reached the second
Confederate line half a mile down the salient it was a confused
aggregation of soldiers separated from their officers and acting without much concert. When the Confederates counterattacked, the
Federals jumped behind the nearest defenses and replied with a
heavy musketry. Banes observed:

The most sanguinary and deadly fight of the campaign began at
this moment. During the entire day and far into the night there

was one continuous roll of musketry. . . . Occasionally both Union
and Confederate flags were on the breastworks at the same moment. . . . The most desperate contest was about the salient, and
in front of it the sight was one of horror. . . .[28]

The Battle Rages Until Midnight

The Confederate counterattack, delivered under the eyes of General Lee, was described as one of "savage desperation."[29]
Wheaton's and Russell's brigades of the Sixth Corps came in to
help Hancock on his right, and the battle became "beyond all comparison the closest and fiercest of the war."[30] The enemies wielded
their bayonets and fired point-blank into the faces of opponents
close at hand.

The 5th North Carolina, the "Bloody Fifth" after Spotsylvania,
was asleep when Hancock struck. Aroused by the heavy firing,
unable to distinguish objects ten paces ahead, not knowing the
position of friend or foe, it was hurried into the gap caused by the
capture of Edward Johnson, where it was caught by an enfilade
fire on both flanks. Five of its officers, including its colonel, were
shot down in fifteen minutes, and before the fighting subsided it had
lost all but 42 of its 450 men.[31] Another regiment of the same brigade lost two thirds in killed and wounded. Such was the intensity
of Hancock's battle.

"Into that bloody space," said Francis Walker, "were advancing
many thousands of stout soldiers, desperately determined to retrieve the fortunes of the day. . . ."[32] Confusion spread on the
Federal side because of the great number of men in the long lines
that had converged into the narrow salient. The turmoil was heightened by the advance of parts of Gibbon's reserve division and the
pressure of Mott's second line.

Barlow saw the disadvantages of piling the reserves into a situation already jumbled and embarrassed by numbers. He went to
Hancock to request that fresh troops be sent in slowly. In the
excitement of the moment he committed a breach of military eti-
quette he was never guilty of before or after. Instead of addressing
his chief as "General," or "Sir," he called him in his excitement
merely "Hancock." The corps commander seemed to understand.
He had learned much since the day when the private failed to
salute him at Fort Leavenworth.[33]

Hancock tended to treat the forward movement of his corps after the trenches had been overrun as spontaneous and unordered, saying:

Our troops could not be restrained after the capture of the intrenchments, but pursued the flying enemy through the forest in the direction of Spotsylvania Court House until they encountered a second formidable line of earthworks, the existence of which was before unknown to us.[34]

The main impetus of the attack had been spent by 6:00 A.M., but there remained eighteen hours of desperate fighting. Gradually the Federals were forced back to the Mule Shoe trenches.[35]

At this stage Hancock managed to get some artillery into position 300 yards outside the old Confederate works, on the right and in front of the Landrum House. With these he fired solid shot over the heads of his own men. Then he sent two sections of artillery up to the breastworks, where the guns fired at close range into the columns of Confederate infantry battling with single-minded abandon to recover their old lines. These guns were particularly effective over the open ground inside the salient west of the McCool House.

Finally the desperation and frenzy of the battle began to subside and Hancock was able to relieve some of the brigades, so that they could be re-formed under cover of the woods. Hancock's ordinarily restrained adjutant, Francis Walker, always seemed to speak in superlatives in dealing with this contest, even in its final phases. "Never since the discovery of gunpowder," he said, "had such a mass of lead been hurled into a space so narrow."

How else was one to speak of a battle where great trees were actually felled by rifle and musket bullets? Both armies were duly impressed when trees came crashing down in this fashion. The South Carolina Brigadier General Samuel Magowan reported that several of his soldiers were killed or wounded when an oak twenty-two inches in diameter was cut through by musket balls. One tree trunk eight to ten inches thick was exhibited in Washington after the battle, cut down mainly by the infantry fire of Miles's brigade. Colonel Hamilton A. Brown of the 1st North Carolina told of a hickory tree falling near his works, cut by Minié balls.[36]

Grant sent a message at 10:00 A.M., saying that Warren seemed reluctant to assault but had been ordered to do so at all hazards. If repulsed, he was to draw in his right and send troops to Wright, now commanding the Sixth Corps, and to Hancock. The message ended "Tell Hancock to hold on."[37] The battle at this stage had become immobile slugging in the clinches. All day long and far into the night of May 12 the unrelenting struggle continued. "Over that desperate and protracted contest Hancock presided, stern, strong and masterful," said his adjutant Walker.[38] The carnage ended at midnight, when the Confederates stopped their counter-attack.

Meantime, as the battle raged, Lee was constructing a new and stronger line in the rear, eliminating the Mule Shoe from his works. His fresh trenches ran roughly parallel to and not far removed from the Brock Road leading to Spotsylvania Courthouse from out of the Wilderness. Next morning when Hancock prepared to renew the assault he found the Confederate army gone from his immediate front. Gibbon, who had borne less of the fighting load than Hancock's three other divisions, was sent forward to define Lee's new position. Confederate skirmishers were driven in near the Harrison House, the fresh trenches were disclosed and the line was felt, but Hancock saw the futility of assailing the strengthened works.

In this last phase of the main battle of Spotsylvania, Hancock lost 650 men. One of his stanchest subordinates, Sprigg Carroll, was critically wounded. He had been wounded a few days before in the Wilderness but had refused to leave his command. Though he recovered and ultimately retired with the rank of major general in 1869—he survived until 1892—after Spotsylvania he was never a part of the Second Corps. His name will always be associated with Hancock's and with some of the greatest moments of the corps. Though he never commanded in battle with a higher rank than colonel, he was a soldier of great capacity and splendid fighting courage, whom Hancock would sorely miss.

The Federals Inflict the Heavier Loss

Grant, always restive when there was a strong enemy line in his front, waited only three days before ordering another assault at Spotsylvania, on the morning of May 18. He had moved Warren and Wright to the army's left. He supposed that Lee would have shifted his army heavily to oppose them and consequently would be weak in his old lines. But the Confederates had made the best of the time, had placed artillery skillfully and had prepared abatis and slashings in front of their trenches.

Grant had been receiving recruits to compensate for his heavy losses in the Wilderness and at Spotsylvania. Under a singular theory that these newcomers would bring fresh enthusiasm from the home front, he placed them in the forward rank, apparently without recalling that the newly dead had not been buried. Hancock's chief of staff, Charles H. Morgan, found the recruits disheartened by the bodies that had been lying in the hot sun for almost a week. Not only was the sight horrible to the eyes but the stench was retching to the stomach. So the last attack was a failure.[39] The new troops could not get through to the enemy and were subjected to a heavy artillery fire. Hancock saw that the assault was proving costly and purposeless and called it off. That ended the fighting at Spotsylvania.

Hancock conceded that his losses were "quite heavy."[40] He calculated the Confederate loss on May 12 in killed, wounded and captured at 10,000. Chief of Staff Humphreys, who always looked into the figures, put Lee's loss at between 9,000 and 10,000 and Grant's at 6,800. The novel feature was that this was the only large battle of the campaign in which the Southern losses were heavier than the Northern. But Grant's losses for the full time he was in front of Spotsylvania aggregated 18,399, greatly exceeding Lee's.

Said Hancock:

The interior of the intrenchments presented a terrible and ghastly spectacle of dead, most of whom were killed by our men with the bayonet. . . . So thickly lay the dead at this point, that at many places the bodies were touching and piled upon each other.[41]

General Brooke said he saw sixty bodies lying in a small spot, every one pierced with a bayonet.

The picture one gets of Grant during this assault—so typical of his generalship—is that of an imperturbable, stubborn man determined to break Lee by hitting him in the middle, but possessing the innate strategical sense to appreciate on second thought that maneuvers of the kind Sherman was practicing so skillfully in

Georgia were a more feasible and less expensive means to final victory than mass assaults. Hancock had won a splendid triumph—about the only one achieved against the Army of Northern Virginia between Gettysburg and Five Forks. Apart from the casualties inflicted on Lee, however, it had gained no more than a mile of trenches which were worthless when a few days later the armies moved to new fields.[42]

Nevertheless, the crushing of the salient and capture of Edward Johnson's division was one of the few glorious victories the Army of the Potomac had to offer the anxious North. It was Hancock's battle and he received a full measure of acclaim for it.

General Steuart Refuses His Hand

While the fighting was in progress, Grant and members of his staff huddled around a campfire—the rain and fog made the morning of May 12 chilly—receiving reports and issuing general orders about a battle he could hear but could not see because of the heavy woods. He heard the shouts and the small arms of the infantry. Finally at 5:30 A.M. an officer brought Hancock's first message, telling the commanding general that the first line of Confederate works was in Northern hands.[43]

Soon Grant had word about prisoners. The capture of 2,000 was reported by 5:50. At 6:30 A.M. the most important of the prisoners, Major General Edward Johnson, was brought to headquarters. He shook hands with his old friend Grant—one gets no picture of how much cordiality existed now between them—and with Meade, who had entered West Point two years ahead of him. They were talking before the fire, which had to be replenished frequently because of the drizzle, when Hancock's laconic message came: "I have finished up Johnson and am now going into Early."[44]

Hancock's experience with Steuart, who had entered West Point the year Hancock graduated, was not pleasant. When Steuart was brought in, Hancock extended his hand but the Confederate held himself aloof and said, "Under the circumstances I must decline to give my hand."

Hancock was quick with his rejoinder. "Under any other circumstances, General Steuart," he said, "I should not have offered mine."[45]

Grant's personal conduct and habits were observed closely during the campaign through the Wilderness and at Spotsylvania. He often sat on the ground, leaning against a tree, or on a stump, usually whittling, the 1863, open-air substitute for modern doodling. He smoked black cigars at the rate of twenty a day. When after Spotsylvania he spoke to Meade regretfully about the heavy losses, the conservative Meade answered in terms a sharper man than Grant would have taken as a rebuke. "General," replied Meade, "we can't do these little tricks without heavy losses."[46]

By the end of the Spotsylvania campaign, roughly three weeks after the crossing of the Rapidan, Grant had lost about 37,500 men, or about one third of his battle force. A candid analysis of this campaign made by Theodore Ayrault Dodge stresses the fact that it had served no purpose that could not have been won by maneuvering. Its losses had disheartened the army. The campaign had not correspondingly weakened the enemy morale but had actually heightened it by their successful resistance to the vastly superior force. Grant, however, did possess spirit and determination, factors lacking in some of his predecessors in command of the eastern theater.

★ ★ ★ 14 ★ ★ ★

Bloody Repulse at Cold Harbor

Brooke and Miles in the Front

Many years ago this writer, visiting a small New England town and going through the cemetery where there seemed an unusually large number of graves of Civil War soldiers, was struck with the number of markers bearing the death date of, or a little after, June 3, 1864. Reflection brought the memory that this was the day of Cold Harbor, the darkest in the history of the Army of the Potomac, a battle in which about 12,000 Northern men fell, most of them in the narrow space of eight minutes.

The town had provided one of the companies that marched, faithful to its orders, into the sheet of flame in front of the Confederate trenches, as Pakenham's had done at New Orleans, and there were many towns like it through the North.

Even with the new implements of destruction in later wars, it is doubtful that like losses have ever been suffered by an American army in so brief a time. The toll was not comparable, of course, with the casualties sustained by civilian populations, now the main target in an offensive, as in World War II. But it was such as to appall the nation, threaten Lincoln with defeat for a second term, earn for Grant the title of the "Butcher," lead to pressure on Lincoln for dismissal of Grant and plunge homes in all parts of the North into mourning.

The brunt of the assault fell on Hancock and his Second Corps, though the Sixth Corps under Major General Horatio G. Wright and the Eighteenth under Major General William F. (Baldy) Smith attacked abreast him. Hancock's assault was resolute and his losses were heaviest.

There were many causes for the appalling sacrifice of young soldiers but the main one was Grant's lack of knowledge. Hopeful of breaking into Richmond, against which Lee had his back, Grant ordered the attack impetuously without making a reconnaissance, and neither he nor the corps commanders knew the nature of the fortifications or the position of Lee's army. Lee's works were not only strong in front but he was drawn up in a crescent that allowed the Southern infantry to enfilade the assailants at close range.

Because of the Spotsylvania and Cold Harbor trenches he required his men to dig, the Confederate commander in chief was acquiring the names of "Old Spades Lee," or "Old Ace of Spades," familiarities adopted by the nimble-tongued Jubal Early.[1]

After Spotsylvania, Grant had moved again to his left and confronted Lee at the crossing of the North Anna River, where Hancock and Warren made ineffectual attacks on Lee's well-prepared defenses. Now Grant moved left again and, as June came to Virginia, he faced Lee once more in the heavily wooded, sparsely settled territory north of the Chickahominy River. The two main points were a crossroads tavern known as Old Cold Harbor, and, to the southwest, New Cold Harbor, or Cold Harbor, the site of another tavern and the center of the battle.

The unusual name, of English derivation, indicated no seaport, but rather a resting place in early colonial time. The original English form appears to have been Cool Arbor, designating a shady haven where foot travelers might tarry on the roadway. Cold Harbor came to imply a resting place without fire. The spelling "Coal Harbor," sometimes employed on old maps, is apparently a corruption, though it may have applied to a resting place with heat. Thus, long before Richmond was ever thought of, Cold Harbor, which became a main defensive position, was a crude shelter on the trail for trappers and traders, a peaceful refuge that was to become the scene of one of the most sanguinary of American battles.

At Old Cold Harbor Grant received heavy reinforcements from the army of Major General Benjamin F. Butler at Bermuda Hundred. The Eighteenth Corps of 16,000 men,[2] under Baldy Smith, moved by boat to the White House on the Pamunkey River. It marched the sixteen miles from the White House to Old Cold Harbor, where it was met by Grant as he extended his lines eastward.

When Butler released Smith's corps to reinforce Grant, Beauregard, who confronted Butler, was able to send the division of Robert F. Hoke as a reinforcement to Lee. Lee had received other acquisitions that made up for the loss of Edward Johnson's division. Pickett's division rejoined Longstreet's corps after a tour in North Carolina, and Major General John C. Breckinridge brought in a small force. These additions aggregated about 14,400, and raised Lee's strength to about 70,000 at Cold Harbor. Grant's army, despite heavy losses, tended to hold its own or grow as the campaign toward Richmond progressed. At Cold Harbor it numbered 113,875.[3]

Some impressions remained with Colonel Lyman during the series of marches of the Federal army to the left: the camp in a clover field while the band played, "Ever of Thee I'm Fondly Dreaming"; the crossing of the Po River over a shaky bridge; the trenches at Madison's Ordinary; and the officer who rode in a hurry to Hancock with the startling news: "General, our breastwork is only bulletproof and the Rebels are shelling us!"

"Killed anybody?" asked Hancock, unperturbed.

"Not yet, sir."

"Well, you can tell the men to take it comfortably," Hancock answered. "The Rebels often throw shells and I am sure I cannot prevent them."[4]

Hancock marched his Second Corps to Cold Harbor through the dark night of June 1, over hot, dusty roads, guided by a young officer of the topographical engineers who managed to confuse the command by taking one division on a short cut through the woods. Hancock lauded his staff officers for being able to reunite his columns, the heads of which reached Cold Harbor at 6:30 A.M. on June 2, exhausted and hungry. They were immediately confronted with orders from Grant and Meade to attack that very morning. Meade had lashed them on as if he cracked a whip: "Every confidence is felt that your gallant corps of veterans will move with vigor and endure the necessary fatigue."[5]

At Hancock's insistence the hour of the attack was postponed until 5:00 P.M., and again until 4:30 A.M., June 3. Even then there

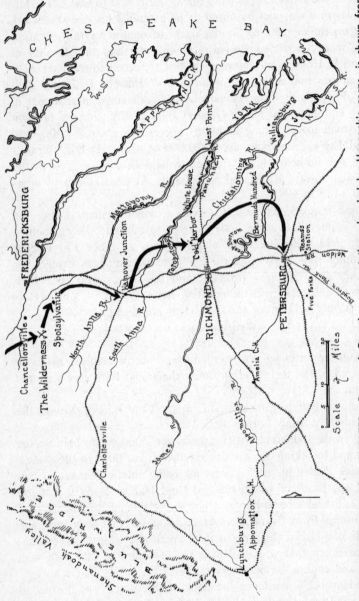

CHESAPEAKE BAY

RICHMOND-PETERSBURG THEATER. Route of Grant's army, at times headed by Hancock's corps, is shown from the Wilderness to the Petersburg campaign south of the James River.

was too little time, but Hancock used it to get his command into
position. His adjutant wondered about the haste, feeling that both
June 3 and 4 could have been utilized beneficially in reconnaissance, which might have developed a weakness somewhere along
Lee's lines.[6] Lee's front extended about six miles from the Chickahominy, touched by his right flank, to the Totopotomy swamp
lands, heavily wooded and impassable on his left. A reconnaissance
was not the duty of the corps commanders but of the commander
in chief and his staff of engineers.[7]

Just as before the Spotsylvania attack, rain fell intermittently on
the night of June 2, but it was more welcome here. The troops
were in position and not on the muddy trails, and rain settled the
dust and broke the heat. Hancock's Second Corps was on the left,
Wright's Sixth Corps in the center and Baldy Smith's Eighteenth
Corps on the right. The Fifth and Ninth Corps, farther to the
right, were out of the area of the main action.[8]

Hancock formed his columns before daylight. Barlow and Gibbon were the assault divisions and Birney was in reserve. After
Spotsylvania Mott's division had been closed out and compressed
into a brigade in Birney's division. Barlow's two leading brigades
under Miles and Brooke, which had come to be the army's shock
troops, were deployed as the front line of the division, while the
second line was formed by the Irish Brigade under Colonel
Richard Byrnes and Frank's old brigade now under Colonel Clin-
ton D. MacDougall.

Gibbon's two leading brigades were commanded by Smyth, who
had been transferred from the Irish Brigade to Carroll's old brigade, and Brigadier General Robert O. Tyler, who had come up
through the Connecticut artillery and had brought in the Corcoran
Legion as recruits to Hancock at Spotsylvania. In Gibbon's second
line were the brigades of Paddy Owen and Colonel Henry Boyd
McKeen.

When Hancock's soldiers looked ahead at the fortifications they
would have to storm, they took out pieces of paper, wrote their
names and pinned the slips to their blouses, so that their bodies
might be identified.[9] Pathetically it suggested the need of the "dog
tags" of later wars.

Azaleas and swamp magnolias were in bloom and their fragrance
permeated the battle line.

"It Was Not War; It Was Murder"

Hancock gave the signal in the dawn of June 3, and Barlow advanced with his customary boldness. Both Brooke and Miles quickly found lodgments in the Confederate works. Brooke encountered a line of graycoats in a sunken road outside their main entrenchments and by impetuous attack was able to drive them and follow them over the parapet, where he captured three cannon, one stand of colors and between 200 and 300 prisoners. But Brooke had scarcely mounted the works when he was shot down, critically wounded. Byrnes, bringing up the Irish Brigade behind him, was killed and with him fell also Colonel Orlando H. Morris of the 66th New York.

Abreast Brooke, Colonel Miles likewise obtained a foothold inside the Confederate lines, but neither his brigade nor Brooke's could maintain their advantage for more than a few minutes. They were attacking a line well supplied with reserves. The assault was quickly becoming a horror-riddled failure at all other points, and isolated units could not hold when their companions were retiring.

Gibbon on the right was even less successful than Barlow. Here trouble stemmed from Grant's failure to make a thorough reconnaissance. When Gibbon moved out in battle order he found his division cut in two by a swamp, an impassable obstacle which widened as his division neared the enemy works. No one on the Federal side had been aware of the existence of this barrier. The two wings of the division pushed on despite it, only to meet a sheet of fire from the Confederate infantry and heavy bursts of shrapnel and shrieking canister as they neared the enemy lines. Tyler was severely wounded as he carried an advanced position, and Colonel James P. McMahon of the 164th New York was dropped as he planted his regimental colors on the main parapet. McKeen, bringing up a supporting brigade, was killed. He, too, went down on the enemy works with his colors in his hand.

Hancock had greatly admired Colonel Henry Boyd McKeen of the 81st Pennsylvania and had said to him as they went into the Wilderness, "Colonel, I am sorry that you do not have more rank, for if you had I would give you a brigade, and be pleased to do so."

McKeen replied, "I am obliged to you, general, but I shall *win* a brigade before this campaign is over."[10]

Depletions due to the Wilderness and Spotsylvania put McKeen in command of a brigade in less than a month, but he exercised it only a few days. Wounded severely in three earlier battles,[11] he was to die at Cold Harbor. Hancock's eyes filled with tears when word was brought to him that McKeen was dead.[12]

Colonel Frank A. Haskell, who followed McKeen in command, was mortally wounded. Part of this brigade as well as part of Smyth's that reached the entrenchments might have held, at least for a time, had not Owen failed to bring up support on Smyth's left. Owen's delay took him out of the army.

Gallant as was the performance of these brigades, their success lasted for no more than a fleeting moment as the great battle roared about them. The Army of the Potomac was receiving the sharpest and most bloody repulse in all its history. How long the attack was sustained was a question. In the frenzy of fighting some counted minutes where others recorded hours. One participant said eight minutes, one nine, one twenty-two, while still others counted it nearly an hour.

Wright and Baldy Smith did not make so much headway as Hancock. All three corps commanders thought their flanks had been left exposed by the failure of the corps next in line to keep abreast them and maintain contact. Here again the fault was not with the corps commanders nor with the men, but with the high command's rush to attack without a reconnaissance. Without recognizing that Lee's concave lines imposed an assault problem, the Federal corps moved forward in straight rank formation and each attacked directly in its front. Each of the attacking corps therefore found its flank exposed to a surprising enfilade from the curved Confederate works, as well as to a fire directly in its front.[13] Hancock was enfiladed on his left, Smith on his right and Wright, the center corps, on both flanks.[14]

Confederate Major General E. McIver Law said that when he came up to the trenches his soldiers were in fine spirits and laughed and talked as they fired. Then he gave his own view of the assault:

I had seen the dreadful carnage in front of Marye's Hill at Fredericksburg, and on the "old railroad cut" which Jackson's men held at the Second Manassas; but I had seen nothing to exceed this. It was not war; it was murder. When the fight ended more than a thousand men lay in front of our works. . . . The loss in my command was fifteen or twenty. . . .[15]

Pickett told the story of Cold Harbor in few words:

The whole Confederate line poured a stream of fire, and thousands of Grant's soldiers have gone to reenforce the army of the dead.

Oh, this is all a weary, long mistake. . . .[16]

The official diary of the First Corps of Lee's army, Anderson's, formerly Longstreet's, bore this entry: "Assault after assault is made, and each time repulsed with severe loss to the enemy. At eight o'clock A.M. fourteen had been made and repulsed."[17] Apparently it meant that fourteen lines of battle were hurled back from Anderson's front in the Confederate center.

The Men Did Not Hear the Attack Order

Though the attack had met with a ghastly repulse, the Federal high command was not satisfied. Grant told Meade to send the men in again.

Meade at 8:45 A.M. wrote a note to Hancock, accompanying it with two notes from Wright, who thought he could carry the main line if Hancock and Smith would make new supporting attacks in their fronts. Meade ended:

It is of the greatest importance that no effort should be spared to succeed. Wright and Smith are both going to try again, and unless you consider it hopeless, I would like you to do the same.[18]

In view of the discretion allowed him by Meade, Hancock decided not to resume the assault, being satisfied that another effort would be fruitless. He did send Birney's division to assist Warren, who felt threatened. Warren was outside the theater of the main engagement.

Badeau explained on behalf of Grant that there were ample reasons for him to order a renewal of the attack. Early returns placed the casualties at no more than 3,000 instead of the 7,000 to 10,000 which later counts showed from the single assault. Hancock had actually broken into the Confederate works, while the other corps had gained ground and captured some of the enemy's rifle pits. Grant, as Badeau interpreted him, was not accustomed to give up after one unsuccessful attempt. All of this caused the commanding general to issue orders that the assault should be renewed as soon as the condition of the troops permitted. Grant did allow Meade some discretion:

The moment it becomes certain that an assault cannot succeed, suspend the offensive, but when it does succeed, push it vigorously, and if necessary, pile in troops at the successful point, from wherever they can be found.

The orders, passed down by Meade, were received with no enthusiasm anywhere along the lines.

One of the Cold Harbor controversies, and there were many, arose from a story that Hancock's men refused to budge when Grant's order to renew the attack was forwarded by Meade.

The story first appeared in a news account by the war correspondent William Swinton and was contained in his book *Campaigns of the Army of the Potomac*. Both Hancock's adjutant Walker and his chief of staff Morgan denied it vehemently.[19] The contemporary historian, John Codman Ropes, who made a careful study of this battle and talked with the officers of the Second and Sixth Corps about it, rejected the newspaperman's version.

Irrespective of what may have come to Walker's or Morgan's attention, there is ample evidence that both officers and men made nothing more than gestures and noise to satisfy Grant that they were attacking again. Though there was no mutiny, there was much dragging of feet.

Lieutenant Colonel Martin T. McMahon, who had long served as chief of staff of the Sixth Corps, felt that the renewed attack was a mere formality to appease Grant. Some troops advanced, some merely opened fire.[20] When the order came for a third attack he said it was transmitted to division, brigade and regimental headquarters without comment; every officer and man of the three corps knew that to move the army forward except by regular approaches was "a simple and absolute impossibility."[21]

According to McMahon, the third order "was obeyed by simply renewing the fire from the men as they lay in position."

Manifestly it would be impossible for Walker and Morgan to deny Swinton's story with finality. They could not be certain they had seen every aspect of the battle that had come to Swinton's attention or heard all the comments he may have heard. Most of the war correspondents were trustworthy, as a review of their dispatches shows. Swinton had an ample supply of news at his elbow and did not need to manufacture more. There seems a deal of professing among the staff that his story was a fabrication.

Swinton seems far from "unprincipled"—to use Walker's word—when he says that after the attack order was renewed, "no man stirred, and the immobile lines pronounced the verdict, silent, yet emphatic, against further slaughter."

Likely, it is true that the men did not refuse to go forward. They merely did not go forward. As Nelson put the telescope to his blind eye at Copenhagen, they had their deaf ears turned to their colonels at Cold Harbor.

Baldy Smith said bluntly, after telling of the repulse of his corps: "Later in the day I received a verbal order from General Meade to make another assault, and that order I refused to obey."[22]

In one respect Lee's works at Cold Harbor differed from those at Spotsylvania in that they were scantily protected by abatis or slashings at the time of the main attack. Later when officers of the Second and Sixth Corps were questioned on this point they could remember no such obstructions.[23] The men were halted by the tremendous fire of the Southern soldiers in their trenches, and in this respect, as well as in regard to the staggering losses, the battle has been compared appropriately to that of New Orleans.[24]

At eleven o'clock Grant rode to the lines to consult with the generals in immediate charge of the operations. Hancock told him flatly that the works in his front could not be carried. The other corps commanders, Smith, Wright and Burnside, were not so positive, but were not enthusiastic for a renewal. Grant thought it over as he was going back, then at 12:30 P.M. ordered Meade to suspend the offensive.

The opinions of the corps commanders not being sanguine of success in case an assault is ordered, you may direct a suspension of further advance for the present. *Hold your most advanced positions* and strengthen them. . . .[25]

The wording of the order was peculiar, because the Southern infantry fire had already caused a "suspension of the advance" and Grant might more nicely have employed other terms.

After the attack Hancock's men held their positions wherever they could find cover and with bayonets and tin plates began to dig ditches. All day they labored with these poor substitutes until regular entrenching tools could be rounded up from the trains and brought in after darkness. Here the war began to take on the aspects of World War I. The hostile armies entrenched at close quarters, the lines at some points only thirty yards apart and at others from fifty to a hundred yards or more. Gibbon's division was especially close. Hancock maintained contact with his front lines by means of covered ways, or communicating trenches.

Owing to the responsibilities of commanding a large corps on timber-covered battlefields where the combat could not be followed by the eye, Hancock had been forced here and in the Wilderness to forgo his custom of directing the battle from the firing line. But he did insist at Cold Harbor on retaining the headquarters he established on reaching the field, though they proved within easy enemy range. Retirement was not an example he would set for the men.

Each night after the battle, while the armies still faced each other in the trenches, Hancock would ride the lines and hurry to any point where he heard heavy firing. Once when he was on such an inspection a shell found his tent and took off the leg of Captain Alexander McCune, assistant provost marshal of the Second Corps, who was standing at the tent flap. McCune died from the wound in a few days. Hancock's diligence had perhaps saved his own life.[26]

The Wounded Are Left Where They Fell

One of the ghastly aspects of the battle was that the Federal wounded lay unattended and the dead unburied for five days on the field, and while extenuating circumstances have been advanced to relieve the Federal high command of the responsibility, there it has appeared to rest.

Grant's delay in sending a flag of truce to Lee requesting an armistice for the burial of the dead was regarded in the army as due to his reluctance to concede that he had been defeated.[27] Thirty years after the battle Walker was adding to the condemnation of Grant for this delay:

It seems now incredible that he should for a moment have supposed that any other view could be taken of that action. But even if it were so, this was a very poor way of rewarding his soldiers who had fallen in the attack or of encouraging their comrades to take similar risks.

By the time the truce was arranged, from 6:00 to 8:00 P.M., June 7, most of the wounded were "past caring for."[28]

John Codman Ropes's analysis of the Cold Harbor campaign brought into focus some glaring faults in Grant's generalship. To Cold Harbor Ropes devoted a paper he read in 1883 before the Military Historical Society of Massachusetts, which he founded.[29] In it he mentioned "the horrible neglect of our wounded men by General Grant." Of Grant he said:

Having lost the battle, he should at once have sent in a flag of truce and asked to remove his wounded and bury his dead. It would, of course, have been a confession of failure, but he would only have confessed a patent fact.

Grant sent no flag until the evening of June 5,[30] when he requested the truce "as a mutual accommodation" instead of on his own behalf. The delays were such that the truce could not be arranged until nearly all the wounded were dead.

Heat, thirst and hunger caused untold anguish to those already in agony from their wounds. One man who managed to live sucked dew from the grass. Baldy Smith said some of his men risked their lives bringing in the wounded, and: "The groans of such as could not be reached grew fainter and fainter until they ceased."[31]

Such neglect would not be calculated to inspire the survivors to unusual sacrifices in subsequent battles. The Army of the Potomac could be credited with great devotion to its cause for its later assaults at Petersburg.

Efforts to spare Grant criticism could not avoid the facts that the men did remain for five days dying between the lines and that the Confederates were not heartless and must surely have recognized any formal plea for their relief. The fault could not be charged to the Federal corps commanders but was assessable only against the commanding general.

Hancock had every right to expect that the high command would devote its first attention after the attack to securing a truce and removing the wounded. Meade called to Grant's attention the fact that had been well established in this and other wars, that the enemy high command would not recognize a communication by flag of truce except when it came from the commanding general.[32] Meade could request no armistice while Grant was present with the army, and, of course, the corps commanders could not.

"McClellan Went There Without Much Loss"

Grant lost on the field of Cold Harbor 12,737 men,[33] and while these casualties were calculated from June 1 to 12, the main fighting took place during the brief period on June 3. The dead were 1,844, wounded 9,077 and missing 1,816.

McMahon timed the assault at eight minutes and said, "In that little period more men fell bleeding as they advanced than in any other like period of time throughout the war."[34]

Hancock's corps lost 3,510. This compares with a loss of 4,194 by the corps in three days at Gettysburg, where also it was the most active participant. At Cold Harbor six colonels—a high rank in this promotion-starved army—were killed. Walker called them "the very flower of the corps."[35] Forty-six officers of lower rank were killed or mortally wounded.

Even Lieutenant Colonel Rufus R. Dawes of the 6th Wisconsin, in the Fifth Corps that had not made the major attack, noticed the way his regiment was dwindling and asked: "How long will it take to whittle us away?"[36]

Baldy Smith thought the formation for the attack of June 3 was "murderous," being in his opinion unsound tactically.[37]

The intrepid young Emory Upton, who was to prove himself one of the best military intellects in the army, likewise used the word "murderous," then repeated it with the explanation, "because we were recklessly ordered to assault the enemy's intrenchments, knowing neither their strength nor position."[38]

Said Upton: "I am disgusted with the generalship displayed."

Historical judgments at times seem arrived at more by reiteration than discernment. Where history has condemned McClellan for the manner of his approach to Richmond, it has acclaimed Grant—though the characteristic of the first was caution and of the second impulsiveness.

Martin McMahon noticed that the men, in their discussions of Cold Harbor, inevitably recalled that McClellan two years earlier had put the army nearer to Richmond with losses that comparatively were very light. McClellan had to beg for reinforcements, Grant could order them up at will and deplete the Washington defenses as he chose.[39]

Grant might hammer through with the great resources put at his disposal, but he seems to have lacked McClellan's deftness. About this Lee, who would be the best judge, had no uncertainty.

Horace Greeley asked the pertinent question, why not take the army there by water at no loss, rather than expend the 60,000 men he calculated Grant had used up taking it there by land.[40]

Between its entry into the Wilderness May 4 and the curtain at Cold Harbor June 3, a period of one month, the army had lost 54,926 men. There was reason for Hancock's sad remark, when he was asked after Cold Harbor where the Second Corps was. "It lies buried," he said, "between the Rapidan and the James."[41]

Trouble with Politics and an Old Wound

Hancock's relations with Grant at this stage were most cordial. At West Point they had been good enough friends for Hancock to call Grant by his familiar nickname, "Sam," and once in the Wilderness the corps commander was quoted as saying, "I love Sam Grant."[42] The remark was made to Grant's brother-in-law, Lieutenant Colonel Frederick T. Dent. Badeau thought Grant entertained the same feeling for Hancock.

Grant's confidence in Hancock, as well as his own good judgment in evaluating intelligence, was evidenced by an incident in the Wilderness, when stragglers brought him word that Hancock had been put to flight. Grant was sitting on the ground busy at his favorite occupation, whittling. All he did was to turn the stick and whittle the other end. When the rumor was repeated, he said flatly: "I don't believe it."

A little later correct information came that Hancock was driving the enemy, which caused Grant to brighten and say with as much enthusiasm as Badeau ever saw him display: "Hancock is a glorious soldier."

Badeau, in recalling the remark during a Philadelphia *Press* interview, went on to say that Grant always gave Hancock the advanced or exposed position; that Hancock carried the heavy load in the Wilderness, made "three terrible assaults" at Spotsylvania, led the army in its march to the North Anna and was in the thickest of the battle of Cold Harbor:

Hancock was given the command which required the most superb daring, the clearest head, the most sustained military ability. More than once I heard General Grant say that if Meade were removed he should give the command of the Army of the Potomac to Hancock."[43]

This cordiality was apparent after Cold Harbor when Grant began his march to the left again, to cross the James River and move against Petersburg. Hancock's name was having its first mention in connection with the Presidency. Though he was a Democrat he had never voted. The anti-Lincoln Republicans, believing Lincoln could not be re-elected, had hit on Hancock, along with Sherman, Ben Butler and Grant, and were passing his name around.[44] Grant took himself out by endorsing Lincoln, and Hancock did not view the matter seriously. Lincoln finally had been nominated for a second term just at the time the country was hearing about Cold Harbor. Not many, including Lincoln himself, would have staked much on his prospects for re-election.

The subject was in the air on the march to the James. While the Second Corps was crossing the Chickahominy River June 13, Grant, Meade and Hancock met, dismounted and chatted pleasantly as the troops moved by. Grant had been able to shake off any regrets he may have felt about Cold Harbor. His mood was as jovial as it ever became. The three generals lay on the grass, their staffs clustered around them, and listened to one another's quips and banter, or what Badeau termed their feeling of camaraderie, which he said was "perfect."[45]

They must have chatted a considerable time, for they covered the old days at West Point, army service on the frontier, the fresh campaign on which they had just embarked and finally hit on poli-

tics. The Pennsylvania legislature had passed a resolution offering
Hancock's name for the Presidency. Grant and Meade, though
neither could be regarded as of felicitous or sprightly wit, amused
themselves at Hancock's expense, poking fun at him because he was
being threatened with a political career. He took it all in good
nature and Badeau thought "it rather tickled him."[46]

Grant had recommended Hancock after Spotsylvania for promotion to brigadier general in the regular army, but the matter had
been ignored for the time in Washington.

Grant was more of a curiosity to the army in these days than he
was to Hancock. Morris Schaff said:

I often looked at him as I might have looked at any mystery, as
day after day I saw him at headquarters, especially after we had
reached City Point—the Wilderness, Spotsylvania, and Cold Harbor, with their frightful losses, lying behind us.

Another anomalous figure around headquarters was John A.
Rawlins, Grant's chief of staff and former neighbor in Galena,
Illinois. He had been conspicuous in Grant's campaigns from the
beginning. General Lew Wallace at Fort Donelson noticed his
"slender figure, large black eyes, hectic cheeks, and sincere, earnest
manner."[47] Sherman, an experienced hand in airing an opinion,
found him "a man of vehement expression."[48] Lieutenant Schaff
agreed that he "talked in a loud, emphatic voice" but found his
face, with its long black beard, one of "sincerity and earnestness."

Apart from the mental anguish, Cold Harbor was unfortunate in
one respect for Hancock personally. His exertions during the battle
and while the hostile forces faced each other later in the trenches
reopened his old Gettysburg wound. Shortly after the army took
up the movement to the James he was seen sitting on the grass
along the Chickahominy with his canteen in his hand.[49] He was
pouring water over the wound, a doubtful remedy perhaps, but
about all he knew to do at the moment.

★ ★ ★ 15 ★ ★ ★

Petersburg Fumble

Grant Neglects to Tell His Orders

Adjutant Francis Walker felt that Hancock did not in 1864 enhance his military reputation as he had in 1863. Walker read a paper before the Military Historical Society of Massachusetts in which he analyzed the causes, the first being that he had reached by 1864 "an almost dangerous elevation in popular reputation, and from which he was far more likely to fall than rise."[1] A second was an almost chronic difficulty with his Gettysburg wound, which was an open sore most of the time and a continual source of weakness.

Another reason—and this was the most important though Walker listed it last—was that the trench warfare into which the armies had settled at Petersburg offered few opportunities for clean-cut battles in the field where resourceful generalship might come into obvious play. That has, of course, remained the depressing condition of trench warfare. World War I, fought sluggishly in the trenches, was barren of those great, spectacular, altogether fascinating duels between armies, with chance often playing a vital part, as at Waterloo and Gettysburg.

Even in the more mobile warfare of World War II, chance and inspiration were relegated to minor roles. Mass and equipment had finally supplanted them; warfare had declined to where the output of the factories was vastly more significant than a flash of genius on the field.

But if Hancock's reputation was not enlarged during the last full year of the fighting, his fame in no manner went into eclipse.

Petersburg was not a battle but a protracted disappointment to both armies. Through the summer, autumn and winter of 1864 and early spring of 1865, Grant faced Lee in the trenches while the war was being won by the North and the hollow shell of the Confederacy was being crushed in, mainly by the armies and the navy in other theaters—by Sherman in his roaming campaigns through Georgia and the Carolinas, Thomas at Nashville, Farragut and Canby at Mobile, Porter and Terry at Fort Fisher.

Lee's army at Petersburg was depleted partly by the attrition of the siege, but more by the general despair of the Confederate cause resulting from this whittling off of territory, defeat of armies and capture of seaports. While Grant sat in front of Petersburg the Confederacy was being sliced away to little more than a strip of southern Virginia and northeastern North Carolina; its contacts with the outside world were being severed even for blockade runners, its civilian wealth destroyed, and its morale and power of resistance broken throughout the greater part of its dwindling domain by the obvious hopelessness of the struggle against the stupendous resources of the North.

In the end the Confederacy died not from any sword thrust by Grant at Richmond but from bleeding through almost countless wounds administered by seasoned, well-led Federal armies on many fields.

The logistics of Grant's march of fifty miles from Cold Harbor to Petersburg, worked out by Humphreys, Meade's chief of staff, were exemplary. The march was described by an onlooker as the finest bit of strategy in the history of the Army of the Potomac to that time.[2]

Hancock's Second Corps headed the march. It crossed the Chickahominy on June 13 and rested that night near Charles City Court House on the James. Hancock was over the James River by 4:00 A.M. on June 15 and took up the march toward Petersburg.

Grant's plan for the capture of Petersburg by co-operation between Baldy Smith's corps of the Army of the James and Hancock's corps of the Army of the Potomac miscarried because of lack of co-ordination and the proper exchange of intelligence, failures to which Grant pleaded guilty in his reflections on the campaign. The plan was for Smith—who after Cold Harbor had been returned by the water route to Butler's Army of the James—to descend on Petersburg rapidly on June 15, while Hancock came to his support.

Grant failed to inform Meade and, in turn, Hancock about Smith's key role in the plan; thus Hancock merely marched on Petersburg without any orders to capture it or assist Smith in the reduction of this lightly garrisoned strong point. All Hancock was required by his orders was to reach the crossing of the City Point Railroad over Harrison's Creek.

Had he been informed he would not have taken time to await the arrival of 60,000 rations at Windmill Point, nor would Meade have given assent to the delay. Hancock marched at a normal rate and found the maps in error respecting the location of Harrison's Creek. He was led into a longer road and it was not until late in the afternoon, when he received messages from both Smith and Grant, that he learned of the proposed assault on Petersburg and the mission expected of him.[3]

Lee was, in fact, caught off guard by Grant's quick descent on Petersburg and would have lost the town and with it Richmond if Baldy Smith had been less timid. With about 16,000 men, Smith came up before Beauregard with about 2,200. Hancock actually was not needed.

Benjamin Butler, commander of the Army of the James, through whom Grant issued the orders for Smith to take Petersburg, had no confidence in Smith, whom he termed a "second grade West Pointer," as well as "obstinate," "disobedient," "insubordinate," "mendacious" and a great many other things.[4] Smith was allegedly given to making reconnaissances when ordered to attack and was "not satisfied with anything that anybody else suggests, and he has not." Butler gave a clinching indictment: "Smith's curse was that he had graduated as a topographical engineer."[5] Most of these things Butler told Grant in opposing Smith to head the Eighteenth Corps. Irrespective of whether or not they were justified, Butler's complaints about Smith's slowness to attack Petersburg on June 15 were altogether warranted, because the attack was long delayed and when delivered was not pushed with vigor.

Smith dawdled around most of the day with his vastly superior force. All Butler could detect in the way of an engagement was "some slight skirmishing." Hancock was four miles away when about 5:50 P.M. he learned that he was expected to go to Petersburg and help reduce it. Birney was hurried off at once, followed by Gibbon, but Barlow was with the trains on another circuit, because of faulty maps, and could not come up until later.

An Unfortunate Yielding of Rank

Hancock reached Smith's position at dusk, when there were not enough minutes of daylight remaining for a reconnaissance. Being ignorant of the enemy's position, the terrain—covered in many places with heavy woods—or the conditions of the battle in which Smith had already taken some redoubts and guns, Hancock waived his seniority in rank, asked Smith to decide if another attack should be made. He offered to form his two divisions at any point Smith might designate. All Smith asked was that Hancock should relieve the Eighteenth Corps men in the captured trenches. This was accomplished at eleven o'clock that night.

Perhaps it was natural for Hancock to defer to his old commander Smith, under whom he had served at Williamsburg, especially since Smith had been on the ground, had made an overabundant number of reconnaissances through most of the day and had already begun something of an engagement with initial success. But it was a decision which he never ceased to regret. It lost Petersburg and led to months of siege. On the night of June 15, the town would have fallen to any kind of aggressive action by the two corps, and aggressive action might have been expected of Hancock. The moon was bright and Butler repeatedly urged on Smith a night attack, but Baldy accepted some unreliable information that Petersburg had been reinforced heavily that afternoon and decided against a night assault. Frank Wilkeson, one of Hancock's artillerymen, looked at the moon and judged the "night was made to fight on."[6]

Neither Grant nor Butler attached blame to Hancock. But Smith was unwilling to accept the responsibility for the failure. His efforts to dodge it finally led to his relief as a corps commander.

Lieutenant John I. Davenport, Butler's staff officer, carried Butler's orders to Smith that night, urging continuation of the assault to the main Confederate works. Smith told Davenport that Hancock's arrival had left him the junior officer. He went no further than that, but the implication remained that the responsibility for further orders was Hancock's. Davenport then went to Hancock and learned that he had waived his rank and was merely taking over the trenches Smith's men had captured. Butler claimed that Smith went into hiding and thus avoided, for the rest of the night, his peremptory orders to continue the attack.[7]

Grant came up the next day but the Smith-Hancock affair, though ended on the field, was merely beginning as one of the prolonged Petersburg controversies. The next episode was the appearance of an account in the New York *Tribune*. It wandered on for almost seven columns but packed a severe wallop against Hancock and left him with the guilt of failing to capture the town. His corps had not arrived until midnight, ran the story, and then he had declined to employ it in co-operation with Smith.

Hancock was deeply incensed at a charge which he believed resulted either from ignorance or malice. He wrote a letter to Meade setting forth the events of his march and arrival and asking that the newspaper story be investigated. Meade's endorsement on the letter when he forwarded it to Grant was a full exoneration: "I do not see that any censure can be attached to General Hancock and his corps."[8]

The author of the article was a correspondent attached to Smith's corps, and Butler had no compunction about charging that the material was fed to him by Smith. Smith denied that he had anything to do with it, but Grant ordered that the correspondent be arrested and sent to headquarters. There Grant interviewed the newsman and satisfied himself that he had written with Smith's knowledge.[9]

Grant not only banished the New York *Tribune* correspondent from the army, but relieved Smith from his command. The reason, according to his chief Butler, was "for having participated in publishing a libel upon his brother superior officer . . . and for denying the truth about it."[10]

Said Butler:

Now, if anything has been proven it is that Hancock arrived early in the evening and offered to co-operate with Smith in every way, even to giving up the command of the movement of his corps to Smith.[11]

Horace Greeley, in whose newspaper the story had been published, took the same view as Butler when he came to write about the matter.[12]

Grant undertook to assuage Hancock's bitterness about the story when he denied his application for an inquiry:

The reputation of the Second Corps and its commander are so high, both with the public and in the army, that an investigation could not add to it. It can not be tarnished by newspaper articles or scribblers. No official dispatch has ever been sent from these headquarters which by any construction could cast blame on the Second Corps or its commander for the part they played in this campaign.[13]

The major shortcoming in the Petersburg fumble was of course Grant's. Apart from his failure to inform Hancock of the role expected from the Second Corps, he might at such an important juncture have been at the front personally. As Lee could be criticized for not having gone to Gettysburg earlier on July 1 to direct the pursuit of the fleeing Federals beyond Cemetery Hill and deprive Meade of that rallying point, so Grant might be charged with a costly dereliction for remaining in the rear during this all-important advance on Petersburg. His presence was the more urgently called for because his plan required co-operation between elements of two separate armies, one commanded by Meade and the other by Butler.

It was reasonable to expect that when these elements met Grant would have taken care of the over-all command, and not left it to negotiation between Hancock and Smith. The treatment of the newspaper correspondent by Hancock, Butler and Grant appears to have been harsh and the characterization of him by Grant as a "scribbler" scarcely seemly. Any correspondent might understandably look on Smith, a major general, as a reliable news source. It was the fashion to denounce the correspondents, but as a whole they were showing in this war a much greater professional competence than many of the generals.

Much other testimony assembled by Butler tended to support Hancock and there is no doubt that the first accountability for the loss of Petersburg belonged elsewhere. Smith could easily have made the capture earlier in the day. Though Hoke's division was returned by Lee to Beauregard late on June 15, the town could have been taken readily that night, after Hancock's arrival.

On this point the defending general, Beauregard, said:

Petersburg at that hour was clearly at the mercy of the Federal commander, who had all but captured it, and only failed of final success because he could not realize the fact of the unparalleled disparity between the two contending forces.[14]

"Oh! That They Had Attacked"

But however free Hancock was of blame, he did not on this occasion rise to the great opportunity opened to him, which probably would have outshone his Gettysburg service. His action in yielding his seniority to Smith was understandable, though scarcely commendable. Grant, it is true, referred to his high reputation and that of his corps and implied that there would be difficulty in adding to it. But Hancock's standing as a general would have been enhanced immeasurably had he taken the command from Smith and stormed into Petersburg with the divisions of Birney and Gibbon. There appears little doubt that he could have forced Beauregard across the Appomattox River and made Richmond untenable for Lee's army.

What effect this would have had on ending the war can only be surmised. Grant and Lee would have been spared the labors of the Petersburg siege. Richmond would have fallen in the summer of 1864. Celerity of movement would have been restored to Lee's army after it had been freed from the necessity of guarding Richmond, but there were no apparent means by which he might have beaten off the vastly superior forces arrayed by the North against him. Had Hancock captured Petersburg on June 15, it is a fair assumption that the war would not have run into the winter of 1864.

Colonel Lyman of Meade's staff saw the opportunity and said in a letter:

Hancock got up that evening and joined the Eighteenth Corps. Their troops were all exhausted, but, oh! that they had attacked at once. Petersburg would have gone like a rotten branch. In war there is a critical instant—a night—perhaps only a half hour, when everything culminates. He is the military genius who recognizes this instant and acts upon it.[15]

If Hancock failed to take full advantage of his numerical superiority on the night of June 15, it was no more than Grant did on the following days, when he had most of the army, a force aggregating perhaps 90,000 men, in front of Petersburg while Lee was still groping about for him, not even certain that he had crossed the James River. Beauregard had not more than 15,000 inside the Petersburg works.[16]

Hancock attacked with Birney's division on the late afternoon of June 16 and again on June 17. Barlow was sent into the front line, with Gibbon in support, and Birney and Barlow stormed the main Confederate line. Though unable to carry it they broke it for a time and captured some redoubts, but these were not worth the serious loss in regimental commanders and enlisted men entailed by the attack. Here fell another of Hancock's trusted subordinates, Colonel Patrick Kelly, commander of the Irish Brigade and earlier commander of the 88th New York. He had commanded the Irish in the Wheat Field at Gettysburg.

Desultory fighting continued. Early on June 18 the arrival of Kershaw's division signaled to the anxious Beauregard that Lee's army was at hand. Lee arrived at 11:30 A.M. and the prolonged siege of Petersburg began.

In mitigation of the criticism of Hancock, it should be said that he was in agony from his Gettysburg wound during this period. For six weeks he had been much in the saddle, with brief rest periods, and the exertions had kept the wound open. Some of the time he had to command sitting on the ground, which was difficult for a man accustomed to looking over the field at a gallop and giving orders from horseback. The incapacity called for a complete readjustment of his command methods. Often he had to retire to an ambulance for rest and he rode in one when the corps was moving. Finally, on June 18, bone fragments began to work their way out of the wound. Hancock was compelled to recognize that he was wholly disabled and to turn over to Birney the command of the Second Corps. He obtained leave of absence for ten days.

Meade mentioned in a letter, June 25, that Hancock's wound had discharged a large piece of bone, following which he showed signs of rapid improvement.[17]

Birney was consuming his vitality by his intense application to his job and would not outlast the Petersburg effort. When Hancock was able to resume his command on June 27, both he and Meade recommended the faithful Birney for command of the Tenth Corps, part of the Army of the James.

Francis Walker called Birney eminently sagacious and said he had an excellent understanding of military principles and in temper was "signally cool and composed." When he left the corps, command of the division went to Brigadier General Gershom Mott, whose earlier division, which had been merged into Birney's, had been routed in the Wilderness. Mott, the Jersey banker, was rated brave, with much natural instinct for leadership, "though lacking a little in that stirring ambition which brings to their highest activity the qualities of a commander."

Grant's confidence in Hancock was expressed again when after Jubal Early had been driven back from his thrust toward Washington, he recommended a unification of four scattered departments, the Susquehanna, Middle, West Virginia and Washington. Writing Lincoln from City Point July 25, 1864, Grant suggested that Meade be placed in command of this unified military division and added: "In this case I would suggest General Hancock for command of the Army of the Potomac, and General Gibbon for command of the Second Corps."[18]

In August Grant renewed his recommendation that Hancock be appointed a brigadier general in the regular army. Lincoln and Stanton complied in two days.

Meade and Hancock—"They Talk and Talk"

Meade's admiration of Hancock was unbroken during this summer period in spite of rumors of controversies. These appear to have no factual basis, except the possibility, always present with a free talker like Hancock and an easily irritated commander like Meade, that spontaneous outbursts might be given greater significance than was warranted.

Meade called these reports of friction "canards," and said, "I have never had a quarrel with either Gen. Hancock or Smith." Nevertheless, his attitude was a bit guarded in the next remark: "Hancock is an honest man, and as he has always professed the warmest friendship for me, I never doubt his statements." Meade went on to stress his "friendly feelings" toward Hancock and "highest appreciation of his talents" and wished him "joy in his promotion."[19] But was there full appreciation of his friend's talents in the notation he made on August 6? He said then that "Hancock with his usual luck, has captured some guns and colors."[20] The reference was to the first Deep Bottom expedition across the James.

Still, the relations between these two generals who had so much in common in the army's history were basically warm and sympathetic.

Meade's visits with Hancock were almost the only relaxation for either during the hot summer. Lyman, who ordinarily accompanied Meade, left an account of a typical meeting in Hancock's temporary headquarters, a half-shattered house on which someone had written the name "Straggler's Rest."[21] Hancock wore on the torrid day a white shirt, blue pants and nothing more. He was stretched out in a covered wagon halted beneath a weeping-willow tree.

Meade anchored himself on the wagon seat with his feet over the footboard and lighted a cigar. "We all knew he was fixed for an hour at least," wrote Lyman, who then explained: "When he gets down with Hancock they talk, and talk, and talk, being great friends. Hancock is a very great and vehement talker but always says something worth hearing."

At length, after the party had been "well fried and dusted," Meade got up as if to depart, but his staff officer was not misled and kept his place, "for I knew he would sit down again. He always rises twice or three times before he finally leaves Hancock."

In late June Meade and Hancock had much entertainment out of what amounted to a popularity contest, a back-home vote to determine which should be the recipient of a sword. Wrote Meade:

We laugh and joke a good deal about it, and whenever a paper comes in we look for the state of the vote. The last date is the 14th and it shows me about one hundred and fifty ahead, which, as I have been behind him all the time, is the source of much merriment.[22]

Meade continued in the lead and ten days later, on June 27, noted in another letter that Hancock was hoping for a big upset at the last minute.

Hancock owed his supply of fresh white shirts to his valet, Shaw, who labored continually over the washboard. Colonel Lyman described him as a "ne'er-do-well, roving, jack-of-all-trades Englishman." He was loyal to his British antecedents, for he "no more picks up anything American than a duck's feathers soak water." His first name does not appear, and to Hancock he was simply "Mr. Shaw." Lyman quoted the general's opinion of him:

That fellow is the most inquisitive and cool man I ever saw. Now I don't mind so much his smoking all my cigars and drinking all my liquors—which he does—but I had a bundle of the most private papers which I had hidden in the bottom of my trunk, and, the other day, I came into my tent and there was Mr. Shaw reading them. And when I asked him what the devil he meant, he said: "Oh, General, I took the liberty of looking at them, and now I am so interested, I hope you will let me finish the rest!"[23]

Hancock's sense of humor was as much a characteristic as his quick flashes of profane anger. Probably he was tolerant with Shaw because the supply of clean white shirts did not cease.

De Trobriand Sees "Political Aims"

Hancock enforced a divorcement of the military from politics as much as possible in his own corps. The Presidential campaign of 1864, which at times grew heated, threatened to break out in the ranks, and partisans of McClellan began to talk in open terms—often not complimentary—of how Lincoln had conducted the war. Hancock, who always seemed to know what was happening among the men, thought this was harmful to the service. He issued an order and had it read at every regimental muster. The point was clear:

Our first duty is to stop the Rebellion, not to talk. When the war is over you can criticize as much as you like. Until then, a soldier's duty is to obey and fight.[24]

For one who had never voted, Hancock took unusual interest in the political campaign and the only explanation is that he appreciated the close relations between military operations and the administration's attitude. As a soldier he practiced what he preached to his men and refrained from partisan discussions. His comments were noncommittal. In a letter August 6 he remarked: "Politics are looking peculiar. It is hard to tell who is going to be President." To that he added, "I do not think either party knows yet who is to be their candidate."[25]

Though McClellan had not been nominated by the Democrats the wind was blowing with unmistakable strength in his direction and Lincoln had been named by the National Union party on June 8. Still, there was continual agitation in Republican ranks against Lincoln because of the war casualties and his call on July 18 for a new levy of 500,000 men. The Grant-for-President movement was revived,[26] and agitation arose in favor of holding a new convention in Buffalo to name a candidate to supplant Lincoln. All of this tended to justify Hancock's doubt about who would finally head the tickets.

Regis de Trobriand came back to the army in mid-July and reported to Hancock for assignment. Meade had heard he was unassigned in New York and had written him to rejoin his old soldiers, though the ghosts of large numbers of them still hovered over the Wheat Field at Gettysburg. De Trobriand met his new corps commander—his old Third Corps having been merged with the Second—about July 15, and gave a picture of Hancock's good and bad points, as he saw them:

General Hancock is one of the handsomest men in the United States army. He is tall in stature, robust in figure, with movements of easy dignity. His head, shaded by thick hair of a light chestnut color, strikes one favorably from the first by the regularity of his features and the engaging expression which is habitual to him. His manners are generally very polite. His voice is pleasant, and his speech as agreeable as his looks. Such is Hancock in repose.

In action he is entirely different. Dignity gives way to activity; his features become animated, his voice loud, his eyes are on fire, his blood kindles, and his bearing is that of a man carried away by passion—the character of his bravery. It is this, I think, which renders him much less fit for an independent command than to act under orders.[27]

The French general, whose relations with his superior became strained before the campaign was much further developed, emphasized that while Hancock was brilliant in the second rank of generals, his luster dimmed in the first. How De Trobriand gained his positive conclusions when Hancock had virtually no opportunity to command independently is not clear. He conceded that in matters of execution "he was admirable." But: "If it was necessary to plan and direct, he was no longer equal to the occasion."[28]

De Trobriand analyzed Hancock's appeal to the army, hinting disapproval of his methods:

His popularity was great, perhaps greater than that of any other officer of his rank. This is easily explained: firstly, by the brilliancy of his service, and also by the particular care he always took to have it known. The correspondents of the principal journals yielded, like everyone else, to his captivating bearing and manners; information was freely given them in the form of reports by the general—often, without doubt to avoid all error—their correspondence was submitted to his inspection, so that the result was sometimes partialities of which they were hardly conscious.[29]

De Trobriand seemed to dwell on the less attractive qualities he found in the corps commander. Hancock's partialities, he contended, were not based on merit or military considerations but "were connected with political aims, in which the general allowed himself to be drawn too easily." Then he found that Hancock had a much warmer attitude toward his first two divisions than his third, which was the remnant of the old Third Corps of Hooker and Sickles. This third division, according to De Trobriand, actually brought him more honor than either of the others.[30] The Frenchman would have found it difficult to sustain that assertion.

Hancock may have had greater affection for the divisions of his old corps which he had led at Gettysburg, but it was never asserted by awarding softer assignments to them. The tough role went usually to Barlow, who led Hancock's own division.

Rambling Talk and Bad Humor

De Trobriand told a story that illustrates how politics did manage to break into the discussions of top officers. A group was in Hancock's tent when an artillery colonel of the Ninth Corps voiced a spirited opposition to emancipation and even declared himself to be in favor of slavery.

This was a strange platform for one of high rank in the Northern army. De Trobriand did not name the colonel other than to say he was the chief of artillery of the corps; it would be difficult to identify him positively because the exact date of the conversation was not given. But De Trobriand "expressed astonishment" at the pro-slavery views of such a high officer.[31]

While the talk was running on, Hancock "preserved a diplomatic silence." He "leaned very near the Democratic party," said De Trobriand. The Frenchman's was the only account of the meeting, incorporated in his later writing, with Hancock having no chance for rebuttal. Of Hancock he continued:

He was strongly of the opinion that, if he had wished, he might have himself been the candidate opposed to Lincoln. It appeared that some politicians, friends of his, had, at the time, made overtures to him on the subject, overtures which he had wisely declined. He had not pronounced for either side, making some general remarks, emphasized by gestures of the head, desiring to run with the hare and hold with the hounds.[32]

That was hardly a fair accusation against Hancock because he was quite obviously at this period—probably it was in September, for De Trobriand's talk indicated that McClellan already had been nominated by the Democrats—wrestling with a problem in which his principles seemed to clash.

In the end he decided to support Lincoln. This determination could not have been reached except by deep reflection and at considerable anguish. Nothing shows more clearly the ardor he felt for the Union cause. His friendship with McClellan was close and sincere. He was by rearing and long devotion a Jacksonian. But before him was the practical matter of winning the war, and that purpose clearly would be advanced, it appeared, by the election of Lincoln. So the lifelong Democrat cast his first vote for Lincoln, the Union Party candidate. Certainly he could never have dreamed then that he would one day become a candidate for President on the Democratic ticket.

Many other War Democrats, among them Major General Ben Butler, followed the same course of reasoning, but 1,835,985 Americans made a contrary decision and it would be a mistake to think that Lincoln got all the carefully reasoned or all the patriotic votes.

Hancock would find later on, when he was a candidate for the Presidency himself, that some of his close friends and former subordinates who admired him would see it as their duty to vote against him out of a belief that the old cause of the Union would be advanced by the triumph of his opponent.

Hancock's impatience with De Trobriand arose out of the conversation at which the artillery colonel spoke approvingly of slavery.

The Frenchman argued for McClellan "as a statesman and as a soldier," though the fact that McClellan was a nominee in the campaign made him recognize that he was "treading on delicate ground." He wrote in detail of his conversation. Unwisely he reached the battle of Williamsburg and criticized the treatment Hooker had received on that field. He judged later that he had been carried away by too much confidence in Hancock's "liberality." But he declared that Hooker was abandoned all morning at Williamsburg without support. Here he seemed to turn critical of McClellan, whose statesmanship and military ability he had just been applauding. McClellan, he declared, had remained back at Yorktown, had come up when the battle was over, had been ignorant of the events of the field, and had sent the dispatch naming Hancock without ever mentioning Hooker, Kearny or John J. Peck.

De Trobriand plunged ahead: "Not that I intend for a moment to underrate in the least the importance of your part in the battle," he told Hancock, who by this time was showing his annoyance. "In that respect there can be but one voice, and, as much as any one can, I appreciate how much your brilliant action on that occasion did you honor." The laudation was getting thick and Hancock could not have been impressed with it. "But I appeal to yourself: what can be thought of a general-in-chief capable of such conduct, and of such injustice toward three generals out of four."

Hancock now was angry. De Trobriand saw that he had "touched a sore spot" and that "the oil I poured upon it did not allay the irritation."

"I understand," Hancock said testily. "You are all alike in the old Third Corps. In your eyes you have done everything in this war, and all others nothing."

Hancock thereupon broke up the meeting. His attitude appeared little more generous than what he attributed to the Third Corps. It could not have been his settled judgment, for he had close personal confidence in Birney and hosts of others in that corps. The rambling conversation of the emotional Frenchman and the pro-slavery Federal colonel had gradually worked him into a lather. De Trobriand attributed his anger to "wounded vanity." "I protested in vain," he said, and added: "By a few words too plainly spoken, I had not only lost the good will of my corps commander, but had also revived his prejudices against the whole Third Division."[33]

★ ★ ★ 16 ★ ★ ★

Defeat Has Bitter Dregs

The Fight Carried Across the River

While there was much argument and political discussion, the army was also fighting.

The long-drawn-out battle of Petersburg, while mainly monotonous, had striking features beyond the race for possession of the town. High drama hovered over the mine dug by bluecoats from the Pennsylvania anthracite fields, and over the sensational explosion; the frightful disaster to the men piled into the crater; Hancock's thrust toward Richmond; the battle of Reams's Station and the verbal wounding of Gibbon. But mainly the story was that of a humdrum siege.

In late July Grant sent Hancock with the Second Corps on a detached mission north of the James River, for the purpose of inducing Lee to send troops north of the James also, so that his army would be depleted at Petersburg when the mine being dug there was exploded. Fighting occurred and both sides suffered. The Second Corps was withdrawn before the mine was set off on July 30, but the battle of the crater turned into a costly fiasco. The whole scheme was abortive.

"We lost a fair chance at Petersburg the other day" was Hancock's observation.[1] He expressed regret that he had been put on the Court of Inquiry to assess the blame for the mine failure. The judicial duty brought his military operations to a standstill.

Then, in mid-August, Hancock was sent north of the James

again on a feint against Richmond at a time when Lee was reported
to have detached three divisions for Jubal Early in the Shenandoah
Valley. Hancock was to be assisted by a corps from Butler's army,
and with the co-operation of Gregg's cavalry was to move to Deep
Bottom and threaten Richmond. The object was to force Lee to
recall his missing divisions or to open up possibilities for an attack
on the Petersburg lines south of the James—if Lee answered the
Deep Bottom expedition by moving a considerable force north of
the river.

Hancock was joined on August 13 by the Tenth Corps, now
commanded by Birney. The Second Corps had marched to City
Point in great haste to get the transports that would convey it to
Deep Bottom. Hancock preferred to ride with his staff and cross
the muffled pontoon bridges maintained by Butler over the Appomattox and James rivers. Butler said Hancock appeared in no
hurry when he stopped for lunch at the headquarters of the Army
of the James. They ate and chatted for an hour, then he went on.
Late that afternoon he picked up Birney and attacked the Confederate works on Newmarket Heights.

Grant earnestly hoped that if Lee had truly weakened his forces
by three divisions, Hancock could turn his feint into a full thrust
and go into Richmond, or else make it possible for Grant to carry
Petersburg. Hancock began his advance up the left bank of the
James, Birney close to the river and Barlow, commanding two
divisions of the Second Corps, on the right. Mott formed the
center. Gregg's cavalry was on the far right, ready to dash into
Richmond if Hancock could penetrate the defenses.

But Hancock met the stiffest sort of resistance and learned that
he faced, not only the Richmond home guards, but also formidable
units of the Army of Northern Virginia. He was confronted first
by Field's division at Deep Bottom, and soon by the divisions of
Wilcox and Mahone and the cavalry divisions of Hampton and
W. H. F. Lee.

Repulsed that evening, he renewed the attack at daylight on the
next day. Birney was swung around the rear of Mott and Barlow
on a flanking movement that proved ineffectual because the circuit
he made was too wide to permit an early attack. Some of Barlow's
men entered a part of the enemy's works and retained possession
for a time of an advanced line of rifle pits. Then Hancock, per-

ceiving that Richmond could not be taken except by a regular investment, returned to the south of the James on the night of August 20.[2] Grant seemed well enough pleased with the operation. Hancock had captured six pieces of artillery and several hundred prisoners and detained troops under marching orders to join Early.[3] Hancock learned that Lee had not detached three divisions to go to Early, but only Kershaw's, which was recalled.

Though Hancock had seemed leisurely to Butler when he stopped for lunch, he was so active during the attack that Walker, his adjutant, rated the day "the most awful in my personal experience as a soldier." In Hancock's effort to envelop the Confederate defenses the corps "literally marched between men lying on both sides of the road dead from the effects of heat and fatigue."[4]

Hancock's movements at Deep Bottom were conducted so rapidly, in fact, that the men began to give the Second Corps the nickname of "Hancock's Cavalry."

The story was told that a curious soldier inquired of his companion when a halt was ordered: "O, Jim, what er we a-stoppin for?"

"The staff is gettin' fresh horses," Jim explained.[5]

Although conducting two corps at Deep Bottom kept him busy, Hancock was still observant of good work by his enlisted men. He noticed a company of New York soldiers commanded by a lagging sergeant. Just then a corporal stepped to the front where the sergeant should have been and began to direct the company like a seasoned officer. When Hancock got back to his headquarters he sent for the corporal. The man must have reported with trepidation, but he left Hancock with a captaincy.[6]

The Corps Is Routed at Reams's Station

Hancock's service at Petersburg was marked by bursts of wrath resulting as much from the frustrations of the campaign as from the heat and continued difficulties with his Gettysburg wound. Among the unfortunate developments was a final break with Major General John Gibbon, his subordinate and second in command at Gettysburg. It is hard to judge who was principally at fault.

The controversy was the outgrowth of Hancock's defeat at Reams's Station, one of the major setbacks of his military career, though not comparable in fatalities with the repulse of his corps at Cold Harbor.

While the siege of Petersburg dragged on, Grant sent Hancock to tear up a stretch of the Weldon Railroad, which he did effectively, on August 24, to about three miles south of Reams's Station. He assigned Gibbon to continue the devastation on the following day, but on the approach of the enemy Gibbon retired to the station and Hancock made a defensive line in some hastily thrown-up trenches. Miles, now commanding Barlow's division, went into position beside Gibbon.

The oncoming Confederates under A. P. Hill made three determined but futile assaults on Hancock's line. Then a battery was put into a position to enfilade the Federals, and Henry Heth, newly arrived, made a fourth try with his fresh division. To the humiliation of Hancock and all his top officers, the divisions of both Miles and Gibbon, which had given to the Army of the Potomac some of the most glorious chapters of its history, broke and retired before the Confederate onslaught. They left three batteries in the hands of the assailants. Miles was able to rally some of his troops, recover one of the batteries and recapture a part of his former position, but the defeat could not be erased. Gibbon conceded:

> My men . . . did not behave well and the enemy beat us badly. . . . It was a severe and terrible battle and a mortifying one to the Second Corps, which is becoming very much used up with its hard work and hard fighting.[7]

Gibbon managed to save the only two pieces he had with him but the loss of artillery elsewhere amounted to nine guns. Hancock lost 1,700 prisoners among about 2,400 casualties, a heavy sacrifice for the number of men engaged.[8] But the proud Second Corps was most humiliated because it lost seven battle flags. Green troops from the draft boards crowded together in indifference or terror and awaited a chance to throw down their arms.

Hancock exposed himself recklessly during the assault, riding the lines, dashing into the retreating troops to rally them, sending his staff officers to all points to quell the panic.[9] He was deeply mortified and incensed and altogether heedless of his own safety. Once, dust-covered and dirty with powder smoke, he rode up to a battery, put his hand on the shoulder of one of his officers and said: "Colonel, I do not care to die, but I pray God I may never leave this field!"[10] Of all the bestowals of fortune, defeat not death, was hardest to accept.

While he was in the center of the action Hancock's horse was hit. The steed dropped almost instantly, apparently dead. He took another horse; then, five minutes later, the first horse, his favorite sorrel, got to his feet, shook himself and looked about the field. He proved in such good shape that the general remounted him, rode him that day and kept him for many years after the war.[11]

What had happened was familiar to horsemen of the Western plains—the horse had been "creased." Horses were captured in the West by this process of "creasing," which involved fine marksmanship. A bullet had to be fired close enough to the horse's spinal column to paralyze the animal temporarily. No permanent injury resulted from "creasing" when the job was properly done.[12]

Chief of Staff Morgan thought Hancock never recovered from Reams's Station. He retreated toward Petersburg that night but got little comfort from the fact that Hill fell back also. Morgan saw a difference between this battle and repulses like Cold Harbor:

He had seen his troops fail in their attempts to carry intrenched positions of the enemy, but he had never before had the mortification of seeing them driven and his lines and guns taken . . . and never before had he seen his men fail to respond to the utmost when he called upon them personally for a supreme effort.[13]

Walker attributed the defeat to the reduced condition of the two divisions, the poor construction of the trenches they defended, and what he described as the enemy's superior force. Of Hancock's mortification he said:

The agony of that day never passed away from that proud soldier, who, for the first time, in spite of superhuman exertions and reckless exposure on his part, saw his lines broken and his guns taken.[14]

The chagrin was heightened by the manner in which the battle was hailed as a triumph in the Northern press. In the next batch of papers received, one carried in big capital letters the headline "Another Great Victory by Gen. Hancock."[15] Manifestly such a story could not be publicly denied; it had to be suffered, with a sense of humiliation and guilt, by Hancock.

Sharp Words over the Defeat

Gibbon had come up through the artillery and had first appeared in the war as McDowell's chief of artillery at First Manassas. He was then thirty-four years old. He had been born in Philadelphia but when he was twelve his father, a physician, moved to Charlotte, North Carolina. John had been appointed to West Point from there. Graduating in 1847, he served in the Mexican War and in the affairs against the Seminoles and in Utah. He was an artillerist, and attained some fame from his book, published in 1859, entitled the *Artillerists' Manual*. Before the war he instructed in the use of the guns at West Point.

Though Gibbon sided with the North and was intensely loyal to the Union cause, three of his brothers chose the Southern armies. One, Dr. Robert Gibbon, often must have been close to his Federal brother, for he served as the surgeon of Lane's North Carolina brigade of Lee's army, which at times, as at Gettysburg and in the Wilderness, faced Hancock's men. Before his assignment under Hancock Gibbon commanded the famous Federal "Iron Brigade" and was rated a highly capable soldier. Lyman referred to him as "steel-cold Gibbon . . . with his sharp nose and up-and-down manner of telling the truth, no matter whom it hurts."[16]

The Hancock-Gibbon rupture had been threatening since Gibbon's failure to throw in Barlow's division against A. P. Hill's flank in the Wilderness. Gibbon's account indicates that Hancock had been unpleasant, on one occasion at least, when there seemed no cause for ill humor. On June 15, the day the corps came up in front of Petersburg, Gibbon was on a road blocked by Baldy Smith's troops. He halted until they cleared, but Hancock, who had just been to a meeting with Smith, rode by and looked him over.

According to Gibbon, Hancock was "out of temper, calling me sharply to account." The fault he complained of was noncompliance with a general order that whenever a division halted one brigade should be deployed in battle formation as a precaution against attack. Gibbon had not regarded this as necessary in an instance where the road ahead was blocked by friendly troops. The explanation, understandable, did not satisfy Hancock. Gibbon, after being reprimanded, returned to his command "in a very bad humor."[17]

Then came the defeat at Reams's Station. Gibbon decided after that battle to recommend to Hancock measures he thought would bolster the corps. He felt that the corps was "fought out," with brigades sometimes under lieutenant colonels, regiments under captains and companies under sergeants. Most of the men were recruits. He called on Hancock and suggested orally the need of a reorganization. He declared the corps could not perform efficiently in its existing condition.

It was Hancock's policy not to blame troops for failure. Whether it was from this consideration or from a growing dislike of Gibbon, he dismissed Gibbon's suggestion and criticized the conduct of Gibbon's command during the battle—"harshly," by Gibbon's account. Gibbon tried to support his case. He said that the regiments with the best records had turned in the worst performance at Reams's Station. The reason was, he thought, that the men who had made the reputations of these regiments were no longer present. In their place was what he called "a mass of newly drafted men, many of whom, it had been reported to me, had in the battle huddled behind their breastworks without firing a piece and allowed themselves to be captured en masse."

Walker made the same point in reviewing the battle, when he referred to the absence of some of the great names of the Second Corps: "Had Tyler, Brooke, McKeen, Haskell, McMahon, Byrnes, Morris and Porter stood over the skeleton regiments at Reams's, the northwest angle would not have been carried. . . ." Hancock himself said some of the officers at Reams's Station could not speak English.[18]

Unquestionably the army was receiving men inferior on the average to earlier recruits. The hiring of substitutes brought out a crop of "bounty jumpers" and lackadaisical soldiers not unwilling to be captured when the end of the war was in sight. The terrible casualties of Grant's campaign had dampened the ardor of draftees and recruits. Standing room in Andersonville was better than six feet in Virginia.

Considering all this, Gibbon had a point when he said that the soldiers were not acting as well as they once did, yet he did not explain how reorganization would correct the fault. Hancock, who could recall his own tireless efforts in drilling his green brigade early in the war, appeared to feel that the trouble was more with the officers than the men. For this or other reasons he was impatient. Gibbon thought it was difficult for a commander to recognize that a brave, efficient body of troops, "once his pride and boast," could have fallen to a much lower standing.

Gibbon Resigns and Reconsiders

Gibbon left the conference unsatisfied. That night he wrote Hancock a note saying he would regret to have his division broken up, but would consent to it if, for the good of the corps, it could be used in some consolidation. Hancock's reply was prompt and, in Gibbon's words, "curt." He sent a private note that "surprised" and "mortified" Gibbon, as well it might, for Hancock suggested perhaps it was in the best interests of the service that Gibbon should surrender command of his division.

"I was more than hurt at this reply," Gibbon said, "which struck me as a distinct intimation that I was *personally* responsible for the condition of my division!" No doubt that was what Hancock meant to convey, but he wrote in anger and while brooding over the loss of the battle. He moved more severely against a worthwhile subordinate than he normally would have done.

Gibbon took the only course open to him. He wrote at once an official application to be relieved from duty in the Second Corps and forwarded it through regular channels, which would take it to Hancock, Meade, Grant and then the War Department.

Hancock was distracted at the time by having to sit on the Court of Inquiry investigating the Petersburg mine disaster. When he received Gibbon's application he asked that general to come to corps headquarters. The meeting resulted in no more than angry exchanges between them. Here, too, the only version is Gibbon's.

Hancock came out when Gibbon arrived, said he wanted to talk about the application but was too busy with the court at the moment. As Gibbon put it, he "said something about wishing me to withdraw the application." Gibbon declined to withdraw it and "with some heat" explained that after Hancock's "insult" he had had but one course. Use of the word "insult" added fuel to Hancock's anger. He started back into the house, saying that if Gibbon regarded it an "insult" he had nothing more to add to the matter. Gibbon sought to hold him by pointing out that he had been summoned to headquarters by Hancock, but the corps commander broke away and returned to the court.

That night Hancock again sent for Gibbon. He had cooled off, and Gibbon found him "in much more pleasant humor." The two were able to talk calmly about the proposal to reorganize the corps. Then picking up Gibbon's application, Hancock said the time was not propitious for Gibbon to request relief from his command—that people would charge him with trying "to desert a sinking ship" and that his "reputation would not stand such an imputation."

"I told him," said Gibbon, "that what 'people said' would have no influence whatever with me; that if my reputation could not stand it, it would have to fall," and that since "he had told me in plain terms I no longer had his confidence as a commander, I could do nothing else than ask to be relieved."

They talked for about two hours but got nowhere. Gibbon stubbornly declined to withdraw his application because of Hancock's note insulting his reputation. Hancock finally asked to see the note he had written. Gibbon handed it over and Hancock read it.

"I was mad when I wrote that letter," he conceded. Gibbon said he was quite aware of it.

"Suppose I withdraw this letter," Hancock suggested.

"All right, General," said Gibbon; "if you withdraw it the matter is ended and I authorize you to stop my application to be relieved."

Hancock held the note to the candle flame and threw the burning paper into the fireplace. Gibbon said they parted "on tolerably good terms." Speaking for himself, he felt that the soreness "never entirely disappeared." No doubt Hancock soon forgot it. He did not record anything about it and with him, when anger left, it left entirely.

A few days later Grant, who does not seem to have any knowledge of this spat, assigned Gibbon to command the Eighteenth Corps temporarily during the sick leave of Major General Edward O. C. Ord, who had supplanted Baldy Smith. Except for a brief period, this marked Gibbon's passing from the Second Corps.[19] He had inscribed his name high in the history of the corps, most notably in its defense of Cemetery Ridge.

Irascible as Hancock may have seemed in some of these matters, Lyman referred to him at different times as "the cheery Hancock" and the "irresistible Hancock."[20] Bitter as was the defeat at Reams's Station, it did not leave him sullen.

That Hancock's great reputation was unmarred in the autumn of 1864 was shown when Rear Admiral David D. Porter, a salty, plain-spoken man, named him as the general preferred to take Wilmington, North Carolina, the most stubborn hold-out among the Confederate ports. Porter, writing to Assistant Secretary of the Navy Gustavus Vasa Fox from his flagship *Malvern* in Hampton Roads, October 19, 1864, asked if troops could not be obtained for the Wilmington expedition and added: "Hancock would be the man to command them if we could get them."[21]

His high standing with the public was evidenced by the collection of a fund by New York residents for the purchase of a handsome barouche. It was presented with the thought that when his wound kept him from the saddle he could ride in the barouche at the head of his troops. The Confederate Lieutenant General Richard S. Ewell, who had lost a leg, campaigned in a buggy. But Hancock did not use the barouche. He preferred the army ambulance.[22]

Parting with the Second Corps

A relatively small affair on the Boydton Road was Hancock's last battle in his long association with the Army of the Potomac. It ended triumphantly with the repulse of Heth's division, an old antagonist, and the capture of about 900 prisoners.

De Trobriand thought he could see in Hancock's report of the affair a reflection of a prejudice against the Third Division, once the old Third Corps, which he said lost more than twice as many on the Boydton Road as the Second Division. He put the alleged distortion into artistic terms:

When a landscape painter finds his subject for a painting in nature, on transferring it to canvas, he puts the lights and shades as pleases him. General Hancock's report was treated somewhat in that manner, and in the division of the light and shade, the relief was for the Second division, and the background for the Third, especially as what concerned my brigade.[23]

De Trobriand was imagining. Hancock was by reputation most diligent to have his aides get the precise facts for his reports, and to give credit where it was due.

Back in Philadelphia Birney was dying in great anguish. He had been a splendid division commander and the Second Corps

was never the same without him. He had risen to high command
from the historic City Troop of Philadelphia. As a colonel he had
served under Phil Kearny; then he commanded a brigade and
finally the division after the intrepid Kearny had been killed. The
malaria which he contracted while campaigning weakened him
and he died at the age of thirty-eight, with characteristic words
on his lips: "Boys, keep your eyes on that flag."

The New York *Herald* correspondent, Thomas M. Cook, wrote
on December 8, 1863, after Mine Run, some comments on Birney
made by Major General William H. French. "He is all soldier. I
never have met a better. Any commander should be proud of
such a subordinate." Hancock always was.

Hancock was having new trouble with his old wound. In November he concluded that the best thing for himself and the service
would be a leave for rest and recuperation. His departure was
without fanfare. It was Thanksgiving Day, November 26, 1864.
He turned over command of the celebrated Second Corps to Major
General A. A. Humphreys, Grant's designee, then circulated his
farewell order, which concluded with words of appreciation:

Conscious that whatever military honor has befallen me during
my association with the Second Corps has been won by the gallantry of the officers and soldiers I have commanded, I feel that
in parting from them I am severing the strongest ties of my military
life.[24]

Mounting the sorrel, he rode away.

When he was gone one of his sergeants, L. Reynols, wrote an
ode to him, set to the meter of the "Star Spangled Banner," ending:

> Farewell! Oh, how painful to break our connection,
> But duty compels it, and sadly we part;
> But nothing can sever the bond of affection,
> That binds to brave Hancock the true soldier's heart.
> As gold to the miser, as the bride to her lover,
> Art thou to those friends who may see thee no more;
> We'll think of thee, Hancock, we'll love thee forever,
> Then remember, brave chieftain, thy bold Second Corps.[25]

Hancock's own sentiments were more simply stated. When a
friend after the war asked him, "Well, General Hancock, how about

the Second Corps?" he laid his hand on the man's shoulder and spoke with feeling: "They are at rest, most of them in Heaven."[26]

"One Felt Safe When Near Him"

While the Second Corps had other commanders—Sumner in the beginning, before the army had been shaken down, then Couch and finally Humphreys in the last few months of the war—the corps was essentially Hancock's and its record was his.

In the four years of war the Second Corps lost roughly 40,000 in killed and wounded. Triumph in this war was measured by the capture of enemy battle flags, and the Second Corps had captured forty-four Confederate colors before it lost one of its own.

General Nelson A. Miles, who had no small part in the great accomplishments of the corps, summed up the record in after years:

It inscribed a greater number of engagements upon its banner than did any other corps of the army, or, I think, more than any other army corps in the history of the world. The graves of its fallen are to be found on every battlefield of the Army of the Potomac from the date of its organization to Appomattox. Its capture of battle flags outnumbered its engagements.

As the war for the Union was unprecedented in the history of the world, so the history of the Second Corps was unexcelled in that war. Its aggregate wounded and killed in battle surpassed that of any other corps. The greatest aggregate of killed and wounded in any division of the army was in the First Division of that corps, and the highest aggregate of killed and wounded in any one regiment of the whole army was in a regiment belonging to the Second Corps. The second highest percentage of regimental loss by death and wounds was also in a regiment of that corps. As to the success and achievements of that famous corps, it captured in a single day as many battle flags, cannon and prisoners of the enemy as it lost in the entire four years of the war.[27]

Among the hundred Federal regiments that sustained the highest casualties of the war, thirty-five were Second Corps regiments.[28]

Hancock's old division lost 2,237 killed and 11,724 wounded in battle. Walker called it:

. . . the division of Sunday morning at Fair Oaks, of the Sunken Road at Antietam, of the Stone Wall at Fredericksburg, the Wheat

Field at Gettysburg, of the Salient at Spotsylvania, of the closing fight at Farmville . . . the division which had been commanded by five such soldiers as Edwin V. Sumner, Israel B. Richardson, Winfield S. Hancock, Francis C. Barlow, and Nelson A. Miles.[29]

Hancock's staff members, the officers who knew him best, were always the most unrestrained in their commendation. Captain H. H. Bingham described him as "handsome in form, commanding in mien and carriage, the soldier marking every feature of his clearcut face, earnest in every word. . . ." He impressed those who met him with "confidence, trust, ability, power, and, above all, self-reliant courage." Then Bingham gave the main quality of Hancock's leadership: "One felt safe when near him."

Walker, his adjutant general, said:

General Hancock was an ideal commander. His presence in the camp or along the line was like an impulse which every soldier felt. It seemed to travel through the army like a great wave. It is needless to say that he was everywhere beloved and admired. It was impossible for it to be otherwise when one saw the force of his character and his enthusiasm and energy. As a military genius he was a tactician of great skill and adroitness, as well as an executor of energy and power. It is seldom that you find these qualities in one man, for it is generally considered as incompatible that a sagacity that was almost cunning should be combined with dash and industry. General Hancock possessed both to a high degree.[30]

· · · 17 · · ·

Mosby and Mrs. Surratt

The Veterans Prefer Their Old Regiments

When Hancock requested leave from the Second Corps, Grant, Stanton and Lincoln all considered that his great prestige might be employed to promote re-enlistments. Consequently he was re-turned to recruiting duty, with headquarters at Harrisburg.

The project seemed reasonable. Many old soldiers had served out their terms and were resting in the North, observing the war from a distance, uncertain about risking their lives again in such an orgy of bloodletting. These men would make the very best soldiers, and the War Department was making every effort to restore them to the ranks. The honorable term of "veteranize" was employed to distinguish their re-enlistment.[1]

When the men were recruited—and Hancock's name was expected to draw them in—they would be assembled into a Veterans' Corps commanded by Hancock. The corps would operate to hem in Lee if he broke away from Petersburg and Richmond in the spring and sought a defensive position in the mountains. Hancock would relieve Sheridan, who commanded in the Shenandoah Valley. Grant's plan at this period was that Sheridan should move out of Virginia and join Sherman, who would be pushing up through the Carolinas.

The recruiting venture met with slight success. Hancock had an abundant amount of prestige, but recruiting in the winter of 1864-

264

1865 had become highly competitive. The quotas were still being assigned to the states, and the states were not partial to enlistments such as Hancock's Veterans' Corps involved. The state received no credit for recruits going directly to Hancock.

Hancock was not opposed; the states merely offered bounties and the scale was continually mounting. What the Federal government could offer in the way of good generalship by Hancock could not outweight the cash-on-the-line from the states. There was one other obstacle. Many veterans who re-enlisted preferred their old regiments to new regiments, new brigades and a whole new set of officers.

By February 1865, Hancock could see that the slow trickle of re-enlistments would never swell into much of a corps and he began to cast about for a better opportunity. When requesting the leave of absence in November he had written to Meade: "I am not ambitious to command Armies or Corps other than the Second (2ᵈ) Corps unless the public service is thought to be in question. . . ."[2]

His stay in Harrisburg had been a series of personal triumphs. One call was from a Philadelphia delegation headed by John W. Everman, the lad he had befriended in Norristown. Everman informed him that he had been voted the freedom of Philadelphia by the city government. He received a greater honor too. A room in Independence Hall—the room in which the Declaration of Independence had been signed—was made available for his use. Few had ever been given that privilege. He went to Philadelphia but could scarcely use the room for an office because of the crowds.

Somebody injecting politics asked Hancock where he stood.

His reply was prompt and discreet: "A good soldier knows no party but his country."[3]

He was about to make overtures to return to the Army of the Potomac preparing for the spring campaign of 1865—the end was in sight but none knew how far down the vista of months they were looking—when Grant revived his plan to use Hancock in the Shenandoah Valley.

Much earlier, when in the summer of 1864 Jubal Early was threatening Washington and the North, Grant had calculated on Meade for the Valley command. In that case Hancock would have taken command of the Army of the Potomac. But Grant, partial to his own boys from the West, had put in Sheridan, thirty-three years old, an experiment, as Lincoln frankly acknowledged in giving approval. One of his top subordinates in the Valley, Brigadier General William H. Emory, commander of the Nineteenth Corps, had been graduated from West Point the year Sheridan was born.

Sheridan had both zest and an ample supply of troops. He succeeded in crushing Early and devastating the Valley even more thoroughly than Sherman had ripped up Georgia, but Grant now changed his plans. Instead of sending Sheridan to help Sherman, he directed him to come in on his own left flank, the result of which was the decisive battle of Five Forks.

When Sheridan was ordered out of the Valley to join in attacking Lee, Grant directed that Hancock take command of what had been designated as the Middle Department, with headquarters at Winchester, Virginia. Explained Grant later:

It was my expectation at the time that in the final operations Hancock should move either up the Valley or else east of the Blue Ridge to Lynchburg, the idea being to make the spring campaign the close of the war.[4]

Gentle Treatment for Former Foes

Hancock relieved Sheridan in Winchester February 26. About the only opposition remaining in the Valley was Colonel John S. Mosby's Rangers. Hancock's main duty after Lee's surrender at Appomattox was bringing about the surrender of this reluctant band.

Hancock's address to the citizens of the Winchester area, published on April 10, 1865, the day after Lee's surrender, foreshadowed the magnanimous policies he would adopt when he came to command one of the military districts of the conquered South. In it he said:

The Major General Commanding trusts that the people to whom this is sent will regard the surrender of General Lee with his army as Lee himself regards it, as the first great step to peace, and will adapt their conduct to the new condition of affairs and make it practicable for him to exhibit towards them every leniency the situation will admit of. Every military restraint shall be removed that is not absolutely essential, and your sons, your husbands, and your brothers shall remain with you unmolested.

He went on to say that it was his purpose to "destroy utterly the haunts" of the marauding bands which invested the territory and that "every outrage committed by them will be followed by the severest infliction."

The negotiations with Mosby were much more prolonged than those between Grant and Lee. Morgan, Hancock's chief of staff, now a brevet brigadier general, sent Mosby copies of the letters exchanged by Grant and Lee and advised him that Hancock was authorized to receive the surrender of Mosby's forces under the same conditions. An officer of equal rank would be sent to meet Mosby.

Mosby replied that he had no other notice of Lee's surrender nor had the emergency arisen that would justify his own surrender. He agreed to suspend hostilities until he could communicate with authorities or get sufficient intelligence to determine his course. The message was carried to Hancock under a flag of truce by a detail which included Dr. A. Monteiro, surgeon of Mosby's Rangers. More interesting than Mosby's reply were the doctor's recollections, written fourteen years later. They suggested that Hancock was at heart warm, sympathetic and gracious to those in misfortune even though they were his enemies. Hancock shook hands pleasantly with the four members of the delegation.

Dr. Monteiro continued:

There was a self-possession, ease and benignant dignity about him that I will never forget. A benevolent expression, illuminated by a powerful intellect, spoke volumes of meaning from his bright and handsome face. It may be that an association of ideas, caused by receiving kind expressions of sympathy and regard, when I expected a harsh, cruel or haughty reception, impressed me favorably with this true gentleman and distinguished soldier. Be that as it may, I have never met a man for whom I have a higher regard, or more profound respect than I have, even at this date, for General Hancock.[5]

Dr. Monteiro said he never had felt ashamed of his old gray uniform until Hancock held his hand, looked kindly and squarely into his face and made a few remarks. He quoted the general as saying:

I sympathize with you in what you believe to be a great misfortune. You have fought bravely and have nothing to be ashamed of. . . . Let us once more kneel down at the same altar, and be like brothers of the same household.

The doctor said that after Hancock spoke he encountered for the first time a doubt as to the righteousness of his cause.

This noble old hero was so kind, considerate and gentle in his manner to us, when we had so little to expect of him, that he conquered me more effectually by his manly sympathy and noble sentiments than could have been done by brute force and military despotism.[6]

Hancock allowed Mosby an armistice of two days provided there were no hostilities, and when the Confederate requested an extension, Hancock granted it. Eventually, after Mosby had disbanded his command and taken his farewell of it, a large group of his men came to Winchester to receive the amnesty. Mosby was in and out of hiding until June, when he finally surrendered and was paroled in Lynchburg.

Hancock's Consideration for Mrs. Surratt

As commanding officer of the department that embraced Washington, Hancock was called on to execute the sentence of the military court which tried the John Wilkes Booth conspirators, though he had no part in the selection of the court, the conduct of the trial or the review of the verdict.

Years later, when he was in politics and it had become evident that Mrs. Mary E. Surratt had been hung in the excitement of the moment by what amounted to a drumhead court-martial and not by a civilian tribunal to which she was entitled, Hancock was subjected to unfair attack on a series of trumped-up charges that held him mainly accountable for the miscarriage of justice. As is often the case in such matters, he was assailed most viciously on the grounds that he failed to do the very acts about which he was the most concerned and punctilious.

Among the charges were those that he confined Mrs. Surratt under brutal conditions, denied her the spiritual consolation of a Catholic priest, refused to obey a writ of habeas corpus issued on her behalf, and debarred her daughter Anna from access to President Johnson to make a final plea for clemency.

Anyone acquainted with Hancock would have known at once that such charges were groundless. However, they came to be circulated so widely that it was necessary for his friends to obtain an exact statement of the circumstances of the trial. Mrs. Surratt's only surviving defense counsel, Judge John W. Clampitt of Illinois, was able to show that Hancock's treatment of her throughout had been most considerate and humane.[7]

Hancock was in Winchester when he heard the shocking news of the assassination of President Lincoln. Mrs. Hancock had arrived that day from Baltimore, intending to remain with the general. That same day Hancock received orders from President Johnson to come immediately to Washington, and he and Mrs. Hancock left at once by special train. They arrived to find the city in a frenzy of uncertainty. Stanton was exercising a virtual dictatorship. A tight censorship soon was imposed on everything relating to the assassins. The country, fearful that the assassination might lead to renewed fighting, breathed a good deal easier when it learned that Hancock was in over-all command of the Washington garrison.

Recognizing that Hancock's presence reassured the people, President Johnson ordered him to remain in Washington until the case against the conspirators was disposed of. The President by executive order of May 1, 1865, appointed Major General John F. Hartranft, already provost marshal of the city, a special provost marshal for the trial by the Military Commission. Since Hartranft derived his powers directly from the President—who imposed on him responsibility for executing the mandates of the court—Hancock had no more than nominal authority over Hartranft and none whatever over the commission. His function was to maintain order, and this he did. Although it was against his principles, he had no other course than to transmit President Johnson's orders to carry out the death sentence imposed on Mrs. Surratt as one of the accessories among the conspirators.

Hancock had come to entertain high personal admiration of Lincoln, as had virtually all of the North and much of the South at the time of his death. About the only Northerner who found consolation was the Dutchman who passed a Baltimore theater and saw the large posters announcing the coming of the "Panorama of Paradise Lost." A bold line proclaimed it "A Rebellion in Heaven." The Dutchman mused a little, then exclaimed, "A Rebellion in Heaven! Mein Gott! That lasts not long now. Uncle Abe is there."[8]

Grieved as he was over Lincoln's death, Hancock nevertheless had profound respect for legal processes and felt that society must treat even its enemies humanely. When he learned that Mrs. Surratt was under close confinement and, in the words of her counsel, was being imprisoned "most carelessly as respects convenience, and in a most brutal manner,"[9] he immediately set about easing these conditions.

Lieutenant Walter F. Halleck, who commanded the guard of the conspirators during the trial, credited Hancock with obtaining for them such consideration as they received:

His humane instructions regarding the treatment of the prisoners (for it was by his order that they were permitted to leave their cells for daily exercise and air in the large yard of the old District penitentiary) deeply impressed me.[10]

Judge Clampitt added his comment. "As counsel for Mrs. Surratt," he said, "I can testify of my own knowledge, that he was deeply moved on her behalf, and distressed on her account." Again he said:

I was myself on the ground and deeply interested in all that occurred, and I know the fact that General Hancock offered to Mrs. Surratt every kindness in his power and was anxious that she should be spared by a pardon. . . .[11]

Hancock took no part in the trial and attended none of the sessions. Colonel H. Kyd Douglas, lately of the staffs of Stonewall Jackson and Edward Johnson, could look down from his place of confinement in the prison at the Arsenal and observe the proceedings. He could see Major General David Hunter, "in the congenial occupation of presiding over a Court of Death with evident pride and satisfaction."[12] No plausible testimony was presented to show that Mrs. Surratt was ever aware of the original plot to abduct Lincoln, and certainly not of Booth's hasty later plan out of which the assassination developed. Hancock's concern about her was due partly to an aversion to the execution of a woman, and apparently partly to his appreciation of the weakness of the case against her. As was afterward contended, "the proof against her was not sufficient to have hung a dog."[13]

According to Clampitt, Hancock was "deeply moved" and "distressed." The Reverend J. A. Walter, Mrs. Surratt's spiritual guide, refuted as "malicious" the charge that Hancock had denied her the consolation of a priest.[14] Clampitt found Father Walter and another priest with her when he came just before the execution to tell her farewell.

Hancock's actions on the morning before the execution showed his great concern and suggest that he hoped to the very end for a pardon or commutation of the sentence. Early on the morning of the execution day, July 7, 1865, Anna Surratt called at Hancock's hotel and asked him what she could do to save her mother from the gallows. He told her there was only one thing remaining—"Go to the President, throw yourself on your knees before him and beg for the life of your mother."[15]

Anna tried to do exactly that. Accompanied by John F. Brophy, a family friend, she went to the White House. There access to the President was barred by two self-appointed guards of the public welfare, Senators Jim Lane of Kansas and Preston King of New York, both destined to be suicides, who stood at the President's door.[16]

Repulsed and heartbroken, Anna and Brophy drove from the White House to the Arsenal in southeast Washington where the sentence was to be carried out between the hours of 10:00 A.M. and 2:00 P.M. En route they saw mounted soldiers at intervals all along the line. These had been stationed at Hancock's order by Mitchell, now his chief of staff, so that notice could be rushed by fast relay in case President Johnson granted a reprieve.[17]

At the Arsenal Anna met Hancock, who with great compassion and sadness told her that he had no further hope. He explained that if any reprieve should be issued it would be addressed to him as the department commander. He said he would remain at the Arsenal until the end, to see personally that any reprieve was made effective.

Meantime Hancock had appeared that morning in the District of Columbia court. Defense counsel had awakened Judge Wylie at

2:00 A.M. and procured a writ ordering the commanding officer of the military district to produce Mrs. Surratt in court at 10:00 A.M. Hancock was accompanied by Attorney General James Speed, who handed to the court an executive order signed by President Johnson suspending the writ and directing Hancock to execute the order previously given to him to carry out the mandate of the Military Commission. Johnson did not then know that the commission itself had petitioned him to commute the sentence against Mrs. Surratt to life imprisonment. This strange procedure by a court that had just imposed the death sentence and did not have the courage to lighten the penalty, but requested the President to do so, was not brought to the President's attention by the Judge Advocate General Joseph Holt.[18] Later Hancock would be charged with disobeying civil authority and declining to appear in court in response to the writ, but at the time he was complimented by the judge for bowing to the civilian law. He might well have allowed the Attorney General to go to court alone and present the executive order suspending the writ. But being summoned, he appeared.

Defense Counsel Clampitt was at the Arsenal when Hancock returned from court. "Are there any hopes?" he asked as the general dismounted.

Hancock shook his head, mournfully, as Clampitt described it, and replied "with a sort of gasping catch in his speech." "I'm afraid not," he said. "No, there is not." He walked off by himself, apparently in deep personal anguish. Returning, he gave directions to some orderlies, then spoke again to Clampitt:

I have been in many a battle and have seen death, and mixed with it in disaster and in victory. I've been in a living hell of fire, and shell and grapeshot, and, by God, I'd sooner be there ten thousand times over than to give the order this day for the execution of that poor woman. But I am a soldier, sworn to obey, and obey I must.[19]

Hancock delivered the death warrant to Hartranft. Mrs. Surratt was executed along with Payne, Atzerodt and Herold.

···18···

A Trial in Statesmanship

Campaigning Again on the Plains

Peace took Hancock again to the Western garrisons. A regular army officer who knew no other career than the military service, he could hope only for favorable assignment in keeping with the high reputation he had earned on the field.

Like Thomas, he stood somewhat apart from the host of officers who had won distinction in the protracted war. He was neither a Lincoln protégé, like Schurz or Ben Butler, who would return to civilian life and find political careers beckoning, nor one of the young subordinates who had risen with Grant, such as Sheridan, Rawlins and Schofield, all destined to receive high recognition. He had his individual opinions about the treatment that should be accorded his late enemies, and he recognized that a harsh peace is rarely an enduring peace.

Congress got around to giving him belated acclaim for his services at Gettysburg, in a resolution adopted April 21, 1866, after everyone was fully aware of how he had been slighted. Gideon Welles recorded the admiration and applause he excited when he appeared in Washington.[1] Grant at this period still retained his admiration and affection for Hancock. In 1866 Congress created the rank of general in the regular army and Grant was elevated to that grade, Sherman was moved up to lieutenant general and Hancock in turn was appointed to fill the vacancy of a major general in the regular army. He had not hesitated to call his qualifications

273

to the attention of Senator James Rood Doolittle of Wisconsin, with
whom he was well acquainted.[2] The choice, he pointed out, would
be among the brigadier generals, McDowell, Rosecrans, Cooke,
Pope, Hooker, Hancock, Schofield, Howard and Terry. Schofield
was his only serious rival.[3] Grant's recommendation of Hancock
was approved by the President and confirmed by the Senate.

His first noteworthy assignment after leaving Washington was
to pacify the Indians on the Western plains. They had grown
hungry and restive because of the dwindling of the buffalo herds,
the increase of overland travel to the Pacific Coast, the building
of railroads and the homesteading of the Western country by discharged soldiers. Sherman was in command at St. Louis, a post
Hancock would have preferred because of his family associations
with that city, but he was ordered to Fort Leavenworth, Kansas,
in command of the Department of Missouri. There he organized
a force of about 1,500 troops, composed largely of the newly
formed 7th U.S. Cavalry, plus some infantry details.[4] Sherman,
writing on March 13, 1867, and telling how Hancock would conduct this force personally into the country of the Kiowas and
Cheyennes, said he would confer with the Indians "to ascertain if
they want to fight, in which case he will indulge them."

The tour of duty gave Sherman a view of Hancock's methods.
"I sometimes joked with him," Sherman said, "about attending to
little details which could have been devolved on his staff, but he
insisted on seeing to everything himself."[5]

Hancock marched into the Indian country and held a series of
pacifying conferences. But neither his show of consideration nor
his strength averted the hostilities which dragged on for many
years under successive commanders in the Northwest.

Interesting personalities were present in this first march of the
7th Cavalry regiment, much of which was to be destroyed nine
years later on the Little Big Horn. Custer, who would lead it to
disaster, was there. Wild Bill Hickok served Hancock as an express rider and guide.[6]

John Rowlands went along. Born in Wales, in 1841, he had
reached New Orleans as a cabin boy in 1859, had taken the name
of his benefactor, Henry Morton Stanley, and had entered the
Confederate army in 1861. Captured at Shiloh and imprisoned at
Chicago, he had secured his freedom by enlisting in the Federal

army but, being sickly, was discharged. He had roamed Europe, knowing nothing but poverty, joined the Federal navy, learned to write in a rapid, moving style and obtained a job at the fancy remuneration of $15 a week on the St. Louis *Democrat.* Now he won the assignment of accompanying Hancock into the Northwest. Surely, nothing in this expedition, about which Hancock submitted an exhaustive report, was of such lasting significance to the nineteenth century as its influence on young Stanley, who found that Hancock "excites admiration and respect wherever he goes."[7]

Stanley noticed that the general was still suffering periodically from his old wound, though four years had passed since Gettysburg. The young correspondent's able dispatches to the St. Louis *Democrat* came to the attention of James Gordon Bennett of the New York *Herald,* who gave him an about-the-world assignment and sent him to Asia, then to Africa to find David Livingstone, which launched him into his career as the greatest of the African explorers.

When Hancock met the chiefs of the Plains Indians he dazzled them by donning his full dress regalia. He was amicable and tolerant but they knew him as a fighting general. In his report he pointed out that because game had virtually disappeared the Indians were forced to roam over wide areas for food. He recommended that they be removed from the lines of main transcontinental travel and brought into reservations, where, since their subsistence had been depleted, they would have to be fed. The chiefs met him with frankness and respect. No doubt relations with the Northwestern tribes would have remained fairly amicable had he been able to continue his firm but temperate command in the Department of the Missouri.

But President Johnson wanted him in one of the Southern military departments and summoned him to Washington. On his return trip an incident at Altoona, Pennsylvania, showed he had not lost the fighting prowess that enabled him to rout the mob of ship desperadoes who had seized his son Russell on the journey up the Pacific to San Francisco. The incident was reported by a Boston writer who happened to observe it.

The reporter was standing in front of the Logan House admiring the physique and carriage of "a superb looking man" who was pacing up and down the station platform waiting for a delayed train.

It was Hancock, though he was not recognized by many in the crowd. A big rowdy with wide shoulders and a truculent air "shambled up near him" and made some offensive comments. Hancock paid no attention other than to look sharply at the intruder, then moved away. The man came on again and now attracted general attention. Mistaking Hancock's silence for timidity, he let fly some oaths about the "damned Yankee general."

The scribe said he "never saw a handsomer blow." It landed squarely on the man's chin and seemed to lift him "neatly and gracefully" into the air, "then stretch him tidily at full length on the platform several feet away."[8]

Dragged into the Reconstruction Row

Hancock's new assignment was to become the military governor of the Fifth Military District, consisting of Louisiana and Texas, with headquarters in New Orleans.

Though a dashing soldier, the preceding governor, "the hot-tempered, South-hating Sheridan,"[9] was a total misfit as an administrator over a defeated people. New Orleans was in continual ferment. He ruled impetuously. One contemporary observed that "before he had been in power a fortnight, he had gone far to reduce the district to the condition of a satrapy."[10] He courted the Congressional Radicals so assiduously that many suspected he was inviting their support for a Presidential nomination in due season.[11] Impulsively he removed local and state officials from office—city councilmen, levee commissioners, the mayor, attorney general, governor. The question devolving on Washington was not so much the merits of the individuals removed as the peremptory method of their removal.

In the midst of a great deal of mobbery and bloodletting President Johnson called to Washington Dick Taylor, son of President Zachary Taylor, who had been among the ablest of the Confederate generals and was a highly respected citizen of New Orleans. Taylor recommended Hancock for military governor, and Johnson immediately acted, appointing Hancock.[12] Stanton, teamed with the Radicals, was out of office as Secretary of War and could interpose no objections.

Johnson on August 12, 1867, had suspended Stanton, to the

anger of a Congress that did not understand that it was only a co-ordinate, and not the paramount, branch of the government. With Stanton out of the way, the President was able to give attention to conditions in New Orleans. Five days after the dismissal of Stanton he relieved Sheridan and assigned Thomas to command the Fifth District. But Thomas was in poor health, and Johnson issued another order, dated August 26, 1867, sending Hancock to the Fifth District and Sheridan to the Missouri.[13]

The condition of the Southern people at the time was summed up succinctly by Josiah Turner, editor of the Raleigh, N. C., *Sentinel*:

We are the poorest people in the world, and our very life blood is being sucked out by insatiate leeches that have floated down from the Northern waters and by the vampires that have come from our own creeks and ponds.[14]

Grant was not setting an attractive example of the proper conduct of a subordinate officer toward his commander in chief. He had no advance knowledge of Hancock's reconstruction views, but when he received Johnson's orders to replace Sheridan, he sent a staff officer to warn Hancock against what his military secretary Badeau termed the "mischievous tendency"[15] of President Johnson. This in itself was a strange course for an administration subordinate, but Grant went even further. When Hancock reached Washington in compliance with Johnson's order, he stopped at the Willard Hotel, where Grant called on him "to put him on his guard."[16] Hancock was altogether frank with him and said he would carry out the instructions of the President, his commander in chief. He would be guided by the President's views on reconstruction and not by any contrary views advanced by Grant.

Certainly Hancock was under no obligation to administer the Fifth District in a manner that would aid Grant to become President. Possibly he saw even then how lacking Grant was in the qualifications for that high office.

Hancock thus went to New Orleans against Grant's wishes, fully intending to implement Johnson's policy, which, in the words of Badeau, "his general-in-chief believed to be almost treasonable, and which he [Grant] was directed by Congress to thwart."[17]

Hancock's administration came at a time when conditions between the President and Congress were worsening and Johnson's impeachment was imminent. Congress entertained a surprising misunderstanding of or indifference to the tripartite nature of the American government. That attitude was reflected by the statement of Thaddeus Stevens: "Though the President is Commander-in-Chief, Congress is his Commander, and, God willing, he shall obey."[18]

Secretary of the Navy Gideon Welles observed Hancock appraisingly while he was in Washington. Welles's diary entry said:

General Hancock talks well, and I hope acts sensibly in Louisiana. The Radicals are a little disconcerted on account of his being here when they wish to make a partisan demonstration for Sheridan.[19]

This visit by Hancock to Washington in late September 1867 developed into an ovation. The capital city had not forgotten Gettysburg. When he entered the theater he was applauded. On September 27 he was the guest at a testimonial party arranged by one of the regimental commanders of his original brigade, Colonel Amasa Cobb, whose drill methods he had vociferously corrected, to the amusement of the Northwestern recruits. Cobb, after his outstanding war service, had been elected a Republican Congressman from Wisconsin. In introducing his "old friend and comrade" before what was described as "an immense audience," he launched into what became the main address. He told not only of the early training days, the rigors of the first winter in front of Washington and the advance to the Peninsula, but also the story of Hancock's turning the enemy flank at Williamsburg and what he described as "saving the day at Antietam." He paid tribute to Hancock for "his kindness of heart, his gallantry as a soldier, and his true greatness as a man."

Hancock made a brief and what seemed a rather unimaginative response, but the observant could recognize he was selecting constitutional heights on which to stand. He asked that the people judge him only by his deeds as military governor. "I am to administer duties rather than discuss them," he said. There was a clear, and, to the Radical leadership of Congress, ominous note, when he declared he could serve "not in the interest of parties or partisans, but for the benefit of my country, the honor of my profession, and

I trúst for the welfare of the people entrusted to my care."[20]

Hancock told President Johnson he was not anxious for the New Orleans assignment, but Johnson insisted. Their reconstruction views proved similar and more in accord with Lincoln's than those of the Radicals of Congress.[21] Hancock returned to St. Louis and took the Mississippi steamer to New Orleans. Before his departure he confided to Mrs. Hancock some beliefs which showed his foreknowledge of how his administration policies would be received:

I am expected to exercise extreme military authority over those people. I shall disappoint them. I have not been educated to overthrow the civilian authorities in time of peace. I intend to recognize the fact that the Civil War is at an end, and shall issue my order or proclamation accordingly. . . . I may lose my commission, and I shall do so willingly, rather than retain it at the sacrifice of a lifelong principle.[22]

He worked at night on the Mississippi River steamboat composing the general order he intended to issue when he reached New Orleans. Mrs. Hancock found him up and writing at the clerk's desk at 4:00 A.M. When he returned to his cabin he had completed the text.

"They will crucify me," he told her. "I warned the President of my intentions. . . . I know I shall have his sympathy, but he is powerless to help me."[23]

A Novel Order Electrifies the Country

Hancock's General Order No. 40, restoring civilian rule to Texas and Louisiana, was issued November 29, 1867. In it he described the state of peace existing in the department and said his purpose as commanding general would be to preserve that peace. He charged the civilian authorities with the faithful execution of the laws. He guaranteed the right of trial by jury, the habeas corpus, liberty of the press, freedom of speech and the preservation of personal and property rights. Crimes would be left to the regular civil tribunals unless they failed to inquire into offenses or administer justice. He would respect the liberties of the people but would instantly suppress any efforts at armed insurrection.

This simple order was a sensation. It was like a breath of fresh air blowing across an oppressed nation stifled with hatred and bitterness. In New Orleans Mrs. Hancock found the gratitude "universal." Even the staid old French element that kept to itself and declined to speak English opened its arms to the Hancocks. She was lavished with gifts, which she returned, and with numerous messages saying, "Thank God we are at peace again," or "Thank God for sending us this great and good man."[24]

When the general visited the St. Vincent Orphan Asylum, the children had prepared a present for him, which he accepted with tears in his eyes because they all rushed up, hugged his knees and covered his hand with kisses. Mrs. Hancock said that young as they were they seemed to understand they were in close unity with him. In New Orleans, peace had broken out almost as suddenly as war had six years before. An atmosphere of suppression and hostility became one of frankness and friendship.

General Order No. 40 was altogether novel in the administration of the defeated South. Virtually every newspaper in the country printed the full text of it. Many in the North as well as the South hailed it as marking an end to the little military despotisms Congress had set up.

Jeremiah S. Black, of Pennsylvania, one of the country's eminent lawyers who had been attorney general in Buchanan's cabinet, was delighted when he read the order in the press. He did not then know that he would later be credited with its authorship, on the ground that it could not possibly have been composed by a general. But he immediately wrote Hancock a letter that was representative of a large segment of public opinion:

Yours is the first, most distinct, and most emphatic recognition which the principles of American liberty have received at the hands of any high officer in a Southern command. It has the very ring of Revolutionary metal. Washington never said a thing in better taste or better time. . . .

I congratulate you—not because it will make you the most popular man in America, for I dare say you care nothing about that—but because it will give you, through all time, the solid reputation of a true patriot and a sincere lover of your country, its law and its government.[25]

He added that his own acknowledgment meant little, but "I am expressing only the feelings of millions."

Dick Taylor, who had recommended Hancock, was pleased that he had restored order in New Orleans at once.

A gentleman, one of the most distinguished and dashing officers of the United States Army, General Hancock recognizes both the great duties of a soldier of the Republic—to defend its flag and obey its laws, discharging the last with a fidelity equal to his devotion to the first in front of battle.[26]

When his old commander Baldy Smith came to sum up Hancock's services, he gave one of the best estimates of his actions in New Orleans:

At a time when military men thirsted for power, when one part of our country was demoralized by poverty and defeat, and when even the people of the North were getting accustomed to the despotism of a long-continued military authority, General Hancock clearly proclaimed the fundamental principles of the subordination of the military power, which is always abnormal, to the civil, which alone has the true interests of mankind in its keeping.[27]

His old antagonist, General John B. Gordon of the Confederate army, was equally impressed:

In the estimation of his Southern countrymen, bereft, as they were, by the contingencies of the war of the protection of courts and of civil environments, and dependent for the time upon his unchallenged power and will, this self-imposed restraint of a great soldier, this subjection of himself and all his military powers to the supremacy of the civil law is a spectacle of moral grandeur almost without a parallel in history. In their estimation no language can exaggerate the honors due General Hancock for this great action, nor overstate its beneficent consequences to their rights and liberties. . . .[28]

Back in Washington canny Gideon Welles was making some penetrating observations. In his diary notations he was unusually severe on Grant. That general, he felt, had undercut President Johnson and gone over completely to the Radicals. General Order No. 40 was discussed in the Cabinet meeting on December 17 and Johnson read a message he intended to send to Congress commending Hancock's respect for the civil law. "Should he send it in," Welles wrote that day, "he will exasperate the Radicals, but it may have the effect of inducing a contrast between the action of Hancock and the other military governors now at the head of departments."[29]

Welles quoted the President as agreeing and saying it "would bring out before the country the weakness of Grant, who, he was sorry to perceive, was becoming identified with the tyrannical and oppressive measures of the military commanders."[30]

Welles recorded the same opinion about Grant. Five days later he summarized his observations obtained from the general's appearances before the Cabinet, at which Hancock's and the other military departments were discussed. Himself an unrestrained hater, Welles wrote:

I am becoming impressed with the idea that Grant may prove a dangerous man. He is devoid of patriotism, is ignorant but cunning, yet greedy for office and power. In discussions, from time to time in Cabinet, when he has been necessarily to some extent drawn out, this shadow of military absolutism has crossed my mind. It struck me more forcibly today when the military government of the South was under consideration. . . .[31]

It is difficult to understand the sensation created in Washington merely because Hancock had announced that he would "make the law the rule of his conduct" and that he would uphold the courts and other civil authorities in the performance of their proper duties. President Johnson sent the message commending Hancock to Congress on December 18, the next day after he read it to the Cabinet. The President analyzed General Order No. 40, showed that Hancock guaranteed the right of trial by jury and the privilege of the writ of habeas corpus, then added for the enlightenment of Congress:

When a great soldier, with unrestricted power in his hands to oppress his fellow-men, voluntarily foregoes that chance of gratifying his selfish ambition and devotes himself to the duties of building up the liberties and strengthening the laws of his country, he presents an example of the highest public virtue that human nature is capable of practicing.

He went on to compare Hancock's action with that of Washington, always a respecter of the civil rights, whose forbearance to assert military power over the people had won the universal admiration of mankind. The President continued:

> I am far from saying that General Hancock is the only officer of the American army who is influenced by the example of Washington. Doubtless thousands of them are faithfully devoted to the principles for which the men of the Revolution laid down their lives. But the distinguished honor belongs to him of being the first officer in high command south of the Potomac, since the close of the civil war, who has given utterance to these noble sentiments in the form of a military order.
>
> I respectfully suggest to Congress that some public recognition is due, if not to him, to the friends of law and justice throughout the country. Of such an act as his at such a time it is but fit that the dignity should be vindicated and the virtue proclaimed, so that its value as an example may not be lost to the nation.[32]

Two days later Johnson called Welles to discuss the Hancock message, with which he felt he had outwitted the Radicals. Welles did not regard it as being so effective as his message suspending Stanton, believing the Radicals would find it difficult to defend the Secretary of War whereas they could make a bitter attack on Hancock—and it was soon forthcoming. But an attack on Hancock, Welles felt, would lead in turn to criticism of the other generals commanding the Southern departments, to their disadvantage.[33]

Thus, while he was being praised in Louisiana and Texas and thanked throughout the rest of the South, and applauded without stint by large numbers in the North, he quickly encountered the open hostility of the Radical majority of Congress and militants elsewhere who favored punitive measures for the South.

The Union League in Philadelphia, which had given him a silver medal for his services at Gettysburg, took down his portrait and sent it to the garret.[34] Radicals planned to strike at him by reducing the number of major generals in the regular army so as to force his resignation or lower his rank to brigadier. The bill to accomplish this was introduced by Representative James A. Garfield of Ohio, who could not then have remotely guessed that in 1880 he would be a candidate against Hancock for the Presidency.

Garfield made an embittered speech against Hancock in the House on January 17, 1868:

We see him issuing a general order, in which he declares that the civil should not give way before the military. We hear him declaring that he finds nothing in the laws of Louisiana or Texas to warrant his interference in the civil administration of those States. It is not for him to say which should be first, the civil or the military, in that rebel community. It is not for him to search the defunct laws of Louisiana and Texas for a guide to his conduct It is for him to execute the laws which he was sent there to administer. . . . Does anybody expect that we will permit an officer of our army to fling back in our faces his contempt of our laws, and tell us what ought to be and what ought not to be?[35]

Garfield did not appreciate that Hancock was basing his action on what he regarded a scrupulous adherence to the law, and not a defiance of it. Years later the Congressman apologized for the speech.

Even Acrimonious Talk Is Legal

Meantime Hancock continued his pacifying efforts. During his brief term as commanding officer of the Fifth District he adhered consistently to the spirit of his general order and governed in sharp contrast with practices in some of the other departments. He discouraged appeals to the United States or trials by military commissions that had been the normal course before him. He refused to be drawn into problems of civilian character. So many were pressed on him that on January 1, 1868, he issued another general order explaining his own limitations. He said:

Applications are being made at these headquarters implying the existence of an arbitrary authority in the Commanding General touching purely civil controversies.

One petitioner solicits this action, another that, and each refers to some special consideration of grace or favor which he supposes to exist, and which should influence this Department.

The number of such applications and the waste of time they involve, make it necessary to declare that the administration of civil justice appertains to the regular courts. The rights of litigants do not depend on the views of the general—they are to be adjudged and settled according to the laws. Arbitrary power, such as he has been urged to assume, has no existence here. It is not found in the laws of Louisiana or of Texas—it cannot be derived from any act or acts of Congress—it is restrained by a constitution and prohibited from action in many particulars. . . .

An example of the pleas to Hancock was one from the mayor of New Orleans requesting him to terminate suits against the city for payment of its corporate notes. Nothing could be less a military problem. Though it had been the custom in the defeated South for Federal soldiers to patrol balloting places on election day, Hancock returned to the civil authorities the responsibility of preserving order at the polls. He issued a special order against military interference with elections. He directed that no soldiers would be allowed at the polls except as voting citizens and then only for voting. Commanders of the army posts would be prepared to act only in case civilian authorities failed to preserve order.

Major E. W. Clark, a member of Hancock's staff, was impressed with his magnanimity during the New Orleans period and told of an instance. A Southern widow claimed compensation for destroyed crops and confiscated provisions and the claim papers were misplaced. Hancock had no more understanding of a lost paper than he had of an accidental discharge of firearms. He called every member of his staff and stopped all proceedings until the paper was found. Major Clark did not say precisely how the case was decided but inferred that the claim was approved when he said "no one was permitted to have rest while the rights of the widow of his late foe were held in abeyance."[36]

Equally strong sentiments in support of local self-government and popular rights were contained in a letter Hancock wrote to embittered, scalawag Governor E. M. Pease of Texas, who in an open letter to the press had criticized his General Order No. 40. It, too, has been called one of the great documents of American civil liberty. Pease had complained because many in Texas remained embittered against the Federal government and obeyed it unwillingly. Hancock stressed the danger to society if either civil or military power was allowed to deal "with the mere opinions or feelings of the people." He continued:

I have been accustomed to believe that sentiments of respect or disrespect, and feelings of affection, love, or hatred, so long as not developed into acts in violation of law, were matters wholly beyond the punitory power of human tribunals.
I will maintain that the entire freedom of thought and speech,

however acrimoniously indulged, is consistent with the noblest aspirations of man, and the happiest condition of his race.

Sentiments of this nature did not make congenial reading for members of the Wade-Stevens-Butler-Sumner clique who had come to dominate Congress and had taken over from the President the responsibility of remaking the South according to their own pattern.

Some of his pronouncements in his orders approached the epigramatic:

Power may destroy the forms but not the principles of justice. These will live in spite of even the sword.

The true and proper use of the military power, besides defending the national honor against foreign nations, is to uphold the laws and civil government, and to secure to every person residing among us the enjoyment of life, liberty and property.[37]

To a friend he wrote:

The President is no longer able to protect me. . . . I may expect one humiliation after another until I am forced to resign. I am prepared for any event. Nothing can intimidate me from doing what I believe to be honest and right.[38]

The uncertain reaction to the plan in Congress of demoting Hancock, who commanded a wide public following, caused the Radical leadership to drop it and bring pressure on Grant to remove him. Grant accomplished this more by harassment than direct action. He overruled Hancock's orders until the subordinate was compelled in humiliation to resign.

The break came after Hancock removed nine aldermen whom he held to have been improperly elected during Sheridan's tenure, and who had arbitrarily appointed a city recorder when that position was elective. He had cautioned them in advance that a choice by them was illegal. Since the council was both insubordinate and improperly constituted, Hancock removed the members—one of his two arbitrary acts during his service in New Orleans. Grant immediately ordered by telegraph that they be reinstated. When Hancock by telegraph asked that the reinstatement be delayed until his report, already forwarded by mail, might be read, Grant censured him for using the telegraph for dispatches which might properly be sent by mail. His answer was in effect that Hancock had the authority to make the removals, but he possessed the authority to countermand them.[39]

"Your order of removal was based on certain charges," said Grant, "which I did not think were sustained by the facts as they were presented to me."[40]

Grant did not disclose where he had obtained his "facts" but it was clear that he trusted other sources than his subordinate officer commanding at New Orleans. Hancock consequently requested that he be relieved. Meantime the aldermen—restored to office by Hancock pursuant to Grant's orders—and their carpetbag followers, staged an early morning mass parade of triumph around Hancock's quarters to demonstrate their contempt for his authority, or lack of it.[41]

Johnson was still confiding in Welles, who had probably been the most solid and unemotional member of the old Lincoln Cabinet and who was as loyal to Johnson as he had been to his first chief. On February 12, 1868, Johnson showed him a telegram from Hancock, advising the President that he had dismissed the aldermen. Grant had ordered the reinstatement which Hancock "mildly remonstrates against, and if the order is persisted in, requests to be relieved."

"I apprehend that Stanton is in this thing," said Welles. "It is a Radical movement. But Stanton means evil, and, while pushing Grant forward, intends to profit himself by the general's weakness and baseness."[42]

"Both have been treacherous," Welles concluded, and, of Grant, added: "He is implicated in the conspiracy against the President—a willing party to it."[43]

Johnson declined at first to accept Hancock's resignation but finally yielded to the inevitable, called him back to Washington for consultation and assigned him to a place under Meade in the Division of the Atlantic.[44] His service in command of a department in the defeated South had lasted only a few months, but it was the brightest spot in the reconstruction picture for the Southern people and for countless others who wanted the war forgotten.

Hancock's difficulties with Grant were not ended. He could not be companionable with the commanding general who, he felt, had harassed and frustrated him in his efforts to give a forthright, non-

partisan administration to Louisiana and Texas. One of less
strength might have truckled, for Grant in the spring of 1868
seemed the inevitable choice of the Republicans for the Presidency.
Hancock was himself being mentioned for the Democratic nomination, though not with sufficient support or in proper quarters for
success.

Grant Incensed by a Cool Hancock

When he reached Washington from New Orleans, Hancock
called first on President Johnson, then went to Grant's headquarters, to which by military custom he was required to report. He
did not ask to see the commanding general—an omission which
Grant always took for a snub—but requested the register ordinarily
kept at such headquarters, to enter his name. He did chat with
members of Grant's staff, with most of whom he was acquainted.
One of them asked if he had seen the commanding general. He
said he had not, then turned to General Rawlins and explained,
as he later worded it:

Under existing circumstances it is probably as well; and if you
will notify the General that I have arrived in the city, and where
my residence is, he will no doubt send for me if he desires to
see me.[45]

His attitude exhibited an undisguised chilliness. Grant never
sent for him. A few days later Grant was standing in front of the
First National Bank, across from the Treasury building, talking
with Governor Benjamin F. Flanders of Florida,[46] when Hancock
emerged from a street car and passed within ten or fifteen feet.
Grant touched his hat and said, "Good morning, General," to
which Hancock, touching his hat, replied, "Good morning, General," and went on. Explaining the incident later, Hancock said,
"I did not feel cordial to him, and so governed my action."[47]

Later Hancock heard stories which he attributed to "those near
to General Grant" of how he had "cut" the general on the street.
The matter became an undercurrent of capital gossip. Suddenly
on May 20, 1870, the New York *World* broke it as a headline sensation. The *World* had gleaned other bits of gossip, some of which
Grant's friends must have fancied, as Hancock had no memory of

them. He was supposed to have turned his back on Grant at a wedding and to have written an insubordinate and disrespectful letter. It was easy to disprove the charge about the letter because there was none on the records. As for turning his back, he very likely did show a lack of warmth, considering the mood in which he had returned from New Orleans, but he denied any intended discourtesy.

He had met Grant at social parties, he said, "and, on at least one or two occasions, happened to be near him, made way for him in a deferential manner, which he appeared to recognize."[48]

He did not support Grant for the Presidency in 1868. Shrewd Gideon Welles had been watching Hancock and was one of the first to regard him a political factor. As the date for the Democratic convention of 1868 approached, Welles wrote: "Hancock seems a fair man. I know not his mental strength, but have a favorable opinion of it. In many respects he would make a good candidate."[49]

Then, as the convention met, he set down his conclusion: "Hancock, if the candidate, will be elected. Seymour, if nominated, will be defeated."[50] Seymour was nominated and defeated, to be sure, but no one can know how Hancock would have fared had he been the candidate against Grant in 1868. The political tide was running strongly in Grant's favor. The Democratic convention gave Hancock 144 votes on the twenty-eighth ballot though he had made no campaign. When doubt was expressed that he would support the ticket he wrote a ringing letter of endorsement, in which he said:

I never aspired to the Presidency on account of myself. I never sought its doubtful honor and certain labor and responsibilities merely for position. . . . "Principles and not rulers," is the motto for the rigid crisis through which we are now struggling. Had I been the Presidential nominee I should have considered it a tribute, not to me, but to principles which I had proclaimed and protected; but shall I cease to regard these principles, because by the judgment of mutual political friends another has been appointed to put them in execution? Never! . . .[51]

The bad feeling was sufficient cause for Grant to pass over Hancock when, on the death of Major General George H. Thomas, he appointed a successor to the command of the Western Division of the Army. Schofield received the assignment though Hancock ranked him. Hancock protested to Sherman, now commander of the army. Sherman took it up with Grant, then replied to Hancock:

The President authorizes me to say to you that it belongs to his office to select the Commanding Generals of Divisions and Departments, and that the relations you chose to assume toward him, officially and privately, absolve him from regarding your personal preferences.[52]

The rebuke was about as severe as the President could administer. Hancock corresponded with Sherman about it and about the New York *World* article. He reviewed and defended his administration at New Orleans, which was at the heart of his misunderstanding with Grant. He insisted on his integrity in all his actions:

It is well known that I never desired the command; I had my opinions upon political matters, but had never obtruded them; I merely wished to be a soldier, not a politician; I had been enabled to go through the war, avoiding politics, and by constantly remaining in the field, to retain the esteem, generally, of all parties in the country. . . . I executed the laws faithfully while there, but not in the interest of partisans.[53]

He said he felt hurt that his commanding officer had not sustained him but had acted in response to the statements of partisans. "I therefore was aggrieved, and felt cold to General Grant," he frankly admitted. But he denied any intention to treat him disrespectfully. He forwarded a letter from Governor Flanders of Florida saying his greeting had been pleasant when he passed Grant on the street across from the Treasury.

Shortly after he became President Grant ordered Hancock to the Department of the Dakotas, perhaps the least attractive assignment available. It amounted to banishment. Sherman tried to ease the tension between the two and felt that he had patched up the relationship. He said later:

I succeeded in reconciling them, but afterwards, when he [Hancock] was a Presidential candidate, the newspapers reported General Grant in the most exaggerated form, and renewed the breach, which was never healed.[54]

What Sherman referred to was an intemperate interview given by Grant at his house in Galena, Illinois, in 1880. Badeau termed it "caustic criticisms to an indiscreet visitor."[55] The words used to describe Hancock were "ambitious, vain and weak," a description which many applied to Grant himself after his eight years in the White House.

When the interview was reported to Hancock he refused to credit it. Grant neither would nor could disavow it to reporters who demanded confirmation or denial. Hancock was "much pained" but the description stood and no doubt influenced some of Grant's friends against Hancock. Badeau, always sympathetic to Grant, referred to it after both generals had died. He told the Philadelphia *Press*:

In his last days, General Grant more than once spoke to me of this circumstance and regretted the pain he had given Hancock. He was generous in his praise, and, though he criticised what he thought foibles and graver faults, he declared that he ought not to have used words which Hancock disliked. This Hancock never knew. . . .[56]

★ ★ ★ 19 ★ ★ ★

Parade and Taps

The Old Soldiers Come for Cash

Meade died on November 6, 1872. Since Sheridan had been pushed along by Grant to be a lieutenant general—this being one of Grant's earliest acts in the White House—Hancock became the senior major general of the Army. As such he was entitled to command the Division of the Atlantic and there was not much Grant could do about it without tearing the service apart. At Sherman's suggestion Hancock moved to New York City and eventually to Governors Island, in New York Bay.

Here, at his headquarters for the last fourteen years of his life, he presided with a charm and dignity that brought to him informed and interesting visitors from all parts of the country and from many foreign lands. Almost for the first time since leaving West Point he had a chance to establish a permanent home life and enjoy the family associations he had yearned for so earnestly during his years of campaigning.

Though he was not a wealthy man, he collected a library of several thousand volumes and read assiduously. Friends and authors sent him war books. The commanding general's house on Governors Island was anything but a mansion; still, the Hancocks were happy there. One of their visitors noticed that the Brussels carpet on the parlor floor was faded and of a design no longer stylish. Everything about the furnishings seemed old-fashioned—the chairs, sofas, mirrors, the whatnot in the corner and the bric-a-brac on the front mantel. The carved piano legs were quaint and crooked, but Mrs. Hancock played rapturously. The hearth rug was an imitation white foxskin, with raised head having glass eyes described as funny and sharp.[1]

The years had reduced the personal fortunes of both the Hancocks, and they were forced to live close inside the limits of a major general's pay of $7,500 annually. The post involved a substantial amount of entertaining. Frugal as he was on most matters, the general could never resist the call of an old soldier for a bit of cash to tide him over, and the word spread so widely that many came. The Governors Island chaplain, the Reverend Edward H. C. Goodwin, said there was never an appeal that did not arouse the general's sympathy. Hancock, companionable and always an eager conversationalist, enjoyed the veterans and liked to talk of the battles, but his staff officers felt that some were imposters who had never heard a shot fired in anger and were only taking advantage of his charitableness.[2]

A story told as typical was that he would read a request and tell Colonel Warde, who had charge of his money, to write that he would like to send fifty dollars but simply didn't have it. Then, next day, he would read the answer, reflect in a disturbed manner, and say, "Warde, I believe that man really needs that money. I guess we will have to arrange it some way." He would scrape the fifty dollars together as best he could and send it.[3]

William P. Wilson, who had served on his personal staff, regarded him as "generous to a fault," and said he was so free of guile he never suspected it in others.[4] Wilson, who was Hancock's lifelong friend, often recalled the time when as a timid and inexperienced young lieutenant he entered Hancock's tent to find his fears suddenly dispelled by the cordiality of the general's greeting.

Thomas B. Musgrave, a New York friend, told of an incident when Hancock visited him at Mt. Desert, Maine. One morning a veteran knocked on the door and said, "Tell the general that Malone is here." He was one of Hancock's old orderlies who had walked twenty-five miles during the night. Hancock met him eagerly. They talked of battle incidents and Musgrave thought a sadness came over the general when it was time for the man to go.

"Malone," he said, "since those war days we old soldiers have

little influence and little money, but here is my walking stick. God
bless you! I am glad you have got a home."[5]

On Governors Island Hancock renewed his interest in tree planting and shrubbery. One of his visitors commented that he had
"improved and beautified the green island till it looked like the lawn
of a wealthy private residence." The observer continued:

This perfect-mannered man was courteous to every human crea-
ture. He was said to be the handsomest man in America, but he
never seemed to know it. Rather strangely, he was finer looking
at 55 than he had been at 35.[6]

Opinions would have varied about that, for at fifty-five he carried 250 pounds. With a height of six feet two inches and a large
frame, he was able to support the load, without damaging his military posture severely, either walking or mounted. The stern vigor
of his countenance had been softened a trifle, perhaps because
there were fewer occasions for his anger to flare.

On visits to Washington it became his custom to have dinner
with other friends at the Georgetown establishment of a liquor
merchant named Esberg. The party would begin with a game of
whist with the stakes going to the servants. Dinner, prepared by
a famed French chef of the capital, would be served at six. One
evening both the chef and party partook lengthily of the liquid ap-
petizers and no dinner was prepared. Hancock, who was not
affected by the afternoon wine, went to the kitchen, cooked up
half a dozen canvasback ducks, dressed the salad and served the
dinner with great delight. "The best dinner I have had since the
war!" he pronounced it as they finished.[7]

He sponsored and helped patriotic and preparedness measures.
He stimulated interest in National Guard units and served as president of the National Rifle Association. Brigadier General George
N. Wingate told of going to him for help at a time when rifle marksmanship was being neglected by a busy, growing country. Hancock
said that if the association were prospering he would not consider
accepting the presidency, but since it needed assistance, he would
do all he could to put it back on its feet. His work added much
to the association's value and growth. He procured for it the
"Hilton Trophy," long contended for by the expert riflemen of the
army and National Guard.[8]

Hancock's greatest joy was his blond daughter Ada, with whom he was at last having opportunity to become acquainted. This child of the Everglades, daughter of two attractive parents, had grown lovelier each year, and the general was very proud of her. The girl could feel pride too as she walked with this big, handsome man who could not pass down the street without being greeted with salutes and lifted hats. He had her picture painted by a celebrated artist of the time, B. F. Reinhart. It shows a soft, sensitive-looking girl with clear, clean features, large blue eyes, high forehead and tresses that must have reached to her waist. She read much and the general lavished books on her; some of the best literature of the day was in her library.

Then, when she was nineteen, she contracted typhoid fever. She died after a brief illness, on March 28, 1875. No other loss had ever struck the general such a blow.

Deeply grieved as was Mrs. Hancock also, a visitor commented that sorrow had not deprived the slender, vivacious lady of her charm.[9] As when "Myra" Hancock had stayed close to the lines during the war, ready for any moments of comfort she could give, so she now by her companionship carried her husband through a much more difficult time.

There remained Russell, the Hancocks' only son, a delightful young man with dancing blue eyes, who seemed to carry a ray of sunshine with him. He was witty, blithe and lovable. As a boy he had spent much time with his Grandmother Russell at their country home near St. Louis, while his father was campaigning. The house was large and imposing, set in spacious grounds, with a great gate.

Russell had attended preparatory school in New Haven, Connecticut, and had gone on to Lehigh, at Bethlehem, Pennsylvania. He had not completed the course owing to his weak health. He was in Louisville about 1872, when he was twenty, working for a local business house. Suddenly he found himself very much in love with one of the "prettiest, brightest" young belles of the city, Miss Elizabeth Gwynn.[10] Her father, Nicholas Gwynn, a cotton broker of substantial means, was not impressed with the idea of his teenage daughter marrying a mere boy, and arranged a trip to Europe to cool the affections she ardently returned. Meantime he barred the young man from his house. Being a stanch, unreconstructed

Southerner, he wanted no connection with "the son of a Yankee soldier."[11]

The youngsters met at a party one night and Russell pleaded with the girl to marry him before she sailed, saying he would set up a home for her during her absence. She readily agreed, and in a few minutes they and one or two close friends were on their way across the Ohio River to Jeffersonville, Indiana, where they were married. The wedding had been altogether unpremeditated until the emergency of the European trip. Russell's mother had been visiting him in Louisville and had departed for New York only the day before, without receiving a hint of the elopement.[12]

News of the ceremony leaked out before Elizabeth could be packed off to Europe. The father was bitterly unforgiving, and the couple moved into a boardinghouse, as attractive a young pair as the country possessed—Russell "blond, merry and frank," and the girl bride "slender, sweet and sensible." A fellow boarder described Russell:

The boy-husband kept everybody, from the waiter to the care-burdened landlady, in a state of laughter, that varied from a smile to an out-and-out roar all the time he was in the house. He remained there nearly a year.[13]

From the time he appeared at the breakfast table until he hung up his smoking jacket and put his guitar in the corner at night, Russell enlivened the crowd with his sparkling personality and witticisms. The boarder continued:

Always the funniest thing said in the most deprecating way; the brightest retorts flashed out without a change of countenance; none of that bitter, sarcastic wit that scorches while it glitters, but a genial, jovial wit, that brightens and lights up life, gurgles with laughter, and sometimes even overflows with tears. . . . A kindlier heart never beat in any bosom.[14]

Russell had neither the commanding height of his father nor the beauty of his mother, but still he gave promise of developing into a handsome man. He had a "slow, preacher-sort" of a smile that seemed to say nothing severe was intended by his jesting and punning.

He was employed by the company headed by Victor Newcomb, a railroad magnate of the period, but after a time he and his wife went to St. Louis. Later, when Elizabeth obtained money, they bought a large plantation along the Little Sunflower River in Coahoma County, Mississippi.

Although the general and the boy's mother were shaken by the clandestine wedding, they were both fond and proud of him and loved his fascinating wife. Mrs. Hancock told a story of the minister who met Russell on a Mississippi River packet and asked how he got his friendly, easy, democratic manner. "I have observed you are as courteous to the boot-black as to the captain," the preacher said.

"I came by it honestly, I suppose." Russell seemed surprised. "My father has always impressed on my mind that all men are born free and equal."

"With such a father," continued the preacher, "it seems to me one would be a little puffed up."

"Not in the slightest," said Russell. "While I am proud of such a father, I claim nothing on his account."[15]

Russell and Elizabeth had two daughters, Myra and Ada, family names, and two sons, Gwynn and Winfield. Winfield died in infancy.

The Civil Courts Have Precedence

Hancock's preference for civil above military authority in peacetime was reflected again in 1875 when he was named to sit on the Military Court of Inquiry appointed to investigate the alleged complicity of Colonel Orville E. Babcock, Grant's private secretary, in the "Whisky Ring" that marred Grant's second administration. Babcock, though serving in a civil capacity, had requested a military court and Grant, holding that the military should take precedence, acceded, much to the puzzlement of newspapers and lawyers. Sheridan was appointed president of the court with Major General Alfred H. Terry the third member. Babcock meantime had come under civil indictment by a St. Louis grand jury.

Hancock, along with some of Grant's Cabinet members, knew the effort to try the secretary before a military commission was illegal and said so. The Lambdin P. Milligan case had been passed on by the Supreme Court, which denied the jurisdiction of a military commission in a civilian offense. A sharp reversal of opinion had taken place against the trial of Mrs. Surratt by a military court, which denied her the constitutional right of trial by jury.

When the Court of Inquiry assembled in Chicago to hear the Babcock case, Hancock at the first session challenged the right of army officers to proceed. He read a well-considered address in support of his position. He had sufficient legal background to register his points with sureness and emphasis. He referred to the difficulties of conducting two trials at the same time in different cities, when the same witnesses and the same voluminous papers and records would be required. Then he touched on constitutional points. He maintained that the military court could not compel the production of these records while they were wanted for the purposes of the civil trial, because the military was subordinate to the civil authority.

He made it clear that the commission could not act as a substitute for the civil court, where the decision would be conclusive on the government, on the accused and on all the world.[16]

The military authorities were dropping the reins of government slowly—largely because of Hancock's continual prodding.

When he had read his statement the court adjourned immediately. Babcock subsequently was acquitted but Grant dismissed him from the White House.

Hancock did not seek office but was continually invited to enter politics. His delegate strength at the 1868 Democratic National Convention had been impressive. The following year leaders of the Pennsylvania Democratic party tendered to him in advance of the state convention, the nomination for governor of his own state. He declined the honor then and on later occasions.[17]

He asked to have his name withheld from consideration by the Democratic Convention of 1872, though the Democrats were hard pressed for a candidate and finally endorsed the arch Republican Horace Greeley. At the convention in 1876 Hancock received seventy-five votes on the first ballot. The scandals in Washington had pointed clearly to the reform governor of New York, Samuel J. Tilden, as the Democratic nominee and he was chosen on the second ballot.

One of Hancock's great services to the nation occurred during the Hayes-Tilden controversy over the election of 1876, which came close to violence between the two parties and possibly another civil war. The young hotheads of 1876 were no different from those on both sides of the Mason-Dixon line in 1860-1861. Hancock, the best-known Democratic general, was talked about as the man who would lead the Tilden forces if it became necessary to sound a call to arms.[18] Rumors spread in the press that to get him out of the way he had been ordered to California but had declined to go. Both statements were groundless.

Far from favoring conflict over the Presidency, he emphasized that it was a good time for people to keep their shirts on. He held that the army, least of all, had a place in the controversy. He was at St. Louis, from where on December 28, 1876, he wrote to Sherman, the general of the army, some clear observations on the controversy. He spoke of the California rumor and made it clear that if so ordered he would go. He said the army should have nothing to do with the selection and inauguration of Presidents. He favored Jefferson's democratic method of being inaugurated. "He rode alone on horseback to the Capitol . . . tied his horse to a rail-fence, entered, and was duly sworn; then rode to the Executive Mansion and took possession." He explained that our system does not provide that one President should inaugurate another, which might be dangerous.[19]

As to the existing dispute, he maintained that if no candidate had a majority in the electoral college, the constitution provided that the election of the President should be made in the House of Representatives and the Vice-President in the Senate:

What the people want is a peaceful determination of this matter, as fair a determination as is possible, and a lawful one. No other administration could stand the test. The country, if not plunged into revolution, would become poorer day by day . . .

He deprecated the use of troops in South Carolina to control who had been elected to the legislature. He said the army had been used unlawfully at times "and we have lost a great deal of the kindly feeling which the community at large once felt for us."[20]

In another letter to Sherman five days later he called attention to an anonymous letter sent to the Secretary of War from Louisville, Kentucky, and forwarded to him. It said the Tilden forces contemplated rising and seizing the Jeffersonville, Indiana, military depot to "clothe the Indiana army of Democrats." The endorsement authorized Hancock to draw a company of troops to protect the depot, but left it to his discretion. He declined. He told Sherman there was no danger and that the movement of troops would create apprehension.[21] In that he was no doubt correct. The situation was so tense that if the army had started moving troops about the country an eruption could have been precipitated.

Democratic Nominee for President in 1880

Recognition came at length to Hancock for his great services and abilities when the Democratic National Convention, meeting in Cincinnati in 1880, nominated him for President. The selection was made on the second ballot. Any elation he might have felt was suddenly stilled by the death of his grandson Winfield on the very day the nomination was officially announced to him.

He had made no campaign for the nomination, and when he had it he made no campaign, in a modern sense, for the election. He had peculiar notions, compared with present-day political standards.

He declined to take money from others to pay for his own campaign costs. Baldy Smith told of a wealthy man, a friend of both Hancock and himself, who went to Hancock with ten one-thousand-dollar bills and urged him to accept them. Putting his hand on the friend's shoulder, Hancock said, "There is no man in this world from whom I would accept money sooner than from you. I thank you for the delicate way in which your friendship has been shown, but I cannot take the money."[22]

Undoubtedly his extreme punctiliousness about money at a time when the opposition party was spending lavishly impaired his prospects.

Wealthy William H. English of Indiana was named his running mate, but it helped little.

The Republicans nominated the Ohio Congressman, James A. Garfield, and as his associate on the ticket, Chester A. Arthur of New York.

Hancock was a good speaker. Some years earlier he had made a talk at Tammany Hall, on the same platform with Thomas F. Meagher, and had been rated fully as effective as the silver-tongued Irishman.[23] But he did no stump speaking. Like Winfield Scott and Grant when they were candidates for the Presidency, he remained in the regular army during the campaign. Delegations went to Governors Island in continual procession. The general was on dress parade but the voters wanted to pick at his uniform to see what was underneath it.

His chances appeared excellent at the time of his nomination and newspaper predictions were in his favor. But he was opposed by one of the tightest political groups in the history of the country, the Grand Army of the Republic veterans, who adhered largely to the Republican party and closed ranks when the assault grew severe. The eagerness with which the South accepted the Hancock nomination caused reflection by many Northern veterans who might have swung to him.

Though scandals under Grant, a Republican, might have been expected to help Hancock, a Democrat, there is no doubt but that the shortcomings of the Grant administration proved a severe handicap to him in some respects. Grant's artlessness and inexperience in civil affairs caused a reaction against a strictly military man in the White House, which was not overcome for eighty years. Garfield, a general but not a professional soldier, was identified more with Congress than with the army. Inconsistent as it might seem, he made good progress with both the veterans and with the anti-military vote.

The campaign came to be focused on this supposed naïveté of military men about the affairs of government. Naïveté developed into the main issue against Hancock. A little booklet was circulated entitled *Hancock's Record;* all the pages were blank.[24] He was called " a good man weighing 250 pounds."[25] Thomas Nast drew a devastating cartoon showing him querying a platform companion, "Who is Tariff and why is he for revenue only?"[26]

Early in October, as the campaign entered the final stretch, Hancock was interviewed by a reporter of the Paterson, New Jersey, *Daily Guardian,* who quoted him as dismissing the main campaign issue by saying, "The Tariff question is a local question."[27] His thinking, of course, was that the tariff concerned mainly the towns having plants that enjoyed protection, but the opposition seized on the remark and heralded it widely as evidence that the candidate had not even a rudimentary knowledge of the affairs of state.

Garfield went into the campaign with some taint from the Credit Mobilier scandal that had rocked Congress after the war. The contest developed free swinging on both sides. Two of the pivotal states were New York and Indiana, both of which Hancock was expected to carry. They, with all the old slave states, would elect him. Indiana was lost mainly by the barnstorming campaign conducted in that state by Benjamin Harrison, a relatively new figure in politics, grandson of President William Henry Harrison. He had risen from second lieutenant to brigadier general in the war. His stump speeches won the attention of the New York *Herald*:

Harrison is a little man, with a long beard and tremendous lung power. He can talk like a streak of lightning on any subject at the smallest notice. . . . This year he has taken an active part in the canvass and spoken somewhere every night.[28]

Eight years later he would land the Presidency himself.

In New York Grant took the stump for Garfield and at Syracuse declared the Democrats in the Southern states would control the country if the Democrats came into power:

It is just as impossible that the limited number of Democrats in the North should control as it is that the dog's tail would wag the dog. . . . If they should get into power that tail would be so powerful that it would sweep down at one stroke all of your industries and prosperity, all of your banks and manufactures and your industries of all sorts and descriptions.[29]

Going on to Buffalo, he declared:

The Democratic party, organized as it now is, is under the control of the rebel brigadiers. . . . We are not willing, and you are not willing, and among the people of the Empire State there are men who will not submit to Southern rule. We want to be ruled by Northern people while we are alive.[30]

Grant had forgotten to whom he had given the tough assignments in the Wilderness, at Spotsylvania and Cold Harbor. His words were a restraint on the Union veterans who might have been thinking of voting for Hancock. In the end, despite Hancock's more outstanding army service, the Union veterans listened to Grant and went down the line for Garfield and Arthur. Even Francis A. Walker, Hancock's adjutant general and historian of the Second Corps, deserted his old chief. He seemed later to regret Hancock's defeat:

Although I did not vote for General Hancock, I am strongly disposed to believe that one of the best things the nation has lost in recent years has been the example and the influence of that chivalric, stately and splendid gentleman in the White House.[31]

George B. McClellan came up from New Jersey and rallied the New York crowds for his old subordinate on the Peninsula.[32] Rosecrans stumped California for him in opposition to Garfield, who had been Rosecran's chief of staff at Chickamauga. One-legged Dan Sickles, a noted haranguer who in the last two campaigns had been for Grant, spoke from his chair with his ready flow of words, "No matter from how great a height the arrows of detraction come, history gathers them all in her sheath and drops them in scorn at Hancock's feet."[33] Thomas F. Meagher of the old Irish brigade worked diligently around New York, where the mood of Tammany seemed uncertain.

Here and there were generous splashes of mud. A writer for the paper *Truth* was hauled into court for libeling Garfield by calling him a liar. Hancock was accused of being pro-Catholic in some quarters, anti-Catholic in others. The Pope was alleged to have sent him $50,000. The execution of Mary E. Surratt became such an issue that the Atlanta *Constitution* sent a reporter to Greeneville, Tennessee, for an interview with the late President Johnson's daughter for her version of the case.

But despite occasional splatterings and bursts of fire, the campain was dull and unexciting. The New York *World,* which gauged its news more by what was interesting than by what was important, gave two columns to the campaign and six and a half to the arrival of the "divine" Sarah Bernhardt.[34]

The outcome in New York turned on the antics of Tammany Hall. A great many Hancock supporters detected that the chief sachem, "stumpy and bullet-headed" John Kelly, was much more concerned about electing a mayor of New York, which he did by a hair, than a President.

When the results were in, Garfield had 214 electoral votes, Hancock 155. The contest was closer than these figures indicate. The shift of New York's 35 electoral votes would have elected Hancock. And a shift of about 12,000 popular votes would have meant victory for him in New York.

Out of more than 9,000,000 votes cast, Garfield's popular plurality was a meager 7,023. Garfield received 4,449,053, Hancock 4,442,030, with scatterings to lesser parties. The Philadelphia

Press quoted a prognosticator on election day as saying the clear sky was worth 100,000 Republican votes. A rain like that at Spotsylvania might have elected Hancock. He carried all the old slave states and made the South for the first time solidly Democratic. General Order No. 40 had not been forgotten. He won New Jersey, Nevada and all of California's six electors except one. But he lost the Middle West and all the East except New Jersey. On the plus side he put the Democratic party in a strong enough position to win four years later under Grover Cleveland.

When Mrs. Hancock woke him at 5:00 A.M. on the morning after the election, he asked the result.

"It has been a complete Waterloo for you," she told him.

"That is all right," he answered. "I can stand it." Then he went back to sleep.[35]

One of the first to reach Hancock was McClellan. These two old soldiers, each buffeted in their turn by the gales of political adversity, were closeted for an hour and a half. Whatever tendency Hancock may have had toward regret was lifted when McClellan departed. Cadmus Wilcox, against whom he had thrown the 1st Minnesota at Gettysburg, and who was now serving in the docile role of doorkeeper of the Senate, arrived with regrets. Dan Sickles, when he saw the defeated candidate in good humor, said, "You are the happiest looking Democrat I have seen since the election."[36]

In an election so close it was natural that charges of fraud should ring from one end of the country to the other. They were swelling into a vociferous volume on any number of counts when Hancock himself put an end to them. Friends and workers rushed to him with demands for a contest, but he would hear nothing of it. The country had been almost torn apart by the contest of 1876. He believed that democratic processes would be weakened or utterly destroyed by another bitter dispute only four years later.

"The campaign is over and the true Christian spirit is to forgive and forget," he said, as the New York *Herald* quoted him.[37]

Other statements of similar purport came from Governors Island. Asked the Democratic New York *Herald* editorially:

What will it avail to trumpet forth charges of wholesale fraud and colonization and to get up a parade of bogus evidence when the candidate . . . resolutely washes his hands of all this tampering with the people's verdict, and declares he would not take an office to which he does not believe that he has been elected.[38]

General St. Clair A. Mullholland, who had commanded a brigade under Hancock, called to solace him. Hancock laughed heartily about some of the campaign incidents, and when Mullholland asked if he would ever go before the people again, the general answered, "No, I am done with that." He qualified it by saying he would swing into action if any great crisis, like that of 1861, arose.[39]

Mrs. Hancock said the only disappointment he ever uttered was over the difference his defeat meant to so many friends. She quoted him as being satisfied with the result. She wrote years afterward that "while it was his firm conviction that he had been really elected, and then defrauded, he would not exchange positions with Garfield for any earthly inducement."[40]

Sherman asked him to come to Washington for Garfield's inauguration and he went. "I have no right to any personal feeling in the matter," he said. "It is clearly my duty as a soldier to obey."[41]

In 1881 he was put in charge of the Yorktown Centennial and was instructed by Secretary of War Robert T. Lincoln to make it a success. He was called on to do much entertaining. American and foreign dignitaries came. In the end he had spent $6,500 of his own money, for which he was never reimbursed.[42]

Governors Island and More Losses

Hancock suffered a great personal and military misfortune when in 1883 his chief of staff, General William G. Mitchell, died. They had been almost inseparable since the young lieutenant of the 49th Pennsylvania Volunteers, in the first winter of the war, reported as an aide. Over the years he had come almost to worship Hancock. The general in turn regarded him with as much affection as he bestowed on one of his family.

Never was there an order to be issued, or appointment to be made, or paper to be found, or praise bestowed, or censure imposed, but that the general's first action was to call, "Mitchell!" The aide—later the chief of staff—would immediately appear. Francis Walker noticed that when Hancock had a secret to confide, it went to Mitchell and remained a secret. Walker looked on him as the beau ideal of the riding staff, but he came to be just as essential in the office. Mitchell was a fearless soldier, an excellent horseman, a judge of men and positions, and a staff officer who was firm in conveying the general's orders, but still friendly and courteous even in haste or emergencies.[43] Hancock had rated him an important factor in the victory at Gettysburg.

Hancock was lost without Mitchell. But he adjusted himself to the void. He would be less active in the sunset years. As books about the war appeared he read them raptly and in some instances made corrections in the margins of facts and spelling. Someone sent him as a present the chatty little book by George Cary Eggleston, *A Rebel's Recollections,* one of the best personal accounts from the Southern side.

He was always disturbed that Grant in his report had not given the Second Corps the recognition to which he felt it was entitled, and feared it would suffer in history as a consequence.

Then, on December 30, 1884, another great sadness came to the Hancocks. Russell died. He had never been robust. His old Louisville friend, the fellow boarder, had heard of his life in Mississippi, "a favorite with his neighbors, in good repute with the world, making money and keeping up his cheery witticisms."[44] He lived only thirty-two years, but they were happy years.

Russell's plantation venture was not as profitable as it seemed. His funds became depleted and his father was called on for help to keep up the irrigation.[45]

With Ada and now Russell gone, life was closing in on the Hancocks.

Hancock's grief was intensified at this period by the moral decline of his twin brother, Hilary, who had become another drain on his dwindling resources. The seat of Hilary's problems seemed to be in his heart. He went to the Northwest because he had been jilted in Norristown by Anna Krause, daughter of the judge of Bucks and Montgomery County. Settling in Minneapolis in 1856, he began a legal career of much brilliance and promise. His earnings, according to newspaper report, reached from $15,000 to $20,000 a year, a tidy income for the period. Then, he "fell a victim to his love for good company and good cheer" and "lost his ambition and sunk into a living death." He "went down like a rocket," as the newspaper account of the day averred.[46]

Perhaps it was not quite so bad, but there is indication that he became a steady drinker. He, too, was "a magnificent looking man,"[47] who became engaged to a beautiful daughter of the woman in whose house he boarded. But the sensible girl saw the danger signals and declined to marry him until he quit drinking and demonstrated that he meant it. Obviously he could not make his sobriety stick. The engagement to the loyal and heartbroken girl ran on for twenty-two years. "The world is full of such unnoticed heroines."[48]

The general for the last fifteen years of his life had to help support his twin. Hilary lived to the age of eighty-four and died in 1908.[49]

Twins can be very far apart—one almost a President, the other almost a tramp.

In November 1885, at the request of map maker Colonel John B. Bachelder, Hancock went to Gettysburg, on his first visit since a quick trip in the summer of 1865 as escort for his beloved daughter Ada. His friend Thomas B. Musgrave accompanied him and at Hancock's request brought along his son Percy. The general took delight in showing the lad about the field and telling what happened. "Your boy will remember what has been said when we have passed away," he told the father. For Bachelder he explained the troop movements during the second and third days and helped this indefatigable student of the battle identify the positions occupied by some Second Corps units. Hancock enjoyed the experience. It rekindled in him the fire and excitement of other days. He relished the conversations with the group of veterans and junior officers who gathered to trudge about the field with him.[50]

The Generals Go Down the Stairs

As Grant neared death he showed quality and character. He died after great suffering on July 23, 1885. To Hancock, as commanding general of the Atlantic Division, fell the task of organizing and conducting the funeral rites. He had charge of the heavily draped train which brought Grant's body from Mount McGregor, near Saratoga Springs, New York, to New York City. Hancock, his staff, and other notables rode in one car, behind which was a car filled with militia officers. They popped champagne bottles and smoked sociably, and were making it a fete beyond what Hancock regarded the proprieties.

He told the train conductor, "Will you please present my compliments to those gentlemen with the request that they stop smoking?"

The crowd sent back their own compliments with notice that they would keep their cigars lighted. Smoking inappropriate for Grant! It did seem that Hancock had grown fretful.

But he still knew how to enforce discipline. "Where is the next switch?" he asked the conductor.

"About five miles below."

"When you reach it, if smoking in that car has not stopped, switch it on a side track and leave it. You may tell the gentlemen what I have said."

The smoking ended.[51]

The Grant funeral, a magnificent pageant, was Hancock's last official public appearance. In front of his staff, he led the tremendous funeral march from City Hall to Riverside Drive. As a tribute to the defeated foe, he directed Lieutenant General John B. Gordon of the Confederate Army to ride beside him along the route.[52] The streets were densely packed with the great New York crowds and those who had come by train and boat. The funeral procession was eight miles long. The funeral car, escorted by a large detachment of the Grand Army of the Republic, was drawn by twenty-four jet black horses each led by a Negro freedman. President Cleveland was accompanied by his Cabinet and was followed by Justices of the Supreme Court and the committees of senators and representatives in Congress. Other distinguished Confederates present included Joseph E. Johnston, Fitzhugh Lee, Wade Hampton, and Simon Buckner. The occasion called for organizational ability and it passed without confusion. Grant's body was placed in the tomb overlooking the North River and the New Jersey Palisades.

Grant's close confidant and biographer, Badeau, saw a final reconciliation between the two generals in Hancock's conduct of what was undoubtedly the most imposing burial rites that had ever been held in the country. He paid tribute to Hancock in a newspaper interview:

With . . . nobility he bore his part in the great funeral over his ancient chief and comrade. The majestic character of those rites that attracted the attention of the world was greatly due to the tender care and chivalrous punctilio of him who thought the dead chieftain had wounded him.

These two soldiers have fought their last fight and ended every difference. Each at the last was full of soldierly and brotherly generosity to the other.[53]

McClellan died three months later and the loss was felt most keenly and more personally by Hancock. He attended the funeral of his old friend and commander at Trenton, New Jersey. Joseph E. Johnston stood between Hancock and William B. Franklin.

Meade and Thomas were gone. The final trumpets were calling the old soldiers. Hancock, upright, vigorous, sixty-one, could not know then that his turn would be next.

Peace at Last in Norristown

He went to Washington on January 27, 1886, attended by Lieutenant John A. DaPray. He registered at Wormleys Hotel and on the next day called on President Cleveland, Secretary of War Endicott and Lieutenant General Sheridan. So annoyed was he by a boil on the back of his neck that on the following morning, the twenty-ninth, he went to the army dispensary and had it lanced, to his great relief.

He returned to Governors Island and for the next few days the boil continued virulent and angry. Dr. John H. Janeway, the departmental surgeon of the army, was called and saw that a carbuncle had developed. Hancock was fed beef tea and milk, then was given hypodermic injections of brandy, whisky, ether and carbonate of ammonia, separately and combined, for the purpose, as the newspapers naïvely explained, of "restoring the sufferer's health."[54]

By February 7 his condition had grown critical. Delirium set in and it was stated that "the malady had touched the brain."[55] For a day his pulse seemed normal and he rested well. Other physicians were called: Colonel Charles Sunderland of the Army and Dr. D. M. Stimson of West 17th Street, a close friend. A consultation agreed that the general was losing strength rapidly, his condition being complicated by diabetes. Some of the doctors felt that the diabetes had caused a "depravity of his blood" which had brought on the carbuncle.

General James B. Fry, his old friend, came to the sickroom. Crowds gathered about the telegraph office in Norristown. The general's faithful orderly, John Ward, waited. Hancock stirred in his sleep, then called out, "Oh, Allie, Myra, good——"[56] Before he could complete the sentence, he died—so quickly that Almira—his Allie, his Myra—could not reach him from the adjoining room.

As Dr. Janeway described the precipitate death, "The general went down to the close of his life like a person descending a flight of stairs."[57]

Almira Hancock asked for a simple funeral without military display. Burial would be at Norristown, where their daughter Ada had rested for nine years.

On Saturday, February 13, the rain fell heavily. The Irish Brigade grieved.[58] Crowds stood with their umbrellas in lower New York as the funeral procession passed with the body of the man who had headed a great political party in a campaign for the nation's highest honor; who had aligned armies and conducted and resisted some of the greatest attacks of history; whose quiet voice and steady courage had rallied faltering brigades. More than any other he had been the Army of the Potomac at the peaks.

The funeral was in Trinity Church. There were no dirges, no military trappings, no long columns of troops. Behind the coffin as it was taken up Broadway, rode Lieutenant General Sherman and Senator Thomas F. Bayard of Delaware, the leading contender against Hancock for the Democratic nomination of 1880. Then came Sheridan and Schofield, and behind them Franklin, Baldy Smith, Terry, John Newton, Nelson A. Miles, Fry, Orlando Willcox, Francis A. Walker and many others. Some had been his friends at West Point; some had helped him write the long and inerasable story of the Army of the Potomac; some had fought by his side in the glorious Second Corps.

At the church his sword and hat were placed on the flag-covered coffin. Nearby was a touching remembrance, a simple wreath of myrtle leaves, with a card that said, "From the hills that shelter the last home of General William L. Mitchell, the friend and associate of the patriot, soldier, statesman, Winfield Scott Hancock."[59]

The Hancock Legion of Brooklyn, bearing an honored name, sent a star of white hyacinths, callas and lilies of the valley. A pillow of white roses bore no other inscription than the "Old Guard." No tickets of admission were required. In the pews were aging veterans mixed with some of the distinguished men of the city: William M. Evarts, Hamilton Fish, Chauncey DePew, John Jacob Astor, Joseph H. Choate. The simple funeral services of the Episcopal Church were read, without address or eulogy. The choir sang "Rock of Ages." Through the rain again, the body, followed by many of the old generals, was started to Norristown.

The funeral train reached Norristown at 3:00 P.M. and the procession moved to the town cemetery, escorted by a famous unit—Battery F, 5th U.S. Artillery.[60] Nothing could have been more fitting than that the ranks of veterans standing at salute when the hearse passed should be members of the Zook Post, Grand Army of the Republic—Zook who was Hancock's heroic brigade commander at Fredericksburg and Chancellorsville, Zook who fell in the Wheat Field at Gettysburg.

Great crowds of home folks lined the streets and were at the cemetery. Sherman headed one line of pallbearers, Senator Bayard the other. Sheridan and Schofield were there. Sixteen artillerymen carried the casket into the Hancock vault.

Battery F fired salvos. Bugler Richard Frank stepped from the ranks and played taps. Winfield Scott Hancock was at rest.

Someone wrote verses about him in which four lines stand out:

> And was he happy all his life?
> Alas! my son—not so;
> It is not thus that Fate rewards
> Her heroes here below.[61]

On the next day, February 14, Hancock's birthday—when he would have been sixty-two—the Reverend Dr. John R. Paxton spoke eloquently but simply[62] in the West Forty-second Street Presbyterian church in New York:

"They buried yesterday my old commander—the ideal soldier—the pure patriot—the noblest man—the stainless name—gentle as a woman, with voice low and caressing as love in the camp . . . but a voice of thunder in the battle to inspire and command.

"And I shall see his face no more. . . . For three years I followed him—from Fredericksburg to Appomattox. My hero, lofty and superb! Glorious Hancock! I see you now at Gettysburg, thrilling me with the accents of command. I see you in the Wilderness, inspiring me with your dauntless courage. My hero . . . my leader . . . farewell!"

NOTES,
BIBLIOGRAPHY,
ACKNOWLEDGMENTS
AND INDEX

Notes

Chapter One: SUMMONED TO THE ARMY

[1] George B. McClellan, *McClellan's Own Story*, 140.

[2] General R. C. Drum to Gen. W. G. Mitchell quotes Meade statement, John W. Forney, *Life and Military Career of Winfield Scott Hancock*, 339; Grant, *Memoirs*, II, 539.

[3] Grand Army *Review*, Vol. I, No. 9, in Hancock Papers, Pennsylvania State Library.

[4] Gideon Welles, *Diary*, III, 204.

[5] Mrs. Hancock, *Reminiscences of Winfield Scott Hancock*, 223. (Hereinafter Hancock, *Reminiscences*.)

[6] James D. Richardson, *Messages and Papers of the Presidents*, VI, 595.

[7] Military Service Institute, *Letters and Addresses*, 70. (Hereinafter *Letters and Addresses*.)

[8] Reprinted in New York *Tribune*, Feb. 13, 1886.

[9] Hancock, *Reminiscences*, 284.

[10] Rev. C. W. Denison (late chaplain) and Captain G. B. Herbert, *Hancock "the Superb," The Early Life and Public Career of Winfield Scott Hancock*, 43. (Hereinafter Denison and Herbert.)

[11] *Ibid.*, 47-48.

[12] Philadelphia *Times* clipping (undated), Hancock Papers, Pennsylvania State Library; Frank H. Norton, *Life and Public Services of Winfield Scott Hancock*, 2, says both of Hancock's grandfathers were in the Revolution. J. R. Cole, *The Life and Public Services of Winfield Scott Hancock*, 18, says the maternal grandfather was imprisoned in Dartmoor. At times it is stated erroneously that Hancock's father was an impressed seaman imprisoned at Dartmoor in the War of 1812.

[13] Scrapbook, Hancock Papers, Montgomery County Historical Society, Norristown, Penna. (Hereinafter called Hancock Papers, Mont. Co.)

[14] Norristown *Herald* story, Scrapbook. Hancock Papers, Mont. Co.

[15] Denison and Herbert, 48.

[16] *Biographical Directory of American Congress,* 1950 edition, 1172.

[17] Denison and Herbert, 34, say he was coached in inflection and emphasis by a local pastor.

[18] Howard M. Jenkins, *Historical Collections Relating to Gwynedd,* 444.

[19] Hancock Papers, Mont. Co. The name of Hancock's group, organized in 1839, was soon changed to the Cabinet of Natural Sciences of Norristown.

[20] *Ibid.* The entries do not appear to be in his handwriting, but the book is indicative of the orderliness of anything he supervised.

[21] Denison and Herbert, 78.

[22] *Ibid.,* 31.

[23] *Ibid.,* 25.

[24] Frederick E. Goodrich, *Life of Winfield Scott Hancock,* 325.

[25] Denison and Herbert, 26.

[26] Goodrich, 326.

[27] Denison and Herbert, 35.

[28] The house is still standing on the east side of the Bethlehem Road. It was enlarged in 1876 for a school. Edward W. Hocker, *Hancock Landmarks,* 15.

[29] Philadelphia *Times* clipping (undated), Hancock Papers, Pennsylvania State Library.

[30] J. Thomas Scharf and Thompson Westcott, *History of Philadelphia,* I, 608.

[31] *Ibid.*

[32] Scrapbook, Hancock Papers, Mont. Co.

[33] Denison and Herbert, 77. DeKalb Street later was extended and the house was removed.

[34] Don Seitz, *The "Also Rans,"* 272. Denison and Herbert, 21.

[35] Denison and Herbert, 24.

[36] O. C. Gardiner, *Sketch of the Life and Public Services of Winfield Scott Hancock* (pamphlet), 7.

[37] Adjutant General's Office, Military Academy Applications, National Archives.

[38] *Letters and Addresses,* 37.

[39] Francis A. Walker, *General Hancock,* 14.

[40] Cole, 24.

Chapter Two: WEST POINT AND MEXICO

[1] Justitia, *Letter to the Hon. Mr. Hawes,* 9.

[2] *Ibid.,* 10.

[3] Grant, *Memoirs,* I, 39.

[4] Justitia, 10.

[5] *Ibid.*

[6] Alvin S. Southworth, *Life of General Winfield Scott Hancock,* 24.

[7] The best answer to the reflections on West Point at this period—in which Horace Greeley and his *Tribune* joined at a slightly later date and which were widespread in the Confederacy—was the performance of the graduates in the most stubbornly contested war of modern history. When the war occurred, 820 West Point graduates held commissions in the regular army. Of these 197 resigned and went with the South, while 623, many of them Southerners, remained with the Federal government. Of the 1200 regular army officers in 1861, two thirds of whom were West Point graduates, 181 were killed in action and 500 were wounded. The casualty rate was about one out of two, apart from the loss by disease which carried off such notable graduates as Major Generals David Birney and John Buford. From *The Regular Army. A Defense of West Point* (author given only as An Officer). Undated letter to Buffalo *Courier* reprinted in Justitia's reply to Hawes. These figures are at variance with those cited by E. Merton Coulter, *The Confederate States of America,* 376-377, from *Southern Historical Society Papers,* XXXVII, 297. (Hereinafter *S.H.S.P.*) Coulter summarizes the attacks on West Point in the South.

[8] James Allen Hardie, *Memoir of James Allen Hardie,* 22.

[9] Cincinnati speech, quoted by Goodrich, 349.

[10] *Letters and Addresses,* 13.

[11] *Ibid.,* 21.

[12] Hardie, *Memoir,* 8 and 9.

[13] *Letters and Addresses,* 46.

[14] *Battles and Leaders of the Civil War,* I, 401. (Hereinafter *B. & L.*)

[15] Walker, *Hancock,* 11.

[16] George Thornton Fleming, *Life and Letters of Alexander Hays,* 9. He draws on Hamlin Garland's *Ulysses S. Grant, His Life and Character,* 33. Other descriptions of West Point life of the period include Perley Poore's *Life and Services of Ambrose E. Burnside,* etc. and Lloyd Lewis' *Sherman Fighting Prophet,* 51-52.

[17] This is in the library of General Hancock's books owned by Edmund A. Hannay, Courtland, Alabama. (See Acknowledgments.)

[18] *Letters and Addresses,* 21.

[19] *Ibid.*

[20] Pleasanton newspaper interview in Fleming, *Hays,* 14-15.

[21] *Ibid.,* 15.

[22] George R. Stewart, *John Phoenix, Esq. The Veritable Squibob,* 30-31.

[23] The class of 1841, three years ahead of Hancock's, included John F. Reynolds, Richard B. Garnett, Nathaniel Lyon, Don Carlos Buell, Horatio G. Wright and Albion B. Howe. In the class of 1842 were

318 HANCOCK THE SUPERB

Longstreet, Abner Doubleday, Lafayette McLaws, John Pope, W. S. Rosecrans, Earl Van Dorn, John Newton, Seth Williams and C. W. Smith. The class of 1843 included Grant and W. B. Franklin. Following Hancock, but cadets while he was at West Point, were Barnard Bee, Fitz John Porter, Gordon Granger, Baldy Smith, McClellan, Stonewall Jackson, Pickett, Cadmus Wilcox, Darius N. Couch, Jesse L. Reno and others who attained generals' commissions or lesser grades.

[24] Hardie, *Memoir*, 7.

[25] Walker, *Hancock*, 13.

[26] The author has been unable to locate the original of this or other Hancock drawings, though a search has been made at the National Archives, Library of Congress, West Point Library, at Norristown, Harrisburg and among remaining family books. A reproduction of "Jineing the Pint" is opposite page 56, Denison and Herbert.

[27] Denison and Herbert, 56-57.

[28] DeGaulle statement in *Time*, Jan. 5, 1959.

[29] *Grand Army Review*, Feb. 1886. Vol. I, No. 9, Hancock Papers, Pennsylvania State Library.

[30] Hardie, *Memoir*, refers to his "august and critical presence."

[31] A distinguished regiment in the old service because it had been Zebulon Pike's.

[32] A.G.O., Mexican War Papers, National Archives.

[33] *Ibid.* "He is much wanted here," wrote the post commander to the adjutant general.

[34] *Ibid.* Denison and Herbert, 63.

[35] Walker, *Hancock*, 17.

[36] His first letter was from Fort Washita, June 30, 1846, National Archives.

[37] Letter of May 8, 1847, National Archives.

[38] Letter of April 7, 1847, National Archives.

[39] Denison and Herbert, 149. The Adjutant General's file, National Archives, shows he wrote applications to go to Mexico May 8 and 25, received orders June 21, and arrived at Vera Cruz July 13, 1847.

[40] Walker, *Hancock*, 18.

[41] D. X. Judkin and Frank H. Norton, *Life of Winfield Scott Hancock*, 24.

[42] Winfield Scott, *Memoirs*, II, 481.

[43] Judkin and Norton, 28.

[44] *Ibid.*

[45] Denison and Herbert, 65.

[46] Fleming, *Hays*, 37-38.

[47] Denison and Herbert, 150-151.

[48] *Ibid.*, 151.

[49] "He has been carried away by successes," the Duke continued. Cited by Goodrich, 49.

Chapter Three: FORMATIVE ARMY YEARS

[1] *Letters and Addresses,* 18.
[2] *Ibid.,* 17.
[3] Hancock Papers, Scrapbook (undated clipping from York, Pennsylvania, *Age*), Pennsylvania State Library.
[4] Hancock, *Reminiscences,* 3.
[5] *Letters and Addresses,* 22.
[6] Hancock, *Reminiscences,* 4.
[7] *Ibid.,* 4-5.
[8] *Ibid.,* 5-6.
[9] *Ibid.,* 8.
[10] *Letters and Addresses,* 15.
[11] A.G.O., General Papers, National Archives.
[12] Hancock, *Reminiscences,* 10.
[13] *Ibid.,* 15.
[14] *Ibid.,* 18.
[15] Denison and Herbert, 82.
[16] *Letters and Addresses,* 27.
[17] *Ibid.,* 22.
[18] Hancock, *Reminiscences,* 34.
[19] *Ibid.,* 34.
[20] *Ibid.,* 29.
[21] *Ibid.,* 30.
[22] Hancock Papers, Scrapbook, Pennsylvania State Library.
[23] Hancock, *Reminiscences,* 42.
[24] *Ibid.,* 40.
[25] Judkin and Norton, 38-39, give summary. The original could not be located in the National Archives or elsewhere.
[26] Hancock, *Reminiscences,* 44.
[27] Walker, *Hancock,* 30.
[28] Reference to the books remaining from Hancock's library is contained under acknowledgments. While there is an assumption involved in determining the books he read, it is clear that his remarkable military insight was based on some study and it is reasonable to believe that his own books were a main source of his information, at the time when there were few public libraries or other opportunities to obtain outside books at army posts.
[29] It is to be noted that no copy of Jomini's work was found among Hancock's books.
[30] J. Mitchell, *Thoughts on Tactics and Military Organization,* 48.
[31] *Ibid.,* 158.
[32] Judkin and Norton, 31.
[33] Walker, *Hancock,* 31-32.
[34] *Letters and Addresses,* 29.
[35] Henry W. Bingham, *Oration at Unveiling,* 5.

[36] *Papers of Military Historical Society of Massachusetts.* (Hereinafter *Mass. Papers.*) Paper read by Francis A. Walker, Vol. X, 51.
[37] *Ibid.,* 51-52.

Chapter Four: PARTING WITH OLD FRIENDS

[1] Hancock, *Reminiscences,* 46.
[2] *Ibid.*
[3] *Ibid.,* 46-47.
[4] *Ibid.,* 49.
[5] *Ibid.,* 51.
[6] *Letters and Addresses,* 36.
[7] Denison and Herbert, 101.
[8] Hancock, *Reminiscences,* 66-67.
[9] *Ibid.,* 54 ff.
[10] J. H. Stine, *History of the Army of the Potomac,* 8.
[11] Goodrich, 81.
[12] Hancock, *Reminiscences,* 67.
[13] *Ibid.*
[14] *Ibid.,* 68.
[15] *Ibid.,* 69.
[16] *Ibid.*
[17] *Ibid.*
[18] Judkin and Norton, 119. Mrs. Hancock gave the book to General Armistead's sister after the war. Hancock, *Reminiscences,* 70.
[19] Judkin and Norton, 118.
[20] Hancock, *Reminiscences,* 70.
[21] Abner Doubleday, *Chancellorsville and Gettysburg,* 195.
[22] Goodrich, 303; O. C. Gardiner, 9.
[23] Denison and Herbert, 99.
[24] Norton, 5.
[25] Hancock, *Reminiscences,* 78.
[26] Walker, *Hancock,* 33.
[27] *Ibid.*
[28] John Frost, *The Pictorial Life of General Washington,* 239.
[29] Walker, *Hancock,* 33-34.
[30] *Ibid.,* 32.
[31] *Ibid.,* 32-33.

Chapter Five: THE CHARGE AT WILLIAMSBURG

[1] Rufus R. Dawes, *Service with the Sixth Wisconsin Volunteers,* 24.
[2] *Ibid.*
[3] *Letters and Addresses,* 91.
[4] Walker, *Hancock,* 39.

[5] *Letters and Addresses,* 91.

[6] Walker, *Hancock,* 38.

[7] Forney, 338-339.

[8] *Ibid.,* 328-329.

[9] Hancock, *Reminiscences,* 82.

[10] *Ibid.,* 82-83.

[11] *Ibid.,* 83.

[12] *Ibid.,* 84-85.

[13] *Ibid.,* 91.

[14] *Pennsylvania at Gettysburg,* II, 1071.

[15] Hancock, *Reminiscences,* 91-92.

[16] Warren W. Hassler, Jr., *General George B. McClellan, Shield of the Union,* 67.

[17] Hassler, 70, points out that they approved the Peninsular plan.

[18] Hassler, 86, cites Hay's letter.

[19] *Ibid.,* 82, quotes Stanton's remarks.

[20] Oliver O. Howard, *Autobiography,* I, 217.

[21] *Official Records,* I, XI, 534. (Hereinafter *O.R.*)

[22] Reprinted in the New York *Herald,* Dec. 25, 1862.

[23] Douglas S. Freeman, *Lee's Lieutenants,* I, 193, cites Charleston *Mercury,* May 20, 1862.

[24] *O.R.,* I, XI, 535.

[25] *Ibid.,* 550.

[26] *Ibid.,* 537.

[27] *Ibid.,* 538.

[28] *Ibid.,* 548.

[29] *Ibid.,* 538.

[30] *Ibid.,* 548.

[31] *Ibid.,* 538.

[32] Quoted in Goodrich, 197 ff. The original of Custer's memorandum could not be found. The Custer Papers were given to the Custer Battlefield National Monument in Montana. There an inventory of the papers was compiled several years ago, but due to more recent shifts of papers from one parcel to another, another inventory is now being made to match the items with their original inventory description. In this process no mention has been found of the Custer notes on the battle of Williamsburg. One unlocated item is a letter from Custer to his step-sister written just after the battle. Mrs. Marguerite Merrington is reported to have destroyed a large number of Custer papers after completing her book, *The Custer Story,* and it is possible that the memorandum on Williamsburg was among them. Goodrich does not state where he copied the memorandum when he wrote in 1886.

[33] *North Carolina Regiments,* I, 283. (Hereinafter *N.C. Regts.*)

[34] Donald Bridgman Sanger and Thomas Robson Hay, *James Longstreet,* 48. Longstreet in *Manassas to Appomattox,* 77, says he ordered that the move not be made.

[35] *O.R.,* I, XI, 550.

[36] The charge caused considerable writing by Southern participants after the War from which the story of the Southern attack is taken. *S.H.S.P.,* VII, 299 ff., and *S.H.S.P.,* VIII, 281 ff.

[37] *O.R.,* I, XI, 608.

[38] Katharine M. Jones, *Heroines of Dixie,* 120. The Richmond *Enquirer* uses similar language respecting the 24th Virginia, June 2, 1862.

[39] *N.C. Regts.,* I, 284. Early praised the 24th Virginia, *O.R.,* I, XI, 608.

[40] Goodrich, 200.

[41] Custer ms., Goodrich, 201.

[42] Use of the word "Gentlemen" in addressing the troops was reported from several sources, as Prince de Joinville, *The Army of the Potomac,* 55, but there was at least one dissent. Captain William H. R. Neel of Germantown, Pennsylvania, who was on Hancock's staff at Williamsburg, was still at the age of ninety-two commuting daily to his Philadelphia office. He remembered as a nonagenarian what a striking figure Hancock was at the critical moment of the attack, but scoffed at the softness of his reported words. Neel must have been listening earlier, for he asserted that "what Hancock actually said would be represented by dashes and asterisks" if any newspaper printed it. Hancock Papers, Mont. Co., Scrapbook.

[43] Hancock in a letter to his wife put his loss at 126 killed and wounded. Hancock, *Reminiscences,* 92.

[44] *McClellan's Own Story,* 330.

[45] *Ibid.,* 331.

[46] Walker, *Hancock,* 43. *B. & L.,* II, 109. The remark occurred in a telegram McClellan sent to his wife. The frequent statement that it was in an official dispatch to Lincoln or Stanton apparently is in error. A careful search of the *Official Records* has failed to disclose a message of this wording. McClellan was laudatory but used a different adjective.

[47] *Maine at Gettysburg,* 408.

[48] *Letters and Addresses,* 45.

[49] *B. & L.,* II, 198-199; Walker, *Hancock,* 43.

Chapter Six: OUR COUNTRY, AND NO ONE MAN

[1] Fleming, *Hays,* 264.

[2] Hancock's Military Record written for Adjutant General, in National Archives.

[3] Walker, *Hancock,* 45; Historical sketch of 49th Pennsylvania Regiment in *Pennsylvania at Gettysburg,* I, 315.

[4] Forney, 336.

[5] Howard, *Autobiography,* I, 299.

[6] Walker, *Hancock,* 48.

[7] Forney, 139, quotes letter from Buffalo *Courier.*

[8] J. B. McClure, editor, *Life of General Hancock,* by Thomas A. Burns, 42.

[9] *Letters and Addresses,* 13-14.

[10] *McClellan's Own Story,* 598.

[11] Denison and Herbert, 162-163.

[12] Walker, *Hancock,* 57.

[13] The danger of mutiny is evident from John Gibbon's observations, *Personal Recollections of the Civil War,* 98.

[14] Thomas L. Livermore, *Days and Events,* 158.

[15] *Ibid.,* 157; Walker, *Hancock,* 54-56. The incident is sometimes placed with less specific details in Grant's Petersburg campaign.

[16] Gibbon, 98.

[17] *Ibid.*

[18] Walker, *Hancock,* 57; Judkin and Norton, 71.

[19] Hancock, *Reminiscences,* 92.

[20] *Ibid.,* 77-78.

Chapter Seven: STORMING MARYE'S HEIGHTS

[1] Walker, *History of the Second Army Corps,* 246. (Hereinafter Walker, *Second Corps.*)

[2] Regis de Trobriand, *Four Years with the Army of the Potomac,* 361.

[3] *Ibid.,* 362.

[4] *B & L.,* 108.

[5] *Ibid.*

[6] Walker, *Second Corps,* 156.

[7] *Ibid.*

[8] A. T. Freed, *The Life and Public Services of Winfield Scott Hancock,* 34-35.

[9] *Ibid.*

[10] *Ibid.,* 27.

[11] Denison and Herbert, 179.

[12] *O.R.,* I, XXI, 226.

[13] Moncure Daniel Conway, *Autobiography. Memoirs and Experiences,* I, 35 and 39. Marye's battery, raised in Fredericksburg, an efficient element of Lee's artillery, opened the battle of Gettysburg.

[14] Walker, *Second Corps,* 152.

[15] R. I. Holcombe, *History of the First Regiment Minnesota Volunteer Infantry,* 267. (Hereinafter Holcombe, *First Minnesota.*) Walker, *Second Corps,* 153.

[16] *Ibid.,* 154.

[17] De Trobriand, 364.

[18] *Ibid.,* 364.

[19] Longstreet speech at Fredericksburg in May 1884, quoted by Stine, 259.

[20] *O.R.,* I, XXI, 570.

21 Freed, 29.

22 *O.R.*, I, XXI, 254.

23 Howard, *Autobiography*, I, 342.

24 New York *Herald*, Dec. 15, 1862.

25 Meagher had been sentenced to death for sedition in England because of his agitation as a member of the "Young Ireland" party, a sentence commuted to banishment for life. He escaped from Van Dieman's Island, became a New York lawyer, and at the first Bull Run was captain in New York's "Fighting 69th" Infantry. He returned to New York and organized the Irish Brigade, which flew the green flag with golden harp alongside the Stars and Stripes on virtually every major eastern battlefield.

26 Walker, *Hancock*, 66.

27 Freed, 29.

28 *O.R.*, I, XXI, 249.

29 George E. Pickett, *Heart of a Soldier*, 66.

30 Quoted by Horace Greeley, *The American Conflict*, II, 345n.

31 Reprinted in New York *Herald*, Dec. 31, 1862.

32 *O.R.*, I, XXI, 235.

33 *Ibid.*, 237.

34 *Ibid.*

35 *Ibid.*

36 *Ibid.*

37 *Ibid.*

38 Frank Moore, *The Civil War in Song and Story*, 132.

39 *O.R.*, I, XXI, 233.

40 *Pennsylvania at Gettysburg*, II, 706. The regiment in its historical sketch strongly makes this claim.

41 *O.R.*, I, XXI, 233.

42 Howard, *Autobiography*, I, 342.

43 *Ibid.*

44 Charles H. Banes, *History of the Philadelphia Brigade*, 157.

45 *Ibid.*, 139-140.

46 Holcombe, *First Minnesota*, 255.

47 Longstreet said the closest body was thirty yards from the wall, with the main mass of the dead something over 100 yards off. *O.R.*, I, XXI, 581.

48 Freeman, *Lee's Lieutenants*, II, 368.

49 Stine, 287.

50 Holcombe, *First Minnesota*, 257; *B. & L.*, III, 114, is similar.

51 Stine, 292.

52 Reprinted in New York *Herald*, Dec. 25, 1862.

53 James H. Anderson, editor, *Life and Letters of Judge Thomas J. Anderson*, 258.

54 Walker, *Hancock*, 67.

55 Walker, *Second Corps*, 189; *O.R.*, I, XXI, 129.

56 Freed, 29.

Chapter Eight: PRAY, COULD WE EXPECT A VICTORY?

[1] J. B. Jones, *A Rebel War Clerk's Diary* (Howard Swiggett, ed.), I, 253. The Adams quotation is cited in a footnote.

[2] Stewart, *John Phoenix, Esq.,* 85.

[3] Glenn Tucker, *Poltroons and Patriots,* II, 498-499.

[4] John Bigelow, Jr., *The Campaign of Chancellorsville,* 6, gives the story as related by the proofreader.

[5] Holcombe, *First Minnesota,* 280.

[6] Gibbon, 107.

[7] Holcombe, *First Minnesota,* 280.

[8] *B. & L.,* III, 156.

[9] Hancock, *Reminiscences,* 95.

[10] Walker, *Hancock,* 83.

[11] *Ibid.*

[12] *B. & L.,* III, 159.

[13] *Ibid.*

[14] *Ibid.,* 161.

[15] Arthur L. Wagner, *Organization and Tactics,* 428n.

[16] Walker, *Hancock,* 86.

[17] *B. & L.,* III, 170.

[18] Bigelow, 366.

[19] Holcombe, *First Minnesota,* 293.

[20] *Grand Army Review,* Feb. 1886, clipping, Hancock Papers, Pennsylvania State Library.

[21] Judkin and Norton, 79.

[22] *Grand Army Review,* Feb. 1886, Hancock Papers, Pennsylvania State Library.

[23] Hancock Papers, Scrapbook, Pennsylvania State Library.

[24] Freed, 34.

[25] Walker, *Second Corps,* 246.

[26] Cole, 88.

[27] Hancock, *Reminiscences,* 93-94.

[28] *Ibid.,* 94-95.

[29] *B. & L.,* III, 170.

[30] Walker, *Hancock,* 93, says: "General Couch had wrought himself into an almost morbid feeling that he could never again lead his troops under Hooker, to what he regarded as purposeless slaughter. In this spirit, with pain inexpressible, he asked to be relieved . . . and on the 10th of June left the Second corps forever." He commanded a division under Thomas at the battle of Nashville.

Chapter Nine: PICKING A BATTLEFIELD

[1] Fleming, *Hays,* 339.

[2] The brush with Stuart's Confederate horse at Haymarket was

accounted by some of Hancock's men the turning point of the campaign. Apart from throwing a few shells into the Federal infantry and scattering some suttlers, Stuart accomplished no more than to capture a messenger going from Hancock at Haymarket to Zook in Gainesville, which gave the Confederates a copy of the Second Corps marching orders. But the brush, as some viewed it, deflected Stuart from the west of the Second Corps and sent him eastward on his long, groping, fruitless ride to find the right of Lee's army as it passed into Pennsylvania. Stuart seemed desperately determined to ride around the Federal army in any event and the skirmish with Hancock may not have been highly significant.

[3] Fleming, *Hays,* 339.
[4] *Ibid.*
[5] *Ibid.,* 405.
[6] *Ibid.,* 402.
[7] Holcombe, *First Minnesota,* 349.
[8] *Letters and Addresses,* 33.
[9] Walker, *Hancock,* 102.
[10] *Pennsylvania at Gettysburg,* II, 620.
[11] Winfield S. Hancock, *Gettysburg,* 821. (Page numbering of pamphlet begins at 821.)
[12] *Ibid.*
[13] *Ibid.,* 822.
[14] *Ibid.*
[15] *Ibid.,* 827.
[16] *Ibid.,* 822.
[17] *Ibid.*
[18] *Ibid.,* 823. In his official report Hancock said he arrived at 3:00 P.M. *B. & L.,* III, 287. In his pamphlet *Gettysburg,* 823, he said "not later than" 3:30, thus showing a lack of specific information. Halstead said he was with Howard at 4:00 P.M. and Hancock arrived later. *B. & L.,* III, 285. Doubleday said 4:30, *Chancellorsville and Gettysburg,* 150. The condition of the battle at the time of his arrival indicates that it was about 4:00 P.M.
[19] Carl Schurz, *Reminiscences of Carl Schurz,* III, 12.
[20] Chief of Staff Morgan's narrative in Appendix A, Hancock, *Reminiscences,* 189.
[21] Doubleday, 151.
[22] *B. & L.,* III, 285.
[23] Hancock, *Gettysburg,* 823.
[24] Schurz, *Reminiscences,* III, 14.
[25] *Atlantic Monthly,* July 1876.
[26] Hancock gave a quotation at the beginning, "The war's over, but the fighting's just begun."
[27] Hancock, *Gettysburg,* 829.
[28] *Ibid.,* 822-823.
[29] Edward N. Whittier, *The Left Attack (Ewell's) at Gettysburg,* 316.

[30] Hancock Papers, Pennsylvania State Library.

[31] Wagner, *Organization and Tactics*, 44.

[32] *Letters and Addresses*, 42.

[33] *Ibid.*, 20.

[34] *Pennsylvania at Gettysburg*, II, 1070.

[35] Schurz, *Reminiscences*, III, 13.

[36] *Ibid.*, 15.

[37] Morgan narrative, Hancock, *Reminiscences*, 191.

[38] Hancock, *Gettysburg*, 827-828.

[39] Richard Meade Bache, *Life of General George Gordon Meade*, 310; Forney, 147.

Chapter Ten: TWO JULY DAYS

[1] *Pennsylvania at Gettysburg*, II, 624.

[2] Denison and Herbert, 206.

[3] Livermore, *Days and Events*, 255.

[4] Holcombe's *First Minnesota*, 339.

[5] Holcombe's account in *First Minnesota* is followed here rather than the version which says that Hancock did not know the identity of the regiment and learned it later by chance.

[6] Walker, *Hancock*, 127. Morgan's narrative, Hancock, *Reminiscences*, 199.

[7] Holcombe's *First Minnesota*, 345. The regiment, with the skirmishers back in the ranks, had 150 men in the battle of July 3.

[8] *Grand Army Review*, Feb. 1886, clipping in Hancock Papers, Pennsylvania State Library. Wilkinson was senator from 1859 to 1865 and later served in the House.

[9] G. G. Benedict, *Vermont at Gettysburg*, 7.

[10] *B. & L.*, III, 313. Howard shows it was not requested, *Autobiography*, I, 429-430; as does Hancock's chief of staff, Colonel Morgan, narrative in Hancock, *Reminiscences*, 204-205.

[11] Gibbon, *Recollections*, 138.

[12] Banes, *Philadelphia Brigade*, 220.

[13] Kane statement in Rothermel Papers, Pennsylvania State Library.

[14] *Grand Army Review*, Feb. 1886, Hancock Papers, Pennsylvania State Library.

[15] Hancock Papers, Scrapbook, Pennsylvania State Library.

[16] Hancock to Rothermel, Hancock Papers, Pennsylvania State Library.

[17] Walker, his adjutant general, said he rode a black horse. Walker, *Hancock*, 139. Hancock gave a fairly complete account of his actions, in his correspondence with the artist Rothermel, which is followed here.

[18] Philadelphia *Times* clipping (undated), in Hancock Scrapbook, Pennsylvania State Library.

[19] Hancock to Rothermel, Dec. 31, 1868, Hancock Papers, Pennsylvania State Library.

[20] Philadelphia *Times* clipping (undated), in Hancock Scrapbook, Pennsylvania State Library.

[21] Letter of Dec. 31, 1868, to Rothermel.

[22] *Ibid.*

[23] *Letters and Addresses,* 21.

[24] Veazey's memorandum, in Walker, *Hancock,* 137.

[25] Freed, 42.

[26] *B. & L.,* III, 375.

[27] *Ibid.,* 386.

[28] Livermore, 259.

[29] Hancock to Rothermel, Jan. 21, 1869. Hancock Papers, Pennsylvania State Library.

[30] *Ibid.*

[31] Walker Paper, *Mass. Papers,* X, 49.

[32] Freed, 44.

[33] George R. Stewart, Berkeley, Calif., to author, July 3, 1959.

[34] Hancock to Rothermel, Dec. 31, 1868. Writing to the artist Rothermel in 1870, Hancock said that while the trefoil had been adopted as the Second Corps badge and was worn by the troops at Gettysburg, the corps flag with that device had not yet been used. He referred the question to General C. H. Morgan, his chief of staff at Gettysburg, who established that the flag was swallow-tailed, of blue silk, bearing a white Maltese cross in the center on which the corps designation appeared in a red figure in the center. This was the flag Private Wells carried. Hancock Papers, Pennsylvania State Library.

[35] Denison and Herbert, 204.

[36] Hancock Papers, Pennsylvania State Library.

[37] *Ibid.*

[38] *Ibid.* The sequence of events is as given by Hancock to Rothermel, Dec. 31, 1868.

[39] Dougherty to Mitchell, Jan. 2, 1869. Hancock Papers, Pennsylvania State Library.

[40] Livermore, 264.

[41] Walker, *Second Corps,* 296.

[42] Bingham to Hancock, Jan. 5, 1869. Hancock Papers, Pennsylvania State Library.

[43] Hancock to Rothermel, Dec. 10, 1870. Hancock Papers, Pennsylvania State Library.

[44] *Ibid.,* Jan. 9, 1869.

[45] *Ibid.,* July 30, 1867.

[46] *Ibid.,* Jan. 21, 1869.

[47] Undated clipping in Hancock Papers, Scrapbook, Pennsylvania State Library.

[48] Bingham to Hancock, Jan. 5, 1869. Hancock Papers, Pennsylvania State Library. He said he talked to Armistead on the crest of the hill in rear of Webb's brigade.

[49] Freeman, *Lee's Lieutenants*, III, 191. Freeman dismissed it.
[50] *S.H.S.P.*, X, 428.
[51] *Ibid.*
[52] *Ibid.*
[53] Schaff, 39-40.

Chapter Eleven: RECOVERY AND HIGH HONORS

[1] Auge, 275-276.
[2] Hancock, *Reminiscences*, 100.
[3] Norristown *Herald* story in Hancock Papers, Scrapbook, Pennsylvania State Library.
[4] Hancock Papers, Scrapbook, Mont. Co. Historical Society.
[5] Gardiner, 16.
[6] *Ibid.*
[7] Denison and Herbert, 215.
[8] A.G.O. General File, National Archives.
[9] Denison and Herbert, 220.
[10] *Ibid.*, 219.
[11] Scharf and Westcott, I, 813; Denison and Herbert, 219.
[12] Goodrich, 826; Denison and Herbert, 221-222.
[13] Hancock, *Reminiscences*, 100.
[14] R. M. Devans, *Our First Century*, 508-514.
[15] *Ibid.*
[16] *Army and Navy Journal* article quoted in Gibbon, 201-205.
[17] Welles, *Diary*, I, 472-473.
[18] *Letters and Addresses*, 15.
[19] New York *Age* clipping, Hancock Papers, Scrapbook, Pennsylvania State Library.
[20] Meade, *Life and Letters*, II, 136.
[21] *Letters and Addresses*, 34.
[22] *Ibid.*, 33-34.
[23] Sedgwick had been sounded out earlier. Tucker, *High Tide at Gettysburg*, 203.
[24] George R. Agassiz, editor, *Meade's Headquarters 1863-1865. Letters of Colonel Theodore Lyman from the Wilderness to Appomattox*, 60. (Hereinafter *Lyman Letters*.)
[25] *Letters and Addresses*, 67-68.
[26] Walker, *Mass. Papers*, X, 53.
[27] *Letters and Addresses*, 18.
[28] Hancock, *Reminiscences*, 303.
[29] *Letters and Addresses*, 18.
[30] *Ibid.*, 41.
[31] Walker, *Mass. Papers*, X, 54.
[32] Banes, *Philadelphia Brigade*, 219.
[33] Quoted in Cole, 40.
[34] Walker, *Hancock*, 34.
[35] Walker, *Mass. Papers*, X, 67.

Chapter Twelve: IN THE WILDERNESS

[1] Fleming, *Hays,* 559.
[2] *Mass. Papers,* IV, 224.
[3] Fleming, *Hays,* 562.
[4] *Ibid.*
[5] *Ibid.*
[6] Schaff, 42.
[7] *Ibid.*
[8] *Lyman Letters,* 82.
[9] *Ibid.*
[10] *B. & L.,* IV, 152.
[11] *Ibid.,* 153.
[12] Schaff, 79-80.
[13] *Ibid.,* 80.
[14] *O.R.,* I, XXXVI, 319.
[15] *Ibid.,* 320.
[16] *Lyman Letters,* 91.
[17] *Ibid.,* 91-92.
[18] John S. C. Abbott, *The History of the Civil War in America,* II, 490.
[19] *Lyman Letters,* 92-93.
[20] Moore, *Civil War in Song and Story,* 134.
[21] Fleming, *Hays,* 656.
[22] *Ibid.,* 658.
[23] *O.R.,* I, XXXVI, 320.
[24] Banes, *Philadelphia Brigade,* 228.
[25] *O.R.,* I, XXXVI, 321.
[26] *Mass. Papers,* IV, 169.
[27] *Ibid.,* 171.
[28] *O.R.,* I, XXXVI, 321.
[29] *Ibid.*
[30] *Ibid.*
[31] *Ibid.*
[32] *Ibid.,* 326.
[33] Freeman, *Lee's Lieutenants,* III, 357; Sanger and Hay, *James Longstreet,* 271 ff.
[34] Walker's *Second Corps,* 427, points out that four brigades, G. T. Anderson's, Davis', Wofford's and Mahone's, struck Birney's flank through the gap Barlow would have filled had Hancock's orders been followed.
[35] Southworth, 87.
[36] Hosmer, 90.
[37] *O.R.,* I, XXXVI, 323.
[38] *B. & L.,* IV, 161; *O.R.,* I, XXXVI, 323.
[39] *Lyman Letters,* 94.
[40] Banes, *Philadelphia Brigade,* 231.

[41] *Ibid.*, 232.

[42] Colonel Lyman quoted Grant as saying at one point at Petersburg that he did not want Mott's troops on his left, that they were no support and he would rather have no troops there at all. *Lyman Letters*, 110.

[43] *Ibid.*, 93.

[44] Longstreet, *Manassas to Appomattox*, 568.

[45] *O.R.*, I, XXXVI, 323.

[46] *B. & L.*, IV, 161.

[47] *Lyman Letters*, 92. It is difficult to tell whether this incident occurred at the first or second break of Mott's division, but it has been placed at the second because, among other considerations, the panic seemed more severe.

[48] Schaff, 276; *O.R.*, I, XXXVI, 324.

[49] *Ibid.*

[50] *Ibid.*

[51] *Ibid.*

[52] Banes, *Philadelphia Brigade*, 233.

[53] De Trobriand, 573.

[54] Hancock, *Reminiscences*, 337.

[55] The implication that he did not receive the orders was in Gibbon's asking Hancock for the names of the aides alleged to have carried them. He did not directly deny their receipt. Gibbon, *Recollections*, 394 ff.

[56] Correspondence in Gibbon, *Recollections*, 389 ff.

[57] *B. & L.*, IV, 242.

[58] Gordon, *Reminiscences*, cited in Commager, editor, *The Blue and the Gray*, 985.

[59] *B. & L.*, IV, 163.

[60] Gordon, *Reminiscences*, 368.

Chapter Thirteen: SPOTSYLVANIA BREAK-THROUGH

[1] *Lyman Letters*, 186. Joe Hayes was a Massachusetts colonel made a brigadier general May 12, 1864.

[2] Wagner, *Organization and Tactics*, 135-136.

[3] Walker, *Hancock*, 196.

[4] Hancock said midnight, *O.R.*, I, XXXVI, 334, but the movement does not appear to have been completed before 1:00 A.M.

[5] Barlow paper on Spotsylvania, *Mass. Papers*, IV, 255.

[6] *Ibid.*

[7] *O.R.*, I, XXXVI, 335.

[8] Walker, *Hancock*, 197.

[9] *B. & L.*, IV, 343.

[10] Gordon, *Reminiscences*, 289, refers to it also as "Hell's Half Acre."

[11] Conway, I, 78-79.

[12] Mary Boykin Chesnut, *A Diary from Dixie*, 232-233.

[13] James K. Hosmer, *Outcome of the Civil War*, 92, quotes Lt. Col. G. F. R. Henderson, biographer of Stonewall Jackson.

[14] Banes, *Philadelphia Brigade*, 245.

[15] Walker, *Hancock*, 197.

[16] John H. Worsham, *One of Jackson's Foot Cavalry*, 214.

[17] *N.C. Regts.*, I, 204.

[18] *Ibid.*, 152.

[19] Worsham, 213.

[20] Banes, *Philadelphia Brigade*, 247.

[21] *Ibid.*

[22] *Ibid.*

[23] Walker, *Hancock*, 199.

[24] Gordon, *Reminiscences*, 274.

[25] *Ibid.*, 275.

[26] *Ibid.*, 276.

[27] *Ibid.*, 278.

[28] Banes, *Philadelphia Brigade*, 248.

[29] Walker, *Hancock*, 199.

[30] Colonel Venable of Lee's staff said it was "perhaps the fiercest struggle of the war." *B. & L.*, IV, 243; the same thought was reflected in *N.C. Regts.*, II, 243 and by others.

[31] *N.C. Regts.*, I, 289.

[32] Walker, *Hancock*, 197-198.

[33] Barlow, *Mass. Papers*, IV, 255.

[34] *O.R.*, I, XXXVI, 336.

[35] Gordon, *Reminiscences*, 280, said every foot of the lost salient was recaptured.

[36] *N.C. Regts.*, I, 152; Walker, *Hancock*, 199.

[37] *Ibid.*, 201.

[38] *Ibid.*, 202.

[39] Morgan memorandum quoted in Walker, *Hancock*, 206-207.

[40] *O.R.*, I, XXXVI, 337.

[41] *Ibid.*, 335-336.

[42] By the time word of Hancock's success reached Washington the facts had been exaggerated in many particulars. Secretary Stanton sent a telegram to Major General Benjamin F. Butler in front of Drewry's Bluff, saying Hancock had captured Jubal Early along with Edward Johnson and had taken forty cannon. In place of two major generals, there was one, and instead of forty cannon, twenty (*Butler's Book*, 651 and 1070-1071). Hancock's first estimate in his message to Grant was that he had taken from thirty to forty guns.

[43] Badeau, II, 174.

[44] *Ibid.*

[45] Hancock, *Reminiscences*, 104; Badeau, II, 175; Greeley, II, 572.

[46] Henry W. Elson, *The Civil War Through the Camera*, page dated May 1864 (no page numbers).

Chapter Fourteen: BLOODY REPULSE AT COLD HARBOR

[1] Pickett, *Heart of a Soldier*, 133.
[2] *Butler's Book*, 671.
[3] *B. & L.*, IV, 187.
[4] *Lyman Letters*, 119.
[5] Walker, *Hancock*, 218.
[6] *Ibid.*, 220.

[7] Hancock had made a careful reconnaissance in his front on June 1, then was ordered to Cold Harbor, marched rapidly, and ordered in so fast that all he had time for was to make his formations, and even for this a delay was required. The responsibility might have been his had he been ordered to attack where and if he judged it promising.

[8] John Codman Ropes, an excellent critic of this campaign in his paper, "The Battle of Cold Harbor," read before the Military Historical Society of Massachusetts (*Mass. Papers*, IV, 349 ff.) in 1883, said the morale of Grant's army had not been severely shaken prior to June 3 in spite of the heavy losses in the Wilderness and at Spotsylvania. There had been some compensation in Hancock's capture of 4,000 and Upton of 1,000 at Spotsylvania; nevertheless, much had been lost by keeping the army continually in contact with the enemy and by attacking unimportant positions for indefinite objects.

That the army had not suffered serious loss of morale was attested by the manner in which it attacked vigorously and promptly at 4:30 A.M. June 3.

[9] Hosmer, 100-101.
[10] Forney, 332-333.
[11] *Pennsylvania at Gettysburg*, I, 441.
[12] Forney, 333.
[13] McMahon in *B. & L.*, IV, 215.
[14] The trenches were strengthened after the attack and probably appear to be more formidable, though they may not be where straightened.
[15] *B. & L.*, IV, 141.
[16] Pickett, *Heart of a Soldier*, 133.
[17] *S.H.S.P.*, VII, 503.
[18] Walker, *Hancock*, 223.
[19] Walker called the author of the news story "an unprincipled writer." *Hancock*, 224. Swinton, *Campaigns of the Army of the Potomac*, 482.
[20] *B. & L.*, IV, 218.
[21] *Ibid.*
[22] *Ibid.*, 227.
[23] Ropes, *Mass. Papers*, IV, 355, said he questioned officers who recollected none, but McMahon, *B. & L.*, IV, 217, makes incidental reference to slashings in front of the works.
[24] Ropes, *Mass. Papers*, IV, 355.
[25] Badeau, II, 291-292.

[26] Judkin and Norton, 307.

[27] Walker, *Hancock*, 225; McMahon in *B. & L.*, IV, 219.

[28] Walker, *Hancock*, 226.

[29] *Mass. Papers*, IV, 349 ff.

[30] Hancock sent a message to Grant at 1:00 P.M. that day saying the wounded were still uncared for, a matter that normally would come to the mind of a commanding general promptly after the end of the fighting. Hancock was puzzled and concerned over the failure of army headquarters to act.

[31] *B. & L.*, IV, 228.

[32] *O.R.*, I, XXXVI, 599.

[33] *B. & L.*, IV, 187.

[34] *Ibid.*, 217.

[35] Walker, *Hancock*, 222.

[36] Dawes, *Sixth Wisconsin*, 282.

[37] *B. & L.*, IV, 229.

[38] Cited by Commager, *Blue and Gray*, 1002.

[39] *B. & L.*, IV, 220.

[40] Greeley, *Conflict*, II, 583.

[41] Norton, 15.

[42] Badeau interview in Philadelphia *Press*. Undated clipping in Hancock Papers, Pennsylvania State Library.

[43] *Ibid.*

[44] J. G. Randall and Richard N. Current, *Lincoln the President. Last Full Measure*, 212.

[45] Badeau Philadelphia *Press* interview, Hancock Papers, Pennsylvania State Library.

[46] *Ibid.*

[47] *B. & L.*, I, 400.

[48] *Ibid.*, IV, 257.

[49] Paper by Colonel Theodore Lyman, Jan. 9, 1882. *Mass. Papers*, V, 19.

Chapter Fifteen: PETERSBURG FUMBLE

[1] *Mass. Papers*, X, 61.

[2] Walker, *Hancock*, 230.

[3] Grant, *Memoirs*, II, 295; Walker, *Hancock*, 233.

[4] *Butler's Book*, 693, 694, 696.

[5] *Ibid.*, 690.

[6] *Ibid.*, 708; Wilkeson's statement quoted, 707-712.

[7] *Ibid.*, 693.

[8] Walker, *Hancock*, 235.

[9] *Butler's Book*, 700.

[10] *Ibid.*, 701.

[11] *Ibid.*

[12] Greeley, *Conflict*, II, 585.

[13] Walker, *Hancock*, 235.
[14] *B. & L.*, IV, 541.
[15] *Lyman Letters*, 162.
[16] *B. & L.*, IV, 541.
[17] Meade, *Life and Letters*, II, 208.
[18] Walker, *Hancock*, 245.
[19] Meade, *Life and Letters*, II, 215.
[20] *Ibid.*, II, 222.
[21] *Lyman Letters*, 189.
[22] Meade, *Life and Letters*, II, 205.
[23] *Lyman Letters*, 191-192.
[24] Goodrich, 195.
[25] Hancock to T. Bailey Myers, Aug. 6, 1864. Hancock Papers, Library of Congress.
[26] Ida M. Tarbell, *The Life of Abraham Lincoln*, II, 199.
[27] De Trobriand, 596-597.
[28] *Ibid.*, 597.
[29] *Ibid.*
[30] *Ibid.*, 598.
[31] *Ibid.*, 657.
[32] *Ibid.*, 658.
[33] *Ibid.*, 659.

Chapter Sixteen: DEFEAT HAS BITTER DREGS

[1] Hancock to T. Bailey Meyers, Aug. 6, 1864. Hancock Papers, Library of Congress.
[2] Stine, 689-690.
[3] *B. & L.*, IV, 577.
[4] *Mass. Papers*, V, 270.
[5] *Lyman Letters*, 221.
[6] Auge, 281.
[7] Gibbon, 258.
[8] *Mass. Papers*, X, 65.
[9] John D. Billings, *Hard Tack and Coffee*, 327.
[10] Walker, *Hancock*, 275.
[11] Billings, 327.
[12] Forney, 330.
[13] *Mass. Papers*, V, 294.
[14] *Ibid.*, X, 65.
[15] Gibbon, 259.
[16] *Lyman Letters*, 107.
[17] This and following material on the threatened rupture is from the account in Gibbon, 243-244, 258-262.
[18] *B. & L.*, IV, 573.
[19] He returned briefly, then went to the command of the Twenty-fourth Corps.

[20] *Lyman Letters,* 233 and 234.
[21] James M. Merrill in *North Carolina Historical Review,* XXXV, No. 4, 466.
[22] Glazier, 351.
[23] De Trobriand, 668-669.
[24] Walker, *Hancock,* 291.
[25] Quoted in Forney, 334.
[26] *Ibid.,* 335.
[27] Bingham oration, 6.
[28] Cited by Bingham, 6.
[29] Walker, *Hancock,* 50.
[30] Goodrich, 196.

Chapter Seventeen: MOSBY AND MRS. SURRATT

[1] Hosmer, 75.
[2] A.G.O. General File, National Archives.
[3] Denison and Herbert, 39.
[4] Grant, *Memoirs,* II, 342-343.
[5] James J. Williamson, *Mosby's Rangers,* 378-379.
[6] *Ibid.,* 379-380.
[7] Clampitt to T. W. Bartley, July 17, 1880, Goodrich, 216.
[8] Baltimore *Clipper,* July 15, 1865.
[9] McClure, *Life of Hancock,* 96.
[10] *Letters and Addresses,* 39.
[11] Clampitt to Bartley, Goodrich, 223.
[12] Kyd Douglas, *I Rode with Stonewall,* 341.
[13] Statement of counsel in later trial of John H. Surratt, in David Miller DeWitt, *The Judicial Murder of Mary E. Surratt,* 173.
[14] Letter from the Reverend Father J. A. Walter, Mrs. Surratt's spiritual adviser, to Hancock, November 14, 1879, Goodrich, 223.
[15] Goodrich, 227.
[16] DeWitt, 121 and 152.
[17] Goodrich, 227.
[18] This was reiterated by President Johnson but denied by Holt. The careful analysis of the case by DeWitt removes any reasonable doubt about President Johnson's veracity and persuades one that the court's recommendation was withheld or concealed. Johnson of course could have modified the sentence on his own initiative had he chosen.
[19] McClure, 97.

Chapter Eighteen: A TRIAL IN STATESMANSHIP

[1] Welles, *Diary,* III, 209. Entry of Sept. 20, 1867.
[2] Hancock to Doolittle, May 14, 1866. Doolittle Papers, Library of Congress.

³ Schofield was pleasant in his references to Hancock, whom he termed "the almost incomparably gallant Hancock." John M. Schofield, *Forty-six Years in the Army,* 456.

⁴ Hancock, *Report on Indian Affairs,* 37.

⁵ *Letters and Addresses,* 10.

⁶ Hancock Papers, Mont. Co., Scrapbook.

⁷ *Ibid.*

⁸ Ed Johnson of Boston *Ideals,* Chicago *News* clipping (undated), Hancock Papers, Pennsylvania State Library.

⁹ Hodding Carter, *The Angry Scar,* 146.

¹⁰ Goodrich, 239.

¹¹ Robert Selph Henry, *The Story of Reconstruction,* 257.

¹² Richard Taylor, *Destruction and Reconstruction,* 241.

¹³ Richardson, *Messages and Papers of the Presidents,* VI, 556-557.

¹⁴ Jonathan Daniels, *Prince of Carpetbaggers,* 199.

¹⁵ Badeau interview (undated), in Philadelphia *Press,* Hancock Papers, Scrapbook, Pennsylvania State Library.

¹⁶ *Ibid.*

¹⁷ *Ibid.*

¹⁸ Henry, *Reconstruction,* 213.

¹⁹ Welles, *Diary,* III, 204. Entry of Sept. 20, 1867.

²⁰ Forney, 422-424.

²¹ Anyone who observes Hancock's reconstruction measures is led to wonder if Lincoln did not discuss the question with him, as he did with others on his trips to the army. The President expressed his views freely. David D. Porter quoted him as saying on a visit to Grant's army that the Confederacy should have the most liberal terms. "Get them to plowing once," Lincoln said, "and gathering in their own little crops, eating pop-corn at their own firesides, and you can't get them to shoulder a musket again for half a century." David D. Porter, *Incidents and Anecdotes of the War by Admiral Porter,* 285. Such was the spirit Lincoln induced into Grant's surrender terms at Appomattox and it was essentially Hancock's during his administration in the South.

²² Hancock, *Reminiscences,* 120-122.

²³ *Ibid.,* 124.

²⁴ *Ibid.,* 125.

²⁵ Goodrich, 247-248.

²⁶ Taylor, *Destruction and Reconstruction,* 241.

²⁷ *Letters and Addresses,* 4.

²⁸ *Ibid.,* 69-70.

²⁹ Welles, *Diary,* III, 241.

³⁰ *Ibid.,* 242. Entry of Dec. 19, 1867.

³¹ *Ibid.,* 245. Entry of Dec. 24, 1867.

³² Richardson, *Messages and Papers of the Presidents,* VI, 595-596.

³³ Welles, *Diary,* III, 242. Entry of Dec. 19, 1867.

³⁴ Hancock, *Reminiscences,* 102.

[35] Pamphlet, *Winfield Scott Hancock's Defiance of the Reconstruction Acts*, 1; Atlanta *Constitution*, July 3, 1880. Garfield pressed his move to have Hancock censured. Representative Charles A. Eldredge, Wisconsin Democrat, complied with President Johnson's recommendation and offered on December 18, 1867, a resolution of thanks to Hancock, which was cut off when Nathaniel P. Banks moved to table the President's message. On January 6, 1868, Eldredge reintroduced his resolution to thank Hancock "for his wise, patriotic and timely recognition of the first rights of the citizen and of the great principles of Constitutional liberty." This was tabled by a vote of 86 to 28. On January 16, Garfield, not satisfied with this result, moved to demote Hancock. He asked for suspension of the rules, which was blocked by Representative Samuel J. Randall of Pennsylvania. At Garfield's request Senator John M. Thayer of Nebraska introduced a similar bill in the Senate. Both bills died in committee.

[36] *Letters and Addresses*, 29.

[37] These and other extracts were culled from Hancock's orders and papers and printed in the Barkley & Co. campaign pamphlet in 1880.

[38] Goodrich, 300.

[39] Hancock to Grant, February 7, 1868, requested Grant to reconsider his countermanding order and added: "To suspend my order, would be to destroy my usefulness here; and in such case, a sense of what I consider due to me and my position, in this matter, would necessitate a respectful request to be relieved from my present command." *Grant-Hancock Correspondence*, 5.

[40] Hancock, *Reminiscences*, 130.

[41] *Ibid.*, 132.

[42] Welles, *Diary*, III, 277. Entry of Feb. 12, 1868.

[43] *Ibid.*, 298. Entry of Feb. 28, 1868. This was four days after the impeachment of President Johnson by the House.

[44] Richardson, *Messages and Papers of the Presidents*, VI, 663.

[45] Hancock to Sherman, July 9, 1870. *Sherman-Hancock Correspondence*, 20.

[46] Flanders was a former Treasury agent in New Orleans whom Sheridan had first installed as Governor of Louisiana.

[47] Hancock to Sherman, July 9, 1870, *Correspondence*, 20.

[48] *Ibid.*, 21.

[49] Welles, *Diary*, III, 394. Entry of July 1, 1868.

[50] *Ibid.*, 397. Entry of July 8, 1868.

[51] Hancock, *Reminiscences*, 138-139.

[52] Sherman to Hancock, *Correspondence*, 6.

[53] Hancock to Sherman, July 9, 1870. *Correspondence*, 6.

[54] *Letters and Addresses*, 10.

[55] Badeau interview (undated), Philadelphia *Press*, Hancock Papers, Pennsylvania State Library.

[56] *Ibid.*

Chapter Nineteen: PARADE AND TAPS

[1] McClure, 105.

[2] General James B. Fry, formerly of Hancock's staff, said the demand of old soldiers was so persistent that despite economical living the Hancocks fell behind. "The salary of his lowest clerk would meet all that he and Mrs. Hancock spent upon themselves," said Fry. "All the rest of their income went for the good of others who needed it." A newspaper clipping apparently from the New York *World* in 1886, but not clearly identified, in the scrapbook of the Hancock Papers, Pennsylvania State Library, said Hancock at Governors Island had been compelled to entertain officially, but at his own expense, the officers of all visiting naval vessels, and added: "The nation expects that no act of courtesy toward visiting officers from abroad will be left undone. But what a miserable exhibition of injustice and niggardliness it is to require the expense for such acts of courtesy to be paid out of the pockets of those who, by reason of their official positions, are obliged to offer them!"

[3] New York *World* clipping, Hancock Papers, Scrapbook, Pennsylvania State Library.

[4] *Letters and Addresses,* 29.

[5] *Ibid.,* 62.

[6] Philadelphia *Times* clipping, Hancock Papers, Scrapbook, Pennsylvania State Library.

[7] *Grand Army Review,* Feb. 1886, p. 147.

[8] *Letters and Addresses,* 48.

[9] Forney, 481.

[10] McClure, 100.

[11] *Ibid.,* 99.

[12] *Ibid.,* 100.

[13] *Ibid.,* 98.

[14] *Ibid.*

[15] Hancock, *Reminiscences,* 167-168.

[16] *Ibid.,* 147-148.

[17] Bliss, 211.

[18] Walker, *Hancock,* 304.

[19] Hancock to Sherman, Dec. 28, 1876. *Letters and Addresses,* 81-82.

[20] *Ibid.,* 83-85.

[21] Hancock, *Reminiscences,* 160-161.

[22] *Letters and Addresses,* 4. Smith said the man came directly to him with the information. The New York *Herald,* Oct. 1, 1880, said English spent $22,000 personally in Indiana and received "no outside favors." The campaign then had more than a month to run.

[23] Southworth, 28.

[24] The full title was: *"A Record of the Statesmanship and Political*

Achievements of Gen. Winfield Scott Hancock, Regular Democratic Nominee for President of the United States. Compiled from the Records. by a Citizen." Hancock supporters, in a veiled reference to Garfield's Credit Mobilier connection, would write on the blank pages "Clean Record."

[25] George Stimpson, *A Book About American Politics*, 294.

[26] Herbert J. Clancy, *The Presidential Election of 1880*, 210-211.

[27] Stimpson, 294.

[28] Oct. 14, 1880.

[29] New York *Herald*, Oct. 27, 1880.

[30] *Ibid.*, Oct. 29, 1880.

[31] Walker, *Hancock*, 306. Walker had become a Federal office holder under Grant and Hayes, having charge of taking the census in 1870 and 1880.

[32] New York *World*, Oct. 27, 1880.

[33] *Ibid.*

[34] Issue of Oct. 28, 1880.

[35] Hancock, *Reminiscences*, 172.

[36] New York *Herald*, Nov. 5, 1880.

[37] Nov. 5, 1880.

[38] Nov. 11, 1880. The New York *World*, Nov. 4, 1880, held that "criminations and recriminations among the vanquished after a defeat are idle." None seemed to relish thoughts of another election dispute.

[39] Philadelphia *Times* clipping, Hancock Papers, Scrapbook, Pennsylvania State Library.

[40] Hancock, *Reminiscences*, 175.

[41] *Ibid.*

[42] General Fry's statement, Goodrich, 347. Hancock entertained at his own expense the admirals of the British, French and German fleets.

[43] Walker, *Hancock*, 309.

[44] McClure, 103.

[45] New York *World* clipping (undated), Hancock Papers, Scrapbook, Pennsylvania State Library.

[46] Hilary's story was contained in an article headed, "General Hancock's Cross in Life," in the Philadelphia *Record*, apparently published just after the general's death in 1886. It is in the Hancock Papers, Scrapbook, Pennsylvania State Library.

[47] *Ibid.*

[48] *Ibid.*

[49] Minneapolis *Journal*, Feb. 26, 1908. Hilary lived from 1881 to 1900 at 1025 Hennepin Avenue, Minneapolis, then moved to Bloomington Avenue South. He had an office in the Prince Opera House, 301 Hennepin Avenue, where he engaged in legal work and sold real estate.

[50] *Letters and Addresses*, 35; Walker, *Hancock*, 312.

⁵¹ Atlanta *Constitution* clipping (undated), Hancock Papers, Scrapbook, Pennsylvania State Library.

⁵² Gordon, *Reminiscences,* 35-36.

⁵³ Badeau interview (undated), Philadelphia *Press,* Hancock Papers, Scrapbook, Pennsylvania State Library.

⁵⁴ Philadelphia *Times* clipping (undated), Hancock Papers, Scrapbook, Pennsylvania State Library.

⁵⁵ York, Pennsylvania, *Daily Age* clipping (undated), Hancock Papers, Scrapbook, Pennsylvania State Library.

⁵⁶ Philadelphia *Times* clipping (undated), Hancock Papers, Scrapbook, Pennsylvania State Library.

⁵⁷ York *Daily Age* clipping. Before their expenses began to accumulate the Hancocks had a substantial amount of property which, had they held it, would have been worth about $150,000 at the time of the general's death. Substantially all of it was spent on his family, his charities for old soldiers and his campaign for the Presidency. About all he had when he died was a $10,000 life insurance policy, personal property valued at $1,000 and some land in Missouri—a "rattlesnake patch," according to a New York *World* story, which, a friend said, "would be rank flattery to call a farm." (Hancock Papers, Scrapbook, Pennsylvania State Library.) A fund was raised for Mrs. Hancock, the first contributor being Samuel J. Tilden. It came to aggregate $55,000. The fund was begun by fifteen subscribers who gave $1,000 each. Among them were Andrew Carnegie, J. P. Morgan, John Jacob Astor, Joseph W. Drexel, August Belmont, Cyrus W. Field, Joseph Pulitzer and W. W. Corcoran of Washington.

⁵⁸ The Irish Brigade members subsequently presented to Mrs. Hancock a testimonial album with resolutions expressing "reverential affection" for the general who had led them in the brigade's glorious achievements. The album was bound in morocco and on the cover was the red clover leaf, the emblem of the First Division, Second Corps, Army of the Potomac.

⁵⁹ New York *Tribune,* Feb. 14, 1886.

⁶⁰ The battery was commanded at the ceremony by Major Wallace F. Randolph, later Chief of Artillery, United States Army.

⁶¹ From "The Story of a Hero," in *Letters and Addresses,* 7.

⁶² New York *Tribune,* Feb. 15, 1886.

Bibliography

ABBOTT, JOHN S. C. *The History of the Civil War in America.* 2 vols. New York, 1863.

ADJUTANT GENERAL'S OFFICE, War Department. Military Academy Applications, 1840. National Archives, Washington, D. C.

AGASSIZ, GEORGE R., editor. *Meade's Headquarters, 1863-1865. Letters of Colonel Theodore Lyman from the Wilderness to Appomattox.* Boston, 1922.

ALEXANDER, E. P. "The Battle of Fredericksburg." *Southern Historical Society Papers,* X, 382.

ANDERSON, JAMES H., editor. *Life and Letters of Judge Thomas J. Anderson and Wife.* 1904.

Atlanta *Constitution.* Various issues.

AUGE, M. *Lives of the Eminent Dead and Biographical Notices of the Prominent Living Citizens of Montgomery County, Pa.* Norristown, 1879.

BACHE, RICHARD MEADE. *Life of General George Gordon Meade.* Philadelphia, 1897.

BADEAU, ADAM. *Military History of Ulysses S. Grant, from April, 1861, to April, 1865.* 3 vols. New York, 1867-1881.

BANES, CHARLES H. *History of the Philadelphia Brigade.* Philadelphia, 1876.

BARCLAY & CO. PUBLISHERS (no author given). *The Life, Brilliant Military Career, and Public Services of Gen. Winfield Scott Hancock.* Philadelphia, 1880.

BARNARD, HARRY. *Rutherford B. Hayes and His America.* Indianapolis, 1954.

BATES, EDWARD. *Diary.* Edited by Howard K. Beale. Washington, D. C., 1933.

Battles and Leaders of the Civil War. 4 vols. New York, 1884.

BENEDICT, G. G. *Vermont at Gettysburg.* Burlington, 1870.

343

BIGELOW, JOHN, JR. *The Campaign of Chancellorsville.* New Haven, 1910.

BILLINGS, JOHN D. *Hard Tack and Coffee or the Unwritten Story of Army Life.* Boston, 1887.

BINGHAM, HENRY W. *Oration at Unveiling of the Equestrian Statue of Major General Winfield Scott Hancock on the Battlefield of Gettysburg, June 5, 1896.* Philadelphia, 1899.

Biographical Directory of American Congress. 1950 ed.

BLISS, F. C. *Our Presidential Candidates and Political Compendium.* Newark, 1880.

BOWERS, CLAUDE G. *The Tragic Era, the Revolution after Lincoln.* Cambridge, 1929.

BRATTON, JOHN. "The Battle of Williamsburg." *Southern Historical Society Papers,* VII, 299.

BURR, FRANK A. *An Original and Authentic Record of the Life and Deeds of General Ulysses S. Grant.* Philadelphia, 1885.

BUTLER, BENJAMIN F. *Butler's Book.* Boston, 1892.

CARTER, HODDING. *The Angry Scar. The Story of Reconstruction.* Garden City, N. Y., 1959.

CHESNUT, MARY BOYKIN. *A Diary from Dixie.* New York, 1905.

CLANCEY, HERBERT J., S.J. *The Presidential Election of 1880.* Chicago, 1958.

COLE, J. R. *The Life and Public Services of Winfield Scott Hancock.* Cincinnati, 1880.

COMMAGER, HENRY STEELE, editor. *The Blue and the Gray.* Indianapolis, 1950.

CONWAY, MONCURE DANIEL. *Autobiography. Memoirs and Experiences.* Boston, 1904.

CONWELL, RUSSELL H. *The Life, Speeches and Public Services of James A. Garfield of Ohio.* Boston, 1881.

COPPEE, HENRY. *Grant and His Campaigns.* New York, 1866.

COULTER, E. MERTON. *The Confederate States of America 1861-1865.* Baton Rouge, 1950.

COX, JACOB DOLSON. *Military Reminiscences of the Civil War.* 2 vols. New York, 1900.

DANIELS, JONATHAN. *Prince of Carpetbaggers.* Philadelphia, 1958.

DAWES, RUFUS R. *Service with the Sixth Wisconsin Volunteers.* Marietta, O., 1890.

DEMOCRATIC NATIONAL COMMITTEE. *Why the People Want a Change.* Campaign Text Book. No place, 1880.

DENISON, REV. C. W. (Late Chaplain). *Winfield The Lawyer's Son and How He Became a Major General.* Philadelphia, 1865.

————, and CAPTAIN G. B. HERBERT. *Hancock "the Superb," The Early Life and Public Career of Winfield Scott Hancock.* Detroit and Chicago, 1880.

DEVANS, R. M. *Our First Century.* Springfield, Mass., 1879.

DeWitt, Daniel Miller. *The Judicial Murder of Mary E. Surratt.* Baltimore, 1895.

Dodge, Theodore A. "Grant as a Soldier." *Papers of Military Historical Society of Massachusetts,* X.

Doolittle, Hon. J. R. Papers. Manuscript Division, Library of Congress.

Doubleday, Abner. *Chancellorsville and Gettysburg.* New York, 1882.

Douglas, Kyd. *I Rode with Stonewall.* Chapel Hill, 1940.

Egle, William H. *An Illustrated History of the Commonwealth of Pennsylvania.* Harrisburg, 1877.

Elson, Henry W. *The Civil War Through the Camera . . . The New Text History.* New York, 1912.

"First Corps, Army of Northern Virginia. Official Diary of the First Corps While Commanded by Lt. Gen. R. H. Anderson, from June 1 to October 18, 1864." *Southern Historical Society Papers,* VII, 503.

Fleming, George Thornton, editor. *Life and Letters of Alexander Hays.* Pittsburgh, 1919.

Forney, Hon. John W. *Life and Military Career of Winfield Scott Hancock.* Philadelphia, 1880.

Freed, A. T. *The Life and Public Services of Winfield Scott Hancock.* Chicago, 1880.

Freeman, Douglas S. *Lee's Lieutenants.* 3 vols. New York, 1942.

Frost, John. *The Pictorial Life of General Washington.* Philadelphia, 1848.

Gardiner, O. C. *Sketch of the Life and Public Services of Winfield Scott Hancock* (pamphlet). New York, 1880.

Gibbon, John. *Personal Recollections of the Civil War.* New York, 1928.

Glazier, Captain Willard. *Heroes of Three Wars.* Philadelphia, 1879.

Goodrich, Frederick E. *Life of Winfield Scott Hancock.* Philadelphia, 1886.

Gordon, John B. *Reminiscences of the Civil War.* New York and Atlanta, 1904.

Grand Army of the Republic. Decoration Day, May 30, 1879. New York, 1879.

Grant, U. S. *Correspondence between General Grant and Major General Hancock Relative to Removal of Members of the City Council of New Orleans.* (No date or place).

———. *Personal Memoirs of U. S. Grant.* 2 vols. New York, 1885.

Greeley, Horace. *The American Conflict.* 2 vols. Hartford, 1867.

Hancock, Mrs. *Reminiscences of Winfield Scott Hancock, by His Wife.* New York, 1887.

HANCOCK, WINFIELD S. Hancock Papers, Pennsylvania State Archives. Harrisburg, Pennsylvania.

————. *Gettysburg. Reply to General Howard.* (Pamphlet.)

HANCOCK MILITARY RECORD. Summary Prepared for Adjutant General. 1864. National Archives. Washington, D. C.

HANCOCK PAPERS. Manuscripts Division, Library of Congress.

Hancock Papers: Scrapbook on Hancock-Garfield campaign at Montgomery County Historical Society, Norristown, Penna.

Scrapbook of Material Relating to Hancock's Tomb at Montgomery County Historical Society, Norristown, Penna.

Scrapbook of newspaper clippings about Winfield Scott Hancock at Pennsylvania State Library, Harrisburg.

Scrapbooks about General Hancock at Montgomery County Historical Society, Norristown, Penna.

Reports of Major General W. S. Hancock upon Indian Affairs with Accompanying Exhibits. Received April 28, 1871. War Department publication.

HARDIE, JAMES ALLEN. *Memoir of James Allen Hardie, Inspector General, United States Army.* Washington, 1877.

Harper's Weekly.

HASSLER, WARREN W., JR. *General George B. McClellan. Shield of the Union.* Baton Rouge, 1957.

HENRY, ROBERT SELPH. *The Story of Reconstruction.* Indianapolis, 1938.

————. *The Story of the Mexican War.* Indianapolis, 1950.

HERBERT, WALTER H. *Fighting Joe Hooker.* Indianapolis, 1944.

HOCKER, EDWARD W. *Hancock Landmarks.* In *Montgomery County, Penna., Historical Sketches,* Norristown, 1925.

HOLCOMBE, R. I. *History of the First Regiment Minnesota Volunteer Infantry.* Stillwater, Minn., 1916.

HOSMER, JAMES KENDALL. *Outcome of the Civil War 1863-1865.* (*The American Nation: A History,* Vol. XXI). New York, 1907.

HOWARD, MCHENRY. *Recollections of a Maryland Confederate Soldier and Staff Officer Under Johnston, Jackson and Lee.* Baltimore, 1914.

HOWARD, OLIVER O. *Autobiography.* 2 vols. 1907.

HUMPHREYS, ANDREW A. *The Virginia Campaign of '64 and '65.* New York, 1883.

JENKINS, HOWARD M. *Historical Collections Relating to Gwynedd, a Township of Montgomery County Settled, 1698, by Immigrants from Wales.* Philadelphia, 1897.

JENKINS, JOHN S. *History of the War between the United States and Mexico.* Auburn, 1851.

JOHNSON, ROSSITER. *History of the War of Secession.* New York, 1910.

JOINVILLE, PRINCE DE. *The Army of the Potomac—Its Organization,*

Its Commander, Its Campaign. Translated from the French with Notes by William Henry Hurlbut. New York, 1862.

JONES, J. B. *A Rebel War Clerk's Diary.* 2 vols. Philadelphia, 1866. New edition, Howard Swigget, editor. 2 vols. New York, 1935.

JONES, J. WILLIAM. "Did General Armistead Fight on the Federal Side at First Manassas or Confess When Dying at Gettysburg that He Had Been Engaged in an "Unholy Cause"?" *Southern Historical Society Papers,* X, 423.

JONES, KATHARINE M. *Heroines of Dixie.* Indianapolis, 1955.

JUDKIN, D. X., and FRANK H. NORTON. *Life of Winfield Scott Hancock.* New York, 1880.

JUSTITIA. *Letter to the Honorable Mr. Hawes in Reply to His Strictures on the Graduates of the Military Academy.* By a graduate. New York, 1836.

LAMBERT, WILLIAM H. *Major General Winfield Scott Hancock.* Pamphlet of oration at Gettysburg, May 29, 1866. Philadelphia, 1886.

LEWIS, LLOYD. *Sherman, Fighting Prophet.* New York, 1932.

LINCOLN, ABRAHAM. Papers. Rare Manuscripts Division, Library of Congress.

LIVERMORE, THOMAS L. *Days and Events.* Boston, 1920.

LLOYD, H. H. (Publishers). *Lloyd's Battle History of the Great Rebellion.* New York, 1866.

LONGSTREET, JAMES. *From Manassas to Appomattox.* Philadelphia, 1896.

LOSSING, BENSON J. *The Pictorial Field Book of the Civil War.* 3 vols. Hartford, 1874.

Maine at Gettysburg. Portland, Me., 1898.

MAURY, COLONEL R. L. "The Battle of Williamsburg and the Charge of the Twenty-fourth Virginia of Early's Brigade." *Southern Historical Society Papers,* VIII, 281.

McCLELLAN, GEORGE B. *McClellan's Own Story.* New York, 1887.

McCLURE, ALEXANDER K. *Abraham Lincoln and Men of War Times.* Philadelphia, 1892.

McCLURE, J. B., editor. *Life of General Hancock, by Thomas A. Burns.* Chicago, 1880.

McRAE, COLONEL D. K. "The Battle of Williamsburg. Reply to Colonel Bratton." Southern Historical Society Papers, VII, 360.

MEADE, GEORGE. *Life and Letters of George Gordon Meade.* 2 vols. New York, 1913.

MERRILL, JAMES M. "The Fort Fisher and Wilmington Campaign: Letters from Rear Admiral David D. Porter." *North Carolina Historical Review.* XXXV, No. 4 (Oct. 1953).

Military Historical Society of Massachusetts, Papers of.

————. *The Wilderness Campaign May-June 1864.* Boston, 1905.

————. *Critical Sketches of Some of the Federal and Confederate Commanders.* Boston, 1895.

MILITARY SERVICE INSTITUTE. *Letters and Addresses Contributed at a General Meeting of the Military Service Institute Held at Governor's Island, New York Harbor, February 25, 1886, in Memory of Winfield Scott Hancock, etc.* New York, 1886.

MITCHELL, LIEUT. COL. J. *Thoughts on Tactics and Military Organization Together with an Inquiry into the Power and Position of Russia.* London, 1838.

MONTGOMERY COUNTY, PENNA. *Historical Sketches. A Collection of Papers Prepared for the Historical Society of Montgomery County, Penna.* Norristown, 1925.

MOORE, FRANK. *The Civil War in Song and Story.* New York, 1889.

MORGAN, JAMES NORRIS. *Recollections of a Rebel Reefer.* Boston, 1917.

NATIONAL ARCHIVES. Adjutant General's Office; General File; Mexican War Papers; Hancock Correspondence, 1844-1861.

NEW YORK *Herald,* various issues.

NEW YORK *Tribune,* various issues.

NEW YORK *World,* various issues.

NICOLAY, JOHN G. Papers. Manuscripts Division, Library of Congress.

NORTH CAROLINA REGIMENTS. Chief Justice Walter Clark, editor. *Histories of the Several Regiments and Battalions from North Carolina in the Great War, 1861-65.* 5 vols. Raleigh, 1901.

NORTON, FRANK H. *Life and Public Services of Winfield Scott Hancock.* New York, 1880.

OFFICER, AN. *The Regular Army. A Defense of West Point.* No place or date. About 1839.

Official Records of the Union and Confederate Armies. Washington, 1882-1900.

OWENS, OSCAR LEE (Chaplain of Sixth Infantry). *A Brief Historical Sketch of the Sixth United States Infantry 1798-1918.* War Department (Unofficial Material). Washington, 1918.

PALFREY, FRANCIS WINTHROP. *The Antietam and Fredericksburg.* New York, 1882.

PARIS, COMTE DE. *The Civil War in America.* 3 vols. Philadelphia, 1876.

Pennsylvania at Gettysburg. 2 vols. Harrisburg, 1904.

PHILADELPHIA *Press.* Various issues.

PHILADELPHIA *Times.* Various issues.

PICKETT, GEORGE E. *Heart of a Soldier.* New York, 1913.

PICKETT, LASALLE CORBETT. *Pickett and His Men.* Atlanta, 1899.

POORE, BEN PERLEY. *Life and Services of Ambrose E. Burnside: Soldier—Citizen—Statesman.* Providence, 1882.

PORTER, DAVID D. *Incidents and Anecdotes of the Civil War by Admiral Porter.* New York, 1885.

RANDALL, J. G. and RICHARD N. CURRENT. *Lincoln the President. Last Full Measure.* New York, 1955.

REDWAY, MAJOR G. W. *Fredericksburg—A Study in War.* New York, 1906.

RICHARDSON, JAMES D. *Messages and Papers of the Presidents.* Washington, D.C., 1896.

RIDPATH, JOHN CLARK. *Life and Work of James A. Garfield.* Cincinnati, 1881.

ROPES, JOHN C. "The War as We Now See It." *Military Historical Society of Massachusetts,* X. Reprint from *Scribner's Magazine,* June 1891.

————. "The Battle of Cold Harbor." *Military Historical Society of Massachusetts,* IV.

ROSEBOOM, EUGENE H. *A History of Presidential Elections.* New York, 1957.

ROTHERMEL PAPERS. Pennsylvania State Library, Harrisburg.

SANGER, DONALD BRIDGMAN, and THOMAS ROBSON HAY. *James Longstreet.* Baton Rouge, 1952.

SCHAFF, MORRIS. *The Battle of the Wilderness.* Boston, 1910.

SCHARF, J. THOMAS, and THOMPSON WESTCOTT. *History of Philadelphia 1609-1884.* Philadelphia, 1884.

SCHOFIELD, JOHN M. *Forty-six Years in the Army.* New York, 1897.

SCHURZ, CARL. *Reminiscences of Carl Schurz.* 3 vols. New York, 1907-1908.

SCOTT, WINFIELD. *Memoirs.* 2 vols. New York, 1864.

SEITZ, DON. *The "Also Rans." Great Men Who Missed Making the Presidential Goal.* New York, 1928.

SHANKS, WILLIAM F. G. *Personal Recollections of Distinguished Generals.* New York, 1866.

SHERMAN, GENERAL W. T. *Correspondence between General W. T. Sherman, U. S. Army and Major General W. S. Hancock.* St. Paul, 1871.

SLOCUM, C. E. *The Life and Services of Major General Henry Warner Slocum.* Toledo, 1913.

SMITH, THEODORE C. *Life and Letters of James A. Garfield.* 2 vols. New Haven, 1925.

Southern Historical Society Papers. Richmond, Va.

SOUTHWORTH, ALVIN S. *Life of General Winfield Scott Hancock.* New York, 1880.

SPECTATOR, THE. *Grant, McClellan, Hancock.* (Pamphlet on the

death of the three illustrious soldiers in the past few months.)
No place, February 1886.

STANTON, EDWIN M. Papers. Manuscript Division, Library of Congress.

STEELE, MATTHEW FORNEY. *American Campaigns.* 2 vols. Washington, D. C., 1909.

STEWART, GEORGE R. *John Phoenix, Esq., The Veritable Squibob. A Life of Captain George H. Derby, U.S.A.* New York, 1937.

STILES, ROBERT. *Four Years Under Marse Robert.* New York, 1903.

STIMPSON, GEORGE. *A Book About American Politics.* New York, 1952.

STINE, J. H. *History of the Army of the Potomac.* Washington, D. C., 1893.

SWINTON, WILLIAM. *Campaigns of the Army of the Potomac.* New York, 1866.

TARBELL, IDA M. *The Life of Abraham Lincoln.* 2 vols. New York, 1900.

TAYLOR, EMERSON GIFFORD. *Gouverneur Kemble Warren.* Boston, 1932.

TROBRIAND, REGIS DE. *Four Years with the Army of the Potomac.* Boston, 1889.

TUCKER, GLENN. *High Tide at Gettysburg.* Indianapolis, 1958.
————. *Poltroons and Patriots.* 2 vols. Indianapolis, 1954.

UPTON, EMORY. *The Military Policy of the United States.* Washington, 1912.

WAGNER, ARTHUR L. *Organization and Tactics.* Kansas City, Mo., 1899.

WALKER, FRANCIS A. *General Hancock.* New York, 1895.
————. *History of the Second Army Corps.* New York, 1887.

WELLES, GIDEON. *Diary of Gideon Welles.* 3 vols. Boston, 1911.

WHITTIER, EDWARD N. *The Left Attack (Ewell's) at Gettysburg.* Military Historical Society of Massachusetts. Boston, 1903.

WILLIAMSON, JAMES J. *Mosby's Rangers.* New York, 1909.

WORSHAM, JOHN H. *One of Jackson's Foot Cavalry.* New York, 1912.

Bibliographical Note and Acknowledgments

In the great recent output of Civil War literature Winfield Scott Hancock has been neglected. Several biographies, some with paper backs, were written for campaign purposes when he ran for President in 1880. Almira Hancock, his widow, wrote her reminiscences of him in 1887.

In that same year Brigadier General Francis A. Walker, who served on his staff during much of the war, wrote a history of the Second Corps of the Army of the Potomac, which Hancock led. Walker drew freely on a memorandum covering the period from November 1862 to November 1864, written by Brigadier General Charles H. Morgan, Hancock's chief of staff. Morgan began work on a history of the Second Corps immediately after the war, but abandoned it in 1867. Walker then published in 1895 a life of General Hancock, using much of the information contained in his earlier history of the corps.

Since that time Hancock, pre-eminent among the Federal corps commanders, has been slighted by biographers, although during these sixty-five years the war has come to be studied intensively and dispassionately and solid judgments about most of the leading participants have been formed.

This biography of General Hancock was undertaken at the suggestion of a number of students of the Civil War, some of whom felt that Hancock was the Federal general who more than any other emerged from the war and its aftermath with the admiration and respect of both sides—of his Northern associates, with relatively few exceptions, and of his former enemies in the South.

Of the political campaign biographies, those by John W. Forney, clerk of the U. S. House of Representatives during the Civil War, and by the two Union army veterans, C. W. Denison and G. B. Herbert, are perhaps the most complete, but also are the most reverential.

Greater source value is attached by this writer to the biographies by

D. X. Judkin and Frank H. Norton, and by J. R. Cole, both written in 1880. It is to be presumed that General Hancock found them accurate. Hancock's personal copies of these books are in the remnants of his library now possessed by Edmund A. Hannay of Courtland, Alabama. In view of the general's practice of editing printed matter and making corrections and marginal notations, the books with which he did not quarrel in any consequential manner would have almost the weight of his own reports. Judkin and Norton and Mrs. Hancock's reminiscences are of much help in dealing with Hancock's early army career and the march of the Sixth Infantry across the plains and mountains to California.

The substantial number of General Hancock's books in Mr. Hannay's possession came to him from his grandmother, Elizabeth Gwynn Hancock, widow of Russell Hancock. After Russell's death she married Ellerton Lodge Dorr, of Boston and Memphis, and Mr. Hannay descends from this union. The general's library, which passed to his daughter-in-law Elizabeth, was presented to the Clarksdale, Mississippi, Carnegie Public Library by Mr. Hannay's mother. Subsequently the library found that it urgently needed space for books in more current demand and asked the Hannays to repossess any of the volumes the family might desire to retain. The library kept others.

Mr. and Mrs. Hannay own both the old Russell Hancock plantation in Coahoma County near Clarksdale and the former Dorr plantation in Alabama. The writer is indebted to them for making available at their home in Courtland, General Hancock's books and other information.

My sincere thanks are expressed to those who provided me with information, made suggestions, answered inquiries and offered encouragement during the research and writing of this book. Among them are:

B. Elizabeth Ulrich, chief reference librarian, and William H. Work, Historical and Museum Collection, Division of Public Records, Pennsylvania State Library, Harrisburg. Mrs. LeRoy Burris, secretary and librarian, Historical Society of Montgomery County, Norristown, Pennsylvania.

David C. Mearns, chief of the Manuscripts Division, Library of Congress, and Peter Draz, head of the Reader Service Section, Manuscripts Division. Colonel Willard Webb, chief of the Stack and Reader Division, Library of Congress.

Victor Gondes, Jr., chief of the Civil War Section, National Archives, Washington; James Kane, archivist, and others of the division. Kenneth W. Rapp, archives assistant, United States Military Academy, West Point. Colonel D. G. Gilbert, chief of the Historical Services Division, Department of the Army. Don Rickey, Jr., Park Historian, Custer Battlefield National Monument, Montana.

Margaret Ligon, head librarian, and members of her staff, Pack Memorial Library, Asheville, North Carolina. Mary Seagle, librarian, Henderson County Public Library, Hendersonville, North Carolina, for obtaining numerous books on interlibrary loans. Hazel Hopper, head of the Indiana Division, Indiana State Library, Indianapolis. Anona Jenkins, librarian, Clarksdale, Mississippi. Neda W. Westlake, assistant curator, Rare Book Collection, University of Pennsylvania Library, Philadelphia. Elizabeth Shepard, Librarian, Sondley Reference Library, Asheville, for answering numerous requests for references and books.

Rodney C. Loehr, professor of history, University of Minnesota. Russell W. Fridley, director, Minnesota Historical Society. Warren W. Hassler, associate professor of American history, The Pennsylvania State University. T. Harry Williams, professor of history, Louisiana State University. James Ripley Jacobs, Easley, South Carolina. Samuel White Patterson, professor-emeritus, Hunter College, New York City. William H. Stauffer, Richmond, Virginia. George R. Stewart, Berkeley, California.

Maurice Franz, Coopersburg; Tom McCrory, Sewickley, and Kent Packard, Paoli, all of Pennsylvania. Mrs. Eileen O'Donnell and Mrs. Walter B. Scott, New York City.

My thanks for permission to use excerpts or quotations are due to Houghton Mifflin Company, for *The Diary of Gideon Welles*; Charles Scribner's Sons, for *Life and Letters of George Gordon Meade* by George Meade; George Hays of Sewickley, Penna., grandson of General Alexander Hays, for *Life and Letters of Alexander Hays,* edited by George Thornton Fleming; Bruce Humphries, Inc., Publishers, of Boston, Mass., for *The Battle of the Wilderness* by Morris Schaff; Mrs. Bancroft Hill (Frances Gibbon Hill) of Baltimore, granddaughter of General John Gibbon, for *Personal Recollections of the Civil War* by General John Gibbon.

For drawing the maps in this volume and assisting in the research, I am indebted, as in previous instances, to Dorothy Thomas Tucker, my wife.

GLENN TUCKER
Route 1,
Flat Rock, North Carolina

INDEX

368

HANCOCK THE SUPERB

Vincent, Lieut. Thomas M., 50, 51
Virginia, 236, 264

Wales, 20, 274
Walker, Francis A., 100, 103, 119,
120, 129, 152, 176, 213, 214,
227, 228, 230, 243, 253, 305, 310;
on Hancock, 27, 34, 55, 57-58,
69-70, 93, 131, 132, 235, 255,
263, 302-303; on Hooker, 121
Wallace, Gen. Lew, 31, 234
Walter, Rev. J. A., 271
Walton, Col., 108
War of 1812, 24, 45, 56
Ward, John, 310
Warde, Col., 293
Warren, Gen. Gouverneur K., 119,
138, 166, 173, 179-187 passim,
197, 214-215, 215-216, 220, 226
Warrenton, Va., 95
Warwick River, 78
Washington, George, 18, 21, 59,
102-103, 129, 190, 280; and civil
rights, 16, 282-283; and profanity,
69
Washington, D. C., 37, 59-60, 67,
68, 74-75, 77, 92, 117, 125, 168,
234, 243, 265, 268-272 passim,
276, 277, 278, 287, 288, 298, 305,
309
Wayne, Anthony, 18
Webb, Gen. Alexander S., 128, 145,
148, 151, 160, 181, 187
Webster, W. E., 167
Weldon Railroad, 254
Welles, Gideon, Secretary of Navy,
171, 172, 273, 283; quoted, 278,
281-282
Wellington, Duke of, quoted, 43
Wells, Private James, 150, 156
West Coast command, 61, 63-64, 77
West Point, Va., 79, 82
West Point Military Academy, 19-
21, 26-27, 28-36 passim, 68, 99,
167, 185, 193, 204, 217, 266, 310
and passim
Westminster, Md., 165
Weston, Mo., 53
Wheat Field, Gettysburg, 141, 242,
262-263, 311
"Whisky Ring," 297

White House, Washington, D. C.,
271, 291, 298, 303
White Oak Swamp, Va., 91
Whittaker House, 80
Whittier, Lieut. Edward N., 135
Wilcox, Gen. Cadmus, 304
Wilderness, battle of, 13, 177-195,
215, 256, 302
Wilderness Church, 182
Wilderness Tavern, 188
Wilkeson, Frank, 238
Wilkinson, Morton Smith, 144-145
Willard, Col. George L., 126, 127,
142
Willard's Hotel, Washington, 68,
277
Willcox, Gen. Orlando B., 30, 32,
46, 51, 99, 310
William and Mary College, 82, 86
Williamsburg, Va., battle of, 13,
14, 79-89, 151, 249, 278
Wilmington, Calif., 61
Wilmington, N. C., 260
Wilson, Brig. Gen. James Grant,
quoted, 174
Wilson, William P., quoted, 293
Wilson, Woodrow, 199
Wilson's Creek, Mo., battle of, 68
Winchester, Va., 266, 268, 269;
address to citizens of, 266-267
Windmill Point, 237
Wingate, Brig. Gen. George N., 294
Wolf Run Shoals, 125
Wormley's Hotel, Washington, 309
Worsham, Sgt. John H., 209
Worth, Gen. William J., 39, 40, 43-
44
Wright, Maj. Gen. Horatio G., 215,
219-220, 223, 225, 226, 228
Wylie, Judge, 271

Xochimilco, Lake, 40

Yellow Tavern, 202
York River, 78, 79, 80
Yorktown, Va., 78-79, 80, 305
Yuma, Ariz., 66

Zanesville, Ohio, 45
Ziegler's Grove, 147, 149
Zook, Gen. Samuel K., 100, 104-
110 passim, 113, 141, 200
Zook Post, G. A. R., 311

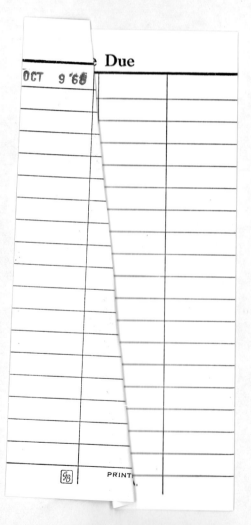